FREE Study Skills Videos/DVD Offer

Dear Customer,

Thank you for your purchase from Mometrix! We consider it an honor and a privilege that you have purchased our product and we want to ensure your satisfaction.

As part of our ongoing effort to meet the needs of test takers, we have developed a set of Study Skills Videos that we would like to give you for <u>FREE</u>. These videos cover our *best practices* for getting ready for your exam, from how to use our study materials to how to best prepare for the day of the test.

All that we ask is that you email us with feedback that would describe your experience so far with our product. Good, bad, or indifferent, we want to know what you think!

To get your FREE Study Skills Videos, you can use the **QR code** below, or send us an **email** at studyvideos@mometrix.com with *FREE VIDEOS* in the subject line and the following information in the body of the email:

- The name of the product you purchased.
- Your product rating on a scale of 1-5, with 5 being the highest rating.
- Your feedback. It can be long, short, or anything in between. We just want to know your impressions and experience so far with our product. (Good feedback might include how our study material met your needs and ways we might be able to make it even better. You could highlight features that you found helpful or features that you think we should add.)

If you have any questions or concerns, please don't hesitate to contact me directly.

Thanks again!

Sincerely,

Jay Willis
Vice President
jay.willis@mometrix.com
1-800-673-8175

SCAN HERE

Series 7

Exam Prep Book 2023-2024

5 Full-Length Practice Tests

Secrets Study Guide with Detailed Answer Explanations for the FINRA General Securities Representative Certification

4th Edition

Written and edited by the Mometrix Financial Industry Certification Test Team

Printed in the United States of America

This paper meets the requirements of ANSI/NISO Z39.48-1992 (Permanence of Paper).

Mometrix offers volume discount pricing to institutions. For more information or a price quote, please contact our sales department at sales@mometrix.com or 888-248-1219.

Mometrix Media LLC is not affiliated with or endorsed by any official testing organization. All organizational and test names are trademarks of their respective owners.

Paperback
ISBN 13: 978-1-5167-2279-2
ISBN 10: 1-5167-2279-5

DEAR FUTURE EXAM SUCCESS STORY

First of all, **THANK YOU** for purchasing Mometrix study materials!

Second, congratulations! You are one of the few determined test-takers who are committed to doing whatever it takes to excel on your exam. **You have come to the right place.** We developed these study materials with one goal in mind: to deliver you the information you need in a format that's concise and easy to use.

In addition to optimizing your guide for the content of the test, we've outlined our recommended steps for breaking down the preparation process into small, attainable goals so you can make sure you stay on track.

We've also analyzed the entire test-taking process, identifying the most common pitfalls and showing how you can overcome them and be ready for any curveball the test throws you.

Standardized testing is one of the biggest obstacles on your road to success, which only increases the importance of doing well in the high-pressure, high-stakes environment of test day. Your results on this test could have a significant impact on your future, and this guide provides the information and practical advice to help you achieve your full potential on test day.

Your success is our success

We would love to hear from you! If you would like to share the story of your exam success or if you have any questions or comments in regard to our products, please contact us at **800-673-8175** or **support@mometrix.com**.

Thanks again for your business and we wish you continued success!

Sincerely,
The Mometrix Test Preparation Team

> **Need more help? Check out our flashcards at:**
> **http://MometrixFlashcards.com/Series**

TABLE OF CONTENTS

Introduction

Thank you for purchasing this resource! You have made the choice to prepare yourself for a test that could have a huge impact on your future, and this guide is designed to help you be fully ready for test day. Obviously, it's important to have a solid understanding of the test material, but you also need to be prepared for the unique environment and stressors of the test, so that you can perform to the best of your abilities.

For this purpose, the first section that appears in this guide is the **Secret Keys**. We've devoted countless hours to meticulously researching what works and what doesn't, and we've boiled down our findings to the five most impactful steps you can take to improve your performance on the test. We start at the beginning with study planning and move through the preparation process, all the way to the testing strategies that will help you get the most out of what you know when you're finally sitting in front of the test.

We recommend that you start preparing for your test as far in advance as possible. However, if you've bought this guide as a last-minute study resource and only have a few days before your test, we recommend that you skip over the first two Secret Keys since they address a long-term study plan.

If you struggle with **test anxiety**, we strongly encourage you to check out our recommendations for how you can overcome it. Test anxiety is a formidable foe, but it can be beaten, and we want to make sure you have the tools you need to defeat it.

Secret Key #1 – Plan Big, Study Small

There's a lot riding on your performance. If you want to ace this test, you're going to need to keep your skills sharp and the material fresh in your mind. You need a plan that lets you review everything you need to know while still fitting in your schedule. We'll break this strategy down into three categories.

Information Organization

Start with the information you already have: the official test outline. From this, you can make a complete list of all the concepts you need to cover before the test. Organize these concepts into groups that can be studied together, and create a list of any related vocabulary you need to learn so you can brush up on any difficult terms. You'll want to keep this vocabulary list handy once you actually start studying since you may need to add to it along the way.

Time Management

Once you have your set of study concepts, decide how to spread them out over the time you have left before the test. Break your study plan into small, clear goals so you have a manageable task for each day and know exactly what you're doing. Then just focus on one small step at a time. When you manage your time this way, you don't need to spend hours at a time studying. Studying a small block of content for a short period each day helps you retain information better and avoid stressing over how much you have left to do. You can relax knowing that you have a plan to cover everything in time. In order for this strategy to be effective though, you have to start studying early and stick to your schedule. Avoid the exhaustion and futility that comes from last-minute cramming!

Study Environment

The environment you study in has a big impact on your learning. Studying in a coffee shop, while probably more enjoyable, is not likely to be as fruitful as studying in a quiet room. It's important to keep distractions to a minimum. You're only planning to study for a short block of time, so make the most of it. Don't pause to check your phone or get up to find a snack. It's also important to **avoid multitasking**. Research has consistently shown that multitasking will make your studying dramatically less effective. Your study area should also be comfortable and well-lit so you don't have the distraction of straining your eyes or sitting on an uncomfortable chair.

 The time of day you study is also important. You want to be rested and alert. Don't wait until just before bedtime. Study when you'll be most likely to comprehend and remember. Even better, if you know what time of day your test will be, set that time aside for study. That way your brain will be used to working on that subject at that specific time and you'll have a better chance of recalling information.

Finally, it can be helpful to team up with others who are studying for the same test. Your actual studying should be done in as isolated an environment as possible, but the work of organizing the information and setting up the study plan can be divided up. In between study sessions, you can discuss with your teammates the concepts that you're all studying and quiz each other on the details. Just be sure that your teammates are as serious about the test as you are. If you find that your study time is being replaced with social time, you might need to find a new team.

Secret Key #2 – Make Your Studying Count

You're devoting a lot of time and effort to preparing for this test, so you want to be absolutely certain it will pay off. This means doing more than just reading the content and hoping you can remember it on test day. It's important to make every minute of study count. There are two main areas you can focus on to make your studying count.

Retention

It doesn't matter how much time you study if you can't remember the material. You need to make sure you are retaining the concepts. To check your retention of the information you're learning, try recalling it at later times with minimal prompting. Try carrying around flashcards and glance at one or two from time to time or ask a friend who's also studying for the test to quiz you.

To enhance your retention, look for ways to put the information into practice so that you can apply it rather than simply recalling it. If you're using the information in practical ways, it will be much easier to remember. Similarly, it helps to solidify a concept in your mind if you're not only reading it to yourself but also explaining it to someone else. Ask a friend to let you teach them about a concept you're a little shaky on (or speak aloud to an imaginary audience if necessary). As you try to summarize, define, give examples, and answer your friend's questions, you'll understand the concepts better and they will stay with you longer. Finally, step back for a big picture view and ask yourself how each piece of information fits with the whole subject. When you link the different concepts together and see them working together as a whole, it's easier to remember the individual components.

Finally, practice showing your work on any multi-step problems, even if you're just studying. Writing out each step you take to solve a problem will help solidify the process in your mind, and you'll be more likely to remember it during the test.

Modality

Modality simply refers to the means or method by which you study. Choosing a study modality that fits your own individual learning style is crucial. No two people learn best in exactly the same way, so it's important to know your strengths and use them to your advantage.

For example, if you learn best by visualization, focus on visualizing a concept in your mind and draw an image or a diagram. Try color-coding your notes, illustrating them, or creating symbols that will trigger your mind to recall a learned concept. If you learn best by hearing or discussing information, find a study partner who learns the same way or read aloud to yourself. Think about how to put the information in your own words. Imagine that you are giving a lecture on the topic and record yourself so you can listen to it later.

For any learning style, flashcards can be helpful. Organize the information so you can take advantage of spare moments to review. Underline key words or phrases. Use different colors for different categories. Mnemonic devices (such as creating a short list in which every item starts with the same letter) can also help with retention. Find what works best for you and use it to store the information in your mind most effectively and easily.

3

Secret Key #3 – Practice the Right Way

Your success on test day depends not only on how many hours you put into preparing, but also on whether you prepared the right way. It's good to check along the way to see if your studying is paying off. One of the most effective ways to do this is by taking practice tests to evaluate your progress. Practice tests are useful because they show exactly where you need to improve. Every time you take a practice test, pay special attention to these three groups of questions:

- The questions you got wrong
- The questions you had to guess on, even if you guessed right
- The questions you found difficult or slow to work through

This will show you exactly what your weak areas are, and where you need to devote more study time. Ask yourself why each of these questions gave you trouble. Was it because you didn't understand the material? Was it because you didn't remember the vocabulary? Do you need more repetitions on this type of question to build speed and confidence? Dig into those questions and figure out how you can strengthen your weak areas as you go back to review the material.

 Additionally, many practice tests have a section explaining the answer choices. It can be tempting to read the explanation and think that you now have a good understanding of the concept. However, an explanation likely only covers part of the question's broader context. Even if the explanation makes perfect sense, **go back and investigate** every concept related to the question until you're positive you have a thorough understanding.

As you go along, keep in mind that the practice test is just that: practice. Memorizing these questions and answers will not be very helpful on the actual test because it is unlikely to have any of the same exact questions. If you only know the right answers to the sample questions, you won't be prepared for the real thing. **Study the concepts** until you understand them fully, and then you'll be able to answer any question that shows up on the test.

It's important to wait on the practice tests until you're ready. If you take a test on your first day of study, you may be overwhelmed by the amount of material covered and how much you need to learn. Work up to it gradually.

On test day, you'll need to be prepared for answering questions, managing your time, and using the test-taking strategies you've learned. It's a lot to balance, like a mental marathon that will have a big impact on your future. Like training for a marathon, you'll need to start slowly and work your way up. When test day arrives, you'll be ready.

Start with the strategies you've read in the first two Secret Keys—plan your course and study in the way that works best for you. If you have time, consider using multiple study resources to get different approaches to the same concepts. It can be helpful to see difficult concepts from more than one angle. Then find a good source for practice tests. Many times, the test website will suggest potential study resources or provide sample tests.

Practice Test Strategy

If you're able to find at least three practice tests, we recommend this strategy:

UNTIMED AND OPEN-BOOK PRACTICE

Take the first test with no time constraints and with your notes and study guide handy. Take your time and focus on applying the strategies you've learned.

TIMED AND OPEN-BOOK PRACTICE

Take the second practice test open-book as well, but set a timer and practice pacing yourself to finish in time.

TIMED AND CLOSED-BOOK PRACTICE

Take any other practice tests as if it were test day. Set a timer and put away your study materials. Sit at a table or desk in a quiet room, imagine yourself at the testing center, and answer questions as quickly and accurately as possible.

Keep repeating timed and closed-book tests on a regular basis until you run out of practice tests or it's time for the actual test. Your mind will be ready for the schedule and stress of test day, and you'll be able to focus on recalling the material you've learned.

Secret Key #4 – Pace Yourself

Once you're fully prepared for the material on the test, your biggest challenge on test day will be managing your time. Just knowing that the clock is ticking can make you panic even if you have plenty of time left. Work on pacing yourself so you can build confidence against the time constraints of the exam. Pacing is a difficult skill to master, especially in a high-pressure environment, so **practice is vital**.

Set time expectations for your pace based on how much time is available. For example, if a section has 60 questions and the time limit is 30 minutes, you know you have to average 30 seconds or less per question in order to answer them all. Although 30 seconds is the hard limit, set 25 seconds per question as your goal, so you reserve extra time to spend on harder questions. When you budget extra time for the harder questions, you no longer have any reason to stress when those questions take longer to answer.

Don't let this time expectation distract you from working through the test at a calm, steady pace, but keep it in mind so you don't spend too much time on any one question. Recognize that taking extra time on one question you don't understand may keep you from answering two that you do understand later in the test. If your time limit for a question is up and you're still not sure of the answer, mark it and move on, and come back to it later if the time and the test format allow. If the testing format doesn't allow you to return to earlier questions, just make an educated guess; then put it out of your mind and move on.

On the easier questions, be careful not to rush. It may seem wise to hurry through them so you have more time for the challenging ones, but it's not worth missing one if you know the concept and just didn't take the time to read the question fully. Work efficiently but make sure you understand the question and have looked at all of the answer choices, since more than one may seem right at first.

Even if you're paying attention to the time, you may find yourself a little behind at some point. You should speed up to get back on track, but do so wisely. Don't panic; just take a few seconds less on each question until you're caught up. Don't guess without thinking, but do look through the answer choices and eliminate any you know are wrong. If you can get down to two choices, it is often worthwhile to guess from those. Once you've chosen an answer, move on and don't dwell on any that you skipped or had to hurry through. If a question was taking too long, chances are it was one of the harder ones, so you weren't as likely to get it right anyway.

On the other hand, if you find yourself getting ahead of schedule, it may be beneficial to slow down a little. The more quickly you work, the more likely you are to make a careless mistake that will affect your score. You've budgeted time for each question, so don't be afraid to spend that time. Practice an efficient but careful pace to get the most out of the time you have.

Secret Key #5 – Have a Plan for Guessing

When you're taking the test, you may find yourself stuck on a question. Some of the answer choices seem better than others, but you don't see the one answer choice that is obviously correct. What do you do?

The scenario described above is very common, yet most test takers have not effectively prepared for it. Developing and practicing a plan for guessing may be one of the single most effective uses of your time as you get ready for the exam.

In developing your plan for guessing, there are three questions to address:

- When should you start the guessing process?
- How should you narrow down the choices?
- Which answer should you choose?

When to Start the Guessing Process

Unless your plan for guessing is to select C every time (which, despite its merits, is not what we recommend), you need to leave yourself enough time to apply your answer elimination strategies. Since you have a limited amount of time for each question, that means that if you're going to give yourself the best shot at guessing correctly, you have to decide quickly whether or not you will guess.

Of course, the best-case scenario is that you don't have to guess at all, so first, see if you can answer the question based on your knowledge of the subject and basic reasoning skills. Focus on the key words in the question and try to jog your memory of related topics. Give yourself a chance to bring the knowledge to mind, but once you realize that you don't have (or you can't access) the knowledge you need to answer the question, it's time to start the guessing process.

It's almost always better to start the guessing process too early than too late. It only takes a few seconds to remember something and answer the question from knowledge. Carefully eliminating wrong answer choices takes longer. Plus, going through the process of eliminating answer choices can actually help jog your memory.

Summary: Start the guessing process as soon as you decide that you can't answer the question based on your knowledge.

7

How to Narrow Down the Choices

The next chapter in this book (**Test-Taking Strategies**) includes a wide range of strategies for how to approach questions and how to look for answer choices to eliminate. You will definitely want to read those carefully, practice them, and figure out which ones work best for you. Here though, we're going to address a mindset rather than a particular strategy.

Your odds of guessing an answer correctly depend on how many options you are choosing from.

Number of options left	5	4	3	2	1
Odds of guessing correctly	20%	25%	33%	50%	100%

You can see from this chart just how valuable it is to be able to eliminate incorrect answers and make an educated guess, but there are two things that many test takers do that cause them to miss out on the benefits of guessing:

- Accidentally eliminating the correct answer
- Selecting an answer based on an impression

We'll look at the first one here, and the second one in the next section.

To avoid accidentally eliminating the correct answer, we recommend a thought exercise called **the $5 challenge**. In this challenge, you only eliminate an answer choice from contention if you are willing to bet $5 on it being wrong. Why $5? Five dollars is a small but not insignificant amount of money. It's an amount you could afford to lose but wouldn't want to throw away. And while losing

$5 once might not hurt too much, doing it twenty times will set you back $100. In the same way, each small decision you make—eliminating a choice here, guessing on a question there—won't by itself impact your score very much, but when you put them all together, they can make a big difference. By holding each answer choice elimination decision to a higher standard, you can reduce the risk of accidentally eliminating the correct answer.

The $5 challenge can also be applied in a positive sense: If you are willing to bet $5 that an answer choice *is* correct, go ahead and mark it as correct.

Summary: Only eliminate an answer choice if you are willing to bet $5 that it is wrong.

8

Which Answer to Choose

You're taking the test. You've run into a hard question and decided you'll have to guess. You've eliminated all the answer choices you're willing to bet $5 on. Now you have to pick an answer. Why do we even need to talk about this? Why can't you just pick whichever one you feel like when the time comes?

The answer to these questions is that if you don't come into the test with a plan, you'll rely on your impression to select an answer choice, and if you do that, you risk falling into a trap. The test writers know that everyone who takes their test will be guessing on some of the questions, so they intentionally write wrong answer choices to seem plausible. You still have to pick an answer though, and if the wrong answer choices are designed to look right, how can you ever be sure that you're not falling for their trap? The best solution we've found to this dilemma is to take the decision out of your hands entirely. Here is the process we recommend:

Once you've eliminated any choices that you are confident (willing to bet $5) are wrong, select the first remaining choice as your answer.

Whether you choose to select the first remaining choice, the second, or the last, the important thing is that you use some preselected standard. Using this approach guarantees that you will not be enticed into selecting an answer choice that looks right, because you are not basing your decision on how the answer choices look.

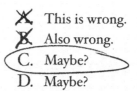

This is not meant to make you question your knowledge. Instead, it is to help you recognize the difference between your knowledge and your impressions. There's a huge difference between thinking an answer is right because of what you know, and thinking an answer is right because it looks or sounds like it should be right.

Summary: To ensure that your selection is appropriately random, make a predetermined selection from among all answer choices you have not eliminated.

Test-Taking Strategies

This section contains a list of test-taking strategies that you may find helpful as you work through the test. By taking what you know and applying logical thought, you can maximize your chances of answering any question correctly!

It is very important to realize that every question is different and every person is different: no single strategy will work on every question, and no single strategy will work for every person. That's why we've included all of them here, so you can try them out and determine which ones work best for different types of questions and which ones work best for you.

Question Strategies

⊘ READ CAREFULLY

Read the question and the answer choices carefully. Don't miss the question because you misread the terms. You have plenty of time to read each question thoroughly and make sure you understand what is being asked. Yet a happy medium must be attained, so don't waste too much time. You must read carefully and efficiently.

⊘ CONTEXTUAL CLUES

Look for contextual clues. If the question includes a word you are not familiar with, look at the immediate context for some indication of what the word might mean. Contextual clues can often give you all the information you need to decipher the meaning of an unfamiliar word. Even if you can't determine the meaning, you may be able to narrow down the possibilities enough to make a solid guess at the answer to the question.

⊘ PREFIXES

If you're having trouble with a word in the question or answer choices, try dissecting it. Take advantage of every clue that the word might include. Prefixes can be a huge help. Usually, they allow you to determine a basic meaning. *Pre-* means before, *post-* means after, *pro-* is positive, *de-* is negative. From prefixes, you can get an idea of the general meaning of the word and try to put it into context.

⊘ HEDGE WORDS

Watch out for critical hedge words, such as *likely, may, can, sometimes, often, almost, mostly, usually, generally, rarely,* and *sometimes*. Question writers insert these hedge phrases to cover every possibility. Often an answer choice will be wrong simply because it leaves no room for exception. Be on guard for answer choices that have definitive words such as *exactly* and *always*.

⊘ SWITCHBACK WORDS

Stay alert for *switchbacks*. These are the words and phrases frequently used to alert you to shifts in thought. The most common switchback words are *but, although,* and *however*. Others include *nevertheless, on the other hand, even though, while, in spite of, despite,* and *regardless of*. Switchback words are important to catch because they can change the direction of the question or an answer choice.

10

⊘ Face Value

When in doubt, use common sense. Accept the situation in the problem at face value. Don't read too much into it. These problems will not require you to make wild assumptions. If you have to go beyond creativity and warp time or space in order to have an answer choice fit the question, then you should move on and consider the other answer choices. These are normal problems rooted in reality. The applicable relationship or explanation may not be readily apparent, but it is there for you to figure out. Use your common sense to interpret anything that isn't clear.

Answer Choice Strategies

⊘ Answer Selection

The most thorough way to pick an answer choice is to identify and eliminate wrong answers until only one is left, then confirm it is the correct answer. Sometimes an answer choice may immediately seem right, but be careful. The test writers will usually put more than one reasonable answer choice on each question, so take a second to read all of them and make sure that the other choices are not equally obvious. As long as you have time left, it is better to read every answer choice than to pick the first one that looks right without checking the others.

⊘ Answer Choice Families

An answer choice family consists of two (in rare cases, three) answer choices that are very similar in construction and cannot all be true at the same time. If you see two answer choices that are direct opposites or parallels, one of them is usually the correct answer. For instance, if one answer choice says that quantity x increases and another either says that quantity x decreases (opposite) or says that quantity y increases (parallel), then those answer choices would fall into the same family. An answer choice that doesn't match the construction of the answer choice family is more likely to be incorrect. Most questions will not have answer choice families, but when they do appear, you should be prepared to recognize them.

⊘ Eliminate Answers

Eliminate answer choices as soon as you realize they are wrong, but make sure you consider all possibilities. If you are eliminating answer choices and realize that the last one you are left with is also wrong, don't panic. Start over and consider each choice again. There may be something you missed the first time that you will realize on the second pass.

⊘ Avoid Fact Traps

Don't be distracted by an answer choice that is factually true but doesn't answer the question. You are looking for the choice that answers the question. Stay focused on what the question is asking for so you don't accidentally pick an answer that is true but incorrect. Always go back to the question and make sure the answer choice you've selected actually answers the question and is not merely a true statement.

⊘ Extreme Statements

In general, you should avoid answers that put forth extreme actions as standard practice or proclaim controversial ideas as established fact. An answer choice that states the "process should be used in certain situations, if…" is much more likely to be correct than one that states the "process should be discontinued completely." The first is a calm rational statement and doesn't even make a definitive, uncompromising stance, using a hedge word *if* to provide wiggle room, whereas the second choice is far more extreme.

11

⊘ Benchmark

As you read through the answer choices and you come across one that seems to answer the question well, mentally select that answer choice. This is not your final answer, but it's the one that will help you evaluate the other answer choices. The one that you selected is your benchmark or standard for judging each of the other answer choices. Every other answer choice must be compared to your benchmark. That choice is correct until proven otherwise by another answer choice beating it. If you find a better answer, then that one becomes your new benchmark. Once you've decided that no other choice answers the question as well as your benchmark, you have your final answer.

⊘ Predict the Answer

Before you even start looking at the answer choices, it is often best to try to predict the answer. When you come up with the answer on your own, it is easier to avoid distractions and traps because you will know exactly what to look for. The right answer choice is unlikely to be word-for-word what you came up with, but it should be a close match. Even if you are confident that you have the right answer, you should still take the time to read each option before moving on.

General Strategies

⊘ Tough Questions

If you are stumped on a problem or it appears too hard or too difficult, don't waste time. Move on! Remember though, if you can quickly check for obviously incorrect answer choices, your chances of guessing correctly are greatly improved. Before you completely give up, at least try to knock out a couple of possible answers. Eliminate what you can and then guess at the remaining answer choices before moving on.

⊘ Check Your Work

Since you will probably not know every term listed and the answer to every question, it is important that you get credit for the ones that you do know. Don't miss any questions through careless mistakes. If at all possible, try to take a second to look back over your answer selection and make sure you've selected the correct answer choice and haven't made a costly careless mistake (such as marking an answer choice that you didn't mean to mark). This quick double check should more than pay for itself in caught mistakes for the time it costs.

⊘ Pace Yourself

It's easy to be overwhelmed when you're looking at a page full of questions; your mind is confused and full of random thoughts, and the clock is ticking down faster than you would like. Calm down and maintain the pace that you have set for yourself. Especially as you get down to the last few minutes of the test, don't let the small numbers on the clock make you panic. As long as you are on track by monitoring your pace, you are guaranteed to have time for each question.

⊘ Don't Rush

It is very easy to make errors when you are in a hurry. Maintaining a fast pace in answering questions is pointless if it makes you miss questions that you would have gotten right otherwise. Test writers like to include distracting information and wrong answers that seem right. Taking a little extra time to avoid careless mistakes can make all the difference in your test score. Find a pace that allows you to be confident in the answers that you select.

⊘ Keep Moving

Panicking will not help you pass the test, so do your best to stay calm and keep moving. Taking deep breaths and going through the answer elimination steps you practiced can help to break through a stress barrier and keep your pace.

Final Notes

The combination of a solid foundation of content knowledge and the confidence that comes from practicing your plan for applying that knowledge is the key to maximizing your performance on test day. As your foundation of content knowledge is built up and strengthened, you'll find that the strategies included in this chapter become more and more effective in helping you quickly sift through the distractions and traps of the test to isolate the correct answer.

Now that you're preparing to move forward into the test content chapters of this book, be sure to keep your goal in mind. As you read, think about how you will be able to apply this information on the test. If you've already seen sample questions for the test and you have an idea of the question format and style, try to come up with questions of your own that you can answer based on what you're reading. This will give you valuable practice applying your knowledge in the same ways you can expect to on test day.

Good luck and good studying!

General Terms

IMPORTANT ORGANIZATIONS IN THE FINANCE INDUSTRY

SECURITIES AND EXCHANGE COMMISSION (SEC)

The Securities and Exchange Commission (SEC) is an agency of the U.S. federal government which was created to protect investors and regulate securities markets. The SEC was formed in response to the stock market crash of 1929, which led to the passage of the U.S. Securities Act of 1933 and the U.S. Securities and Exchange Act of 1934. The SEC is charged with oversight of investment advisers, broker-dealers, transfer agents, securities exchanges, clearing agencies, mutual funds, exchange traded funds and SROs. The SEC has the authority to file civil suits against those who violate its rules and share information obtained through its investigations with criminal prosecutors. Securities issues must be registered with the SEC before they can be sold to investors and financial services firms and representatives must be registered with the SEC to sell investment products.

FINANCIAL INDUSTRY REGULATORY AUTHORITY (FINRA)

The **Financial Industry Regulatory Authority (FINRA)** is a self-regulatory organization (SRO). It is accountable to and under the oversight of the Securities and Exchange Commission (SEC), and it governs securities trading and investment banking firms. The FINRA promulgates rules and regulations for these firms and their employees and associates, and it enforces the rules. FINRA also settle disputes between member firms and settles disputes between customers from the general public and firms. Anyone who trades securities must be registered with FINRA.

MUNICIPAL SECURITIES RULEMAKING BOARD (MSRB)

The Municipal Securities Rulemaking Board (MSRB) is a self-regulatory organization (SRO) tasked with developing rules for banks and securities firms when underwriting, trading, and selling municipal securities. This includes the requirement to provide continuing disclosure on the financial health and operating condition of the municipality. The MSRB is subject to SEC oversight, and while it generates rules for firms to follow, it is not authorized to enforce violations of such rules. The enforcement of MSRB rules is handled by the Securities and Exchange Commission (SEC), the Financial Industry Regulatory Authority (FINRA), the Office of the Comptroller of the Currency (OCC), the Federal Deposit Insurance Corporation (FDIC), and the Federal Reserve Board (FRB), depending on the type of institution.

CHICAGO BOARD OPTIONS EXCHANGE (CBOE)

The **Chicago Board Options Exchange (CBOE)** is not only an options exchange—the largest options exchange in the United States—but also a self-regulatory organization (SRO). The CBOE creates rules for options exchanges and enforces them.

SEC RULE 405 TERMS

Affiliate - a person who directly or indirectly controls or is under common control with the specified person.

Amount - for debt, it means the principal; for shares it means the number of shares; and it means the number of units if relating to any other security.

Associate - in reference to an organization, it is a person who is an officer, partner, or the beneficial owner of at least 10% or more of any class of securities. In reference to a trust or estate, it is anyone who is a trustee or has any interest in it. Relatives are also associates.

15

Automatic shelf registration statement - a shelf registration filed by a WKSI (well-known seasoned issuer).

Business combination related shell company - a company formed to combine multiple other businesses, or to change the corporate domicile of an existing company.

Dividend or interest investment plan — a plan that allows current security holders to reinvest dividends or interest.

Electronic filer — a person or entity that submits filings according to Rule 100 and 101.

Electronic filing — document submitted to the SEC in electronic format.

Employee — does not include director, trustee, or officer.

Employee benefit plan — a written purchase, saving, option, bonus, appreciation, profit sharing, thrift, incentive, pension, or similar plan available to employees.

Equity security — any stock, certificate of interest, transferable shares, limited partnership interest, joint venture interest, and certificate of interest. Any security entitling a person to interest in equity.

Executive officer — any president, vice president, or other policy making officer.

Fiscal year — either calendar year or other annual accounting period.

Foreign government — government of foreign country.

Foreign issuer — a foreign government, foreign person, or organization formed under the laws of a foreign government.

Foreign private issuer — certain foreign issuers other than foreign governments.

Free writing prospectus — a written communication that is an offer to transact a security meeting certain requirements.

Graphic communication — all forms of electronic media that are not being communicated in real-time (live).

Ineligible issuer — an issuer who has not met certain filing requirements put forth by the Securities Exchange Act of 1934 or violated other SEC rules and regulations.

Majority-owned subsidiary — a subsidiary of which the securities with voting rights are more than 50% owned by one parent.

Material — describes a fact to which a reasonable person would likely attach importance.

Officer — president, vice president, secretary, treasurer, principal financial officer and accounting officer, or any person performing these same functions, in an organization.

Parent — of a person is an affiliate that controls it either directly or indirectly.

Predecessor — a person that previously owned the majority portion of a business and assets before an acquisition.

Principal underwriter — the underwriter in privity of contract with the issuer.

Promoter — any person that takes initiative to found and organize an issue, or any person with a connection to the founding and organizing of an issue that receives more than 10% of the proceeds of the issue.

Prospectus — a prospectus that meets the requirements in section 10(a) of the Securities Act of 1933.

Registrant — issuer of securities that has filed for registration.

Share — a share of corporate stock or unit of interest in other types of organizations.

Shell company — a registrant other than an asset-backed issuer that has little-to-no operations and little-to-no assets.

Significant subsidiary — a subsidiary of a registrant that comprises more than 10% of the registrant's total assets.

Smaller reporting company — certain issuers that are not investment companies or asset-backed issuers and that have less than $75 million in public float.

Subsidiary — an affiliate control directly or indirectly by a specific person.

Succession — direct acquisition of assets by merger, consolidation, purchase, or other direct transfer.

Totally held subsidiary — a subsidiary that is owned 100% by its parent or its parents' other subsidiaries and is not significantly indebted to any other person.

Voting securities — securities that provide the owners with the right to vote on election of directors.

Well-known seasoned issuer — a status given by the SEC to certain well-known issuers that have a market value of $700 million or more.

Wholly owned subsidiary — a subsidiary, the outstanding voting securities of which are owned 100% by a parent or a parent's other wholly owned subsidiaries.

Written communication — any communication via written, printed, radio, television, or graphic media.

FINRA RULE 9000 (CODE OF PROCEDURE) TERMS

General Counsel — the Chief Legal Officer of FINRA.

Head of Enforcement — the individual designated by the FINRA CEO to manage the Department of Enforcement.

Hearing Officer — an attorney employed by FINRA that acts in an adjudicative role regarding disciplinary proceedings.

Hearing Panel — an adjudicator that conducts a disciplinary proceeding.

Market Regulation Committee — a FINRA committee designated to consider federal securities laws and FINRA rules in relation to securities quotes, transaction execution and reporting, and trading practices.

Panelist — a member of an FINRA panel that is not a Hearing Officer.

Primary District Committee — the District Committee designated to provide a panelist for a disciplinary proceeding.

Statutory Disqualification Committee — a subcommittee of the National Adjudicatory Council that makes a recommended decision to grant or deny an application for relief from FINRA eligibility requirements.

FINRA RULE 6320A TERMS

Designated securities — NMS stocks defined in Rule 600(b)(47).

Normal market hours — 9:30 AM Eastern Time to 4:00 PM Eastern Time.

Normal unit of trading — 100 shares, unless otherwise determined.

Otherwise than on an exchange — a transaction that takes place somewhere else than on a national exchange.

Round lot holder — any holder of a normal unit of trading.

Stop stock price — the price at which a stop stock transaction will be executed.

Stop stock transaction — a transaction that executes at a stop stock price or better.

Terms defined here are to have the same meaning as in FINRA by-laws and rules; Rule 600 of Regulation NMS; and the Joint Self-Regulatory Organization Plan Governing the Collection, Consolidation, and Dissemination of Quotation and Transaction Information for NASDAQ-Listed Securities Traded on Exchanges on an Unlisted Trading Privilege Basis, unless otherwise defined.

FINRA RULE FOR PAYMENTS IN MARKET MAKING

Payments for market making (FINRA Rule 5250) - a member may not receive payment from an issuer of a security in exchange for publishing a quote or acting as a market maker in a security.

FINRA RULE FOR QUOTE AND ORDER ACCESS REQUIREMENTS

Quote and order access requirements (FINRA Rule 6250) - an ADF trading center, for each security displays a bid and/or offer, must provide other ADF trading centers direct electronic access. This access is to include access for broker-dealers that are not ADF trading centers. The ADF trading center is required to keep certain information for each order they receive to include a unique order identifier; order entry firm; order side; order quantity; issue identifier; order price; order negotiable flag; time in force; order date; order time; minimal acceptable quantity; market making firm; and trade-or-move flag.

SEC ACT OF 1934

The **Securities Exchange Act of 1934** is the foundational law of American stock trading. After the 1929 stock market crash, many critics blamed the crash and subsequent depression on rampant speculation in an unregulated stock trading atmosphere, including selling short, buying on margin, and selling on margin. In response, the Congress passed the SEC Act, which established rules and regulations for stock trading in America, including the formation of the **Securities and Exchange Commission** (SEC) to enforce those laws.

In addition to creating the Securities and Exchange Commission, the SEC Act of 1934 requires that stock exchanges file their registration papers with the SEC and requires any companies that trade on the exchanges to file their registration papers. It also established capital requirements and set rigid limits on borrowing and lending for purposes of buying on margin. It set rules governing insider trading and created general rules for trading stocks and other securities, including how customer accounts are handled, and the "customer protection rule." In addition, it set standards for ownership and administration of exchanges and broker firms.

SROs

SROs are self-regulatory organizations. These types of non-governmental organizations set standards and regulate a specific industry. Members of an SRO agree to be bound by its rules or face penalties or possible expulsion. Examples of SROS are the Financial Industry Regulatory Authority (FINRA), the Municipal Securities Rulemaking Board (MSRB), the New York Stock Exchange (NYSE), National Association of Securities Dealers Automated Quotations (NASDAQ) and the Chicago Board Options Exchange (CBOE). Though SROs do not receive their power from the government, they may be overseen by a government agency. For example, FINRA is overseen by the Securities and Exchange Commission (SEC).

NASD RULE 1032 AND REGISTRATION REQUIREMENTS FOR REPRESENTATIVES

General Securities Representative - any representative associated with a member is required to register as a General Securities Representative, unless his activities are limited enough to qualify him for one of the limited categories of representation.

Limited Representative - Investment Company and Variable Contracts Products - a representative associated with a member may register as a Limited Representative - Investment Company and Variable Contracts Products if his activities are limited to the solicitation, purchase, or sale of certain investment companies' redeemable securities, certain closed-end investment companies' securities, and certain exempt variable contracts and insurance premium funding programs, and the person passes a corresponding Qualification Examination.

Limited Representative - Direct Participation Program - a representative associated with a member may register as a Limited Representative - Direct Participation Program if his activities are limited to the equity interests in or the debt of direct participation programs, and the person passes a corresponding Qualification Examination. A person seeking this registration must already have been registered as a Limited Representative - Corporate Securities or Limited Representative - Government Securities.

Limited Representative - Options and Security Futures - a representative associated with a member may register as a Limited Representative - Direct Participation Program if his activities involve solicitation or sale of option or security futures contracts, and the person passes a corresponding Qualification Examination.

REGISTRATION, CONTINUING EDUCATION, AND TERMINATION OF REGISTERED REPRESENTATIVES (RR)

All candidates for brokerage must have a **sponsoring broker** before they register to take the Series 7 exam. Usually, this occurs by means of a firm that has hired the candidate. The sponsoring firm needs to file an application form and pay processing fees with the **Central Registration**

Depository (CRD). The applicant must submit his fingerprints through an approved facility (such as a local police station) and schedule his exam time.

Among the continuing education requirements for RRs is to complete an exam covering various topics of regulation. This exam needs to be taken two years after one gains his license and then every three years after that. In addition to these exams, there is a "broker-age firm element," which is a requirement for broker dealers to ensure that their employed RRs are up-to-date on various topics related to their particular jobs.

Regarding the termination of a registered representative from his firm, a broker dealer is required to issue a form explaining the reason for the RR's departure, including the relevant ethical and legal factors.

STATE REQUIREMENTS FOR BECOMING A LICENSED STOCKBROKER

After the Series 7 exam, there might be **additional licensing exams** which one would need to pass in order to ensure that a particular state grants him a stockbroker's license. Some states, for example, require that one pass the Series 63 and Series 65 exams, while others may simply require that one pass the Series 66 exam. States also have varying requirements for continuing education.

Seeking Business

Contacting Customers and Developing Marketing Materials

SEC REGULATION ANALYST CERTIFICATION (AC)

Securities & Exchange Commission (SEC) Regulation Analyst Certification (AC) requires investment analysts to attest to the fact that their research reports are truthful and accurate and the views they express in their public appearances are honest and complete. In addition, under SEC Regulation AC, analysts must disclose what compensation they have received that is related to their opinions and views.

FINRA RULE 2210

Communications with the public (FINRA Rule 2210) - a qualified registered principal must approve all retail communication before its use or filing with FINRA, unless another member has already filed it and it has been approved and the member has not altered it. For institutional communications, members are to establish written procedures for review by a qualified registered principal of institutional communications. The procedures are to be designed to ensure that institutional communications company with the standards. All communications, retail and institutional, are to be retained according to requirements, and must include:

- a copy of the communication
- the name of any registered principal approving of the communication
- if not approved by a registered principal prior to first use, the name of the person who prepared it
- information about the source of information used in graphic illustrations
- if approval is not required for retail communication, the name of the member that filed it with FINRA, as well as the letter from FINRA

Under FINRA Rule 2210 Communications with the Public, specified retail communications are required to be filed with FINRA at least 10 business days prior to first use, while others are required to be filed within 10 business days of first use.

Retail communications that must be filed **at least 10 business day prior to first use** include:

- communications of new FINRA members for one year from the effective date of membership, including website; newspaper, magazine, telephone directory or other advertisements; television or radio commercials; telephone or audio recordings; video displays, signs or billboards; and motion pictures
- communications that include rankings or performance comparison information that is not generally published or that is created by the investment company
- security futures communications
- communications concerning options used prior to delivery of the options disclosure document

21

Retail communications that must be filed **within 10 business days of first use** include:

- registered investment company communications that promote or recommend a specific registered investment company or family of registered investment companies
- communications concerning any structured or derivative product registered under the Securities Act
- communications concerning public direct participation programs
- communications concerning collateralized mortgage obligations registered under the Securities Act
- final filmed versions of television and video communications previously filed in draft form

CATEGORIES OF PUBLIC COMMUNICATION

Under FINRA Rule 2210, Communications with the Public, FINRA classifies all communications into three categories:

1. "Correspondence" means any written (including electronic) communication that is distributed or made available to 25 or fewer retail investors within any 30 calendar-day period. Reviews of correspondence and internal communications must be conducted by a registered principal and must be evidenced in writing, either electronically or on paper.
2. "Retail communication" means any written (including electronic) communication that is distributed or made available to more than 25 retail investors (any person other than an institutional investor, regardless of whether the person has an account with a member) within any 30 calendar-day period. An appropriately qualified registered principal of the member must approve each retail communication before the earlier of its use or filing with FINRA's Advertising Regulation Department.
3. "Institutional communication" means any written (including electronic) communication that is distributed or made available only to institutional investors, not including internal communications. Institutional investors include government entities, employee benefit plans, and qualified plans. Institutional communication must be reviewed by an appropriately qualified registered principal in accordance with a firm's written procedures. No member may treat a communication as having been distributed to an institutional investor if the member has reason to believe that the communication or any excerpt thereof will be forwarded or made available to any retail investor.

INSTITUTIONAL INVESTORS

For purposes of FINRA Rule 2210 "Institutional investor" is defined as any:

- Person or entity described under Rule 4512(c): (a) a bank, savings and loan association, insurance company or registered investment company; (b) an investment adviser registered either with the SEC under Section 203 of the Investment Advisers Act or with a state securities commission (or any agency or office performing like functions); or (c) any other person (whether a natural person, corporation, partnership, trust or otherwise) with total assets of at least $50 million
- Governmental entity or subdivision thereof
- Employee benefit plan, or multiple employee benefit plans offered to employees of the same employer, that meet the requirements of Section 403(b) or Section 457 of the Internal Revenue Code and in the aggregate have at least 100 participants, but does not include any participant of such plan

- Qualified plan, as defined in Section 3(a)(12)(C) of the Exchange Act, or multiple qualified plans offered to employees of the same employer, that in the aggregate have at least 100 participants, but does not include any participant of such plans
- Member or registered person of such a member
- Person acting solely on behalf of any such institutional investor

STANDARDS FOR FINRA MEMBERS INVOLVED IN PUBLIC APPEARANCES

When sponsoring or participating in a seminar, forum, radio or television interview, or other public appearances or speaking activities that are unscripted and do not constitute retail communications, institutional communications, or correspondence ("public appearance"), persons associated with members must follow the standards:

- If an associated person recommends a security in a public appearance, they must have a reasonable basis for the recommendation.
- If an associated person recommends a security in a public appearance, they must disclose if they have a financial interest in any of the securities of the issuer, and the nature of the financial interest, and any other actual, material conflict of interest.
- Each member must establish appropriate written procedures to supervise its associated persons' public appearances. Such procedures must provide for the education and training of associated persons who make public appearances, including the firm's procedures, documentation of such education and training, and surveillance and follow-up to ensure that such procedures are implemented and adhered to. Evidence that these supervisory procedures have been implemented and carried out must be maintained and made available to FINRA upon request.
- Any scripts, slides, handouts or other written (including electronic) materials used in connection with public appearances are considered communications and must meet general content standards, including being based on principles of fair dealing and good faith, being fair and balanced, and providing a sound basis for evaluating the facts.

REQUIREMENTS FOR THE ADVERTISEMENT OF INVESTMENT COMPANY PRODUCTS

FINRA requires that advertisements for investment company products not be **misleading**, even in part. The term "misleading" is intentional, since it goes beyond mere falsity. Whether an advertisement is misleading is determined according to the context, intended audience, and clarity of the advertisement.

Moreover, FINRA guidelines specifically analyze advertised claims of **tax-free or tax-exempt returns** (since there are questions of whether the taxes are actually deferred, in addition to whether the taxes in question are local, state, or federal), comparisons (which must be clear, fair, and balanced), and predictions or projections (which are allowed only if stated as theoretical extensions of mathematical principles).

REQUIREMENTS FOR THE ADVERTISING VARIABLE CONTRACTS AND MUTUAL FUNDS

All advertisements for investing companies, including those advertisements for variable contracts and mutual funds, are required to be registered with the **Advertising Regulation Department** of FINRA within ten business days of the advertisement's first use or publication. This requirement for such advertisements also includes written or electronically distributed form letters which are to be delivered to twenty-five or more potential customers.

A number of SEC regulations also exist for advertisements of variable contracts and mutual funds. These include SEC Rule 482 (the "Omitting Prospectus Rule"), SEC Rule 433 (which applies to free writing prospectuses), SEC Rule 135a (which permits a general discussion of product attributes without a specific identification of the product), and SEC Rule 34b-1 (which requires performance data for mutual fund and variable annuity advertisements to comply with Rule 482).

OPTIONS-RELATED COMMUNICATIONS

Options communications:

- must comply with the general standards of content, which prohibit untrue or misleading statements or omissions of material fact, promises of specific results, or statements reflecting availability of a secondary market.
- may contain projected performance figures (including projected annualized rates of return), provided that they are accompanied or preceded by the options disclosure document; parameters relating to such performance figures are clearly established and all relevant costs are disclosed; and
- may feature records and statistics that portray the performance of past recommendations or of actual transactions, provided that all such communications are accompanied or preceded by the options disclosure document; any such portrayal is done in a balanced manner and consists of records or statistics that are confined to a specific "universe"; the price and date of each such recommendation or transaction is disclosed; and a determination is made by Registered Options Principal that the records or statistics fairly present the status of the recommendations or transactions.

EXEMPT AND NON-EXEMPT OPTIONS COMMUNICATIONS UNDER SECURITIES ACT RULE 238

Options communications **exempted under Securities Act Rule 238** used prior to options disclosure document delivery must be limited to general descriptions of the options being discussed; must contain contact information for obtaining a copy of the options disclosure document; and must not contain recommendations or past or projected performance figures.

Options communications regarding options **not exempted under Securities Act Rule 238** used prior to delivery of a prospectus that meets the requirements of Section 10(a) of the Securities Act must conform to Securities Act Rule 134 or 134a, as applicable.

All retail communications issued by a member concerning options must be approved in advance by a Registered Options Principal, and communications concerning standardized options used prior to delivery of the applicable current options disclosure document or prospectus must be submitted to the Advertising Regulation Department of FINRA at least ten calendar days prior to use.

PUBLISHING OPTION INFORMATION

Tables displaying options for sale list not only the security, date, type of option (call or put), strike price, bid price, and ask price, but also have a number of other factors which are meant to be useful to investors in evaluating options. These factors include **extrinsic bid/ask price**, which measures the time premium value of the option, the **implied volatility** of the option, and a number of Greek factors: Delta, Gamma, Vega, and Theta.

OVER-THE-COUNTER (OTC) OPTIONS

Over-the-counter (OTC) securities are securities traded apart from an exchange. Since they do not abide by any particular exchange rules, OTC options can come in a variety of forms and contain unusual features. OTC options thus are characterized by both increased flexibility and increased risk.

MUNICIPAL FUND SECURITIES ADVERTISEMENTS

DISCLOSURES

Municipal fund securities, in addition to not being materially false or misleading, must include certain disclosures. These disclosures can be divided into basic disclosures and additional disclosures for identified products.

- **Basic disclosures** include statements that an investor ought to consider his objectives, risks, charges, and expenses before investing, that he can gain additional information about municipal fund securities in the issuer's official statement, and that the official statement ought to be carefully perused before investing.
- **Additional disclosures** for identified products are complex and vary according to the products. An example is that if the advertised municipal security has the characteristics of a money market fund, the advertisement must include a statement noting that the security is not guaranteed by any government agency.

Municipal securities advertisements are also required to offer a legend explaining the relevance of performance data, noting that future results cannot be guaranteed on the basis of past performance, that an investor may lose more than his original investment, and that even current performance may be worse than the (past) performance indicated in the advertisement.

Additionally, such advertisements should note any sales loads or other nonrecurring fee, including whether such fees are reflected in the advertisement's performance data.

Lastly, to whatever extent this is applicable to the performance data, the advertisement should include the total annual operating expense ratio of municipal securities (gross of fee waivers or expense reimbursements).

STANDARDS AND APPROVAL

The general standard for all municipal securities advertisements is that they may not be **materially false or misleading**. The prohibition of misleading information includes an appraisal of the clarity of the information, its emphases, its intended audience, and other relevant factors which go beyond the technical accuracy of the information.

Advertisement for municipal securities must be approved in writing by a municipal securities principal or a general securities principal prior to the advertisement's first display. Records of this approval should be maintained by each broker dealer and municipal securities dealer involved.

TYPES OF ADVERTISEMENTS

Professional advertisements are advertisements related to the skills, services, or facilities of some professional broker or dealer of municipal securities. The requirements for these advertisements are the same as the more general requirements for municipal securities advertisements; they must not be materially false or misleading.

Product advertisements are advertisements related to specific municipal securities, issues of municipal securities, or features of municipal securities. These also must not be materially false or misleading.

New issue advertisements are specific types of product advertisements dealing with the new issue of municipal securities. These advertisements have specific requirements related to accuracy at the time of sale (if showing initial reoffering prices or yields for securities, the date for such information must be provided) and accuracy at the time of publication (there must be a disclaimer

25

noting that the advertised securities may no longer be available at the time of publication, or that they may be available only at a different price).

MUNICIPAL SECURITIES BUSINESSES AND POLITICAL CONTRIBUTIONS

To ensure that traders in the municipal securities industry are not engaging in "**fraudulent and manipulative acts and practices**," the MSRB prohibits brokers and dealers from doing business with municipal securities issuers if they have made any political contributions to officials of those issuers. Moreover, brokers and dealers are obligated to disclose their political contributions and related information to the public.

The more specific and exhaustive rules governing political contributions are found in MSRB Rule G-37.

INFORMATION BARRIERS AND QUIET PERIODS

FINRA Rule 2241 addresses conflicts of interest related to the publication and distribution of equity research reports. The Rule requires written policies and procedures that establish information barriers or other safeguards reasonably designed to ensure that research analysts are insulated from the review, pressure or oversight of persons engaged in investment banking services activities or other persons, including sales and trading personnel, who might be biased in their judgment or supervision.

It also requires quiet periods after an initial public offering (IPO) or secondary offering and before and after the expiration, waiver or termination of a lock-up agreement. Quiet periods are defined as a minimum of 10 days following the date of an IPO, and a minimum of three days following the date of a secondary offering, during which the member must not publish or otherwise distribute research reports, and research analysts must not make public appearances, relating to the issuer if the member has participated as an underwriter or dealer in the IPO or, with respect to the quiet periods after a secondary offering, acted as a manager or co-manager of that offering. FINRA interprets the date of the offering to be the later of the effective date of the registration statement or the first date on which the securities were bona fide offered to the public.

RESEARCH REPORTS

Research reports are any documents which communicate information related to the characteristics, strengths, and weaknesses of some particular stock, financial instrument, industry, commodity, or geographic region. These reports are generally prepared by **investment research teams** (or individuals) in stock brokerages or investment banks, and they ordinarily include "actionable" recommendations, i.e., recommendations for investment.

Research reports need not be done "in house," but can also be performed by a third party. Third parties in such situations are defined as persons or entities lacking any affiliation or contractual relationship with the entity being researched or any of the entity's affiliates who would have an interest in the report's contents, and making all decisions about the content of their report independently of the input of the entity being researched or its affiliates.

A number of regulations govern the distribution of research reports by brokers, such as ones clarifying whether the distribution of a research report constitutes an offer to sell. These regulations also differ according to the differing content of the reports.

TRADING AHEAD OF RESEARCH REPORTS

Trading ahead of research reports occurs when a person expects a security to be affected by the release of a research report. The reasons for the trade determine the **ethicality** of the trade. If a trade desk is placing the trade based on public knowledge and they only expect a change, then the trades placed are legal and ethical under FINRA Rule 5280. However, if the trade desk is privy to material non-public information concerning the security, whether or not they have non-public access to the research report, a trade would be illegal and unethical according to FINRA Rule 5280. A firm that trades ahead of a research report should document their reasons well, and have proof that the reasons are public knowledge.

ADVERTISEMENTS FOR GOVERNMENT SECURITIES, COLLATERALIZED MORTGAGE OBLIGATIONS (CMOS), AND CERTIFICATES OF DEPOSIT (CDS)

Advertisements for government securities are required to be filed with FINRA's Advertising Regulation Department within ten business days of the advertisements' first use.

Advertisements for **collateralized mortgage obligations (CMOs)** must likewise be filed within ten days of their first use with the Advertising Regulation Department. Specifically, the advertisements must be filed for review, and they cannot be used until all the changes designated by the department have been made. Moreover, the **National Association of Securities Dealers (NASD)** is concerned with the possibility of CMO advertisements being materially misleading, inasmuch as they are advertised as alternatives to certificates of deposit (CDs), implicitly communicating that CMOs offer the same level of security and guarantee as CDs.

Advertisements for certificates of deposit (CDs) generally have the same regulations governing them as for other types of advertisements.

FINRA RULE 2210

The FINRA Content standards for communications with the public are found in Rule 2210:

A. All member communications are to be based in fair dealing and good faith. They must be fair, balanced, and provide a sound basis for evaluating facts.

B. It is prohibited to make false, exaggerated, unwarranted, promissory, or misleading statements.

C. Information can only be based in a footnote if the placement does not inhibit the readers understanding of the information.

D. Statements are to be clear and not misleading in the context in which they are made.

E. Members must consider the nature of the audience and are to provide details and explanations when appropriate.

F. Communications cannot predict or project performance, imply that past performance will recur, or make exaggerated or unwarranted claims.

IM-2210-2

Communications with the public about variable life insurance and variable annuities - in addition to the standards in FINRA Rule 2210, additional guidelines must be met regarding communications with the public about variable life insurance and variable annuities. All communications must clearly describe the product as a variable annuity or life insurance policy. There is to be no representation that the investments are short term, and all references to liquidity must include clear language that describes the negative aspects of early redemption. The relative safety of guarantee must not be overemphasized, and there can be no representation that a guarantee applies to the investment return or value of the account.

FINRA RULE 2212

FINRA Rule 2212 defines "Ranking Entity" as any entity that provides general information about investment companies to the public, that is independent of the investment company and its affiliates, and whose services are not procured by the investment company or any of its affiliates to assign the investment company a ranking.

Members may not use investment company rankings in any retail communication other than:

(1) rankings created and published by Ranking Entities, or

(2) rankings created by an investment company or an investment company affiliate but based on the performance measurements of a Ranking Entity.

A headline or other prominent statement must not state or imply that an investment company or investment company family is the best performer in a category unless it is actually ranked first in the category.

Retail communications containing an investment company ranking must disclose the following information: the name of the category (e.g., growth); the number of investment companies in the category; the name of the Ranking Entity; the length of the period (or the first day of the period) and its ending date; and criteria on which the ranking is based (e.g., total return, risk-adjusted performance).

Other required disclosures include: the fact that past performance is no guarantee of future results; for investment companies that assess front-end sales loads, whether the ranking takes those loads into account; whether a waiver or advancement had a material effect on the total return or yield for that period, a statement about the publisher of the ranking data (e.g., "ABC Magazine, June 2011"); and if the ranking consists of a symbol (e.g., a star system), the meaning of the symbol.

Any investment company ranking included in a retail communication must be, at a minimum, current to the most recent calendar quarter ended prior to use or submission for publication. If no ranking that meets this requirement is available then a member may only use the most current ranking available, unless use of the most current ranking would be misleading. Retail communications may not present any ranking that covers a period of less than one year unless the ranking is based on yield. An investment company ranking must be based only on (A) a published category or subcategory created by a Ranking Entity or (B) a category or subcategory created by an investment company or an investment company affiliate but based on the performance measurements of a Ranking Entity.

FINRA RULE 2213

For purposes of FINRA Rule 2213, the term "bond mutual fund volatility rating" is a description issued by an independent third party relating to the sensitivity of the net asset value of a portfolio of an open-end management investment company that invests in debt securities to changes in market conditions and the general economy and is based on an evaluation of objective factors.

Members may distribute a retail communication that includes a bond mutual fund volatility rating only when the following requirements are satisfied;

- The rating does not describe volatility as a "risk" rating;
- The retail communication incorporates the most recently available rating and reflects information that, at a minimum, is current to the most recently completed calendar quarter ended prior to use;
- The criteria and methodology used to determine the rating is based exclusively on objective, quantifiable factors;
- The rating and the disclosure that accompanies it are clear, concise, and understandable.
- The entity that issued the rating provides detailed disclosure on its rating methodology to investors through a toll-free telephone number, a website, or both.

Members must also provide a description of the rating in narrative form, containing the following disclosures: (i) a statement that there is no standard method for assigning ratings; (ii) whether consideration was paid in connection with obtaining the issuance of the rating; (iii) a description of the types of risks the rating measures (e.g., short-term volatility); and (iv) a statement that there is no guarantee that the fund will continue to have the same rating or perform in the future as rated.

FINRA RULE 2216

Under FINRA Rule 2216, Communications with the Public about CMOs, a "collateralized mortgage obligation" (CMO) is a multi-class debt instrument backed by a pool of mortgage pass-through securities or mortgage loans, including real estate mortgage investment conduits (REMICs).

All retail communications and correspondence concerning CMOs must meet the following requirements:

- include within the name of the product the term "Collateralized Mortgage Obligation";
- may not compare CMOs to any other investment vehicle, including a bank certificate of deposit;
- must disclose, as applicable, that a government agency backing applies only to the face value of the CMO and not to any premium paid; and
- must disclose that a CMO's yield and average life will fluctuate depending on the actual rate at which mortgage holders prepay the mortgages underlying the CMO and changes in current interest rates.

Before selling the CMO to anyone other than an institutional investor, the member must offer the investor educational material that discusses the characteristics and risks of CMOs, the structure of a CMO, and the relationship between mortgage loans and securities, must indicate questions an investor should ask before investing, and must provide a glossary of terms.

To promote a specific CMO, the member must satisfy a detailed list of disclosure requirements.

Using Historical Performance of Past Recommendations With Prospective Customers

Note that option communications are governed by FINRA Rule and Cboe Rule 9.15. Both have similar criteria related to presenting historical performance of past recommendations or of actual transactions, and both allow approval by the other.

1. All such communications are accompanied or preceded by the ODD.
2. Any such portrayal is done in a balanced manner, and consists of records or statistics that are confined to a specific "universe" that can be fully isolated and circumscribed and that covers at least the most recent 12-month period.
3. Such communications include the date of each initial recommendation or transaction, and the relevant dates and prices.
4. All relevant costs, including commissions, fees, and interest charges (as applicable) are disclosed.
5. Whenever such communications contain annualized rates of return, all material assumptions used in the process of annualization are disclosed.
6. An indication is provided of the general market conditions during the period(s) covered, and any comparison made between such records and statistics and the overall market (e.g., comparison to an index) is valid.
7. Such communications state that the results presented should not and cannot be viewed as an indicator of future performance.
8. A Registered Options Principal determines that the records or statistics fairly present the status of the recommendations or transactions reported upon and so initials the report.

FINRA Rule 2330

Application - this rule applies to recommended purchases and exchanges of **deferred variable annuities** and **recommended initial subaccount allocations**. The Rule states that documents can be created, stored, and transmitted in electronic or paper form, and electronic signatures are acceptable as well as written form.

Principal review and approval - before submitting a customer's application to an insurance company for processing, a member must have the application package approved by a registered principal.

Supervisory procedures - a member must implement procedures for surveillance to determine if associated persons have rates of effecting deferred variable annuity exchanges that raise for review, whether such rates are consistent with FINRA or SEC rules. A member must also have policies and procedures designed to implement corrective measures addressing inappropriate exchanges.

Training - a member must develop and document training policies or programs designed to ensure that associated persons who effect and registered persons who review transactions of deferred variable annuities are compliant.

A member is not to recommend to a customer, a deferred variable annuity unless the member believes that the customer has been **informed of the features** of deferred variable annuities, the customer would benefit from such features, and the specific annuity is suitable for the customer. The same standard applies to the exchange of a deferred variable annuity, but the member must also take into account any surrender charge, product enhancements, and other deferred variable annuities the customer may have had in the last 36 months. Prior to recommending, a member must make a reasonable effort to get important information from the customer material to investment decisions, such as age, income, financial situation, investment objectives, risk tolerance, etc. After receiving all information necessary to complete an application for a deferred variable annuity, it must be sent to an **office of supervisory jurisdiction.**

FINRA Rule 2360

FINRA Rule 2360 requires members to keep a central file at their principal place of business to log complaints. The central file should make it easy to identify and retrieve information concerning complaints. This central file should at least include the identity of the complainant, the date that the firm received the complaint, the registered person servicing the account, a description of the complaint, and a record of the action taken by the member to resolve the complaint. The rule further goes on to require that the firm retain the options trading agreement at both the servicing branch and the OSJ branch. Additionally, statements must be maintained at both locations for at least six months, unless easily accessible (i.e., electronically stored), in which case statements need only be stored in one location.

Rule 156 of the Securities Act of 1933 and Material Facts

Pursuant to **Rule 156 of the Securities Act of 1933**, there are 2 requirements related to material facts. The first requirement is that investment company sales literature may not contain an untrue statement of material fact. Additionally, investment company sales literature may not omit to state a material fact that is necessary in order to make a statement made not misleading. Each circumstance is considered within the context in which the statement is made, and will be evaluated in conjunction with other statements made in connection with the sale of the same security and the absence of other explanations or qualifications that are necessary to make a statement not misleading, among others. Potential investors need to be made aware of all materials facts related to an investment company security to allow them to make an informed investment decision.

Prohibitions Relating to Interstate Commerce and Mails-Sales Literature

Section 5 of the Securities Act of 1933 states that it is unlawful for any person, directly or indirectly, to make use of interstate commerce or the mails to sell an unregistered security, a security for which a registration statement has been filed but for which the prospectus does not meet the requirements of Section 10, or a security for which the registration statement is the subject of a refusal order, a stop order or (prior to the effective date of the registration statement) any public proceeding or examination.

Investment Company Advertising

Rule 482 of Section 5 of the Securities Act of 1933 relates to investment company (i.e., mutual fund) advertising. It states that all investment company advertisements must provide the following disclosures:

- a statement advising recipients to "consider the investment objectives, risks, and charges and expenses of the investment company carefully before investing"
- information about the availability of a prospectus
- a statement encouraging recipients to carefully read the prospectus before investing

For advertisements that include performance data, Rule 482 also requires the following disclosures:

- that performance data quoted is past performance, past performance does not guarantee future results, and current performance may be lower or higher than the performance data quoted
- that an investment's return and principal value will fluctuate such that an investor's shares, when redeemed, may be worth more or less than their original cost
- either a telephone number or a Web site where an investor may obtain performance data current to the most recent month-end
- if a sales load or any other nonrecurring fee is charged, the maximum amount of the load or fee and, if not reflected, that the performance data does not reflect the deduction of the sales load or fee, and that, if reflected, the load or fee would reduce the performance quoted

MAILS-PROSPECTUSES FOR OPEN-END COMPANIES

Rule 498 of Section 5 of the Securities Act of 1933 requires key information to appear in a standardized form at the front of the mutual fund Statutory Prospectus. It also permits a mutual fund Summary Prospectus to be given or sent to investors, as long as a Statutory Prospectus is made available online. Mutual funds must also send the Statutory Prospectus upon request. The rule was adopted to improve mutual fund disclosure by providing investors with key information in plain English in a clear and concise format, while enhancing the means of delivering more detailed information to investors.

SEC RULE 15C2-12

Rule 15c2-12 requires dealers that underwrite certain types of municipal securities to ensure that the state or local government issuing the bonds enters into an agreement to provide specific information to the Municipal Securities Rulemaking Board (MSRB) about the securities on an ongoing basis. These continuing disclosures should provide up-to-date information about the municipality's financial and operating condition, as well as events that could impact the value of the bonds or the state or local government's ability to pay investors. Annual disclosures must be submitted by the date specified in the Continuing Disclosure Agreement, while information about events must be submitted within 10 days of occurrence. Disclosures are made available to investors and the public on the MSRB's Electronic Municipal Market Access (EMMA®) website.

CUSTOMER PROTECTION-RESERVES AND CUSTODY OF SECURITIES

According to Rule 15c3-3 of the 1934 Act, a broker or dealer must promptly obtain and thereafter maintain the physical possession or control of all fully-paid securities and excess margin securities carried by the broker or dealer for the account of customers. Securities under the control of a broker or dealer shall be deemed to be those that are in the offices or in transit between offices of the broker or dealer, or in accounts at clearing organizations or banks in the name of the broker dealer, or in any other location deemed adequate by the Commission.

The provisions of this section do not apply to brokers or dealers that meet the following requirements:

- pass through all transactions to banks or other broker/dealers
- act as dealer (as principal for its own account) in redeemable securities of registered investment companies or of interests or participations in an insurance company separate account

- act as broker (agent) in the sale and redemption of redeemable securities of registered investment companies or of interests or participations in an insurance company separate account, the solicitation of share accounts for savings and loan associations insured by an instrumentality of the United States, and the sale of securities for the account of a customer to obtain funds for immediate reinvestment in redeemable securities of registered investment companies
- transmit all funds and deliver all securities received in connection with its activities as a broker or dealer, and do not otherwise hold funds or securities for, or owe money or securities to, customers

CBOE RULE 9.8

Cboe Rule 9.8 states that no Trading Permit Holder (TPH) [member] organization shall address any communications to a customer in care of any other person unless either (a) the customer, within the preceding 12 months, has instructed the TPH [member] organization in writing to send communications in care of such other persons, or (b) duplicate copies are sent to the customer at some other address designated in writing by him.

CBOE RULE 9.9

Cboe Rule 9.9 requires that every TPH [member] organization deliver a current options disclosure document to each customer, at or prior to the time such customer's account is approved for options transactions. A copy of each amendment to an options disclosure document must be furnished to each customer who was previously provided the options disclosure document, not later than the time a confirmation of a transaction in the category of options to which the amendment pertains is delivered to such customer. When such customer is a broker or dealer, the TPH [member] organization must take reasonable steps to see to it that the broker or dealer is furnished reasonable quantities of current options disclosure documents, as requested by him, in order to enable him to comply with the requirements of this Rule.

CBOE RULE 9.15

According to Cboe Rule 9.15, an "options communication" must be approved by a Registered Options Principal prior to use. Options Communications include:

- **Advertisements** - any material concerning options that is published or used in any electronic or other public media
- **Sales Literature** - any written or electronic communication concerning options other than an advertisement
- **Correspondence** - any written letter or electronic mail message or market letter distributed by a TPH member to: (A) one of more of its existing retail customers; and (B) fewer than 25 prospective retail customers within any 30 calendar-day period
- **Institutional Communication [Sales Material]** - any written (including electronic) communication concerning options that is distributed or made available only to institutional investors
- **Public Appearances** - any participation in a seminar, forum (including an interactive electronic forum), radio, television or print media interview, or other public speaking activity, or the writing of a print media article concerning options
- **Independently Prepared Reprints** - any reprint or excerpt of an article issued by a publisher concerning options

OPTIONS COMMUNICATIONS

Options Communications as defined by Cboe 9.15 are subject to specific approval and record retention requirements. All advertisements, sales literature, and independently prepared reprints issued by a TPH organization pertaining to options must be approved in advance by a Registered Options Principal designated by the organization's written supervisory procedures.

If the communication is not accompanied or preceded by the current Options Disclosure Document (ODD), it must be submitted to the Exchange for review and approval at least ten calendar days prior to use. Exceptions to this requirement include:

- the TPH could submit the communication to a different SRO that has similar standards to Cboe (like FINRA)
- the TPH does not need approval if the communication simply lists their services

Communications must be retained by the TPH organization for the time periods specified under Rule 17a-4 of the Securities Exchange Act of 1934, along with the names of the persons who prepared the options communications, the names of the persons who approved the options communications, and the source of any recommendations contained therein.

REQUIREMENTS FOR OPTIONS COMMUNICATIONS THAT FEATURE RECORDS AND STATISTICS

Options communications may feature records and statistics which portray the performance of past recommendations or of actual transactions, provided that:

- All such communications are accompanied or preceded by the ODD
- Any such portrayal is done in a balanced manner, and consists of records or statistics that are confined to a specific "universe" that covers at least the most recent 12-month period
- Such communications include the date and price of each initial recommendation or transaction, and the date and price of each recommendation or transaction at the end of the period or when liquidation was suggested or effected, whichever was earlier
- All relevant costs, including commissions, fees, and interest charges (as applicable) are disclosed
- Whenever such communications contain annualized rates of return, all material assumptions used in the process of annualization are disclosed
- An indication is provided of the general market conditions during the period(s) covered, and any comparison made between such records and statistics and the overall market (e.g., comparison to an index) is valid
- Such communications state that the results presented should not and cannot be viewed as an indicator of future performance
- A Registered Options Principal determines that the records or statistics fairly present the status of the recommendations or transactions reported upon and so initials the report

"ADVERTISEMENT" ACCORDING TO MSRB RULE G-21

For purposes of MSRB Rule G-21, the term "advertisement" means any material published or used in any electronic or other public media, or any written or electronic promotional literature distributed or made generally available to customers or the public. The term does not apply to preliminary official statements or official statements.

All advertisements by a broker/dealer must be based on the principles of fair dealing and good faith, must consider the nature of the audience to which the advertisement will be directed and must not predict or project performance, or imply that past performance will recur. There is a standard set of disclosures that must accompany advertisements, such as maximum charges, fees, or loads, and warnings like "consider the objectives, risks, and charges and expenses" and "past performance does not guarantee future results". Each advertisement must be approved in writing by a municipal securities principal or general securities principal prior to first use.

In recent years a new form of advertisement has been created: Interactive Content. Interactive content that is an advertisement and that would be posted or disseminated in an interactive electronic forum is exempt from the requirement to be approved in writing by a municipal securities principal or general securities principal prior to first use. However, each broker, dealer and municipal securities dealer must supervise and review interactive content in the same manner in which they supervise and review correspondence under Rule G-27.

SUBTYPES OF PRODUCT ADVERTISEMENT

MSRB Rule G-21 defines certain specific types of advertisements and standards for each:

- Professional Advertisement - means any advertisement concerning the facilities, services or skills with respect to municipal securities of such broker, dealer or municipal securities dealer
- Product Advertisement – means any advertisement concerning specific securities or securities from specific issuers

There are two subtypes of Product Advertisement:

New Issue Product Advertisements – these advertisements may show the initial reoffering prices or yields for the securities, or the prices or yields of the securities as of the time the advertisement is submitted for publication. Each advertisement must also indicate, if applicable, that the securities shown as available from the syndicate may no longer be available from the syndicate at the time of publication or may be available from the syndicate at a price or yield different from that shown.

Municipal Fund Security Product Advertisements – these advertisements must provide the following disclosures: an investor should consider the investment objectives, risks, and charges and expenses associated with municipal fund securities before investing; more information about municipal fund securities is available in the issuer's official statement; that the broker, dealer or municipal securities dealer publishing the advertisement is the underwriter for one or more issues of such municipal fund securities; and the official statement should be read carefully before investing.

Describing Investment Products to Customers

REQUIRED DISCLOSURES FOR SPECIFIC TRANSACTIONS

Offering documents are disclosures provided by issuers of securities providing specific and detailed financial information concerning both the issuer and the offering itself.

Prospectuses are formal documents which brokers are legally required to file with the SEC. They provide information about investments being offered for sale to the public, giving information so that investors can make intelligent and informed decisions. Stocks and bonds have two types of prospectuses, preliminary and final.

Red herrings are preliminary prospectuses. They are called such, not because they are misleading (as are "red herrings" in logic and rhetoric), but because they include a statement in red lettering on the cover declaring that they are preliminary, and thus that some items might be subject to change.

Statements of additional information, sometimes abbreviated as SAIs, are supplementary documents which are added to prospectuses for mutual fund offerings. These statements provide further details on the fund, although they are not strictly necessary for investors to make informed decisions, and therefore they are not legally required by fund companies to include. (However, they must provide such information for free to customers upon request.)

Material events are any events which substantively impact a prospective investor's decision to invest or not. These can be economic events, political events, or anything else. Brokers should be aware of these and report them to customers as is appropriate.

In order to avoid conflicts of interest and thereby protect customers, brokers are required to disclose any control relationships they have with the issuer of securities, bonds in particular. Although the initial disclosure can be merely verbal, before a transaction actually goes through, the customer must be informed in writing of the control issue. This usually takes place at confirmation.

SHELF REGISTRATION

Under SEC Rule 415, a shelf registration statement is a registration that allows an issuer to register a security without a specified issuance date or terms. The issuer then has three years to sell the entire issue. A shelf registration gives the issuer flexibility to quickly offer the securities when it deems market conditions are favorable.

BLUE SKY LAWS

Blue sky laws are state laws designed to protect investors from fraud in securities transactions. These laws require all securities offerings and sales, brokerage firms, and brokers to register with the customer's home state. The security issuer is thus responsible to register not merely with the SEC, but with each state where the securities are sold.

COOLING-OFF PERIOD AND DUE DILIGENCE MEETINGS

Issuers of securities are required to file with the SEC for the new offering. At the date of filing, a cooling-off period commences, at the end of which the issue is either cleared or rejected for public sale. The cooling-off period lasts at least twenty days, and during it, underwriters can advertise for the offering and solicit (nonbinding) indications of interest. Syndicate members are permitted to leave the underwriting agreement within the cooling-off period, but forbidden once the period has ended.

Near the end of the cooling-off period, the underwriter holds a meeting to give information for the new offering to syndicate members, selling groups, brokers, institutions, and any other interested parties. This is the due diligence meeting, designed to ensure that all material information related to the offering is disclosed to potential investors.

PRELIMINARY PROSPECTUS AND FINAL PROSPECTUS

The preliminary prospectus must be submitted along with the registration statement for the issuance of new securities, as the preliminary prospectus is required to be available to potential investors during the cooling-off period. This prospectus includes the general but important facts regarding the securities issuance, but does not include the public offering price or the date when the issue will first be sold. Preliminary prospectuses are also called red herrings because they include a statement in red lettering on the cover declaring that they are preliminary, and thus that some items might be subject to change.

The **final prospectus** is prepared near the end of the cooling-off period. It includes the public offering price, as well as the underwriter spread and the date when the securities will be available (the delivery date).

INFORMATION REQUIRED IN A REGISTRATION STATEMENT

When a company files a registration statement with the SEC, so that it may publicly issue its securities, the **registration statement** must include the following information:

- issuer's name
- description of issuer's business
- names and contact information of the issuer's control persons (officers, directors, and >10% owners of the company's securities)
- the purpose of raising the money with the issuance
- the company's capitalization
- the company's complete financial statements
- legal proceedings being filed against the company, if material

FILING DATE AND EFFECTIVE DATE FOR SECURITIES REGISTRATION

The **filing date** is the date when the (hopeful) issuer of securities files the requisite registration statement with the SEC. This filing date initiates the cooling-off period, which is at least twenty days long.

The **effective date** is the date when the cooling-off period ends, that is, once the securities are cleared for public sale.

SECURITIES ACT OF 1933

The **Securities Act of 1933** can also be called the Truth in Securities Act, the Paper Act, the Full Disclosure Act, the Prospectus Act, or the New Issues Act. It was enacted by Congress in response to the 1929 stock market crash, and it regulates new issuances for corporate securities, requiring any issuers to fully and truthfully disclose information for the new issue of securities.

TOMBSTONE ADVERTISEMENTS

Tombstone advertisements are ads in newspapers to proclaim an announcement of new securities for sales, receiving their name due to their austere, black-and-white appearance, looking like a tombstone. These advertisements are given during the cooling-off period for the securities (being the only allowed ads during that period), and therefore they are not offers for sale. They merely provide information concerning the basic facts of the securities to be issued, and they generally inform potential investors of how to obtain a prospectus for the securities.

METHODS OF UNDERWRITING MUNICIPAL BOND ISSUES

The first is a **negotiated underwriting**. When this method is used, the municipality selects one investment banker to do the underwriting. Revenue bonds are typically done through a negotiated underwriting. The underwriter and the issuer work together on the details, such as interest rates and price. Most general obligation bonds use a process called **competitive underwriting**, in which bids are taken from several different sources, and the underwriting is awarded to the lowest qualified bidder.

COMPETITIVE SALES AND NEGOTIATED SALES

Competitive sales occur when underwriters make proposals to purchase a new issue of securities, with the securities going to the underwriter (or the underwriting syndicate) offering the lowest bid. This can also be called a **public sale** or a **competitive bid**.

Negotiated sales differ from competitive sales, for they occur when the issuer simply selects an underwriter (or syndicate) to whom to sell the new issue of securities. This can also be called **negotiated underwriting**.

Both competitive sales and negotiated sales are means of **primary financing**—that is, obtaining financing within the securities' primary market.

PUBLIC OFFERINGS, PRIVATE PLACEMENTS, AND ADVANCE REFUNDING

Public offerings occur when an entity sells shares to the public for the purpose of raising funds.

Private placements occur when an entity sells share to a small number of specific investors, again for the purpose of raising funds. Investors in private placements are usually larger ones, such as banks and mutual funds.

Advance refunding is used for debt securities, issuing bonds at a lower rate in order to pay off bonds outstanding. It is often used for municipal bonds, giving governmental entities an opportunity to delay their required debt payments.

UNDERWRITING SYNDICATES

After an issuer (such as a state or local government body) has announced plans to issue bonds, the next step is to find an **underwriter**, someone willing to bring the securities to the public on the issuer's behalf. Because of the large sums of money and the financial risk involved, a **syndicate** (a group of firms that have banded together in order to lower their individual risk and investment) often performs the underwriting. Members of the syndicate must sign a syndicate agreement as part of a syndicate contract, or agreement among underwriters. The contract contains the official terms: how much each firm is obliged to underwrite, how long the obligation lasts, the person officially in charge from each member firm, and so on.

SELLING GROUPS

If an underwriting syndicate need additional assistance in selling securities, they can recruit other brokerage firms that are not components of the syndicate itself. These firms constitute **selling groups**. Members of selling groups do not purchase shares from the issuer, although they perform the service of selling them to the public. Because they are not responsible to the issuer for unsold shares, they receive a smaller commission per share sold.

REGIONAL DIFFERENCES

There are two different ways to assign the financial obligations of syndicates. The first is the **Western-style syndicate**. Under this arrangement, the financial obligations are divided between the firms, and each firm is only held responsible for selling its own allocation of bonds. Under an **Eastern-style syndicate**, each firm receives an allocation, but any unsold bonds are the responsibility of the entire syndicate, and they are divided proportionally. So even though a member firm sells all its allocation, it may be required to purchase unsold bonds from other allocations.

MANAGER'S FEES, TAKEDOWNS, CONCESSIONS, AND REALLOWANCES

The spread for an underwriting syndicate is composed of two factors, the manager's fee and the takedown. The **manager's fee** is the profit earned by the syndicate manager, and is generally the smallest of fees for the share's sale. The **takedown** is the profit earned by the members of the syndicate; since they are assuming the risk to sell the securities they purchased from the issuing company, they deserve most of the profits.

Whenever underwriters employ selling groups to assist the selling of their securities, they give a percentage of the takedown to the selling groups; this percentage is the **concession**. The remainder of the takedown is the **additional takedown**.

Firms not part of the syndicate or a selling group can still profit through the selling of an issuing company's securities. Any portion of the takedown earned by these companies is the **reallowance**.

SPREAD IN UNDERWRITING BONDS

When shares are issued for an underwriting syndicate to sell, they're sold to the syndicate at a certain price. The syndicate hopes to make money by turning around and selling the shares to the public (individual and institutional investors) at a higher price. The price the public pays is the **re-offering price**. This is part of what makes underwriting a share so difficult: a syndicate has to be the lowest bidder and to sell the shares at a price that the public wants, but still make a profit. The difference between the re-offering price (at which the shares are sold to the public) and the price at which the shares are bought from the issuer is the **spread**. This spread can be subdivided into the syndicate manager's fee and the takedown.

COMPONENTS OF WINNING UNDERWRITING BIDS

Syndicate members will look at the proposed bond and crunch the numbers to determine the selling price and terms necessary for them to both sell the bonds and make a profit. Their profit comes from the **spread**, or the difference in the price they pay the issuer for the bonds and the price at which they sell the bonds to the public. In addition, they receive a **management fee** for each bond sold.

Syndicate members then write the **scale**, which determines the actual price for each series of bond. They then submit their bid at the lowest price at which they think they can make a profit. The bid with the lowest net interest cost to the issuer is the winner. Syndicates must be very sure of their numbers, because they can't back out of a winning bid, even if it turns out they calculated wrong and will lose money.

TYPES OF UNDERWRITING AGREEMENTS

Before an offering occurs, an underwriter gauges demand through indications of interest. Despite this, sometimes all the shares of an offering are not sold. The underwriting agreement addresses this situation in advance by outlining the underwriters' responsibilities. There are generally four types of underwriting agreements:

1. Best Efforts – states that the underwriters will do their best to sell all the securities of the issue but if they are unable to, they are not obligated to purchase the securities for their own account.
2. Mini Max – states that the offering will not become effective unless a minimum number of securities are sold. This protects both the issuer and underwriter. Until the minimum is met, all funds are held in escrow and if the issuance is cancelled investors receive refunds.

3. All or None – states that the issuer will sell either all of its offering or none. Similar to the mini max agreement, all funds are held in escrow and if the issuance is cancelled investors receive refunds.
4. Standby – states that the underwriter agrees to buy any unsold securities. This transfers the risk from the issuer to the underwriter.

NORMAL ALLOCATION PRIORITY IN BOND UNDERWRITING

When a bond issue is oversubscribed, the underwriting syndicate must use allocation priorities to determine who gets the opportunity to purchase the bonds. Orders are filled in the following sequence:

1. **Pre-sale** - orders that are entered before the syndicate wins the bid. These customers indicated willingness to buy the bonds without knowing the specific terms of the offering.
2. **Group net** - orders that are placed in the syndicate bank account and distributed to members of the syndicate according to their participation upon completion of the underwriting.
3. **Designated** - orders that specify which member of the syndicate is going to receive credit for the order.
4. **Member** - orders that are placed by members of the syndicate looking to buy bonds for their own account.

SEC REGISTRATION STATEMENTS

When an investment company files a **registration statement** with the SEC, it consists of two parts. The first part is the **prospectus**. This is the information that every potential investor in the company must be provided with before they're allowed to purchase the company's shares. The prospectus is also known as a summary prospectus, or an NI-A prospectus. The second part is the information that must be on file with the SEC and available for public inspection, but is not required to be provided to all potential investors. It is also called the **statement of additional information (SAI)**.

STATEMENTS OF ADDITIONAL INFORMATION

All information that an investment company is required to provide to investors before they purchase shares in the company is provided in the prospectus. However, some investors and members of the public may desire additional information about the company beyond what's provided in the prospectus. This additional information, such as the history of the company, or a detailed financial profile, are in the **statement of additional information (SAI)**, and must be provided to potential investors upon request. These days, the SAI is commonly provided on the company website.

ALLOWABLE INFORMATION RELEASES FOR NEW SECURITIES
INFORMATION RELEASES IN THE PRE-FILING PERIOD

The **pre-filing period** is the entire time before the issuing company files to register the securities-to-be-issued with the SEC. During this period, offers to sell the securities are restricted. The regulations forbid all oral or written "offers to sell," but this term has a very broad meaning. It does not refer to offers in the sense of contract law, but refers to any attempts to increase or incite interest among possible buyers—in other words, any attempt to get people interested at all. This restriction exists to prevent issuing companies from "jumping the gun" in advertising the securities.

However, the important of full, public disclosure presses the other way, encouraging companies to reveal information. For this reason, securities law has exemptions to the release of information for securities-to-be-issued, such as SEC Rules 137, 138, and 139. (These rules apply to the cooling-off and post-registration periods as well.)

INFORMATION RELEASES IN THE COOLING-OFF PERIOD

Within the **cooling-off period**, the period between the initial filing of securities to be registered with the SEC and their approval (also known as the "filing period"), offers to sell the securities are more widely permitted. While brokers may not make offers in the sense of contract law—that is, offers which legally bind the other party to purchase—they can still seek indications of interest. This is done through **tombstone advertisements,** which are the only allowed types of ads during the cooling-off period.

INFORMATION RELEASES IN THE POST-REGISTRATION PERIOD

During the **post-registration period**, securities are allowed to be offered as normal. There are still normal regulations governing securities sales, but nothing additional for this period. For example, written offers to sell and confirmations of sales must be qualifying prospectuses, and no security can be delivered for sale unless a qualifying prospectus attends or precedes it.

The post-registration period can also be called the **post-effective period**, since it follows the effective date, when the securities are approved for public sale.

OFFICIAL STATEMENTS FOR MUNICIPAL BOND SECURITIES

Official statements of a municipal bond issue must contain all the information prospective investors will need to evaluate the bond and must be signed by an officer of the issuer. Information that must be part of the official statement includes:

- terms of the offering
- purpose of the bond
- whether the bond can be redeemed prior to maturity
- how principal and interest will be repaid
- any collateral or security
- any legal proceedings affecting the bond
- tax status of the bond
- financial condition of the issuer

An official statement for municipal bonds is similar to a prospectus for other securities. Municipal bonds also have a preliminary official statement, which is roughly equivalent to a preliminary prospectus for other securities.

NOTICES OF SALE

Notices of sale are announcements made by municipal entities to declare that the entity is now accepting bids from underwriters (or underwriting syndicates) to purchase the issue of a new bond. They should include the following:

- amount and kind of bonds
- purpose for selling the bonds
- interest payment dates and maturity schedule
- bond counsel that prepared the legal opinion
- location and time for bids to be delivered
- good faith deposit (a refundable deposit displaying intent to purchase)

ACCREDITED INVESTORS FOR LIMITED PARTNERSHIPS

The average man on the street is not qualified to take part in a limited partnership sold by private placement. The government requires that anyone taking part in a privately placed limited partnership have substantial income and/or substantial net worth.

According to the SEC, to qualify as an **accredited investor**, a person must either have a net worth of more than one million dollars on his own or together with a spouse, or the person must have had an income of over $200,000 for each of the last two years, plus have a reasonable expectation that he will continue to receive the same level of income.

REGULATION A OFFERINGS

Regulation A offerings are any offerings of securities which are worth $5 million or less within a twelve-month period. Due to the smaller size of these offerings, the offerings are exempt from the more stringent registration requirements for other securities. Regulation A offerings need only a simplified or abbreviated registration statement. Moreover, an **offering circular** must be given to potential investors in the issued securities.

The name for these offerings arises from the fact that SEC Regulation A governs offerings of this sort.

REGULATION D OFFERINGS

Regulation D provides the rules by which securities can be exempted from the ordinary SEC registration requirements. The purpose of this is to aid smaller companies who could not afford to pay for all the registration fees. The exemptions also improve the rate at which these smaller companies can raise funds for themselves.

Regulation D offerings are also called **private placements**. They can be given to a maximum of 35 "unaccredited investors," as defined according to the regulation.

SECURITIES EXEMPTED FROM REGISTRATION

Some securities are **exempt** from the registration requirements applicable to other securities per the Securities Act of 1933. This is due either to the **credit standing** of the issuer, which is perceived to be high, or to the **authority** belonging to a government regulatory agency. (In the case of fixed annuities, they are exempt because the insurance company guarantees them.) The exempt securities include the following:

- securities issued by the federal government or its agencies
- municipal (local government) bonds
- securities from banks, savings institutions, and credit unions
- public utility securities
- securities issued by nonprofit, educational, or religious institutions
- fixed annuities and insurance policies
- notes, bills of exchange, bankers' acceptances, and commercial paper with an initial maturity of at most 270 days

SECTION 3(A)(11) OF THE SECURITIES ACT OF 1933 RULE 147

The exemption from registration for intrastate offerings is codified in **Section 3(a)(11)** of the Securities Act of 1933, including Rule 147. The rule required that, for the offering to qualify as exempted, the issuing company must be incorporated in the state where it is selling the securities, it must conduct 80% of its business in that state, and all its customers must be residents of that state. These securities would not be exempted from state-level registration, however.

REGULATION S

Regulation S exempts offshore offerings from Section 5 registration requirements provided that certain conditions are met:

- the offer or sale must be made in an "offshore transaction"
- no "directed selling efforts" may be made in the United States

Since the 1990 adoption of Regulation S, abuses had been identified that resulted in flow back of unregistered securities into the U.S. To address these abuses, securities eligible for exemption were divided into three categories based on their susceptibility to flow back.

- Category #1 is an offer that has no substantial US market interest and must only meet the general conditions.
- Category #2 includes equity securities of a reporting foreign issuer, and debt securities of a reporting U.S. or foreign issuer, or a non-reporting foreign issuer. These securities require a holding period of 40 days during which the securities may not be resold.
- Category #3 includes debt or equity securities of non-reporting U.S. issuers, equity securities of reporting U.S. issuers, and equity securities of non-reporting foreign issuers for which there is a substantial U.S. market interest. Debt securities classified as Category #3 require a 40-day period during which the securities cannot be resold. Equity securities classified as Category #3 require a holding period of six months if the issuer is a reporting company, and a period of one year otherwise.

Regulation S exemptions are not available for the offer and sale of securities issued by open-end investment companies, unit investment trusts, or closed-end investment companies.

EXCHANGE CONTROLS

Since national governments have a vested interest in what their currency's exchange rate is, they will sometimes erect **exchange controls** in order to modify the rate as they see fit. This can include banning (or restricting) the use of another currency within their country, banning their own citizens from even possessing another currency, fixing exchange rates (rather than permitting them to float), and controlling the quantity of a foreign currency which is imported or exported.

Generally speaking, financially weaker countries are more prone to implement exchange controls.

FINRA RULE 3160

Networking arrangements between members and financial institutions (FINRA Rule 3160) - a member that is a part of a networking agreement under which it conducts broker-dealer services on or off the premises of a financial institution is subject to the Rule.

Setting - the member is to be clearly identified and have its services distinguished from the services of the financial institution, have its name displayed where it conducts business, and maintain its services physically separate from that of the financial institution if at all possible.

FINRA RULE 3170

FINRA Rule 3170 states that each member that is either notified by FINRA or otherwise has actual knowledge that it is a taping firm shall establish, maintain, and enforce special written procedures for supervising the telemarketing activities of all its registered persons. A taping firm is member firm that meets one of the three following criteria, based on how many registered employees have been associated with one or more disciplined firms in a registered capacity within the last three years:

- a member with 5-9 registered persons, where 40% or more have been associated with disciplined firm(s)
- a member with at least 10-19 registered persons, where four or more have been associated with disciplined firm(s)
- a member with 20+ registered persons where 20% or more have been associated with disciplined firm(s)

All tape recordings made pursuant to the requirements of this rule must be retained for a period of not less than three years, the first two years in an easily accessible place. Each taping firm must catalog the retained tapes by registered person and date. By the 30th day of the month following the end of each calendar quarter, each taping firm must submit to FINRA a report on its supervision of the telemarketing activities of its registered persons.

A firm can reduce its size within 30 days of receiving notice to avoid taping, but then cannot increase its size for 180 days. The firm must notify FINRA in writing to identify the terminated employee(s).

FINRA RULE 5110

Underwriting compensation and arrangements - all underwriting terms and agreements have to be fair and reasonable. All compensation in relation to underwriting a security has to be fair and reasonable.

Items included in compensation - all items of value received or that will be received by an underwriter in connection with a distribution starting from 180 days before the filing date are considered to be compensation and have to be disclosed in the prospectus.

Valuation of non-cash compensation - a security cannot be received by an underwriter as compensation in connection with a public offering unless the security is identical to the security issued to the public or the security can be accurately valued. Calculated compensation value is usually in some way based on, or derived from, the market price or public offering price.

Non-cash compensation - is restricted, and includes small gifts, occasional meals, and entertainment events.

FINRA RULE 5121

Public offerings of securities with conflicts of interest (FINRA Rule 5121) - no member with a conflict of interest can participate in certain public offerings unless the conflict is properly disclosed, a qualified independent underwriter has prepared it, the security is investment grade, and there is a bona fide public market.

Offerings resulting in affiliation or public ownership of member - when comprising more than 5% of the offering, it creates a conflict of interest.

Escrow of proceeds - any member offering securities under the Rule must place all proceeds in an escrow account where they must stay until the member is able to prove that they meet the net capital requirement, which requires the member to have enough funds to pay off certain obligations such as non-subordinated debt.

Discretionary accounts - no member with a conflict of interest may sell to a discretionary account.

FINRA RULE 5130

FINRA Rule 5130 was established to ensure that **initial public offerings (IPO)** are executed on a fair and unbiased basis. Rule 5130 applies to new issues, and its goals are to ensure that members do not keep a portion of the IPO for themselves or others that might entice them to and to prevent insiders from taking advantage of a new issue that retail investors may not have the same insight into. FINRA Rule 5130 established a list of persons prohibited from buying new issues. This list includes members of FINRA and their employees, representatives of the underwriters that underwrote the new issue, a shareholder that owns more the 10 percent of a FINRA member firm, portfolio managers, and immediate family members of the preceding. Rule 5130 also prohibits "spinning," or the act of sending an unfair proportion of the IPO to a person that may be able to send business back.

FINRA RULE 5131

FINRA Rule 5131 prohibits the following practices when allocating and distributing new issues.

Quid Pro Quo Allocations - No member or person associated with a member may offer or threaten to withhold shares it allocates of a new issue as consideration or inducement for the receipt of compensation that is excessive in relation to the services provided by the member.

Spinning - No member or person associated with a member may allocate shares of a new issue to any account in which an executive officer or director of a company or a person materially supported by such executive officer or director, has a beneficial interest, if the company:

- is currently an investment banking services client of the member
- has received compensation from the company for investment banking services in the past 12 months
- may provide investment banking services to the company in the future

Flipping - No member or person associated with a member may directly or indirectly recoup any portion of a commission or credit paid to an associated person for selling shares of a new issue that are subsequently flipped by a customer, unless the managing underwriter has assessed a penalty bid on the entire syndicate.

REPORTING

The book-running lead manager must provide to the issuer's pricing committee or its board of directors) the following reports:

- a regular report of indications of interest
- after the settlement date of the new issue, a report of the final allocation of shares to institutional investors
- any lock-up agreement or other restriction on the transfer of the issuer's shares by officers and directors of the issuer
- the agreement between the book-running lead manager and other syndicate members requiring that any shares trading at a premium that are returned by a purchaser to a syndicate member after secondary market trading commences be used to offset the existing syndicate short position

FINRA Rule 5141

FINRA Rule 5141 is intended to protect the integrity of fixed price offerings by ensuring that securities in such offerings are sold to the public at the stated public offering price or prices, thereby preventing FINRA members from granting an undisclosed better price. It states that no member or person associated with a member that participates in a selling syndicate or selling group or that acts as the single underwriter in connection with a fixed price offering shall offer or grant, directly or indirectly, to any person or account that is not a member of the selling syndicate or selling group or that is a person or account other than the single underwriter any securities in the offering at a price below the stated public offering price ("reduced price").

A member of a selling syndicate or selling group, or a member that acts as the single underwriter, is permitted to sell securities in the offering to an affiliated person, provided such member does not sell the securities to the affiliated person at a reduced price under this Rule.

The requirements of this Rule do not apply until the termination of the offering or until a member, having made a bona fide public offering of the securities, is unable to continue selling such securities at the stated public offering price. For purposes of this Rule, securities in a fixed price offering shall be presumed salable if the securities immediately trade in the secondary market at a price or prices which are above the stated public offering price.

Nothing in this Rule prohibits the purchase and sale of securities in a fixed price offering between members of the selling syndicate or selling group.

FINRA Rule 5160

Each underwriter member of a syndicate can either sell the securities on its own or enlist the aid of agents, such as brokers or dealers, to sell the securities. These agents along with the underwriter that enlisted them are considered a selling group. The underwriter and the agents that agree to sell shares enter into a selling group agreement. The agents receive compensation from the underwriter member in the form of a concession, which is usually a markup (spread) between the discounted syndicate price and the price to the public.

FINRA Rule 5160 requires that selling syndicate agreements or selling group agreements set forth the price at which securities are to be sold to the public or the formula by which such price can be ascertained and state clearly to whom and under what circumstances concessions, if any, may be allowed.

There are two different types of agreements among underwriters that divide the liability of any unsold portion of the issue:

1. Undivided (Eastern Account Basis) - each syndicate member is responsible for all the unsold securities in an issue according to their percentage of participation.
2. Divided (Western Account Basis) - each syndicate member is only responsible for the unsold securities of their portion of the issue.

FINRA Rule 5190

FINRA Rule 5190 outlines the required notifications for new public offerings. It provides requirements for securities subject to a restricted period under SEC Regulation M as well as actively traded securities:

A. Securities subject to a restricted period - a written notice must be submitted relaying to FINRA information regarding whether a one-day or five-day restricted period applies (according to Rule

101 of SEC Regulation M), the name and symbol of the security, the type of security, identification of participants and purchasers, the pricing, and the number of shares offered, among other things.

B. Actively traded securities - a written notice must be submitted relaying to FINRA information regarding the fact that no restrictive period applies, the name and symbol of the security, the type of security, identification of participants and purchasers, the pricing, and the number of shares offered, among other things.

FINRA Rule 5190 outlines the required notifications for **penalty bids** and **syndicate covering transactions**. When a member is imposing a penalty bid or is conducting a syndicate covering transaction, a written notice must be submitted relaying to FINRA information regarding the intent to carry out the activity and identification of the security and symbol, before imposing the bid or conducting the transaction. A confirmation is to be submitted to FINRA within one business day of the completion of the activity, including identification of the security and symbol, the total number of shares, and the date of the activity.

EXEMPTED TRANSACTIONS - COMMUNICATIONS NOT DEEMED A PROSPECTUS

Under Rule 134 of the Securities Act of 1933, a communication is not considered a prospectus if it is limited to the following types of information:

- Factual information about the legal identity and business location of the issuer
- The title of the security and the amount being offered
- A brief indication of the general type of business of the issuer
- The price of the security, or if the price is not known, the method of its determination
- In the case of a fixed income security, the final maturity and interest rate provisions
- In the case of a fixed income security with a fixed (non-contingent) interest rate provision, the yield or the probable yield range
- A brief description of the intended use of proceeds of the offering
- The name, address, phone number, and e-mail address of the sender of the communication and the fact that it is participating, or expects to participate, in the distribution of the security
- The type of underwriting
- The names of underwriters participating in the offering, and their additional roles, if any, within the underwriting syndicate
- The anticipated schedule for the offering and a description of marketing events
- A description of the procedures by which the underwriters will conduct the offering
- Whether, in the opinion of counsel, the security is a legal investment for savings banks, fiduciaries, insurance companies, or similar investors under the laws of any State or Territory, and the permissibility or status of the investment under ERISA
- Whether, in the opinion of counsel, the security is exempt from specified taxes
- Whether the security is being offered through rights issued to security holders, and, if so, the class of securities the holders of which will be entitled to subscribe
- Any statement or legend required by any state law or administrative authority
- The names of selling security holders
- The names of securities exchanges or other securities markets where any class of the issuer's securities are, or will be, listed

- The ticker symbols, or proposed ticker symbols, of the issuer's securities
- The CUSIP number assigned to the securities being offered
- Information disclosed in order to correct inaccuracies previously contained in a communication permissibly made pursuant to this section

EDUCATIONAL MATERIALS EXEMPT FROM DISCLOSURE

Educational materials are exempt from disclosure if the material complies with SEC Rule 134A. In order to comply, the educational material must meet the following guidelines:

- The risks involved in options trading and the strategies addressed in the material must be explained.
- Performance figures and annualized rates of returns cannot be used in the material.
- There is no recommendation to purchase or sell an option contract.
- The only securities identified are those that are exempt from registration, index options and foreign currency options.
- The name and address where an options disclosure document can be obtained must be listed in the material.

RULE 144

Rule 144 is an SEC rule governing the sale of restricted, unregistered, and control securities. (**Control securities** refer to securities that effectively give the owner control over the entity.) The rule establishes five requirements which must be met for the securities to be permissibly sold:

1. A specific holding period must pass. This can involve the seller to wait between six months and twelve months before being allowed to sell.
2. An "adequate" amount of information concerning the securities' past performance has been publicly disclosed.
3. The amount of securities to be sold is no more than 1% either of the outstanding shares or of the average weekly trading volume over the previous four weeks.
4. A seller desiring to sell over 500 shares or $10,000 must file a form with the SEC prior to making the sale.
5. Other requirements for ordinary trades have been fulfilled.

RULE 144A

Rule 144a is an SEC rule which provides exemptions from ordinary registration requirements for specific securities transactions. These transactions must be private resales of at least $500,000 units of restricted securities, and they must be made with a **qualified institutional buyer (QIB)**, which generally refers to an institution with at least $100 million in assets to invest. An institution's status as a QIB depends upon its presentation of specific documents to the SEC, including audited financial statements.

This rule permits securities to be more liquid than otherwise, since there are fewer restrictions on their ability to be transferred. In fact, one particular purpose of the rule is to encourage foreign institutions to sell their securities in U.S. markets.

This rule is distinct from rule 144; the two should not be confused.

48

RULE 145 OF THE SECURITIES ACT OF 1933

Under Rule 145 of the Securities Act of 1933, the following situations, when approved by a security holder vote, constitute the sale of a security and require a new registration to be filed:

- the substitution of one security for another
- the merger, consolidation, or similar plan or acquisition through which the securities of one entity are exchanged for another
- the transfer of assets where the consideration paid is securities of the purchaser corporation or entity

SEC RULE 164

Rule 164 - provides for some leniency in the free writing prospectus requirements for certain offerings.

Conditions for WKSIs - A WKSI can use a free writing prospectus as long as a registration statement has been filed that includes a prospectus.

Conditions for non-reporting and unseasoned issuers - if the issuer is to give compensation for the dissemination of the free writing prospectus, a registration statement has to have been previous filed that includes a prospectus. The free writing prospectus has to be accompanied by the original prospectus.

SEA RULE 10B-1, SEA RULE 10B5-2

Prohibitions with respect to securities exempted from registration (Rule 10b-1) - it is prohibited to use any manipulative or deceptive device in connection with securities exempt from registration pursuant to the SEA.

Duties of trust or confidence in misappropriation insider trading cases (Rule 10b5-2) - a duty of trust and confidence exists:

A. when a person agrees to maintain information in confidence;

B. when the persons involved in communicating the material nonpublic information have a history or practice of sharing confidences to the extent that the communicator trusts the information will remain confidential;

C. or when a person receives information from a spouse, parent, child, or sibling.

RULE 10B-5 OF THE SECURITIES ACT OF 1934

Rule 10b-5 of the Securities Act of 1934 prohibits manipulative or deceptive practices in the sale of securities. These practices include:

- spreading market rumors for the purpose of influencing others to buy or sell a security
- frontrunning, which is when a broker or financial advisor buys securities for their personal account before buying them for their clients, or sells them from their personal account before selling them from their clients' accounts
- churning, which is when a broker excessively trades in a client's account only to generate extra commissions
- commingling, which is when a broker or financial adviser combines personal money with client money without the client's permission to do so

PROHIBITED ACTIVITIES FOR BROKERS

Brokers are legally prohibited from engaging in a number of behaviors designed to unduly benefit themselves or hurt others.

They are not permitted to **prearrange trades**, which would be an agreement between a broker and a customer to buy back some security at a given price.

They are not permitted to **guarantee against losses**, since that would be frankly misrepresenting the riskiness of investments.

They are not permitted to **pay for referrals** by compensating others (whether with cash or something else) for finding, introducing, or referring a client.

They are not permitted to make **unsuitable recommendations**, which is simply to say that they ought to recommend good investments. If this is serious enough, customers can sue brokers for failing in their obligations.

SEA RULE 10B-3, SEA RULE 10B-5

Employment of manipulative and deceptive devices by brokers or dealers (Rule 10b-3) - it is prohibited for a broker or dealer to purchase or sell a security otherwise than on a national exchange with an act that is manipulative, deceptive, or fraudulent. The same is also prohibited for municipal securities dealers and municipal securities.

Employment of manipulative and deceptive devices (Rule 10b-5) - it is prohibited for any person to employ and device, scheme, or artifice to defraud; to make any untrue statements of material fact; or to engage in any act, practice, or course of business that would be a fraud or deceit upon any person in connections with the purchase or sale of any security.

SECURITIES EXCHANGE ACT RULE 10B-18

Rule 10b-18 provides issuers "safe harbor" from liability for manipulation solely by reason of the manner (i.e., timing, price, volume) of repurchases of their common stock. To be eligible for safe harbor, an issuer must satisfy four conditions on a daily basis:

- Purchases are made from or through only one broker or dealer in a single day
- Purchases are not the opening purchase reported in the consolidated system, or made within 10 minutes of the close of the principal market for securities with an average daily trading volume of $1 million or more or a public float value of $150 million or more, or within 30 minutes for all other securities
- Purchases are made at a price that does not exceed the highest independent bid or the last independent transaction price, whichever is higher, quoted in the consolidated system or, if not applicable, any national securities exchange or on inter-dealer quotation system that displays at least two priced quotations for the security, or at a price no higher than the highest independent bid obtained from three independent dealers
- Purchases do not exceed 25% of the average daily trading volume

SEC RULE 15c2-8

SEC Rule 15c2-8 states that a broker or dealer must deliver a copy of the preliminary prospectus to any person who is expected to receive a confirmation of sale at least 48 hours prior to the sending of such confirmation.

A broker or dealer must take reasonable steps to furnish a copy of the preliminary and final prospectus to the following individuals:

- any person who makes written request
- associated persons who are expected, after the effective date, to solicit customers' orders for such securities
- if serving as a managing underwriter, all other brokers or dealers participating in such distribution

A preliminary prospectus must be supplied between the filing date and a reasonable time prior to the effective date of the registration statement to which such prospectus relates and a final prospectus must be supplied between the effective date of the registration statement and the later of either the termination of such distribution, or the expiration of the applicable 40- or 90-day period under section 4(3) of the Securities Act of 1933.

SEC RULE 17A-3

Memorandum of each brokerage order given or received for the purchase or sale of securities (for customer and firm accounts) - whether executed or unexecuted. The memorandum is to show the terms and conditions; the account for which entered; the time the order was received; the time of entry; the price it was executed; the identity of any associated persons responsible for the account; the identity of the person who entered or accepted the order; and the time of execution or cancellation.

Memorandum of each purchase and sale for the account of the firm - including the price, the time of execution, and if the transaction was with a customer other than a broker or dealer, a memorandum of each order received showing the time of receipt, the terms and conditions; the identity of each associated person responsible for the account; and the identity of the person who entered or accepted the order.

SEC RULE 17A-3

Blotters or other records of original entry - are to contain an itemized daily record of all purchases and sales of securities, all receipts and deliveries of securities, all receipts and disbursements of cash, as well as all other debits and credits.

Copies of customer confirmations - and copies of notices of all other debits and credits for accounts of customers.

Identification data on beneficial owners of all accounts - all cash and margin accounts are to have identification data including the name and address of the beneficial owner of the account.

Ledgers or other records reflecting all assets and liabilities - including income and expense and capital accounts.

RULE 415 OF REGULATION C OF THE SECURITIES ACT OF 1933

Rule 415 of Regulation C of the Securities Act of 1933 pertains to shelf registrations where the statement permits multiple offerings on the same registration. It can be used for primary offerings, secondary offerings, or a combination of both. Securities are registered for sale either on a continuous or delayed basis. In a "continuous offering," securities are offered promptly after the effective date of the registration (within two days) and will continue to be offered in the future. In a "delayed offering," there is no present intention to offer securities at the time of the effective date.

RULE 427 OF REGULATION C OF THE SECURITIES ACT OF 1933

Rule 427 of Regulation C of the Securities Act of 1933 allows the contents of a prospectus used for more than nine months after the effective date to omit outdated required information if the prospectus contains updated required information including the latest certified financial statements. However, the time period of the replacement information must be within 16 months prior to the use of the prospectus.

PROSPECTUS FILING REQUIREMENTS FOUND IN SEC RULE 430, 430A, AND 430B

Prospectus for use prior to effective date (Rule 430) - prospectus can be used prior to effective date so long as all requirements are met.

Prospectus in a registration statement at time of effectiveness (Rule 430A)- a prospectus submitted as part of a registration statement can omit certain details so long as certain requirements are met, such as the securities only being offered for cash.

Prospectus in a registration statement after effective date (Rule 430B) - a prospectus filed with a registration statement can omit certain unknown or unavailable information.

REGULATION D
EXEMPTED TRANSACTIONS

Regulation D relates to transactions exempted from the registration requirements of Section 5 of the Securities Act of 1933. Such transactions are not exempt from the antifraud, civil liability, or other provisions of the federal securities laws. Users of Regulation D exemptions must keep in mind the following:

- Nothing in Regulation D removes the need to comply with any applicable state law relating to the offer and sale of securities.
- Attempted compliance with any rule in Regulation D does not act as an exclusive election; the issuer can also claim the availability of any other applicable exemption.
- Regulation D is available only to the issuer of the securities and not to any affiliate of that issuer or to any other person for resales of the issuer's securities.
- Regulation D is not available to any issuer for any transaction or chain of transactions that, even if in technical compliance with Regulation D, is part of a plan or scheme to evade the registration provisions of the Act.
- Securities offered and sold outside the United States in accordance with Regulation S need not be registered under the Act. For example, persons who are offered and sold securities in accordance with Regulation S would not be counted in the calculation of the number of purchasers under Regulation D.

CATEGORIES OF ACCREDITED INVESTOR

The definition of Accredited Investor continues to evolve, as more types of investors are added. As of October 2020, the following categories are defined by Regulation D, section 501:

- any bank or any savings and loan association or other institution acting in its individual or fiduciary capacity
- any broker or dealer
- any investment adviser
- any insurance company
- any investment company
- any Small Business Investment Company or Rural Business Investment Company

- any employee benefit plan with assets exceeding $5 million
- any private business development company
- any business trust, partnership or LLC not formed for the specific purpose of acquiring securities with assets exceeding $5 million
- any director, executive officer, or general partner of the issuer of the securities being offered or sold
- any natural person whose individual net worth, or joint net worth with that person's spouse or spousal equivalent, exceeds $1,000,000, excluding their primary residence
- any natural person whose income is >$200K in the prior two years (>$300K for joint/married income) and who has a reasonable expectation of the same income this year
- any natural person with a professional certification recognized by the Commission or considered a "knowledgeable employee"; and any "family office" or "family client" defined by the Investment Company Act of 1940

TERMS AND CONDITIONS RELATED TO TIMEFRAME AND REQUIRED INFORMATION.

All sales that are part of the same Regulation D offering must meet all the terms and conditions of Regulation D, Section 502.

1. Timeframe - Offers and sales made within six months before or after the completion of a Regulation D offering are part of the same offering.
2. Required Information - An issuer selling securities under Regulation D must furnish the following types of information:
   a. non-financial statement information as required by the registration statement,
   b. financial statement information as required based on the size of the offering,
   c. the issuer's annual report for the most recent fiscal year,
   d. exhibits required to be filed with the SEC as part of a registration statement, other than an annual report to shareholders,
   e. for any purchaser who is not an accredited investor, a brief description in writing of any material written information concerning the offering that has been provided by the issuer to any accredited investor,
   f. the opportunity to ask questions and receive answers concerning the terms and conditions of the offering and to obtain any additional information,
   g. for business combinations or exchange offers, written information about any terms or arrangements of the proposed transactions that are materially different from those for all other security holders,
   h. for any purchaser who is not an accredited investor, any information regarding limitations on resale.

TERMS AND CONDITIONS RELATED TO GENERAL SOLICITATION AND RESALE

All sales that are part of the same Regulation D offering must meet all the terms and conditions of Regulation D, Section 502.

1. No General Solicitation - Neither the issuer nor any person acting on its behalf may offer or sell the securities by any form of general solicitation or general advertising, including, but not limited to, advertisements, articles, seminars, or generally solicited meetings.
2. Restriction on Resale - Securities acquired in a transaction under Regulation D cannot be resold without registration or an exemption from registration.

RULE 503

Rule 503 of Regulation D requires any issuer offering or selling securities in reliance on § 230.504 or § 230.506 to file with the SEC a notice of sales containing the information required by Form D (17 CFR 239.500) for each new offering of securities no later than 15 calendar days after the first sale of securities in the offering.

An issuer may file an amendment to a previously filed notice of sales on Form D at any time and must file an amendment to correct a material mistake, as well as annually, on or before the first anniversary of the filing of the notice of sales on Form D or the filing of the most recent amendment to the notice of sales on Form D, if the offering is continuing at that time.

Immaterial changes do not require amendments. Examples include any changes like amounts, commissions, issuers or investors that do not change the Regulation D qualification.

If an issuer files an amendment for any reason, the issuer must update all required information, regardless of why the amendment was filed.

A notice of sales on Form D must be filed with the SEC in electronic format by means of the Commission's Electronic Data Gathering, Analysis, and Retrieval System (EDGAR). Every notice of sales on Form D must be signed by a person duly authorized.

RULE 504

Rule 504 of Regulation D provides an exemption from registration requirements for some companies when they offer and sell up to $10,000,000 of their securities in any 12-month period.

To be eligible for exemption, the company must satisfy the provisions of Rules 501 and 502, except the prohibitions on soliciting or advertising their securities to the public, and selling securities that are not restricted, and meet at least one of these State Requirements:

- The company registers the offering exclusively in one or more states that require a public registration statement to be filed and disclosure documents to be delivered to investors.
- A company registers and sells the offering in a state that requires registration and disclosure delivery, as well as in a state that does not, as long as the company delivers the disclosure documents required by the state where the company registered the offering to all purchasers (including in the state that has no such requirements).
- The company sells exclusively according to state law exemptions that permit general solicitation and advertising for companies selling only to "accredited investors."

Companies that are not eligible to use the Rule 504 exemptions include Exchange Act reporting companies, investment companies, companies that have no specific business plan or have indicated their business plan is to engage in a merger or acquisition with an unidentified company or companies and companies that are disqualified under Rule 504's "bad actor" disqualification provisions.

RULE 506

Rule 506 of Regulation D of the Securities Act of 1933 provides for two types of exemptions from registration. The first (Rule 506(b)) requires a company seeking exemption from registration to meet the following requirements:

- cannot use general solicitation or advertising to market the securities
- securities can be sold to an unlimited number of accredited investors but only 35 non-accredited investors, who must be, or be represented by, a sophisticated investor
- to accredited investors the company must provide information that is free from false or misleading statements and material omissions, and to non-accredited investors the company must provide the disclosure documents required under Regulation A, as well as any information provided to accredited investors
- the company must be available to answer questions from prospective purchasers

The second type of exemption (Rule 506(c)) allows a company to be exempt from registration and to broadly solicit and advertise if the company only offers the securities to accredited investors and takes reasonable steps to verify that the investors are accredited, including the review of W-2s and tax return documentation.

For both types of exemptions, companies can raise an unlimited amount of money, but investors own "restricted" securities, meaning they cannot be sold for at least six months.

RULE 507

Regulation D Rule 507 disqualifies exemptions under Regulation D Rules 504 or 506 if an issuer, or any of its predecessors or affiliates, has ever failed to comply with Rule 503, which requires the filing of a notice of sales containing the information required by Form D for each new offering of securities no later than 15 calendar days after the first sale of securities in the offering. However, the SEC may determine, upon a showing of good cause, that it is not necessary under the circumstances that the exemption be denied.

RULE 508

Regulation D Rule 508 states that a failure to comply with a term, condition or requirement of Rule 504 or Rule 506 will not result in the loss of the exemption from the requirements of section 5 of the Act for any offer or sale to a particular individual or entity, if the person relying on the exemption shows:

- the failure to comply did not pertain to a term, condition or requirement directly intended to protect that particular individual or entity
- the failure to comply was insignificant with respect to the offering as a whole
- good faith and reasonable attempt was made to comply with all applicable terms, conditions and requirements

REGULATION M

Regulation M was created to prevent manipulation by individuals with a financial interest in the outcome of an offering and prohibits activities and conduct that could artificially influence the market for an offered security. Regulation M is composed of Rules 100 to 105.

Rule 100 defines certain terms used in Regulation M. Rule 101 regulates bids and purchases by distribution participants (including underwriters and selling group members) and their affiliated purchasers. Rule 102 regulates bids and purchases by issuers, selling securityholders and their affiliated purchasers. Rule 103 governs the extent to which distribution participants that are also NASDAQ market makers can continue to engage in certain passive market making activities. Rule 104 addresses permissible stabilization arrangements that may be used to facilitate an offering. Rule 105 restricts short selling activities that may take place in connection with certain types of offerings.

REGULATION S OFFERINGS

Regulation S exempts offshore offerings from Section 5 registration requirements provided that two conditions are met: the offer or sale must be made in an "offshore transaction" (offer is not made to a person in the United States and either the buyer is outside of the United States or the transaction is executed on an established foreign securities exchange); and no "directed selling efforts" (any activities that condition the U.S. market for such securities, such as a roadshow in the U.S., placing an advertisement in a U.S. newspaper, etc.

TRUST INDENTURE ACT OF 1939

The Trust Indenture Act (TIA) of 1939 was created to strengthen the rights of bondholders. It prohibits bond issues exceeding $50 million from being offered for sale without a formal written agreement (an indenture). It also requires that a trustee be appointed for all bond issues so that the rights of bondholders are protected. Both the bond issuer and the trustee must sign the indenture, and it must fully disclose the details of the bond issue.

The provisions of the Trust Indenture Act of 1939 do not apply to any security that has been or will be issued otherwise than under an indenture; any security that has been issued or will be issued in accordance with the provisions of Regulation A; or any security which has been or is to be issued under an indenture which limits the aggregate principal amount of securities at any time outstanding to $10,000,000 or less, but this exemption shall not be applied within a period of thirty-six consecutive months to more than $10,000,000 aggregate principal amount of securities of the same issuer.

BOND INDENTURES

For any bond, the interest rate, frequency of interest payments, maturity date, characteristics of the bond (e.g., convertibility, callability), and the principal amount need to be disclosed in a contract between the bond issuer and the bond buyer. This contract is called an **indenture**.

MSRB RULE G-11

MSRB Rule G-11 requires an underwriter or syndicate to establish priority provisions for the allocation of securities which give priority to customer orders over orders by members of the syndicate for their own accounts or orders for their respective related accounts. Prior to the first offer of any securities by a syndicate, the senior syndicate manager shall furnish in writing to the other members of the syndicate and to members of the selling group:

- a written statement of all terms and conditions required by the issuer
- a written statement of all of the issuer's retail order period requirements, if any
- the priority provisions
- the procedure, if any, by which such priority provisions may be changed

- if the senior syndicate manager or managers are to be permitted on a case-by-case basis to allocate securities in a manner other than in accordance with the priority provisions, the fact that they are to be permitted to do so
- if there is to be an order period, whether orders may be confirmed prior to the end of the order period
- all pricing information

The senior syndicate manager must within 24 hours of the sending of the commitment wire, complete the allocation of securities and notify all members of the syndicate and selling group members, at the same time, via an industry-accepted electronic method of communication, that the issue is free to trade. Then, within two business days following the date of sale, disclose to the other members of the syndicate and the issuer, in writing, a summary, by priority category, of all allocations of securities which are accorded priority over members' take-down orders.

MSRB RULE G-28

MSRB Rule G-28 states that no broker, dealer or municipal securities dealer may open or maintain an account in which transactions in municipal securities may be effected for a customer who it knows is employed by, or the partner of, another broker, dealer or municipal securities dealer, or for or on behalf of the spouse or minor child of such person unless such broker, dealer, or municipal securities dealer first gives written notice with respect to the opening and maintenance of such account to the broker, dealer or municipal securities dealer by whom such person is employed or of whom such person is a partner.

No broker, dealer, or municipal securities dealer may affect a transaction in municipal securities with or for an account subject to this rule unless it sends simultaneously to the employing broker, dealer or municipal securities dealer a duplicate copy of each confirmation sent to the customer and acts in accordance with any written instructions which may be provided by an employing broker, dealer or municipal securities dealer.

The provisions of this rule are not applicable to transactions in municipal fund securities or accounts that are limited to transactions in municipal fund securities.

MSRB RULE G-32

Under **Rule G-32**, underwriters of a primary offering of municipal securities are required to send an official statement to **Electronic Municipal Market Access (EMMA)** within 1 business day after receipt of the statement from the issuer. If the official statement is not submitted by the underwriter by the closing date, the underwriter must submit to EMMA the following information:

1. The date that the official statement will be available and a commitment to send it when available
2. The preliminary official statement and a commitment to send the official statement when available
3. The fact that no official statement has been prepared because it is an exempt offering

MSRB RULE G-34

Under MSRB Rule G-34, each broker/dealer that acquires a new issue of municipal securities or is acting as a financial advisor in a competitive sale of a new issue shall apply in writing to the Board or its designee for assignment of a CUSIP number or numbers to such new issue. The CUSIP number assigned to the security must be imprinted on or otherwise affixed to the security. If the new issue refunds or alters any prior issues, the broker/dealer must apply in writing to the Board to reassign the CUSIP appropriately.

Prior to acting as underwriter for a new issue of municipal securities eligible for submission to New Issue Information Dissemination Service (NIIDS), each broker, dealer or municipal securities dealer must register to use NIIDS with DTCC and shall test its capability to use NIIDS.

The Board operates a facility for the collection and public dissemination of information and documents about securities bearing interest at short-term rates (the Short-term Obligation Rate Transparency System, or SHORT System). Information submitted to the Board pursuant to Auction Rate Securities or Variable Rate Demand Obligations shall be submitted in the manner described in the written procedures for SHORT System users.

MSRB RULE G-38

MSRB Rule G-38 prohibits any broker, dealer or municipal securities dealer from making a direct or indirect payment to any person who is not an affiliated person of the dealer for a solicitation of municipal securities business. An affiliated person of a dealer is any partner, director, officer, employee or registered person of the dealer or of an affiliated company. An affiliated company of a dealer is any entity limited solely to the solicitation of municipal securities business.

Opening Accounts

Informing Customers of Account Types and Providing Disclosures

TYPES OF ACCOUNTS

Cash accounts are ordinary brokerage accounts where the customer deposits cash to purchase various securities. Regulation T requires that customers with cash accounts pay for their securities within two days of having bought them.

Margin accounts are brokerage accounts where, instead of paying his own cash, the customer is lent cash from the broker, with various securities and cash being used as collateral.

Options accounts are brokerage accounts where the customer can trade various options, which are generally riskier than ordinary stocks or bonds.

Retirement accounts are brokerage accounts aimed for the purposes of providing retirement income.

Day trading accounts are brokerage accounts opened specifically for the purposes of trading various financial instruments within the same day, depending upon speculation for one's profits.

Prime brokerage accounts are brokerage accounts where special customers receive a special set of services. These services can include cash management and securities lending, as well as mutual funds.

Delivery Versus Payment (DVP) accounts involve a procedure where a security buyer's payment is due at the time of delivery.

Receive Versus Payment (RVP) accounts involve a procedure where a security buyer's payment is due at the time of receipt.

Advisory accounts are brokerage accounts where the customer works closely with a financial advisor but retains the final say over investment decisions.

Fee-based accounts are brokerage accounts where a customer's financial advisor is compensated as a percentage of the client's assets rather than according to commissions.

Discretionary accounts are accounts where brokers have the authority to engage in securities transactions apart from the client's consent. These accounts require the client and broker to sign a discretionary disclosure. (These are also called managed accounts.)

SPECIFIC RULES RELATED TO DISCRETIONARY ACCOUNTS

All discretionary accounts must have a power of attorney giving the investment adviser the power to make decisions on behalf of the client. The POA could have specific provisions or rules (how much margin is allowed, types of securities, etc.). All discretionary accounts must be reviewed and approved by a principal. The principal must review the account periodically to ensure that no improper trading practices are occurring, such as churning or trading ahead. All orders for these accounts must be marked Discretionary.

OPTIONS DISCLOSURE DOCUMENT (ODD)

Options are riskier than other types of investments, so before engaging in their first options transaction, investors are required to receive an **Options Disclosure Document (ODD)** that articulates these increased risks and their tax implications. (For instance, if the investor is selling call options, he could have an unlimited maximum loss potential.) The investor must read and sign this document before his brokerage account is permitted to include options.

WRAP ACCOUNTS

One type of discretionary account is marketed to customers as a "wrap" account. These accounts come with a list of services, which typically include asset management and general account maintenance. Instead of paying the firm for separate services and trade commissions, wrap accounts have all of their services "wrapped" up into one fee.

Wrap account fees are usually charged as asset under management (AUM) fees. For example, a customer with a $100,000 account would pay an annual fee of $1,000 if their wrap account fee was 1% of AUM.

Wrap accounts are considered investment advisory products and require financial professionals to be properly licensed as investment adviser representatives in order to sell them. This typically involves passing the Series 65 or Series 66 exams.

TYPES OF ACCOUNT REGISTRATION

Brokers can register accounts for a number of different businesses, not simply individuals. They can register accounts for **sole proprietorships** (individually-owned businesses), **partnerships** (businesses owned by two or more individuals who manage and operate it), and **corporations** (a business legally separate from its owners).

Furthermore, brokers can open accounts for **unincorporated associations**, which are voluntary unions of individuals for some common purpose, generally non-profit ones. They can also open accounts for **marital property** (or community property), where property acquired by either spouse is owned by the author as well, and **trust accounts**, where a trustee manages an account for the sake of another.

Among the different types of account registrations are:

- Custodial accounts - accounts managed on behalf of a minor (under 18 or 21 years old, depending on the relevant state's legislation). These accounts can be either a Uniform Transfers to Minors Act (UTMA) account (able to hold almost any type of asset) or a Uniform Gifts to Minors Act (UGMA) account (can only hold financial assets).
- Numbered accounts - accounts where the account holder's name is replaced with a multi-digit number.
- Transfer-on-death (TOD) accounts – accounts whereby a named beneficiary or beneficiaries receive the assets upon the account holder's death without going through probate.
- Estate accounts - accounts held in the name of the estate of a deceased person and handled by his or her representative (the executor or executrix).

- Joint Tenants with Rights of Survivorship (JTWROS) – accounts where all the individuals on the account have equal rights to the account's assets when one of the account holders dies.
- Joint Tenants in Common (JTIC) - accounts where if one account holder dies, the surviving account holders don't necessarily receive the assets of the deceased account holder. For instance, the deceased account holder may choose to bequeath the assets to other beneficiaries through a will.

A broker may create a joint account with a customer provided that a brokerage company principal approves the account and the customer and broker sign a Proportionate Sharing Agreement, however, this is not an advisable practice.

FINRA RULE 3210

FINRA Rule 3210 states that a person who is associated with a member ("employer member") must receive prior written consent from the member before opening an account with another member ("executing member") or at any other financial institution in which securities transactions can be affected and in which the associated person has a beneficial interest. Prior to opening such an account, the person must also notify the executing member, or other financial institution, in writing of his or her association with the employer member. Following opening of the account, executing member must, upon written request by an employer member, transmit duplicate copies of confirmations and statements.

FINRA RULE 4512

FINRA Rule 4512 states that to open a new account for a customer, members must obtain the following information:

- customer's name and residence
- whether customer is of legal age
- name(s) of the associated person(s), if any, responsible for the account, and if multiple individuals, a record indicating the scope of their responsibilities
- if the customer is a corporation, partnership or other legal entity, the names of any persons authorized to transact business on behalf of the entity
- name of and contact information of a person who may be contacted about the customer's account

Members must also make reasonable efforts to obtain, prior to the settlement of the initial transaction in the account, the following information to the extent it is applicable to the account:

- customer's tax identification or Social Security Number
- occupation of customer and name and address of employer
- whether customer is an associated person of another member
- suitability information, such as other investments, investment horizon, investment objective, and risk tolerance

Each new account must be approved in writing by signature of a partner, officer or manager denoting that the account has been accepted in accordance with the member's policies and procedures.

INDIVIDUAL RETIREMENT ACCOUNTS (IRAS)
APPROVED INVESTMENTS

Almost any type of security can be held in an IRA, including stocks, bonds, mutual funds, exchange-traded funds, unit investment trusts, and annuities.

Investment types that cannot be held in an IRA include life insurance, collectibles (e.g., stamps, coins, art, etc.), certain types of derivative instruments, and real estate.

TRANSFERS AND ROLLOVERS

Transfers and rollovers are different way of moving funds from one account to another. The movement can be between different IRA accounts (e.g., to switch from Traditional to Roth, or because the IRA holder is dissatisfied with the investment-management in a particular account), or between employer plans, or between IRAs and employer plans.

The terms are not synonymous. **Transfers** are direct movements of funds without the individual possessing the assets for any period. **Rollovers** involve a temporary period when the individual can hold the assets without any early withdrawal penalties or taxes.

There are rules restricting rollovers, however. As one example, an individual cannot roll over funds between IRAs more than once within a twelve-month period.

"TAX-ADVANTAGED" STATUS AND CONTRIBUTION LIMITS

The term "tax-advantaged" refers to any type of investment, financial account, or savings plan that is either exempt from taxation, tax-deferred, or that offers other types of tax benefits. Examples of tax-advantaged investments are municipal bonds, partnerships, UITs, and annuities. Tax-advantaged plans include IRAs and employer-sponsored qualified retirement plans such as 401(k)s.

Contribution Limits: For employer-sponsored qualified retirement plans, the limit on total employer and employee contributions is currently $66,000, or 100% of employee compensation, whichever is lower (as of 2023). For workers aged 50 and up, the limit is $73,500 ($66,000 plus the $7,500 catch-up contribution).

For IRAs, the limit on total contributions to all traditional and Roth IRAs is $6,500 ($7,500 for those age 50 or older) (as of 2023). The Setting Every Community Up for Retirement Enhancement Act (SECURE Act), which was signed into law on December 20, 2019, removed the age limit of 70½ on contributions to IRAs, allowing account holders to invest indefinitely.

Rollovers - A rollover occurs when a withdrawal of cash or other assets from one eligible qualified retirement plan is contributed, all or in part, to another eligible retirement plan within 60 days. This rollover transaction is not taxable, unless the rollover is to a Roth IRA, but is reportable on federal tax returns.

Distributions - For qualified retirement plans (employer-sponsored retirement plans and IRAs), a tax penalty of 10% of the taxable amount of the distribution is assessed if taken before age 59½.

Investors in qualified retirement plans must begin taking distributions upon reaching a specified age. The SECURE Act increased the age that minimum distributions must begin from 70½ years to 72 years.

DISTRIBUTIONS

Anyone who owns an IRA may begin taking money out of it without suffering a penalty after reaching the age of 59 ½ years. **Withdrawals** before the required age are subject to a 10% penalty in addition to any income tax on the money withdrawn. There are a few exceptions in which money may be withdrawn before the age of 59 ½ years without incurring a penalty: if the person become disabled; if taking out the money to purchase a first home which the person will be using as a residence; to pay education-related expenses for himself, his spouse, or their children or grandchildren; and for certain medical expenses. IRA owners must begin withdrawing the money by the first day of April after reaching the age of 72 years, or they will pay a 50% penalty on their withdrawals.

TRADITIONAL AND ROTH IRAS

The two different types of IRAs vary in terms of their tax benefits.

Traditional IRAs allow for tax-deductible contributions, and the investments in them grow tax-deferred, but distributions are taxed. In other words, someone placing contributions in his Traditional IRA can deduct that amount from his taxes for that year, and he doesn't have to pay any taxes on capital gains (or dividends, or interest income, or whatever) which his investments earn. However, he does have to pay income tax at the applicable rate whenever he withdraws money.

Roth IRAs have after-tax contributions, but grow tax-free and have tax-free distributions. After the contributions are made, no taxes ever have to be paid on the account.

REQUIRED MINIMUM DISTRIBUTIONS (RMDS)

In order to maintain the tax advantages for an IRA without penalty, the individual must make certain **required minimum distributions** (RMDs) on the account, though there is no maximum limit.

The RMD is determined by the value of the account and the age of the IRA holder. The IRS has a table listing factors for RMDs, so that, for any given year, the RMD equals the value of the total IRA divided by that year's factor. The factors decrease as the individual's age increases, so that the fraction of the IRA which must be distributed increases from year to year.

The first RMD must be paid by April 1 after the individual turns 72, and then they are required to be distributed annually by December 31 of subsequent years. (If the first RMD is due on April 1 in the year after the IRA holder turns 72—e.g. if the individual turns 72 in May and then has the first RMD by next April—then the next RMD will be due on December 31 of that same year.)

SEP IRAS AND SIMPLE IRAS

Simplified Employee Pension (SEP) IRAs are designed for owners of small businesses and self-employed persons, as well as their employees. (That is, eligible employers can directly make contributions to their employees' SEP IRAs.) While the tax benefits mirror those of Traditional IRAs, SEP IRAs are noteworthy for their increased contribution limits.

In SEP IRA plans, only the employer contributes - For 2022 & 2023, the maximum contribution limit is 25% of income or $61,000/$66,000, whichever is less - the employees are 100% vested, the employer has no filing requirements. Eligible employees must be over 21 and have worked at the company for 3 of the last 5 years. Also, the employee must have earned more than $650/$750 in the year for 2022/2023.

Savings Incentive Match Plan for Employees (SIMPLE) IRAs are similar to SEP IRAs, in that they have the tax benefits of a Traditional IRA and are designed for small business owners and self-employed persons. Their main difference is that they permit employees to make contributions to the plan themselves. Moreover, employers are required to contribute a certain amount, either a match or a percentage of income. SIMPLE IRAs also have higher contribution limits.

These plans - SEP IRAs and SIMPLE IRAs largely replaced Keogh Plans, which were an earlier form of retirement planning for self-employed individuals. Since the tax code was changed in 2001, Keogh Plans are now rarely used for very high-income individuals.

KEOUGH PLANS

The maximum contribution to a Keogh by the owner is the same as for SEP IRAs—for 2023, the lesser of 25% income or $66,000. However, if a person establishes a **Keogh plan** for his own benefit, that person is legally obligated to cover any employees who work for him (and are age 21 or above and worked 1,000 hours or more), but at a lesser amount. This makes Keoghs a very unattractive option for anyone with more than a handful of employees.

Unlike IRAs, you can't set up a Keogh plan between the end of the year and your tax-filing deadline. The plan must be set up during the year for which it's effective.

Unlike IRAs, business owners with Keogh plans must file Form 5500 annually to report information on their plan to the IRS.

UGMA AND UTMA ACCOUNTS

UGMA stands for the Uniform Gift to Minors Act, which governs fiduciary accounts set up for minors (that is, accounts managed by a custodian on behalf of a minor). Anyone may contribute either cash or securities to an UGMA account; however, the gift is irrevocable. UTMA stands for the Uniform Transfer to Minors Act. UTMA accounts are very similar to UGMA accounts, but allow for more asset types (e.g., real estate, art, etc.) to be held in the accounts. Since 1986, many states have amended their laws related to UGMA and UTMA accounts, so brokers need to know their state's rules. FINRA has enforced discipline related to UGMA and UTMA accounts by referencing the Know Your Customer Rule (Rule 2090). UGMA/UTMA accounts are registered under the minor's Social Security number, and earnings are taxed at the minor's tax rate up to a specified limit. The account administrator, or custodian, trades on behalf of the minor, and may use proceeds of the account to pay for the minor's living expenses, education, etc., when appropriate. The minor has no control over the funds until reaching adulthood. Only one minor and one custodian can be on each account, although a minor can be the beneficial owner of more than one account, and a custodian can manage more than one account.

RESPONSIBILITIES OF A UGMA OR UTMA FIDUCIARY

To meet the requirements of Rule 2090 and Rule 3110 as they relate to UGMA/UTMA accounts, member firms must have a supervisory system and procedures in place that are reasonably designed to:

- address the termination of the custodianship upon the beneficiary reaching the relevant age
- verify whether the custodian has authority to manage assets in the UTMA/UGMA after the beneficiary reaches the relevant age

As fiduciary of the UGMA/UTMA account, the custodian must invest prudently ("prudent man rule") with the minor's best interests in mind. Margin activity is prohibited in UGMA and UTMA accounts, and the custodian is not allowed to use the assets of the account as collateral on a loan. Any cash coming into the account, along with interest and dividends, must be invested within a reasonable period of time. The custodian is not allowed to borrow money from the account, although he or she can make loans to the account. Note that a custodian does not typically have the power to name another custodian outside of the guidelines of the account. The supervisory system should address changes in custodianship.

DEFERRED COMPENSATION RETIREMENT PLANS

In a deferred compensation retirement plan, an employee agrees to forego some present income on the condition that his employer will pay that portion after the employee retires from the company. The advantage of this type of plan is that many employees who take advantage of it will be in a lower tax bracket after retirement and will therefore pay lower taxes on the income than if they had received it at the time it was earned. Risks of a deferred compensation plans to employees are that the company could go bankrupt before the employee retires, or the employee could leave the firm before becoming vested, impairing their ability to collect the income.

Tax law requires a deferred compensation retirement plan to be in writing and the plan document(s) to specify the amount to be paid, the payment schedule, and any triggering event that will result in payment. The employee must make an irrevocable election to defer compensation before the year in which the compensation is earned.

Deferred compensation plans can be qualified or non-qualified. Qualified plans place the funds in a trust that is separate from the business' assets. Non-qualified plans include the funds as part of the company's assets and may be used for business purposes.

CORPORATE PENSION PLANS

There are two types of private, corporate pension plans:

Defined benefit plan - the corporation promises to pay the employee a certain amount after the employee retires. The corporation makes the investment decisions and assumes the investment risk. Contributions are calculated by actuaries based on the desired stream of fixed payments, which are determined by employee salary histories and length of service. Defined benefit plans were once quite common but are now becoming increasingly scarce due to the complexity of accurately estimating pension liabilities and investment returns.

Defined contribution plan – the employee makes regular contributions to an account, usually a fixed percentage of their paycheck, and the employer may make matching contributions up to a specified percentage for the purpose of funding the employee's retirement. Employee contributions are made on a pre-tax basis, and earnings are not taxed until withdrawal are made. The employee makes the investment decisions and assumes the investment risk.

DEFERRED COMPENSATION PLANS

Contribution limits vary depending on the type of deferred compensation plan. For 457 plans, the contribution limit is the lesser of the elective deferral limit of $19,500 or 100% of the participant's includible compensation (may allow catch-up contributions for participants over age 50). For defined benefit plans, the limit is the lesser of $230,000 or 100% of the participant's average compensation for his or her highest three consecutive calendar years. Distribution provisions also vary by plan type. For 457 plans, distributions can be taken at any time without incurring a tax penalty. For defined benefit plans, distributions generally begin upon retirement and are typically taxed at the participant's ordinary income rate upon receipt (monthly payments or lump sum).

PROFIT-SHARING PLANS

Profit-sharing plans boost an employee's retirement savings without increasing their taxable income in a given year. The combined total of employer contributions and employee contributions to all plans made for a participant cannot exceed the lesser of $58,000 or 100% of the participant's compensation.

Profit-sharing contributions are tax-deductible to the employer up to 25% of a participant's total compensation up to a compensation limit of $285,000 and are not subject to Social Security or Medicare withholding. A profit-sharing plan can allow employers to make greater contributions to (highly compensated employees) HCEs without failing IRS compliance limits for nondiscrimination testing. Employers have the option to choose a contribution vesting schedule based on the employee's length of service. If employees leave the company before their contributions are fully vested, they forfeit the unvested portion. Employees who take distributions before age 59½ face a 10% penalty.

INCENTIVE STOCK OPTIONS (ISOs) AND NONQUALIFIED STOCK OPTIONS (NSOs)

Incentive stock options (ISOs) are employee stock options which carry tax benefits with them, whereas **nonqualified stock options (NSOs)** are ones which don't. When an employee has an NSO, he will have to pay taxes on the gain he acquires when he exercises it, even though he receives no cash in the transaction. For example, if a stock option entitles an employee to 20 shares at $20 per share, and the market value of the shares at the date he exercises the option is $25 per share, then, with an NSO, he would have to report income of $100 (20 shares x $5/share) and pay income tax on it. The cost basis of his investment would then be $500 (20 shares x $25/share), and any capital gains or losses would be determined against this basis.

But with ISOs, any taxes are deferred to the time when the stock is sold. When the employee exercises the stock, he is to use the exercise price as his cost basis (in the above case, $20/share), and the only tax he has to pay is on any capital gains he might have. The sale of an ISO must occur at least two years from the granting of the option and one year from the exercising of the option, however, or the tax benefits will be forfeited due to a **disqualifying disposition** of the stock.

QUALIFIED AND NON-QUALIFIED RETIREMENT PLANS

There are all sorts of retirement plans, and they all have unique features. But one key feature that sets many of them apart from others is the fact that contributions to them are tax-deductible. Plans that feature tax-deductible contributions are known as **qualified plans**; the ones that don't are known as **nonqualified plans**. Two of the best-known nonqualified plans are **payroll deduction plans** and **deferred compensation plans.**

Nonqualified plans still benefit from tax-deferred growth. For qualified plans, distributions are taxed entirely as income, but for nonqualified plans, since the original contributions were from after-tax dollars, only the distributions in excess of the original contributions are taxed as income.

PAYROLL DEDUCTION RETIREMENT PLANS

Under a **payroll deduction retirement plan**, an employee allows the employer to take out a certain amount or percentage of the employee's wages and invest that money. The money comes out of the employee's net pay after taxes have been paid. Payroll deduction plans are often confused with 401(k) plans, but they are not the same, though they share similarities. Payroll deduction plans are considered nonqualified retirement plans. 401(k) plans, on the other hand, are classified as qualified plans, because they are considered to be salary reduction plans, not payroll deduction plans.

401(K) PLANS, 403(B) PLANS, AND 457 PLANS

Most corporations now use 401(k) plans to fund their employee retirement pensions. With a **401(k)**, employees contribute a portion of their wages or salary, which are not counted as part of their gross income. Their contributions and the earnings on the contributions are tax deferred until withdrawal. In addition, the corporation may choose to match part of the employee's contribution. Most companies will have a variety of investment vehicles that an employee can choose to contribute to; the employee may put all his money in one or spread the money out among several.

403(b) plans are also called **tax-sheltered annuity (TSA) plans**. They are only available to people who work in educational institutions, including college, universities, elementary schools, middle schools, high schools, religious institutions, private hospitals, and institutions with an educational purpose, such as zoos and museums. In addition, the employees must be at least 21 years old, and must have at least one year of service before being eligible for coverage. The benefits of 403(b) plans are very similar to 401(k)s.

457 plans are nonqualified plans available to government employers (as well as certain non-government employers), similar in structure to 401(k)s and 403(b)s. They are deferred-compensation plans, and unlike 401(k)s and 403(b)s, they have no penalty on early distributions, even though distributions are taxed as income.

WEALTH EVENTS

A wealth event is an event that causes a sudden increase in wealth. The event can be expected or unexpected and may include the following:

- Inheritance
- Sale of a business
- Sale of real estate
- Legal settlement
- Exercise of stock options
- Lump-sum retirement payout

Wealth events can be life-changing from a financial perspective and may require the advice of a financial professional and/or other professionals to help an individual or family make sound decisions regarding their wealth. If the event is anticipated, address the potential tax consequences and event timing, and establish a cash flow budget. After the event, avoid large expenditures and consider a "waiting period", and determine an appropriate liquid and secure structure in which to hold cash.

AUTOMATED CUSTOMER ACCOUNT TRANSFER SERVICE (ACATS)

A customer wishing to transfer his account between broker-dealers needs to complete an **account transfer form** with the new broker-dealer, stating whatever securities he held with the old broker-dealer. At this point, the new broker-dealer can send transfer instructions to the old broker-dealer.

After the new broker-dealer sends these instructions to the old one, the old broker-dealer has three business days to confirm or else make an exception for some information in the request (e.g. an invalid account number of Social Security number). Once the account is validated, the old-broker dealer then has three more business days to execute the account transfer.

A common means of account transfers is through the **Automated Customer Account Transfer Service (ACATS).** Using this service requires membership in the **National Securities Clearing Corporation (NSCC).**

PROCESSES FOR ACCOUNT REGISTRATION CHANGES

Accounts can be registered under different categories, such as individual, joint, and custodial. If a customer desires to **change the registration** for his account, different firms will ordinarily have some process and form for the customer to fill out, requiring the signatures of all the owners involved.

These processes are different if certain owners are dropping from the account. Doing so may require the notarized signatures of the other owners of the account. If the primary account holder is dropping from the account, then a new account may need to be opened.

INTERNAL TRANSFERS

Internal transfers are transfers which customers make with funds between or among their own accounts (or accounts with which they are closely associated).

Transfer on death (TOD) permits securities to pass from an account owner directly to some assigned TOD beneficiary upon the owner's death. The benefit of this is that such a transfer eliminates the need to go through probate. In this type of transfer, however, the beneficiaries need to ensure that the transferred funds and assets are re-registered in their own names.

Divorce transfers can vary according to the terms specified by the parties to be divorced. It is not uncommon for brokerage accounts to be split 50-50.

DAY TRADING RISK DISCLOSURE STATEMENT

Day Trading Risk Disclosure Statement (FINRA Rule 2270) - in addition to providing the customer with the risk disclosure statement, the member must post the same disclosure on the member's website. The risks disclosures include: day trading is extremely risky; be cautious of claims of large profits from day trading; day trading requires knowledge of securities markets; day trading requires knowledge of a firm's operations; day trading will generate substantial commissions, even if the per trade cost is low; day trading on margin or short selling may result in losses beyond your initial investment; and potential registration requirements.

APPROVAL PROCEDURES FOR DAY-TRADING ACCOUNTS

Approval procedures for day-trading accounts (FINRA Rule 2130) - a day-trading member may not open an account for a non-institutional customer without furnishing to the customer a risk disclosure statement and without having approved the customer's account for day trading according to certain criteria. In lieu of approving the customer's account, the member can obtain a written agreement from the customer stating the customer does not intend the account to use for day-trading activities.

FINRA RULES 4512 AND 4515

(FINRA Rules 4512 and 4515 describe the exact information that a broker-dealer is required to have on file prior to opening an account for a new customer. The information includes the following:

- Name
- Address
- If the customer is of legal age
- Name of any other individuals that will be responsible for the account
- Signature of the partner, officer, or manager indicating that the account is good standing

68

- The names of anyone who is authorized to make trades in the account
- Tax ID or Social Security number
- Occupation of the customer, including the name and address of the employer

FINRA RULE 4514

FINRA Rule 4514 states that no member or person associated with a member shall obtain from a customer or submit for payment a check, draft or other form of negotiable paper drawn on a customer's checking, savings, share or similar account, without that person's express written authorization, which may include the customer's signature on the negotiable instrument. Where the written authorization is separate from the negotiable instrument, the member shall preserve the authorization for a period of three years following the date the authorization expires. This provision shall not, however, require members to preserve copies of negotiable instruments signed by customers.

CBOE RULE 9.1

Cboe Rule 9.1 states that no TPH organization shall accept an order from a customer to purchase or write an option contract unless the customer's account has been approved for options transactions in accordance with the provisions of the rule. A TPH organization must obtain the following information, at a minimum, and make a record of such information which must be retained in accordance with Rule 9.2.

- Investment objectives (e.g., safety of principal, income, growth, trading profits, speculation)
- Employment status
- Estimated annual income from all sources
- Estimated net worth
- Estimated liquid net worth (cash, securities, other)
- Marital status, number of dependents
- Age
- Investment experience and knowledge (e.g., number of years, size, frequency and type of transactions for options, stocks and bonds, commodities, other)

A Registered Options Principal must approve in writing the customer's account for options transactions.

DISCLOSURES REQUIRED IN OPENING AN OPTIONS ACCOUNT

At or prior to the time a customer's account is approved for options transactions, a TPH organization must furnish the customer with current options disclosure documents. Within 15 days after the customer's account has been approved for options transactions, the background and financial information upon which the account has been approved must be sent to the customer for verification. Also within 15 days, a TPH organization must obtain from the customer a written agreement that the account shall be handled in accordance with the Rules of the Exchange and the Rules of the Clearing Corporation.

SUPERVISORY PROCEDURES FOR TRADING IN UNCOVERED OPTIONS

In addition to the requirements for opening a covered options account, for investors wishing to trade in uncovered options, the Cboe also requires that the TPH organization have written procedures in place that address the following:

- Specific criteria and standards to be used in evaluating the suitability of a customer for uncovered short option transactions
- Specific procedures for approval of accounts engaged in writing uncovered short option contracts
- Designation of a specific Registered Options Principal as the person(s) responsible for approving accounts which do not meet the specific criteria and standards for writing uncovered short option transactions
- Establishment of specific minimum net equity requirements for initial approval and maintenance of customer uncovered option accounts; and
- Requirements that customers approved for writing uncovered short options transactions be provided with a special written description of the risks inherent in writing uncovered short option transactions, at or prior to the initial uncovered short option transaction.

INDIVIDUAL RETIREMENT ACCOUNTS (IRAs)

Individual Retirement Accounts (IRAs) were created in the early 1980s so that people could supplement whatever retirement plans and Social Security they had with their own savings and investments. IRAs are given **preferential tax treatment** in order to encourage people to save for their own retirement. Unlike many retirement plans, anyone may open an IRA, regardless of whatever other plans they're covered under. For 2023, people with earned income may contribute up to $6,500 per year ($7,500 if the person is age 50 or older), or up to $13,000 per year if the person has a spouse that doesn't work ($15,000 if both are age 50 or older).

Any contributions in excess of the maximum amount are subject to a tax on 6% of the excess per year until the excess (and any gains it has produced) is removed from the IRA.

LIMITS ON BENEFITS AND CONTRIBUTIONS OF QUALIFIED PLANS

Section 415 of the Internal Revenue Code provides for dollar limitations on benefits and contributions under qualified retirement plans.

- The annual benefit for a participant under a defined benefit plan cannot exceed the lesser of: 100% of the participant's average compensation for his or her highest three consecutive calendar years, or $265,000 for 2023.
- The limitation on contributions for a participant under a defined contribution plan cannot exceed the lesser of: 100% of participant's compensation, or $66,000 for 2023.
- The limits are required to be adjusted annually for cost-of-living increases.

529 PLAN COLLEGE SAVINGS ACCOUNTS

529 plans, named after section 529 of the Internal Revenue Service code, are another way, besides Coverdell Educational Savings Accounts, for parents to pre-fund their child's college education. Taxes are deferred on the money invested in 529 plans, the money is generally not taxed in most states, and it isn't taxed by the federal government when withdrawn if applied directly to legitimate college educational expenses of the named beneficiary.

There are two kinds of 529 plans. One is a **pre-paid tuition plan**, which allows a parent to purchase a certain number of units of tuition, "locking in" the units, which will be used in the future, at today's rates, thereby protecting against rises in tuition over the years. The other kind of 529 is a **savings plan**. Plans vary greatly state by state, but one thing they have in common is that, because contributions to 529 plans are gifts, there are certain restrictions on contributions. However, these are much more lenient than for Coverdell accounts. 529 plans generally have lifetime contribution limits rather than annual limits.

COVERDELL EDUCATION SAVINGS ACCOUNTS

Coverdell Education Savings Accounts (CESAs), formerly known as Coverdell IRAs, were created by Congress to enable parents to help fund their children's future college education. For 2023, the maximum contribution per year is $2,000, and anyone is allowed to contribute (i.e. not just the parents), so long as the sum total of all contributions for one child is no more than $2,000. Contributions must cease once the child turns 18, but the earnings are not taxed if directly applied to the beneficiary's educational expenses. However, for 2023, anyone making over $95,000 per year ($190,000 for couples) can't give the full $2,000, and anyone making over $110,000 per year ($220,000 for couples) is not allowed to participate.

EMPLOYEE RETIREMENT INCOME SECURITY ACT (ERISA)

The **Employee Retirement Income Security Act** (ERISA) was passed in 1974 with the purpose of protecting the retirement assets of American employees in qualified retirement plans. Since employees invest assets for retirement in a fund of plan assets, the growth of that investment is very important. ERISA requires plans to inform employees about these investment strategies and makes fiduciaries in charge of those plan assets accountable to the employees for any asset mismanagement.

Updating Customer Information and Documentation and Identifying Suspicious Activity

ELEMENTS OF CUSTOMER SCREENING

The **Customer Identification Program (CIP)** was implemented in various companies as a result of the Patriot Act, requiring financial institutions to better assess persons who wish to engage in financial activity. Each institution must employ its own CIP as befits its size and ordinary operations. CIP programs seek to assess the riskiness of their customers and verify their identities.

Know Your Customer (KYC) forms are documents specifically designed to acquire relevant information about customers, so that brokers or other agents can assess the client's willingness to assume risk, his knowledge of investments and finance, and his actual assets.

Important information about the client includes his place of residence and citizenship. Brokers should seek to gain this kind of information from their clients, such as whether they qualify as bona fide foreign residents.

Corporate insiders are individuals who are particularly privy to a corporation's "**inside**" information; this definition includes directors and officers for the company in addition to anyone owning over 10% of the voting shares, and really anyone who has access to **material but non-public knowledge**. These insiders have an extra set of restrictions for any securities transactions they wish to make, and brokers should consider them accordingly.

Another consideration which brokers have to make is whether their clients are employees of a broker-dealer. Just as corporate insiders are subject to various trading restrictions based upon their inside knowledge, so also employees of broker-dealers (especially of competing broker-dealers) carry their own set of risks. Particularly, the broker's company must receive consent from the employee's own institution.

Employees of self-regulatory organizations (SROs) likewise are subject to these restrictions. As with employees of other broker-dealers, brokers are required to obtain the consent of a client's institution if he is employed for an SRO.

INFORMATION SECURITY

Since registered representatives are required to handle a great deal of important proprietary and personal information, it is important for them to take significant steps in developing **information security**. This can be as simple as safeguarding laptops with security and password protection, as well as encrypting one's email interactions.

DISCLOSING NONPUBLIC PERSONAL INFORMATION ABOUT CONSUMERS

A financial institution must provide its customers with a notice of its privacy policies and practices and must not disclose nonpublic personal information about a consumer to nonaffiliated third parties unless the institution discloses to the consumer clearly and conspicuously that such information may be disclosed and the consumer has not elected to opt out of the disclosure. For customers, the notice must be provided at the time of establishing a customer relationship. For consumers who are not customers, the notice must be provided before disclosing nonpublic personal information about the consumer to a nonaffiliated third party.

This does not prevent a financial institution from providing nonpublic personal information to a nonaffiliated third party to perform services for or functions on behalf of the financial institution, including marketing of the financial institution's own products or services, or financial products or services offered pursuant to joint agreements between two or more financial institutions that comply with the requirements imposed by the regulation, if the financial institution fully discloses the providing of such information and enters into a contractual agreement with the third party that requires the third party to maintain the confidentiality of such information.

TYPES OF ACCOUNT AUTHORIZATIONS

One means of account authorization is **power of attorney (POA)**, where the authority to represent someone in legal, private, or business matters is held by another person; these must be formalized in writing.

Another means is by **corporate resolution**, where a corporation as a unit performs some action. This is usually accomplished with a legal document, voted upon by the corporation's board of directors.

Trading authorization can serve as a lesser substitute for power of attorney. There are different degrees of trading authorization, where the client grants a level of power to a broker (or some other agent) for the trading of his securities. This is less than the authorization granted in power of attorney, since it applies only to trading (and only to the trading that the client specifies).

Discretionary accounts are accounts where a broker is authorized to make securities transactions on the client's behalf without the client's consent. These require the signing of a discretionary disclosure for written confirmation.

TYPES OF TRUSTS

Trust Accounts are accounts administered by a trustee. Trusts have several types:

- Revocable trusts are created during the lifetime of the trustmaker and can be altered, changed, modified or revoked entirely. Often called a living trust, these are trusts in which the trustmaker transfers the title of a property to a trust, serves as the initial trustee, and has the ability to remove the property from the trust during his or her lifetime
- An irrevocable trust is one that cannot be altered, changed, modified or revoked after its creation
- A special needs trust is one that is set up for a person who receives government benefits so as not to disqualify the beneficiary from such government benefits.

Trusts can be simple or complex:

- A simple trust must annually distribute to the beneficiaries any income it earns on trust assets, cannot distribute the principal of the trust, and cannot make distributions to charitable organizations.
- A complex trust must retain some of its income and not distribute all of it to beneficiaries, must distribute some or all of the principal to the beneficiaries, and must distribute some funds to charitable organizations.

FINRA RULE 408T

FINRA Rule 408T states that no member or employee of a member organization shall exercise any discretionary power in any customer's account or accept orders for an account from a person other than the customer without first obtaining:

- written authorization of the customer,
- the signature of the person or persons authorized to exercise discretion in the account (and of any substitute so authorized), and
- the date such discretionary authority was granted.

The member or employee may not exercise the power without approval from an authorized principal. Orders must be identified as discretionary, and each transaction must be appropriate for the customer's profile and not be excessive in size or frequency give the financial resources of the customer. Discretionary accounts must be frequently reviewed according to written supervisory procedures.

The rule does not apply to discretion as to the price at which or the time when an order given by a customer for the purchase or sale of a definite amount of a specified security shall be executed.

FINRA KNOW YOUR CUSTOMER AND SUITABILITY RULES

Know your customer (FINRA Rule 2090) - members of FINRA are to use reasonable diligence when opening and maintaining accounts for customers, and to get to know essential facts about the customer and concerning the authority of each person acting on behalf of a customer.

Suitability (FINRA Rule 2111) - a member must have a reasonable basis to believe that an investment or strategy is suitable for the customer based on the information the member has gained, according to the "know your customer" rule. Pertinent information includes the customer's age, other investments, financial situation, tax status, objectives, experience, investment time horizon, liquidity needs, and risk tolerance. For an institutional customer, the member is to have reasonable belief the customer is capable of evaluating risks and has indicated that it is exercising independent judgment.

"INVESTMENT DISCRETION" AND REPORTING REQUIREMENTS OF INSTITUTIONAL INVESTMENT MANAGERS

A person exercises "investment discretion" with respect to an account if, directly or indirectly, such person:

- is authorized to determine what securities or other property can be purchased or sold by or for the account,
- makes decisions as to what securities or other property can be purchased or sold by or for the account, even though some other person may have responsibility for such investment decisions, or
- otherwise exercises such influence with respect to the purchase and sale of securities or other property by or for the account as the Commission, by rule, determines, in the public interest or for the protection of investors, should be subject to the operation of the provisions of this chapter and the rules and regulations thereunder.

Per Section13(f) of the Securities Exchange Act of 1934, every institutional investment manager that exercises investment discretion with respect to accounts holding section 13(f) securities (equity securities of a class described in section 13(d)(1) of the Act that trade on a national securities exchange or are quoted on the automated quotation system of a registered securities association) having an aggregate fair market value on the last trading day of any month of any calendar year of at least $100,000,000 must file a report on Form 13F with the Commission within 45 days after the last day of such calendar year and within 45 days after the last day of each of the first three calendar quarters of the subsequent calendar year.

REGULATION S-P

Regulation S-P is the SEC rule pertaining to privacy notices and safeguard policies of investment advisers and broker-dealers. Regulation S-P requires an investment adviser or broker/dealer to:

- provide a clear and conspicuous notice to its customers of its privacy policies and practices at the time the customer relationship is established,
- provide annual notices of its privacy policies and practices, and
- provide notice to customers that explains their right to opt out of some disclosures of non-public personal information about the customer to nonaffiliated third parties.

CBOE RULE 9.4

Cboe Rule 9.4 states that no TPH organization shall exercise any discretionary power with respect to trading in options contracts in a customer's account unless the customer has given prior written authorization and the account has been accepted in writing by a Registered Options Principal.

Approval and Review - Each firm shall designate specific Registered Options Principals to review the acceptance of each discretionary account and shall maintain a record of the basis for each determination. Discretionary accounts must receive frequent appropriate supervisory review by a Registered Options Principal specifically delegated such responsibilities, who is not exercising the discretionary authority, and who uses written supervisory procedures, preferably using computerized surveillance tools.

Discretionary Orders - Every discretionary order shall be identified as discretionary on the order at the time of entry. A record must be made of every options transaction for an account for which a

TPH organization has any discretionary power, which must include name of the customer, designation, number of contracts, premium, and date and time. The transactions made must be appropriate for the customer's financial resources and account profile. If the TPH uses a program to systematically execute a strategy, the TPH must give the customer an explanation of the program according to Cboe Rule 9.15.

Obtaining Customer Investment Profile Information

FINRA RULE 2090 AND "ESSENTIAL FACTS"

FINRA Rule 2090 requires broker-dealer member firms to use reasonable due diligence in opening and maintaining customer accounts and to know and retain the essential facts concerning every customer. This obligation begins at the start of the relationship and continues through its termination.

The Rule defines "essential facts" as those that are required to (1) effectively service the customer's account, (2) act in accordance with any special handling instructions for the account, (3) understand the authority of each person acting on behalf of the customer, and (4) comply with applicable laws, regulations and rules.

Rule 2090 must be interpreted in conjunction with Rule 2111, which requires that a firm have a reasonable basis to believe that a recommended transaction or investment strategy is suitable for the customer based on the information obtained through the due diligence of the member firm to ascertain the customer's investment profile.

According to the Rule, a customer's investment profile must include, but is not limited to, the following information:

- Customer age
- Other investments
- Financial situation and needs
- Tax status
- Investment objectives
- Investment experience
- Investment time horizon
- Liquidity needs
- Risk tolerance
- Any other information the customer may disclose to the member or associated person in connection with such recommendation

REGULATIONS RELATING TO ESSENTIAL FACTS

Members must follow several regulations to gather essential facts related to customer relationships. Among them are FINRA Rules 2090 (Know Your Customer), 2111 (Suitability), 2214 (Requirements for the Use of Investment Analysis Tools), SEC Regulation Best Interest, and MSRB Rule G-19 (Suitability of Recommendations and Transactions).

Generally, essential facts are used to determine a customer's investment profile. A member or associated person must make reasonable efforts to obtain and analyze the information, unless they have "a reasonable basis to believe, documented in writing, that such information is not relevant to suitability. Members are required to keep records on the essential facts of each customer, as well as identify each person who has authority to act on the customer's behalf.

75

FINANCIAL FACTORS USED WHEN ASSESSING A CUSTOMER'S INVESTMENT PROFILE

Many investors are not sure how much risk they should be taking, and it is the broker's job to help them figure this out. **Primary financial factors** in making this determination include the client's household income, his net worth (his total assets—including deferred assets, like retirement plans, and marketable securities—minus his liabilities), including his liquid net worth (the component of his net worth which can easily be converted to cash), the money he has available for investment, and additional background items, such as:

- whether he is a homeowner
- whether he has employee stock options
- what insurance he has, including life and disability insurance
- what his credit score is
- what his tax bracket is

NONFINANCIAL FACTORS USED WHEN ASSESSING A CUSTOMER'S INVESTMENT PROFILE

Many investors are not sure how much risk they should be taking, and it is the broker's job to help them figure this out. **Various nonfinancial factors** in making this determination include:

- the investor's age (older couples should generally employ less risk, since they have less time to gain from investment)
- his marital status (couples who are recently married might desire something relating buying a house)
- his dependents (the more dependents, the less desired risk)
- his educational needs (including those of his children)
- his employment situation
- his previous investment experience

INVESTMENT STRATEGIES

Investors can pursue a range of investment strategies, from very conservative to very risky:

Capital preservation, also referred to as a defensive or conservative investment strategy, is an investment strategy with a goal of preserving capital and avoiding losses. For this type of investor, safety is critical, even if it means foregoing potential returns. The primary risk of this strategy is that investments will not keep pace with inflation. Types of financial products that a person pursuing a capital preservation strategy might utilize are bank CDs, U.S. Treasury securities, and savings accounts.

Income investing is an investment strategy that is focused on generating regular income. The primary risk of this strategy is that by using the income generated from investments instead of reinvesting, investors are foregoing the benefits of compounding. Income may come from dividends on stocks, real estate investment trusts (REITs) or yield and interest payments from high quality bonds.

Long-term growth investing is an investment strategy that is focused on increasing the value of a portfolio over many years. The long-term investment horizon of this strategy allows the investors to take more risk, and therefore favors stocks over bonds, and the reinvestment of dividends allows the investor to benefit from compounding. The primary risk of this strategy is that the value of the investments will be down when the investor needs to begin making withdrawals.

Growth investing is an investment strategy that is focused on increasing capital. It is typically a stock-buying strategy that invests in companies expected to grow at an above-average rate compared to their industry or the market. Growth investors tend to favor small, young companies that are expected to experience a significant increase in earnings growth. While this strategy offers the potential for high returns, there is a high risk that some investments will not meet their growth expectations.

Speculation is an investment strategy that focused on maximizing returns, even if that means accepting a significant amount of risk. This is typically a short-term investment strategy where the investor is seeking to capitalize on price fluctuations. While speculation offers the potential for very high returns, relative to other strategies, the risk is much higher that the investor could lose all or most of their investment.

FINRA RULE 2111

FINRA Rule 2111 lists three main suitability obligations for firms and associated persons:

Reasonable-basis suitability requires members/associated persons to make an objective inquiry into whether there is "a reasonable basis to believe, based upon reasonable diligence, that the recommendation is suitable for at least some investors."

Customer-specific suitability requires "that a member or associated person have a reasonable basis to believe that the recommendation is suitable for a particular customer based on that customer's investment profile, as delineated in Rule 2111(a)."

Quantitative suitability requires a member or associated person [who has actual or de facto control over a customer account] to have a reasonable basis for believing that a series of recommended transactions, even if suitable when viewed in isolation, are not excessive and unsuitable for the customer when taken together in light of the customer's investment profile, as delineated in Rule 2111(a).

SUITABILITY REQUIREMENTS AND "HOLD" RECOMMENDATIONS

In addition to the suitability obligations prescribed by FINRA Rule 2111 that must be met when recommending a new purchase, sale or exchange of an investment, firms and associated persons must also ensure that explicit recommendations to hold an investment are suitable. An explicit recommendation to hold constitutes a type of advice upon which a customer can be expected to rely. The rule would apply, for example, when a registered representative meets (or otherwise communicates) with a customer during a quarterly or annual investment review and explicitly advises the customer not to sell any securities or make any changes to the account or portfolio or to continue to use an investment strategy.

WAYS TO VERIFY THAT AN INDIVIDUAL IS AN ACCREDITED INVESTOR

Some firms seek to qualify for exemption from registration under SEC Rule 506 by selling exclusively or primarily to accredited investors. To rely on this exemption, firms must take reasonable steps to ensure that investors are accredited. Ways in which firms can verify accreditation include:

- verification of a natural person's income by looking at US tax documentation and a statement that the customer expects to maintain this income level
- verification of a natural person's net worth by looking at a US credit report for liabilities and bank statements, brokerage statements, real estate appraisals, etc., for assets

- written confirmation from another broker, attorney, CPA, that the purchaser demonstrated accreditation in the last three months
- the investor was accredited before 2013 and still holds the investments

ADDITIONS TO THE DEFINITION OF "ACCREDITED INVESTOR"

In 2020, the SEC expanded the definition of "accredited investor" as delineated in Rule 501. Below is a list of the types of individuals and entities that were added.

- Natural persons who possess certain professional certifications, designations or credentials as determined by the SEC. These include holders in good standing of Series 7, Series 65, and/or Series 82 licenses. This also provides the SEC with flexibility to reevaluate or add certifications, designations, and credentials in the future.
- Natural persons who are "knowledgeable employees" of a private fund.
- SEC- and state-registered investment advisers, and rural business investment companies.
- Any entity, including Indian tribes, governmental bodies, funds, and entities organized under the laws of foreign countries, that own "investments," as defined in Rule 2a51-1(b) under the Investment Company Act, in excess of $5 million and that was not formed for the specific purpose of investing in the securities offered.
- Family offices with at least $5 million in assets under management and their family clients, as defined under the Investment Advisers Act; and
- Spousal equivalents, so that spouses may pool their assets for the purpose of qualifying as accredited investors.

The amendments also expand the definition of "qualified institutional buyer" in Rule 144A to include limited liability companies and RBICs if they meet the $100 million in securities owned and invested threshold.

"INVESTMENT ANALYSIS TOOLS" AND FINRA RULE 2214

For purposes of Rule 2214, an "investment analysis tool" is an interactive technological tool that produces simulations and statistical analyses that present the likelihood of various investment outcomes if certain investments are made or certain investment strategies or styles are undertaken, thereby serving as an additional resource to investors in the evaluation of the potential risks and returns of investment choices.

A member may provide an investment analysis tool (whether customers use the member's tool independently or with assistance from the member), written reports indicating the results generated by such tool and related retail communications only if the tool, written report or related retail communication:

- describes the criteria and methodology used, including the investment analysis tool's limitations and key assumptions
- explains that results may vary with each use and over time
- if applicable, describes the universe of investments considered in the analysis, explains how the tool determines which securities to select, discloses if the tool favors certain securities and, if so, explains the reason for the selectivity, and states that other investments not considered may have characteristics similar or superior to those being analyzed
- displays the following additional disclosure: "IMPORTANT: The projections or other information generated by [name of investment analysis tool] regarding the likelihood of various investment outcomes are hypothetical in nature, do not reflect actual investment results and are not guarantees of future results."

REGULATION BEST INTEREST (REG BI)

In June 2019, the SEC passed Regulation Best Interest (Reg BI), which establishes a "best interest" standard of conduct for broker-dealers and associated persons when they make a recommendation to a retail customer.

Regulation Best Interest includes the following components:

Disclosure Obligation: Broker-dealers must disclose material facts about the relationship and recommendations, including the capacity in which the broker is acting, fees, the type and scope of services, conflicts, limitations on services and products, and whether the broker-dealer provides monitoring services.

Care Obligation: Broker-dealers must exercise reasonable diligence, care and skill when making a recommendation to a retail customer. The broker-dealer must understand potential risks, rewards, and costs associated with the recommendation and consider these factors in light of the retail customer's investment profile.

Conflict of Interest Obligation: Broker-dealers must establish, maintain, and enforce written policies and procedures reasonably designed to identify, disclose or eliminate conflicts of interest. Conflicts may include incentives for the firm's financial professionals to place their interest or the interests of the firm ahead of the retail customer's interest; material limitations on offerings, such as a limited product menu or offering only proprietary products, and sales contests, sales quotas, bonuses, and non-cash compensation that are based on the sale of specific securities.

Compliance Obligation: Broker-dealers must establish, maintain, and enforce policies and procedures reasonably designed to achieve compliance with Regulation Best Interest.

MSRB RULE G-19

MSRB Rule G-19 requires that, prior to trading in a retail customer's account, the registered individual must collect suitability information regarding the customer's financial status, tax status, investment objective concerning the municipal security being traded, and any other information that might be required to ensure that the transaction meets the customer's suitability needs. The claim that the security is a suitable investment must be supported by complete and accurate information obtained from the customer for that purpose, and information provided by the issuer. MSRB G-19 also addresses suitability issues concerning discretionary accounts, and requires that the investment be suitable in such accounts. Finally, G-19 expressly forbids churning in accounts through multiple transactions, or unreasonably large transactions to provide larger commissions to the registered person.

Obtaining Supervisory Approvals Required to Open Accounts

SUPERVISION REQUIRED BY FIRM PRINCIPALS

FINRA Rule 3110 requires each member to establish and maintain a system to supervise the activities of each associated person that is reasonably designed to achieve compliance with applicable securities laws and regulations, and with applicable FINRA rules. As part of the Rule, members must designate an appropriately registered principal(s) with authority to carry out the supervisory responsibilities of the member for each type of business in which it engages. Additionally, members must designate one or more appropriately registered principals in each Office of Supervisory Jurisdiction (OSJ) and one or more appropriately registered representatives or principals in each non-OSJ branch office with authority to carry out the supervisory responsibilities assigned to that office by the member.

FINRA Rule 3120 requires members to designate principal(s) to be responsible for establishing, maintaining and enforcing a firm's Supervisory Control Policies and Procedures (SCPs). The designated principal(s) must prepare, at least annually, a report detailing the firm's supervisory control system and submit it to senior management. The report must include a summary of the test results and significant identified exceptions, and any additional or amended supervisory procedures created in response to the test results.

SAFEGUARDING PHYSICAL ASSETS

Since the broker is acting for the sake of the client's assets, it is imperative that he appropriately receive and guard any **physical assets** owned by the client and given to the broker's care, such as cash, cash equivalents, and checks. Measures for the **physical safeguarding** of these assets generally include something as simple as a safe or a locked drawer, with access being provided only to authorized persons. Brokers should periodically modify safe codes and other means of access in order to stave off the risk of theft.

SAFEGUARDING SECURITIES

In order to receive securities, customers must have the **cash on hand**, or **line of credit**, or **stocks** to cover a transaction at the time of the transaction. It is the job of the registered representative to ensure this. If stocks are required, and the customer doesn't have them on hand, but says they're listed in a street name at another firm, the rep must call the other firm and confirm this before making the trade.

The broker is generally required to safeguard the client's securities, that is, to hold the securities on the client's behalf. Since some securities come with physical certificates, it can also be the broker's job to ensure that these physical assets are appropriately safeguarded.

REFUSING TO TRADE FOR A CUSTOMER

Under certain circumstances a broker may refuse a transaction or freeze an account:

1. If an order does not make sense in the context of the market (e.g., a stop order at the current price, a limit order 1000% higher than the current price).
2. If a customer does not have funds to settle, the broker may require payment in advance. Specifically, if the investor has not paid for a prior transaction, the broker may refuse to make any further transactions unless they are paid for in advance.
3. Orders that violate day trading or margin rules.
4. Regulatory agencies may freeze an account that has suspicious activity and/or is related to potential criminal activity.

Although brokerage firms are not required to monitor whether day-trading accounts fall below the $25,000 minimum throughout a given trading day, customers must cover any losses incurred in their accounts from the previous day's trades before they are allowed to continue day trading. If a day trader exceeds the four times leverage rule during the day, a brokerage firm can impose additional restrictions on the account. An official stock transaction is settled three days after the date of the trade, meaning that day traders frequently are buying and selling stocks before their transactions are officially settled.

RESTRICTIONS ON DAY TRADERS

Day traders cannot free ride, meaning they cannot buy a security and sell it an hour later without first having enough funds to cover the settlement of the initial trade. If a trader buys a stock or other security, he or she must have the funds to cover the initial trade even if the security is sold for a profit within the same day. A margin account with leverage of four times excess equity is what enables day traders to get around this rule. All the trader needs to have is sufficient cash to pay for the shares or sufficient reserve in his or her margin account. Brokers can restrict use of margin funds for three days until a stock transaction is settled, but they are not required to do so.

INSTANCES WHEN ACCOUNT ACTIVITY CAN BE RESTRICTED OR REFUSED

Account activity can be restricted in different ways for different accounts.

A **mutual fund, or open-end investment company**, must state in its prospectus whether it intends to engage in the following practices and how big a part these activities will play in their investment portfolio: buying stocks and bonds on margin, short selling, taking part in joint investment accounts, or distributing its own securities without an underwriter. If these activities aren't listed in the prospectus, in detail, the investment company is forbidden from participating in them.

Since **money market funds** are not insured by the FDIC, the SEC requires that the front cover of a money market prospectus plainly state that federal government does not guarantee the money, and that there is no guarantee that the fund will be able to maintain a net asset value of one dollar. Another restriction on money market funds is that they must stay mainly invested in short-term securities—the average maturity in their portfolio cannot exceed 90 days, and no security in the portfolio can have a maturity of more than 13 months.

Additionally, customers with **cash brokerage accounts** are not permitted to sell securities before they have fully paid for the shares. Doing so subjects one's account to trading restrictions for ninety days.

COMPONENTS OF A SUPERVISION SYSTEM ACCORDING TO FINRA RULE 3110

FINRA Rule 3110 states that each member must establish and maintain a system to supervise the activities of each associated person that is reasonably designed to achieve compliance with applicable securities laws and regulations, and with applicable FINRA rules. A supervisory system must include the following:

- establishment and maintenance of written procedures
- designation of an appropriately registered principal(s)
- registration and designation as a branch office or an office of supervisory jurisdiction (OSJ) of each location
- designation of one or more appropriately registered principals in each OSJ and one or more appropriately registered representatives or principals in each non-OSJ branch office
- assignment of each registered person to an appropriately registered representative(s) or principal(s)
- use of reasonable efforts to determine that all supervisory personnel are qualified
- participation of each registered representative and registered principal, no less than annually, in an interview or meeting conducted by persons designated by the member at which compliance matters relevant to the activities of the representative(s) and principal(s) are discussed.

ACTIVITIES THAT A SUPERVISION SYSTEM MUST GOVERN

Each member must establish, maintain, and enforce written procedures to supervise the types of business in which it engages and the activities of its associated persons. Procedures must address the following requirements:

- review by a registered principal, evidenced in writing, of all transactions relating to the investment banking or securities business of the member
- review of incoming and outgoing written (including electronic) correspondence and internal communications
- procedures to capture, acknowledge, and respond to all written (including electronic) customer complaints
- documentation of supervisory personnel, including titles, registration status, and locations of the required supervisory personnel and the responsibilities of each and a record, preserved by the member for a period of not less than three years, of the names of all persons who are designated as supervisory personnel
- procedures to prohibit associated persons who perform a supervisory function from supervising their own activities or reporting to a person they are supervising and to prevent conflicts of interest

REQUIREMENTS OF RULE 3110 RELATED TO RECORDKEEPING

A copy of a member's written supervisory procedures must be kept each OSJ and at each location where supervisory activities are conducted, and each member must promptly amend its written supervisory procedures to reflect changes in applicable securities laws or regulations and as changes occur in its supervisory system.

Each member must conduct a review, at least annually (on a calendar-year basis), that is reasonably designed to assist the member in detecting and preventing violations of, and achieving compliance with, applicable securities laws and regulations. Reviews must include the periodic examination of customer accounts to detect and prevent irregularities or abuses. Each member must also retain a written record of the date upon which each review and inspection is conducted.

Each member must include in its supervisory procedures a process for the review of securities transactions that are reasonably designed to identify trades that may violate the provisions of the Exchange Act, the rules thereunder, or FINRA rules prohibiting insider trading and manipulative and deceptive device that are effected for the accounts of the member; accounts introduced or carried by the member in which a person associated with the member has a beneficial interest or the authority to make investment decisions; accounts of a person associated with the member that are disclosed to the member pursuant to Rule 3210; and covered accounts. Each member must ascertain by investigation the good character, business reputation, qualifications and experience of an applicant before the member applies to register that applicant with FINRA. If the applicant previously has been registered with FINRA or another self-regulatory organization, the member shall review a copy of the applicant's most recent Form U5.

REQUIREMENTS OF A SUPERVISORY CONTROL SYSTEM

FINRA Rule 3120 states that each member must designate and specifically identify to FINRA one or more principals who are responsible for establishing, maintaining, and enforcing a system of supervisory control policies and procedures that:

- test and verify that the member's supervisory procedures are reasonably designed to achieve compliance with applicable securities laws and regulations, and with applicable FINRA rules
- create additional or amend supervisory procedures where the need is identified by such testing and verification

The designated principal or principals must submit to the member's senior management no less than annually, a report detailing each member's system of supervisory controls, the summary of the test results and significant identified exceptions, and any additional or amended supervisory procedures created in response to the test results. Each report provided to senior management in the calendar year following a calendar year in which a member reported $200 million or more in gross revenue must include, to the extent applicable to the member's business:

1. a tabulation of the reports pertaining to customer complaints and internal investigations made to FINRA during the preceding year
2. discussion of the preceding year's compliance efforts, including procedures and educational programs, in each of the following areas: trading and market activities; investment banking activities; antifraud and sales practices; finance and operations; supervision; and anti-money laundering

CBOE RULE 9.2

Cboe Rule 9.2 requires that by April 1 of each year, each TPH organization that conducts a non-TPH customer business submit to the Exchange a written report on the TPH organization's supervision and compliance effort during the preceding year and on the adequacy of the TPH organization's ongoing compliance processes and procedures. Each TPH organization that conducts a public customer options business shall also specifically include its options compliance program in the report.

The report shall include, but not be limited to, the following:

- tabulation of customer complaints (including arbitrations and civil actions) and internal investigations
- identification and analysis of significant compliance problems, plans for future systems or procedures to prevent and detect violations and problems, and an assessment of the proceeding year's efforts of this nature
- discussion of the preceding year's compliance efforts, new procedures, educational programs, etc. in each of the following areas: antifraud and trading practices; investment banking activities; sales practices; books and records; finance and operations; supervision; internal controls, and anti-money laundering
- designation of a general partner or principal executive officer as Chief Compliance Officer
- a certification signed by the TPH organization's Chief Executive Officer that the organization has in place processes to establish, modify, and test policies and procedures reasonably designed to achieve compliance with applicable Exchange Rules and federal securities laws and regulations

MSRB RULE G-27

Rule G-27 of the Municipal Securities Rulemaking Board (MSRB) states that all municipal securities firms are required to employ a principal to oversee the company's representatives, and to write and maintain a written manual of supervisory procedures. Further among the responsibilities of the **financial and operations principal**, or **FinOp**, are to approve or reject (in writing) the opening of new accounts, approve or reject in writing all municipal securities transactions, approve or reject in writing steps taken to resolve client complaints, and approve or reject in writing correspondence pertaining to the trading of municipal securities. All broker/dealers (not including bank dealers) must employ FinOps to keep financial records and books.

Information Exchange

Informing Customers About Investment Strategies, Risks and Rewards, and Relevant Market, Investment, and Research Data

CUSTOMER-SPECIFIC FACTORS AFFECTING THE SELECTION OF SECURITIES

The customer-specific factors which affect the selection of his securities for investment purposes can be categorized into three sections: his **risk tolerance,** his **investment time horizon**, and his **investment objectives**. Risk tolerance and investment time horizon are dependent upon a number of financial and nonfinancial factors which a broker must grasp in assessing a customer's investment profile.

The investment objectives of a customer include how much emphasis he puts on the following goals:

- capital preservation
- increased current income
- capital growth
- total return (i.e. growth with income)
- tax advantages of different investments
- diversification in one's portfolio
- liquidity
- acquiring trading profits
- balancing short-term and long-term risks

SECURITIES

Securities are fungible and tradable financial instruments used to raise capital in public and private markets. They have variable performance, and expose the owners to risks of loss (and potential gain). A fixed annuity or most indexed annuities are not considered securities because they are not variable, but a Variable Annuity is considered a special type of security.

There are primarily three types of securities: equity—which provides ownership rights to holders; debt—essentially loans repaid with periodic payments; and hybrids—which combine aspects of debt and equity.

Public sales of securities are regulated by the SEC.

Self-regulatory organizations such as Cboe, MSRB, NYSE, and FINRA also play an important role in regulating securities.

A security is different than an account. For example a 401(k) or IRA are not securities - they are accounts.

PORTFOLIO DIVERSIFICATION

Diversification for portfolios or accounts is the possession of several varied types of securities, usually so that different parts of one's portfolio offset risks in other parts. (And it can be contrasted with **concentration**, which involves an emphasis upon some specific type of asset.) Part of diversification involves **asset allocation**, where one takes an investor's portfolio and divides it into different categories, such as cash, stocks, and bonds.

85

Strategic asset allocation seeks to structure a portfolio for long-term investment (e.g., having fewer stocks for older investors, all other things being equal), whereas **tactical** asset allocation seeks to structure a portfolio in response to particular market conditions (e.g., decreasing stocks in the short term if the market as a whole is expected to fare poorly).

An important characteristic of a portfolio is its **volatility**, that is, its tendency to fluctuate in its returns or losses according to the market's own fluctuations. Generally, portfolios follow the principle that an increased chance of return comes with an increased risk.

A broker should also help an investor construct his portfolio according to the various tax ramifications of the assets in question.

INTEREST-RATE-SENSITIVE STOCKS

Interest-rate-sensitive stocks are shares of stock whose value is extremely sensitive to changes in interest rates. The price of these stocks will fluctuate widely, for instance, with a modification in the risk-free rate. These stocks will have large beta factors according to the capital asset pricing model. Their sensitivity to interest rate changes can be due to the type of industry of which they are a part and to the degree to which the company operates off of debt.

PORTFOLIO THEORY

Portfolio theory is a branch of finance theory which mathematically seeks to maximize the return and/or minimize risk for a given portfolio.

A widely used model in portfolio theory is the **capital asset pricing model (CAPM)**, which functions according to the following formula:

$$E(R_i) = R_f + \beta_i(E(R_m) - R_f)$$

$E(R_i)$ = expected return on the capital asset

R_f = risk-free rate of return, such as interest from government bonds

β_i = beta, or the sensitivity of the asset to the market as a whole (where 1 means that stock prices change with the market, and >1 means that they change more than the market does)

$E(R_m)$ = expected return of the market

The concept of an asset's **beta coefficient** is an important feature of portfolio theory, as is an alpha coefficient in other models. An asset's **alpha coefficient** is a measure of an asset's return after its risk is accounted for, i.e. after the compensation for the risk is deducted.

ANNUAL REPORTS

An **annual report** is intended to comprehensively summarize a company's activities for investors (and others) over the past year. (**Interim reports** are reports issued more frequently.) Annual reports include financial statements (such as income statements, balance sheets, and statements of cash flows), notes to the financial statements, accounting policies, statements and reports from management, directors, chairmen, and/or auditors, material risk disclosures, and other information.

A broker is responsible for informing his customer of various actions taken by corporations in which the customer has some share or interest. This includes notifying the customer about **annual reports** for the corporation (as well as interim reports, if necessary) and notices of various corporate actions. If a corporation has split its stock, tendered new stock, established some kind of shareholder voting by proxy, announced plans to repurchase stock, or done some other action which is worthy of the customer's attention, the broker should seek to notify him.

ROLE OF FUNDAMENTAL ANALYSTS

Technical analysts try to determine when to buy a security by tracking its price patterns over time, but **fundamental analysts** focus on information concerning the company itself in order to determine the intrinsic value of ownership in the company (stock), which is then compared to the stock's actual price.

The type of information analyzed by fundamental analysts includes its management, its financial statements, its industry, the overall economy, and competitor companies.

DEPRECIATION, DEPLETION, AND GOODWILL

Depreciation refers to the systematic decreasing of an asset's value over its useful life. It would not be proper for an asset like a building or a machine to be recorded at its historical cost and then removed in its entirety from the balance sheet when it is discontinued, so its book value must be steadily lowered over the course of its useful life.

Depletion refers to the systematic decreasing of natural resources as they are extracted over time, such as timber or oil. Since natural resources do not have a fixed useful life, the strategy for allocating depletion costs over time is different, and usually is calculated by dividing the total cost by the estimated total resource to give a depletion charge per unit of resource. The total cost includes acquisition of asset, exploration costs, development costs and restoration costs following extraction.

Goodwill is recorded as an intangible asset on a company's balance sheet, and refers to the general value of the company in excess of its assets' book value. For instance, goodwill would include the value of having a well-known brand name, skilled employees, good customer relations, and other things.

BALANCE SHEETS

A **balance sheet** is a monetary representation, meeting the standards of generally accepted accounting principles, of assets, liabilities, and owner's equity for a given date. It is intended to show what a company possesses at a given point in time (assets), and of those assets, what the company owes (liabilities) and what it owns (equity). Thus, for a balance sheet, it should always be the case that assets = liabilities + equity.

OWNER'S EQUITY SECTION

Owner's equity is the remaining interest in assets after liabilities have been deducted. Originally created by the investments of the owners, it can increase by the addition of investors and decrease when it is distributed amongst its investors. It can also fluctuate because of business operations.

When there is a sole owner, owner's equity is called **proprietor's equity**. In a partnership, equity accounts are set up for each partner, allowing for individualized accounting of investments, income, or withdrawals.

When a corporation is formed, accounts are determined by their source. Minimum contributed capital is determined by incorporation regulations or state law. **Retained earnings** are a result of accumulated earnings minus losses and dividends and are considered a resource to use when growing the business.

TYPES OF ASSETS

Some different kinds of **assets** are current assets, fixed, assets, and intangible assets.

Current assets are a company's most liquid assets. Current assets are one of the major considerations when determining a company's value. They include any cash on hand and everything the company owns that will be converted into cash in the next year, such as accounts receivable, money market funds, inventory, etc.

Fixed assets are what a company owns that couldn't quickly be sold to raise cash, such as plants and equipment. These things aren't very liquid, as there is usually not a big market for them, and they often aren't worth much due to depreciation. But they do have some value, and could conceivably be sold for some amount eventually.

Intangible assets are nonphysical assets, which include patents, intellectual property rights, trademarks, goodwill, and other things.

LIABILITY SECTION

Liabilities are the debts and obligations of a business, and are listed on the balance sheet by due date and current or long-term status.

1. **Current Liabilities** – Debts that must be paid in the short-term, generally within a year. Usually presented in order of payment due date or priority of payment.
2. **Long-Term Liabilities** – Business debts that are due over the longer term, which is generally considered longer than one year.
3. **Valuation Accounts** – Similar to valuation accounts for assets, these are associated with the original liability, i.e., not separate assets or liabilities. The changes, such as discounts on bonds, affect the amount of the liability.

INCOME STATEMENTS

A company's **income statement** reports its revenues and expenses for a given period of time, showing how the revenues result in a given net income, thus indicating the success or failure of a company's profitable activities. The expenses listed on the income statement include all the charges against the revenues, such as write-offs and taxes. The main components can be listed as follows:

$$Net\ Sales - Cost\ of\ Goods\ Sold\ (CGS) - Operating\ Expense - Interest\ Expense = Taxable\ Income$$

$$Taxable\ Income - Taxes\ = \ Net\ Income$$

$$Net\ Income - Dividends\ = \ Retained\ Earnings$$

INTERMEDIATE CALCULATIONS

Besides net income (also called **net profit**), there are a number of intermediate income calculations made on an income statement. In order, these include:

- *EBITDA* – earnings before interest, taxes, depreciation, and amortization
- *EBIT* – earnings before interest and taxes
- *EBT* – earnings before taxes

The name of the calculation tells where it is located on the income statement. EBITDA appears before operating expenses are subtracted (since those include depreciation and amortization), but after cost of goods sold is subtracted. EBIT appears before interest expense is subtracted, and EBT appears before taxes are subtracted.

STATEMENTS OF CASH FLOWS

A **statement of cash flows** is responsible for communicating to readers the amount and uses of cash funds for a business over a time period. It is divided into three sections: operating, investing, and financing.

The operating section involves all those cash flows tied up with the company's main operations, that is, the same activities which are used to determine net income.

The investing section tracks the cash movement for transactions involving securities (available-for-sale and held-to-maturity) and property, plant, and equipment, in addition to collections and sales on purchased loans.

The financing section includes cash from the repayment of debts, the payment of dividends, the issuance of stock, and any other finance activities (such as derivatives).

METHODS FOR VALUING A COMPANY'S INVENTORY

When determining the value of its inventory, a company can choose to use either the first in, first out (FIFO) method or the last in, first out (LIFO) method.

Using the **LIFO method**, when a company sells a product from its inventory, it calculates the cost of that sale based on the newest item in its inventory. For instance, if 600 objects were purchased on Jan. 1 at $10 apiece and 400 more on Feb. 1 at $12 apiece, and if there were 750 objects remaining on Feb. 15, then the inventory value would be $(600 \times \$10) + (150 \times \$12) = \$7,800$.

Using the **FIFO method**, when a company sells a product from its inventory, it calculates the cost of that sale based on the oldest item in its inventory. For instance, given the above example, the inventory value on Feb. 15 would be $(400 \times \$12) + (350 \times \$10) = \$8,300$.

TYPES OF DEPRECIATION

Except for real estate, pretty much all physical property owned by a company depreciates (loses value over time) due to obsolescence and wear and tear. There are different ways to reflect this depreciation, but two general approaches. In the **straight-line method**, the cost of a physical asset is divided by the number of years of expected useful life. So if a company buys a new machine for five million dollars, and its useful life is estimated at 20 years, the company could use straight-line depreciation and depreciate $250,000 a year for each of the 20 years. Or the company could use **accelerated depreciation**, and write off larger amounts in the first years of owning the property and smaller amounts in the later years of its use. Accelerated depreciation can come in different forms, particularly the **double-declining balance (DDB) method** and the **sum-of-the-years'-digits (SYD) method**.

LIQUIDITY

Liquidity is a company's ability to quickly convert its assets into cash. Several different measures can serve to analyze it.

$$Working\ capital\ =\ current\ assets\ -\ current\ liabilities$$

$$Current\ ratio\ =\frac{current\ assets}{current\ liabilities}$$

$$Quick\ assets\ =\ current\ assets - inventory$$

$$Acid\ test\ ratio\ = \frac{cash + \frac{A}{R} + short-term\ investments}{current\ liabilities}$$

CAPITALIZATION RATIOS

Capitalization refers to a company's equity plus its long-term debt. A capitalization ratio is a measure of the proportion of debt in a company's overall capital structure. Among the capitalization ratios are:

- Debt-to-Equity ratio: total liabilities / equity – this ratio measures the percentage of the balance sheet that is financed by outside parties, such as creditors or suppliers, against the percentage that is owned by shareholders. A high ratio means that the company is highly leveraged.
- Long-term Debt-to-Capitalization ratio: long-term debt / total capitalization – this ratio measures the proportion of debt the company is using to finance its operations. Again, a high ratio means the company is highly leveraged.
- Common Stock-to-Capitalization ratio: common stock equity / total capitalization – this ratio measures the proportion of stock the company is using to finance its operations. A high ratio means the company is mostly funded through the issuance of common stock shares.

INVENTORY TURNOVER RATIO

Inventory turnover is a ratio of cost of goods sold divided by the average inventory (beginning inventory plus ending inventory divided by two). If the number is low, it represents slow-moving items, which is a bad sign for business. If the inventory is perishable, such as food, then the inventory turnover ratio should be high. The inventory turnover ratio is an indicator of how hard the inventory is working for the business.

PROFIT MARGIN

Profit margin is the ratio of a company's net profit (i.e., net income) to the revenue (i.e., net sales) for a given time period. Generally, a lower profit margin means that an investment in the company will be riskier. Profit margin can be a helpful measure for comparing companies within the same industry.

BOOK VALUE PER SHARE

Book value per share is the measure of how much each share of stock would actually be worth if the company were to be sold to satisfy creditors. Book value per share is an important figure for more conservative investors. Book value per share is determined by subtracting all liabilities (such as creditors and preferred stock holders, since they are paid before holders of common stock) from the total value of all tangible assets. This is the book value, or **net asset value (NAV)**, of the company. What's left over is divided by the number of shares of common stock outstanding, and the result is the book value per share.

The NAV can also be divided by the number of bonds a company has, to arrive at the net asset value per bond.

INTEREST COVERAGE RATIO

A company's **interest coverage ratio** shows how easily a company can pay the interest expense on its outstanding debt. It is calculated by dividing the earnings before interest and tax (EBIT) by the interest expense for a given period. A lower number for this, such as 1.5 or less, signifies a heavy debt burden that the company must deal with.

This ratio can also be applied to particular kinds of interest expense. For instance, the **bond interest coverage ratio** equals the EBIT divided by the total bond interest expense.

EARNINGS PER SHARE (EPS)

Earnings per share (EPS) is the percentage of a company's net profits per outstanding share of company stock. EPS is calculated as: EPS = (net income – preferred dividends) / avg. shares outstanding.

The higher the EPS the more profitable the company. If a stock split occurs, the shares outstanding increase. If a buyback occurs, the shares outstanding decrease.

Another variation on earnings per share is Fully Diluted Earnings per Share. This ratio includes both outstanding shares of common stock plus all sources of convertible shares (e.g., stock options and convertible bonds) and generally results in lower EPS.

PRICE/EARNINGS RATIO, THE DIVIDEND PAYOUT RATIO, AND RETURN ON EQUITY (ROE)

The **price/earnings (P/E) ratio** is calculated by dividing the current price of a share of stock by the company's current earnings per share. A stock with a high P/E ratio is considered expensive, all other things being equal, and a stock with a low P/E ratio is considered a bargain, all other factors being equal.

The **dividend payout ratio** measures the company's earnings which are paid out to stockholders. It is calculated by dividing the dividends by the net income for a given period. Or, equivalently, it is calculated by dividing dividends per share by a company's EPS.

Return on equity (ROE) measures how much income the company makes based upon its shareholder's equity. It is calculated by dividing net income by shareholder's equity (which excludes preferred shares). This also can be called **return on net worth (RONW)**.

NOMINAL YIELD AND CURRENT YIELD

Yield is the value of the interest payments received from a bond compared to the bond's value. There are several ways to measure a bond's yield. The **nominal yield**, also known as the **coupon yield**, is the interest rate with which the bond was sold. However, as market conditions change, and interest rates go up and down, the value of a bond goes up and down in inverse proportion to interest rates. So **current yield** is a more accurate measure of bond value, and it is determined by dividing the coupon rate by the current market price.

COMPARATIVE PERFORMANCE ANALYSIS

Comparative Performance Analysis is comparing current ratios to either past ratios or the ratios of other companies, in the same or different industries. Comparative analysis allows for the identification of significant trends and areas of outperformance/underperformance relative to other companies. A key profitability ratio that companies use when conducting Comparative Performance Analysis is Return on Common Equity (ROCE), which is net income, divided by the average common stockholders' equity. It is similar to Return on Equity, but specific to common shareholders as it excludes preferred stock.

Another useful tool in conducting Comparative Performance Analysis is common-size financial statements (income statement, balance sheet, etc.), for which statement values are translated into

percentages. For the income statement, the nominal amounts would be translated to a percentage of Total Revenue, while for the balance sheet each amount would be changed to a percentage of Total Assets.

SEC RULE 14E-3

SEC Rule 14e-3 states that when a person has taken steps to commence a tender offer, it constitutes a fraudulent act for any person who is in possession of material information related to the tender offer, which information he/she knows or has reason to know is nonpublic and was acquired directly or indirectly from a person connected to the issuer, to purchase or sell such securities, unless within a reasonable time prior to any purchase or sale such information and its source are publicly disclosed by press release or otherwise.

A person will not be deemed in violation of the Rule if such person shows that the individual(s) making the investment decision on their behalf did not know the material, nonpublic information and they implemented policies and procedures to ensure that individual(s) making investment decision(s) would not violate the Rule. A purchase or sale of any such security by a broker or by another agent on behalf of an offering person shall not be deemed in violation of the Rule.

It is unlawful for the offering person, the issuer of the securities, or anyone acting on their behalf to communicate material, nonpublic information relating to a tender offer to any other person under circumstances in which it is reasonably foreseeable that such communication is likely to result in a violation of the Rule.

Except that this does not apply to a communication made in good faith to persons involved in the planning, financing, preparation or execution of such tender offer.

SEC RULE 14E-4

SEA Rule 14e-4 states that it is unlawful for any person acting alone or in concert with others, directly or indirectly, to tender any subject security in a partial tender offer unless at the time of tender, and at the end of the proration period or period during which securities are accepted by lot, he has a net long position equal to or greater than the amount tendered in the subject security or an equivalent security and will deliver or cause to be delivered such security for the purpose of tender to the person making the offer within the period specified in the offer. The Rule is designed to preclude persons from tendering more shares than they own for the purpose of avoiding or reducing the risk of pro rata acceptance in a partial tender offer.

CBOE RULE 9.3

Cboe Rule 9.3 states that a Trading Permit Holder, Registered Options Principal or Registered Representative who recommends to a customer the purchase or sale (writing) of any option contract cannot recommend a purchase or sale of options unless they:

- have reasonable grounds for believing that the recommendation is not unsuitable for such customer on the basis of the information furnished by such customer after reasonable inquiry as to his investment objectives, financial situation and needs, and any other information known.

- have a reasonable basis for believing at the time of making the recommendation that the customer has such knowledge and experience in financial matters that he may reasonably be expected to be capable of evaluating the risks of the recommended transaction and is financially able to bear the risks of the recommended position in the option contract.
- ensure that the customer has previously engaged in an options transaction before engaging in a Delayed Start Option Series.

Reviewing and Analyzing Customers' Investment Profiles and Product Options to Determine that Investment Recommendations Meet Applicable Standards

AUTHORIZED STOCK, ISSUED STOCK, AND OUTSTANDING STOCK

Authorized stock is the maximum number of shares that a company has been approved to sell on the market. They may sell them all immediately, or hold them back for sale at a later date, or for other purposes, such as employee stock options. Holding stocks back is fairly common, and authorized shares often exceed the actual shares issued for sale on the market. Once all authorized shares have been sold, or issued, the company may not sell any more shares without getting approval from current stockholders, because the company charter must be amended.

Issued stock is the number of shares that have ever been sold and held, even if they have since been repurchased by the company or retired.

Outstanding stock is the number of shares that are currently held by investors and tradeable in the market. If no shares have been repurchased or retired, then issued stock = outstanding stock.

TREASURY STOCK

Shares that have been issued and sold are sometimes bought back by the company. The stock that is bought back from the market and held by the company is known as **treasury stock**. The corporation may hold the stock for future use, such as employee stock options, or they may retire it for good. Stock buybacks are usually seen as an indicator of a company's belief in the strength of its value, and are often followed by an increase in share value, as investors will interpret the buyback as a sign of strength. Even if the share price remains the same, the earning per share should go up, since the number of shares outstanding that will share in company earnings has been reduced. The rights that apply to outstanding stock still on the market, such as voting rights and dividend rights, don't apply to treasury stock.

STOCKS VS. EQUITY

Stocks and equity are often used synonymously. Both represent ownership in a company. Equity is a broader term meaning ownership of assets after debt is paid, while stock generally refers to traded equity.

PAR VALUE FOR STOCKS

The **par value** for a stock is the value stated on the stock certificate. This is the requirement which the company is legally obligated to pay a shareholder in exchange for ownership in the company, no matter how worthless the stock certificate might be on the open market. Consequently, the par value for stocks tends to be very low, $1 or even $0.01 per share, in order to lower the company's obligation in the event of stock devaluation.

Predictably, stocks with a par value are known as **par value stocks**, and stocks lacking a par value are known as **no par value stocks**.

RIGHTS OF COMMON STOCKHOLDERS

Common stockholders enjoy a number of rights, including:

- voting on major issues, such as the election of directors and changes affecting the company such as mergers or liquidation
- pro rata share of dividends
- ability to inspect corporate books and records, such as company bylaws and board of director minutes
- preemptive rights, which give a shareholder the opportunity to buy additional shares in any future issue of common stock before the shares are made available to the general public
- residual claim on corporate assets after debt has been paid in the case of bankruptcy

VOTING POWERS FOR COMMON STOCKHOLDERS

Common stockholders generally receive one vote for each share they own per issue to be decided. For instance, a stockholder owning 1,000 shares in a corporation, voting for candidates to fill 5 different positions on the board of directors, will have a total of 5,000 votes to expend. However, how votes are allocated can differ:

- Statutory voting – this the most common type of voting and requires the stockholder to split up his votes evenly among the issues. For instance, in the above example, the shareholder will have 1000 votes maximum to expend on each of the five different positions being filled.
- Cumulative voting – this type of voting allows shareholders to distribute their votes as they please. For instance, the above shareholder, if he chose, could use all 5,000 votes on one candidate running for a single position on the board of directors.

Since it is often unfeasible for all common stockholders to physically attend annual corporate meetings, they can exercise their voting rights through a form of absentee ballot called a proxy.

PREEMPTIVE RIGHTS

A **preemptive right** is the right of a shareholder (though not of just any shareholder) to maintain his current percentage of share ownership in case the corporation decides to issue more stock. If a company decides to issue more stock, the company must give these privileged shareholders first crack at buying the shares before the company offers the shares to the general market (and usually below market price). Current shareholders will receive a subscription rights certificate, which will spell out the terms and conditions of the offer, such as the date, price, and how many shares they're entitled to buy based on their current ownership.

SPINOFFS

A **spinoff** occurs when a corporation "spins off" (or splits off) one of its divisions/sections, making it a separate entity altogether and endowing it with particular facilities and assets.

When this occurs, shareholders in the original corporation also receive stock in the spinoff entity. Spinoffs can increase the value of stocks previously held in the one corporation before the spinoff, since it gives investors the option to choose whichever section of the company they think will be more profitable.

EFFECT OF COMPANY CONSOLIDATION ON STOCKS

Consolidation refers to the combining of the assets and liabilities of two companies. Mergers and acquisitions are examples of consolidation. The acquiring firm can pay cash for all the equity shares of the target company and pay each shareholder a specified amount for each share, or the acquirer can provide its own shares to the target company's shareholders according to a specified conversion ratio (a stock-for-stock merger), or they can do a combination of both.

This type of consolidation is the result of negotiations between the executives of the acquiring company and the target company, followed by a vote by each organization's board of directors, then a shareholder vote. The target company must hold a shareholder vote, while the acquiring company only needs to hold a shareholder vote if 20% or more of its shares will be issued to the target company's shareholders.

No shareholder of the target company who votes against the transaction is required to accept shares in the acquiring company. Instead, he or she may exercise appraisal rights and be paid the fair market value for his or her shares.

In a cash-for-stock merger, the investor may have to pay capital gains taxes on the transaction. In a stock-for-stock merger, **the IRS does not look on this as a taxable transaction for shareholders of the target company and the shareholder has the same tax basis as before the merger.**

Instead of a merger occurring through negotiations, a potential acquirer can appeal directly to the shareholders of the target company through a tender offer. In the case of a takeover attempt, the tender may be conditional on the potential acquirer being able to obtain a certain amount of shares, such as a controlling interest in the company. The price offered per share is usually higher than market value to incent shareholders to tender their shares.

For tax purposes, the acceptance of a tender offer constitutes a sale. This means the investor may have to pay capital gains taxes on the transaction.

PENNY STOCKS

Penny stocks are shares of very small publicly traded companies, generally traded as over-the-counter stocks, not on major exchanges. These stocks are prone to speculative and volatile price changes and manipulation, thus being very risky. They are also characterized by **illiquidity**; that is, they are difficult to trade to others. Because of this, a broker must acquire his customer's written consent before facilitating any penny stock transactions for him.

There are special rules accompanying **penny stock transactions**. A broker wishing to facilitate such a transaction is required by the SEC to give the customer a document outlining the risks of penny stock investments, the market price for the stock, and the compensation the brokerage firm will receive for executing the transaction. Brokerage firms also must send monthly statements to penny stock investors, disclosing the value of their penny stocks.

TYPES OF PREFERRED STOCK

Cumulative preferred stock is preferred stock that gives the stockholder the right to missed dividend payments from the company. Should the company miss a dividend payment to owners of cumulative preferred stock, the company must make up the payment at a later date, as it stays on the books as a debt until paid. This is opposed to straight (or non-cumulative) preferred stock, which has a fixed dividend payment (like cumulative preferred stock), but if the company misses any payments, they are not made up later.

Participating preferred stock entitles the stockholder to a portion of the profits that remain after dividends and interest have been paid by the corporation. These are so called because they permit stockholders to participate further in the company's profits.

Participating preferred stockholders also have special rights should the corporation liquidate.

95

Convertible preferred stock consists of shares that can be converted into common stock if the owner so chooses. The conversion price is preset, and convertible preferred shares tend to rise and fall in value along with common shares because of this feature. They also usually have lower dividend payments than other preferred stocks.

Callable preferred stock consists of shares that the company reserves the right to buy back at a future date at a specific price. When a company calls a preferred share, it will pay a premium over the stated price to make up for loss of future dividends. This can also be called **redeemable preferred stock**.

Callable preferred stock is ordinarily covered by a **sinking fund provision**. In the same way that corporations can repurchase bonds with a sinking fund, the same can be done for their repurchasing of preferred stock.

Normal preferred stock pays dividends at a fixed rate, but **adjustable-rate preferred stock** has the level of dividend payment change periodically. These payments are altered according to a benchmark, usually the risk-free rate on U.S. Treasury securities. Despite the fact that these types of stocks can change in their return, they are generally acknowledged to be more stable than preferred stocks with a fixed rate.

DIFFERENCES BETWEEN COMMON STOCK AND PREFERRED STOCK

The vast majority of stocks issued are **common stock**. Some corporations issue a limited number of **preferred stocks**. Holders of preferred stock do not have voting rights under most circumstances. But there are financial benefits to owning preferred stock instead of common stock. If a company goes bankrupt, preferred stock owners take precedence over common stock holders when it comes to distributing whatever assets are available. And preferred stock usually comes with a fixed dividend paid on a regular basis, so that even if the owners of common stock don't receive a dividend, preferred stock owners will. And because the dividend is fixed, owners of preferred stock can depend on a regular income. Because of these differences, the prices of preferred stocks tend to rise and fall with relation to interest rates, and not with other factors that affect the price of the common stock.

REASONS TO ISSUE PREFERRED STOCK

Preferred Stock is often issued as an alternative to issuing debt. The Par value of preferred stock is typically $100 per share.

Preferred stock is a form of equity, or a stake in the company's ownership. Instead of being a form of debt equity, preferred stock works more like a bond than it does like a share in a company. Companies issue preferred stock as a way to obtain equity financing without sacrificing voting rights. This can also be a way to avoid a hostile takeover - a ""flip in"" poison pill provision would allow only existing shareholders to buy preferred stock at a discount under certain situations.

Some companies like to issue preferred shares because they keep the debt-to-equity ratio lower than issuing bonds and give less control to outsiders than common stocks.

Preferred stocks attract investors looking for dividends, which provide owners with a fixed rate of return rather than returns that rise and fall with the stock market.

RIGHTS OFFERINGS

In a **rights offering** (also called a **rights issue**), a company will issue the right to purchase additional stocks to current stockholders in the company. The company will set a predetermined number of shares and price per share, giving shareholders the right to purchase such shares in the future, sometimes within a set time period.

Since rights offerings can give an incentive for shareholders to purchase further stock, they are often used as a means to raise capital for the company.

WARRANTS

Warrants are the right to buy a stock at a specified price, which is almost always higher than the price the stock is trading at when the warrant is issued. If the stock price rises above the warrant price, the warrant becomes very valuable, much like a call option, as the warrant owner has the right to purchase stock below the market price. The owner may choose to exercise the warrant and buy the stock, may sell the warrant, or may continue to hold it hoping the stock goes even higher, until the expiration date. Most warrants are good for five years.

ANTI-DILUTION PROVISIONS

With options and convertible securities, their main value derives from the fact that stocks can be purchased for a price lower than the market price. Because of this, holders of options and convertible securities would dislike any additional issuance of stock, which would dilute the value per share by spreading out the total equity of the company over more shareholders.

Consequently, certain options and convertible securities will have an **anti-dilution provision** (or **anti-dilution cause**), which guarantees that the company will not dilute shares through further stock issuance.

PINK SHEETS

Pink sheet stocks are stocks that are traded in the over-the-counter market rather than on exchanges like the New York Stock Exchange (NYSE). Pink sheet stocks are issued by companies that either cannot meet the requirements for listing on a U.S. stock exchange or wish to avoid the high costs and regulatory requirements of listing on an exchange. The pink sheets market gets its name from the fact that its stock quotes used to be published on pink paper; however, trading is now done electronically. Stocks listed on pink sheets are typically penny stocks, which means they have low market capitalizations and share prices of $5 or less. There is generally limited information available about the companies offering pink sheet stocks and they tend to be more volatile and riskier than exchange-listed stocks.

OVER-THE-COUNTER (OTC) MARKET

The **over-the-counter (OTC) market** is also known as the **second market** (not to be confused with the secondary market, which encompasses all the various ways of trading stock besides new issues). It consists of a nationwide network of brokers and dealers connected by phone and computer who trade non-listed stocks from their offices. NASDAQ, Bulletin Board, and Pink Sheet stocks comprise the second market, with the most prominent distinction being between NASDAQ issues and non-NASDAQ issues.

OVER-THE-COUNTER BULLETIN BOARD (OTCBB)

The **over-the-counter bulletin board** (OTCBB) is a regulated electronic medium for trading over-the-counter (OTC) securities, displaying quotes, recent sale prices, and volume information. Stocks trading on the OTCBB include the suffix .*OB* in their stock symbol, and they are generally considered riskier than stocks trading on the NASDAQ exchange.

THREE-QUOTE RULE

For bulletin board stocks and pink sheet stocks traded on the OTC, there may not always be much indicated **trading interest** on the part of market makers. So when a broker or dealer gets a trade order for a bulletin board or pink sheet stock, the broker or dealer must first check and see if there are at least two market makers making firm quotes for the security. If not, the broker or dealer must consult at least three other brokers or dealers to come up with a price.

AUCTION MARKETS

Auction markets are arrangements where prospective buyers and prospective sellers compete with another to make bids and offers. Securities traded in auction markets will naturally be traded according to the highest bid and lowest ask price. The execution of orders in auction markets involves matching compatible bids and asks.

Examples of auction markets include the Philadelphia Stock Exchange (NASDAQ OMX PHLX), NYSE Euronext, NYSE MKT LLC (formerly NYSE Amex Equities), and NYSE Arca.

NEW YORK STOCK EXCHANGE (NYSE)

The **New York Stock Exchange (NYSE)** is the biggest stock market by total market value in the country, and it is often referred to as the "big board." In general, older, larger, and more established company's shares are traded on the NYSE. The **Dow Jones Industrial Average** is an index based on thirty of the largest and most heavily traded stocks on the NYSE. Much of the trading on the NYSE still occurs on the actual floor between human beings bidding against each other in person.

NYSE MKT LLC

One of the world's foremost equities exchanges is the NYSE MKT, or **NYSE MKT LLC**, formerly the American Stock Exchange (AMEX) and, after that, NYSE Amex Equities. It is designed for small-capital companies. Like the NYSE it handles stocks of companies from all over the United States. The regulations under which the NYSE MKT operates are typically somewhat more lenient than those governing the NYSE, so it therefore has a larger representation of stock issued by smaller companies. It is also known as "the curb."

LISTING REQUIREMENTS FOR EXCHANGES

Different exchanges have different requirements which companies must fulfill before being permitted to participate in trading on the exchange. These are called **listing requirements**, or **listing standards**. These requirements are entirely up to the discretion of the exchanges, not regulated by the SEC.

The standards include both financial and non-financial requirements. The requirements can be based on stock price and the number of publicly traded shares and shareholders, among other considerations.

ELECTRONIC COMMUNICATION NETWORKS (ECNs)

Electronic communication networks (ECNs) are systems which aim to facilitate more direct trading between traders and brokerage firms. ECNs allow orders to be executed without a third party, especially orders executed by a market maker. ECNs are often utilized by institutional investors who do their own trading of massive quantities of shares twenty-four hours per day. The three biggest ECNs for stock trading are Island, Archipelago, and Instinet.

DARK POOLS OF LIQUIDITY

For some orders, the volume of securities traded can be hidden from public knowledge. This is usually done by institutional investors, to keep their trades secret from other (competing) institutional investors. These types of trades are said to involve **dark pools of liquidity**, since the actual trades are concealed or cloudy.

AMERICAN DEPOSITORY RECEIPTS (ADR)

An **American Depository Receipt (ADR)** is a financial instrument created so that the stocks of foreign companies can be bought and sold on stock markets in the United States. Each ADR represents a certain number of shares of a foreign company, usually somewhere between one and ten shares. Each individual share is known as an **American Depositary Share**. ADRs are bought and sold just like other common stocks listed on the exchanges, and ADR owners have the same rights as other stock holders, including voting and receiving dividends, which are paid in dollars. An ADR is technically owned by a bank, which handles the ADR, and is held in the buyer's name. An ADR can fluctuate in value due to changes in currency rates.

TAX TREATMENT OF EQUITY SECURITY SALES

Selling securities creates either a capital gain or loss, generally determined by subtracting the tax basis (the cost of the investment plus broker commissions or other costs of buying plus reinvested dividends) from the sale proceeds. The IRS presumes a first-in, first-out (FIFO) rule. If the taxpayer wants to treat the transaction differently, then he must identify the specific stock sold by using one of the methods acceptable to the IRS.

If the holding period for the security exceeds one year, then the capital gain or loss is considered long-term, if it is less than one year, it is considered short term. Short-term gains are subject to the ordinary income tax rate, which ranges from 10% to 37%. Long-term gains are subject to a 0% rate, a 15% rate, or a 20% rate, depending on the taxpayer's filing status and annual income. For instance, a single taxpayer earning less than $44,625 would not pay capital gains tax, while one earning greater than $492,300 (for 2023) would be subject to a capital gains rate of 20%. Additionally, taxpayers with incomes of at least $200,000 ($250,000 for joint filers) must pay the new 3.8% Medicare surcharge on net investment income. Capital losses can be netted against capital gains realized in the same tax year, but only up to $3,000 can be deducted from earned or other types of income, such as wages, in that year. Losses beyond this amount can be applied to future years' taxes up to $3,000 per year.

Brokerage firms are required to report to the IRS the cost basis of the shares sold, if known. Investors must report sales of securities on Form 1040, Schedule D, Capital Gains and Losses. The trade date determines the year in which the transaction is taxable. As an example, gains/losses on a stock sold on December 30 must be reported in that tax year, even though the settlement date was in the following year.

TAXATION FOR DIVIDENDS

Dividends can be reinvested or distributed as cash. Cash dividends are subject to taxation in the year they were paid. Dividends are classified as either qualified or nonqualified. Qualified dividends are those paid by U.S. companies, foreign companies whose stocks are traded on a major U.S. stock exchange, and foreign companies residing in countries eligible for benefits under a U.S. tax treaty. Qualified dividends are taxed at a lower rate compared to nonqualified dividends. Qualified dividends are tax-free for taxpayers in income tax brackets <12%, rising to a 20% tax rate for taxpayers in income tax brackets >35%. Nonqualified dividends do not meet the requirements of

qualified dividends and are treated as short-term capital gains and are taxed at the taxpayer's income tax rate.

WASH SALES

The IRS generally permits investors to offset investment gains with capital losses up to $3,000 a year. However, a capital loss may not be used to offset gains if the investor, within thirty days after taking the loss, then buys the same security, or one that is "substantially identical," which would include warrants, rights, options, and convertible bonds in the same stock. If the investor purchases the same security or a substantially identical one within thirty days of the loss, it is considered a **wash sale**, and cannot be factored in with net capital losses to offset gains or income.

CAPITAL GAINS AND LOSSES

Capital gains occur when an asset (usually a security) is sold for a price greater than the price at which the investor purchased it. Similarly, **capital losses** occur when the investor loses money on the sale of the asset. Note the gain or loss when the asset is sold - any change in value before sale is simply called appreciation or depreciation and it not taxable until a sale occurs.

Capital gains and losses are subject to federal, state, and local taxes. The taxation depends upon the holding period of the security, that is, how much time passed between when the asset was purchased and when it was sold.

If the holding period is one year or less, then any capital gain or loss is classified as short-term, and gains are consequently taxed as if they were ordinary income (i.e., by the investor's tax bracket).

Long-term capital gains or losses occur for holding periods exceeding one year. In 2023 the capital gains tax rates are either 0%, 15% or 20% for most assets held for more than a year. Capital gains tax rates on most assets held for less than a year correspond to ordinary income tax brackets (10%, 12%, 22%, 24%, 32%, 35% or 37%).

Additionally, in 2013 the US added a 3.8% investment tax on investment income for high income individuals.

TAXATION EFECTS OF CAPITAL LOSSES ON CAPITAL GAINS

While investors are taxed on **capital gains**, the amount of capital gains on which they are taxed can be reduced by their **capital losses**. An investor with $10,000 in long-term capital gains and $5,000 in long-term capital losses during the year will have to pay taxes only on $5,000 worth of long-term capital gains.

Only short-term losses can offset short-term gains, and only long-term losses can offset long-term gains.

Besides offsetting capital gains, capital losses can also offset **ordinary income** if there are no capital gains left to offset. However, ordinary income can be offset by a maximum of $3,000 per year, with the remaining balance being carried forward to the next year. For example, if an investor had long-term capital gains of $5,000 and long-term capital losses of $15,000 for the year, then he would pay no taxes on the capital gains, deduct $3,000 from his ordinary income, and carry the remaining $7,000 balance to the next year, which can offset future capital gains or income.

TAX IMPLICATIONS FOR STOCKS ACQUIRED THROUGH CONVERSION

If stock is acquired through **conversion**, such as by exercising the conversion feature on convertible bonds, then any gain or loss acquired through the conversion is not immediately relevant to capital gains or losses. Instead, the **basis** of the stocks is equal to the value of the debt at the point of conversion. This basis is then the reference point for determining future capital gains or losses on that stock.

For example, if a convertible bond with a basis of $1,000 is converted into 20 shares of stock selling at that date for $55 apiece, then the basis of the stock investment will still be $1,000 (effectively $50 per share), and the investor will recognize no capital gain or loss at that point. (That is, he will not recognize a gain of $100 at the date of conversion, even though the stock is valued at $1,100 and the bond at $1,000.) However, if the investor were to then sell the stocks at $60 per share one year later, then that would be taxable event upon his capital gain of $10 per share sold.

The **holding period** for the stock begins at the date of the debt issuance, not at the date of conversion.

TAX CONSIDERATIONS FOR THE BEQUEATHING OF SECURITIES

Individuals can gift up to $15,000 each year tax-free to an unlimited number of recipients. Gifts toward education and medical expenses do not count toward the $15,000 annual limit. Gifts in excess of that amount require the donor to file an estate and gift tax return, but there would be no tax implications unless the gift exceeded their lifetime gift and estate tax exemption.

The recipient of the stock does not owe any capital gains taxes until the shares are sold. If the recipient sells the stock for a gain, the donor's cost basis and purchase date is used to determine the realized capital gain. For example, if the donor bought the stock more than a year ago, it is considered a long-term gain, with tax rates of 0%, 15%, or 20%, depending on the recipient's income tax bracket. If the recipient sells the shares for a loss, the cost basis is the lower of the donor's cost basis or the fair market value (FMV) on the transfer date.

Inherited stock, or stock that is bequeathed to a beneficiary upon the death of the stockholder, is not taxed on the appreciation from the time the decedent purchased it to the time or his or her death. The beneficiary is only taxed on the change in value from the time they inherited it to the time of sale. This is referred to as stepped-up basis.

DIVIDENDS

A **dividend** is a portion of the company's profit that is returned to shareholders. A dividend can come in the form of cash, in which case a check is sent to the owner or to the owner's brokerage account. When the company announces dividends, there will be some dollar amount per share distributed to shareholders. When dividends are paid in cash, they are considered income, and taxes must be paid on them during the tax year they're received.

Dividends can also be in the form of additional shares of stock given to shareholders. These are not taxable until they're sold, just like all stocks. Because this type of stock dividend increases the number of outstanding shares, it decreases the market value of each share, but does not affect the total market value of the company.

STOCKS' COST BASIS

The **cost basis** (or **tax basis**) for stocks is the reference point to be used when determining one's capital gains or losses. If your stock's cost basis is $5,000 and you sell it for $5,500, then you have a capital gain of $500. Cost basis will often be listed as **cost basis per share**.

The cost basis for stock is not ordinarily the purchase price of the stock. When buying stock, the basis will be increased by fees and commissions paid to the broker or dealer.

EFFECT OF DIVIDENDS ON STOCKS' COST BASIS

If **dividends** are gained on stock and then reinvested in the stock, the dividends are still treated as income, in which case their reinvestment increases the cost basis of the stock by the amount reinvested.

Moreover, all reinvested dividends are still taxable.

FIFO, LIFO, AND SPECIFIC SHARE IDENTIFICATION

With the **first in, first out (FIFO) method** for valuing one's stocks, given a list of how many shares were bought or sold on which day (and at what price), the investor assumes for simplicity's sake that any shares sold are the oldest ones he possesses. If he bought 100 shares at $15 per share two years ago and 100 shares at $20 per share last year, then if he sells 150 shares today, it will be as if he sold $2,500 worth of shares: (100 shares x $15/share) + (50 shares x $20/share). $2,500 would be the basis against which he compares the selling price to determine capital gains or losses.

Under the **last in, first out (LIFO) method**, the newest stocks are assumed to be the ones sold. In the above example, the cost basis of the sold shares would be $2,750: (100 shares x $20/share) + (50 shares x $15/share).

Specific share identification involves the most work, since the investor (or mutual fund manager) must keep track of the buying and selling prices for every transaction of stock at the time it was transacted. The benefit of this is that it tends to reduce one's taxes.

Other methods are **high cost, first out (HCFO)** and **low cost, first out (LCFO)**, where the basis is determined by the relative prices of the acquired shares, not the time at which they were purchased.

UNIT INVESTMENT TRUSTS (UITS)

One type of investment company is the **unit investment trust (UIT).** Unit investment trusts operate by issuing shares entitling the owner to a portion of the investment portfolio owned by the trust. These shares can't be sold on the market, but only bought back, or redeemed, by the trust itself, and the trust is obligated to purchase them when an investor wants to sell. Unit investment trusts don't have boards of directors, and they don't have investment managers or advisers (and thus no fees for them). They usually invest in government bonds or in mutual funds.

Since UITs are not traded on the secondary market and have a finite number of shares that must be redeemed with the original issuer, one of their characteristics is **limited liquidity**.

UNIT INVESTMENT TRUSTS AND CLOSED-END FUNDS

There are a variety of mutual funds depending on the investments which the funds make. These include growth, income, balanced, sector, international, and other types of funds. Other investment companies, such as unit investment trusts and closed-end funds, can likewise have these different kinds of funds, even though (open-end) mutual funds tend to have the greatest variety.

EXCHANGE-TRADED FUNDS (ETFS)

Exchange-traded funds (ETFs) are types of mutual funds which are, like stocks, traded on an exchange. Many exchange-traded funds are designed to track an index, which is a passive type of investing and so requires smaller managing fees. Thus, the advantage of ETFs is that they provide the diversification which comes with mutual funds, the lower fees which come with index funds, and the flexibility of trade which comes with ordinary shares of stock.

BENEFITS FOR MUTUAL FUND INVESTORS

There are many reasons it makes sense for investors to choose to invest by way of **mutual funds** instead of selecting their own stocks. They may have little or no experience in investing, and can feel bewildered at all the investing options available today. A mutual fund solves this problem. A professional experienced investment adviser uses his knowledge and skill for the investors' benefit. Their investment dollars are automatically diversified, giving them the benefit of reduced risk and opportunities for gains in several areas. The cost to get started is often only a few hundred dollars. A professional custodian protects their investment. In addition, all investors in a mutual fund are on an equal footing, since there's no such thing as preferred stock, and everyone owns the same class of shares. And should the investor decide to liquidate their holdings, the mutual fund is required to buy them instantly.

MONEY MARKET FUNDS

Investors use **money market funds** to park cash while they are out of the market. They receive interest income, and have maximum liquidity, and generally face lower risk than with securities. Money market interest rates are always changing, and the net asset value is always at one dollar, although this is not actually guaranteed. During times of volatility in the stock markets, many investors will look to money market funds for liquidity and capital preservation.

TYPES OF INVESTMENT COMPANIES

The SEC defines an "investment company" as a company (corporation, business trust, partnership, or limited liability company) that issues securities and is primarily engaged in the business of investing in securities.

An investment company receives money from investors and invests it collectively, with each investor participating in the profits and losses on a pro rata basis.

There are three categories of investment companies:

- Mutual funds (legally known as open-end companies) – mutual funds are actively traded investment portfolios that can offer an unlimited number of shares on an ongoing basis and investors can redeem their shares whenever they choose.
- Closed-end funds (legally known as closed-end companies) – closed-end funds issue a fixed number of shares. Closed-end funds are not redeemable. Instead, investors can sell their shares in the secondary market.
- UITs (legally known as unit investment trusts) – UITs are fixed portfolios of securities that have an expiration date based on the securities held. Like mutual funds, UITs are redeemable at any time before the expiration date.

OPEN-END MANAGEMENT INVESTMENT COMPANIES

Unlike closed-end management investment companies (MICs), **open-end MICs** do not issue a fixed number of shares. When they register with the SEC, they do so as an open offering, which gives them the right to raise more investment capital by issuing and selling shares continuously. In addition, the shares of open-end MICs do not trade on the secondary market. Anyone who wants to purchase shares must buy them directly from the MIC, and the **offering price** is determined by dividing the net asset value of the MIC by the number of shares outstanding and then adding a sales charge. Fractional shares can be bought, not just whole shares. And when a shareholder wants to sell, the shareholder must sell the shares back to the company, not on the secondary market.

TYPES OF FUNDS

INDEX FUNDS

Index mutual funds are one of the more conservative mutual fund choices. Because these funds deliberately choose stocks to achieve the same performance as a broad based market index, (often the S&P 500), the portfolio will usually achieve roughly the same rate of return as the general market. Generally speaking, there is not much risk with this kind of approach, and there usually is not opportunity for extraordinary profits, although there are obviously exceptions to both of these rules. But many investors like this approach, and because of the much lower number of trades involved in an index fund, costs are often much lower than with other types of funds.

VALUE FUNDS

Value funds are mutual funds which aim to hold stocks that have an undervalued price and tend to pay out dividends. Since the share prices are undervalued, they are expected to rise in time and give the fund investors capital gains.

GROWTH FUNDS

Growth funds are only suitable for aggressive investors who are comfortable with a high degree of risk. Because growth funds invest in younger, less established companies that are growing fast, the risk with this type of fund is greater than that of investing in an index fund of established companies across the spectrum of the American economy. Growth funds are for people who are looking for maximum capital gains and are not interested in income, as the types of corporations in which growth funds invest do not pay dividends.

INCOME FUNDS

Income funds, like index funds, are generally considered more conservative, and are more suitable for investors with a strong aversion to risk. Income funds are not designed for capital gains, or for spectacular contrarian plays, but for safe, predictable, steady income. They buy shares of companies who are well established and have been paying dividends for a long time.

BALANCED FUNDS

Balanced funds, unlike many mutual funds, invest in both stocks and bonds. For this reason, balanced mutual funds are also commonly known as **hybrid funds**. The objective is a balance between capital gains and income. The general mix is 60 percent stocks to 40 percent bonds, although this is not a hard and fast rule, and many fund managers use their own ratio, especially as market conditions change. Balanced funds are considered to be pretty suitable for all investors.

INTERNATIONAL FUNDS

International funds are not usually suitable for investors with low tolerances to risk. They can post spectacular gains, but the risks attendant to investing in foreign companies is very high. Some funds are made up of shares of companies from around the world, while many of them focus on buying shares of companies in one particular country or region. Many of these countries and regions do not have the economic history and political stability that we enjoy in the United States. Foreign funds are therefore only suitable for investors who understand the risks and are comfortable with them.

SECTOR FUNDS

Sector funds invest in only one area, or sector, of the stock market, or one industry, etc. Many popular sector funds are in gold mining stocks, utility stocks, technology stocks, etc. While generally not as high-risk as foreign funds and special situation funds, there is certainly risk attached to investing in a sector fund. It is the risk of putting all your eggs in one basket. Many sector funds pop up only after the sector has had a huge run up, and investors are clamoring to get in on the market. By then, many times market conditions have changed and future investors don't get the same returns, and in fact often experience losses. Sector funds are for investors who know what they're doing, and understand that sector investing may not be the riskiest kind of fund, but it is also not the safest.

Sector funds are also called **specialized mutual funds**.

LIFE-CYCLE FUNDS

Life-cycle funds are a type of asset allocation fund that change the investment allocation as the investor ages. If the investor is younger, the allocation will involve stocks to increase risk, but as the investor ages, the allocation will involve more bonds to decrease risk. Since this is based on the age of the investor, these funds are also called **age-based funds**.

ASSET ALLOCATION FUNDS

Asset allocation funds are generally considered to be less risky than most other types. These funds allocate their assets between stocks, bonds, and cash, depending on market conditions. They will also adjust the percentages of each allocation as conditions change—it's not necessarily a uniform split among the three. Risk is lessened, but as always, with lower risk comes lower potential gains. For investors primarily concerned with safety, asset allocation funds are a good choice.

NET ASSET VALUE (NAV)

Net asset value (NAV) is the value of one share of a mutual fund. NAV is always changing, and must be calculated every day at the end of the trading day. Although it is quite a complicated calculation, in principle it is very simple. The fund's total liabilities are subtracted from the fund's total assets, which leaves the net asset value of the fund. That figure is then divided by the total number of shares outstanding, which gives the NAV per share. Usually, when NAV is mentioned, it refers to share NAV, not fund NAV.

There are only two things that cause a mutual fund's share net asset value to rise. One is when new investors come in and add cash to the mutual fund. The second is when the value of the securities in their portfolio goes up. Just the same, there are only two things that drive down a share's net asset value. One is when capital gains and/or income are paid out to shareholders. The other is when the value of the portfolio securities decreases. The buying and selling of stocks has no effect on net asset value, and when the fund redeems investors' shares, there is no effect on net asset value, because cash is being traded for securities, and vice versa.

FORWARD PRICING AND LATE TRADING

Since the net asset value (NAV) of open-end mutual fund shares is recalculated at the end of each trading day, and since investors wish to buy or sell mutual fund shares during the day, there has to be a sensible way to put a price tag on their transaction. This is done by **forward pricing**: using the next available NAV for each share bought or sold. This ordinarily involves waiting for the NAV to be computed at the end of the trading day.

Late trading involves purchasing mutual fund shares after the market has closed for the day but still obtaining that day's closing price, not the next day's price. This practice is illegal.

PUBLIC OFFERING PRICES OF MUTUAL FUND SHARES

A mutual fund's **public offering price** is the price the general public pays, no matter if they buy the share directly from the fund, or from a dealer, or from an underwriter, or a combination of any of the above. Broker/dealers and underwriters get a discount from the public offering price (POP) and they make their money on the difference between what they pay the fund for the shares and what they charge the investing public for the shares.

NO-LOAD FUNDS

Many mutual funds charge a **load**, or fee, to investors who participate in the fund. This fee goes to reimburse underwriters and dealers who market the fund to investors. But a mutual fund can choose to distribute its shares to investors without using underwriters and dealers. If they do so, and therefore don't charge a fee to cover their sales expense, they are known as a **no-load fund**.

In addition, a 12b-1 fund with a 12b-1 fee of 0.25% or less is also classified as a no-load fund.

12B-1 FEES

12b-1 fees are fees paid annually on mutual funds, ordinarily between 0.25% and 1% of the fund's net assets, to cover marketing and distribution costs for the fund. Their name is based upon the section from the Investment Company Act of 1940 bringing them into existence. When originally created, the fee was thought to help investors, since the marketing and distribution benefits presumably outweighed the cost of the fee. That assumption is more challenged today, however.

MARKETING OF LOAD FUNDS

Load funds may market and distribute their shares through one of two ways: (1) utilizing an underwriter only, who sells the shares to the investing public, or (2) utilizing an underwriter who sells the shares to brokers and dealers, with the brokers and dealers then selling the shares to the investing public. In either case, there is a profit built into the process for all parties between the fund and the investor. This is what the load is for, to cover sales expenses.

CALCULATION OF LOAD

There is a simple way of **calculating a mutual fund's load**. If you know the public offering price, and the net asset value per share, you can subtract the NAV from the POP. This will give you the load in dollars. You then divide that figure by the POP, and you'll have the load expressed as a percentage. Likewise, to determine the public offering price, simply add the dollar amount of the load to the net asset value.

CLASSES OF SHARES IN MUTUAL FUNDS

Although all mutual fund shares are common stock, and mutual funds do not issue preferred stock, there are three classifications of shares bought by investors in the funds. What separates the three is the amount of the sales charges the investor will pay, and the manner in which the investor pays them. **Class A shares** are bought with a front-end load, and the load can be lowered by investing in large enough amounts to qualify for breakpoints. **Class B shares** are bought with a back-end load, which decreases over time. **Class C shares** are 12b-1 shares.

FEATURES OF CLOSED-END MANAGEMENT INVESTMENT COMPANIES

When closed-end management investment companies begin trading, they issue a **fixed number of shares** that are available for purchase by the public, issued at the IPO price. These shares then trade on the secondary market, just like other securities. They may also issue preferred stocks and sell bonds. Unlike in open-end funds, in closed-end funds only whole shares can be bought (never fractional shares). The market determines the price of a share of a closed-end MIC.

Moreover, while open-end funds always trade their shares at their NAV, closed-end funds, being subject to the forces and influences of the secondary market, can sell with a premium or discount to their NAV.

FRONT-END LOADS AND BACK-END LOADS

When mutual funds use broker/dealers or underwriters to sell their shares to the public, they must pay for their services. To cover these sales and marketing services, mutual funds charge a fee, called a load. Loads vary fund by fund, but by law they cannot exceed 8.5 percent of the public offering price.

Mutual funds that use a **front-end load** charge the fee when the investor buys shares.

When a mutual fund charges the fee when the investor withdraws shares (instead of when the investor buys the shares), it is called a **back-end load**. Back-end loads encourage investors to invest for the long-term because the load decreases the longer the investor holds the shares. If investors hold the shares long enough, the load eventually drops to zero. Because of this feature, back-end loads are also known as **contingent deferred loads**.

COSTS AND FEES ASSOCIATED WITH INVESTMENTS

Mutual funds have portfolio managers who get paid a certain percentage, and in order to encourage investors to invest more, this percentage decreases for higher investment amounts. The point at which the percentage decreases is the **breakpoint**. (Brokers and dealers are forbidden from making "breakpoint sales": sales that seek to maximize commission income by encouraging investors to invest just below the breakpoint.)

Rights of accumulation (ROAs) are closely related to breakpoints. Investors can receive the reduced sales charge (the percentage paid to the portfolio manager) if the dollar amount of investments purchased, when combined with the fund investment they already possess, surpasses the breakpoint level.

Letters of intent (LOIs) can be signed by investors to permit them to receive the desired reduction in the sales charge immediately, so long as they pay the remaining amount needed to reach the breakpoint within a given time period.

DOLLAR-COST AVERAGING

Dollar-cost averaging (DCA) is an investment strategy that aims to reduce the impact of volatility on large purchases of financial assets, such as equities. DCA occurs when a customer invests a fixed amount of money into a mutual fund or other investment on a regular basis (monthly, quarterly, etc.), regardless of the asset price at that time of purchase. Dollar-cost averaging takes the guesswork out of trying to time the market; it avoids making the full investment when the security may be at its highest market price, while also prevents money sitting on the sidelines waiting for better price. A potential disadvantage of dollar-cost averaging is that the market tends to go up over time, meaning that a larger amount invested earlier could deliver a better return than smaller amounts invested over a longer period of time.

FAMILIES OF FUNDS AND CONVERSION PRIVILEGES

Many mutual fund companies offer more than one mutual fund. It is quite common for mutual fund companies to offer many, many choices for investors with different investment goals, or to provide for investors who want to divide their portfolio for balance, diversification, and risk aversion. The group of funds offered by an individual mutual fund company is known as a **family of funds**. Many mutual fund companies allow investors in their fund to transfer their money in and out of different

funds in the family without incurring sales charges. This is known as a **conversion (exchange) privilege**.

REDEMPTION OF MUTUAL FUND SHARES

Mutual fund shares are not traded on the secondary market. An investor buys them directly from the company, or one of its underwriters or broker/dealers. When a mutual fund shareholder wants to sell, the mutual fund company **redeems the shares**; that is, the mutual fund company buys the shares back. When shares are redeemed, they are destroyed, as mutual funds are constantly issuing new shares. When a customer notifies the mutual fund company that he wants to sell his shares back, the company must redeem the shares within seven calendar days, except in extraordinary circumstances.

SYSTEMATIC MUTUAL FUND WITHDRAWAL PLANS

Many mutual funds allow investors to withdraw funds on a pre-planned, systematic basis. These methods are called **withdrawal plans**.

There are three basic approaches to systematic withdrawal. The first is when the customer wants to receive a fixed dollar amount at every interval. In this case, the fund redeems however many shares necessary at the current net asset value to raise the amount of money requested by the customer. The second is where the customer doesn't specify a fixed dollar amount, but rather specifies a fixed percentage or number of shares to be redeemed at every interval. Lastly, the customer may choose to redeem shares over a stated amount of time, known as a **fixed-time withdrawal plan.**

RESTRICTIONS ON MUTUAL FUND REDEMPTION

Since mutual funds differ from ordinary stocks, in that shares are constantly being newly issued or destroyed upon redemption, the situation for mutual funds is more vulnerable than for other stock transactions. Consequently, there are various **restrictions on mutual fund redemption** to protect mutual funds from a rapid or sudden redemption of fund shares.

TAXATION OF MUTUAL FUND'S INVESTOR'S PROFITS

The tax rate that a mutual fund investor pays depends on several different factors, and tax rates can be quite different, depending on how the profit being taxed was derived. Income from dividends is taxed differently based on whether they are qualified or not. If they are not qualified, the dividends are ordinary income. To be qualified, the dividends must be paid by a US or qualified foreign corporation and held by the fund for >60 days +/- the ex-dividend date. If the dividends are qualified, then they become capital gains and can be netted with capital losses. Realized capital gains are divided into two categories, short-term and long-term. Capital gains earned from holdings of less than 1 year are taxed as ordinary income. Capital gains earned from holdings of greater than 1 year and are taxed from 0% in the lower income brackets, up to 20% for the highest tax brackets.

DEALING WITH CAPITAL GAINS FROM MUTUAL FUNDS

A mutual fund investor can be impacted by two types of gains: the gains from the investor's sale of the mutual fund, or gains distributed to investors when the mutual fund sells a stock from the portfolio. Mutual funds often make capital gains distributions at the end of each year for all the gains made on stocks sold during the year. When mutual funds distribute capital gains, investors have two choices. They can either reinvest the proceeds to purchase additional shares of the fund, or they can take the distribution in cash. In either case, the investor must pay taxes on the distribution, unless he or she owns the fund in a tax-deferred retirement plan. Capital gains distributions from a mutual fund are always long-term capital gains, regardless of how long the investor has owned the mutual fund.

AVERAGE BASIS METHOD FOR MUTUAL FUNDS

Mutual funds make the calculation of capital gains and losses to be much trickier, since the customer is often unaware of all the securities transactions executed by the fund manager. One common method is the **average basis method**.

According to this method, the total money paid for shares is divided by the total number of shares to give the investor an average basis per share. Then, whenever he sells any shares, the basis is lowered accordingly: the quantity of shares decreases, but the basis per share remains the same.

If an investor purchased 100 shares for $15/share two years and 100 shares for $20/share last year, then if he sold 150 shares today, the cost basis to which he would compare the selling price would be $2,625 (150 shares x $17.50/share). The remaining cost basis on his other 50 shares would be $875 (50 shares x $17.50/share).

It can be difficult to determine whether capital gains are short- or long-term with average basis methods. To solve this, there used to be average cost single category (ACSC) and average cost double category methods (ACDC), but ACDC has been discontinued by the IRS since April 2011.

AUTOMATIC REINVESTMENT OF DISTRIBUTIONS IN MUTUAL FUNDS

Mutual funds must offer **automatic reinvestment of distributions** in order to be allowed to charge the maximum sales charge of 8.5 percent. Additionally, many mutual funds that don't charge the maximum also allow automatic reinvestment of distributions. Normally, investors in mutual funds would receive any dividends and/or capital gains in cash, by a check issued by the mutual fund. However, customers of funds that offer automatic reinvestment of distributions may choose to have their dividends and capital gains automatically reinvested in the mutual fund instead of receiving cash.

CHARGES AND EXPENSES PAID BY MUTUAL FUND INVESTORS

Mutual fund investors pay two types of fees and expenses, shareholder fees and annual fund operating expenses.

Shareholder fees are assessed on the investor's total investment amount and may include:

Sales load – a commission paid to a broker or advisor who sold the mutual fund. It is a percentage that is assessed on the investor's total investment amount. For some funds, investors may qualify for a lower sales load percentage, if they invest a larger amount.

Redemption fee – some funds charge a percentage fee on the investment amount if the investor redeems their shares within a certain amount of time after purchase. Redemption fees may not exceed 2%.

Annual operating expenses are assessed on the mutual fund's total assets and may include:

Management fee – a percentage fee that is paid to the advisor that manages the mutual fund portfolio.

Distribution, or 12b-1, fee – a percentage fee that is paid to the fund's distributor for the costs associated with marketing and selling the fund. Rule 12b-1 is the SEC rule that authorizes mutual funds to charge these fees.

Other expenses – additional expenses not included under management fees or 12b-1 fees, such as shareholder service expenses, transfer agent expenses, legal fees, etc.

ANNUITIES

Life insurance companies sell **annuities**. Purchasers of annuities are buying a regular payment from the company, guaranteed for life. This guarantee makes an annuity different from virtually all other investments. Purchasers make either a one-time lump sum payment or a series of regular payments, and later they are entitled to regular withdrawals of income payments.

Annuities can also have **riders**: provisions built into the policy but purchased as a separate entity, entitling the annuitant to additional benefits other than the usual coverage. For example, a life insurance could have, as a rider, an "accelerated death benefit," which permits the policy holder to receive some of the coverage before death, such as in the case of severe illness. The coverage provided by the company at the policy holder's death would then be reduced by the accelerated amount. But in order to have this accelerated benefit, it would have to be separately purchased as a rider on the ordinary life insurance contract.

IF THE PURCHASER OF AN ANNUITY DIES BEFORE PAYMENTS BEGIN

There is generally a long period of time between the purchase of an annuity and the time before payments begin. If the purchaser should die, in most cases the annuity's **beneficiary** will get all the money the purchaser paid in plus any gains that have accumulated by the day of the purchaser's death.

In cases where the account has lost money, the beneficiary will receive the total of what the purchaser paid in.

The age of the beneficiary is not a factor, and the beneficiary is not subject to early withdrawal penalties.

FIXED AND VARIABLE ANNUITIES

A **fixed annuity** guarantees a specific rate of return. Investors' premiums are deposited into the insurance company's general accounts. Fixed annuities are not considered securities, because all the risk is on the insurance company, not the buyer.

Variable annuities are considered securities, because the purchaser is taking the risk. With variable annuities, investors' monies are deposited into an account separate from the insurance company's general account, and the company invests these funds. Variable annuities guarantee payments for life, but don't guarantee the amount of the payments or the rate of return on the investment.

Variable annuities are insurance products issued by insurance companies that are designed to provide regular, periodic income. Variable annuities invest in subaccounts, which are diversified investment portfolios that are very similar to mutual funds. The value of a variable annuity is based on the performance of its underlying subaccounts. Variable annuities can either be deferred or immediate. Deferred annuities are structured to pay periodic income (i.e., monthly, quarterly, annual) beginning at some point in the future, while immediate annuities begin paying periodic income upon purchase.

Unlike mutual funds, which can be redeemed at any time, variable annuities charge a surrender fee if the contract holder makes a withdrawal within the surrender period, typically six to eight years after purchase. Variable annuity investments grow tax-deferred, while mutual funds only grow tax-deferred if they are purchased in a tax-deferred retirement account, such as a 401(k) or an IRA. In addition to periodic income payments, a feature that mutual funds do not offer, variable annuities also provide a death benefit, which means that if periodic payments have not begun or have not reached a specified level at the time of the contract holder's death, a beneficiary is entitled to a death benefit. From a tax perspective, periodic payments from variable annuities are taxed at ordinary income rates, while distributions from mutual funds are taxed at capital gains rates.

PHASES OF VARIABLE ANNUITIES

The time during which the purchaser of an annuity is paying into the annuity, up until the time the purchaser begins receiving income payments, is called the **accumulation phase**. The period after payments begin is called the **annuity phase**. The purchase is accumulating units, which are called either **accumulation units** or **annuity units**, and which determine how much the purchaser receives during the annuity phase.

STRUCTURES OF VARIABLE ANNUITIES

Annuities can be purchased through a single, lump-sum payment or a stream of periodic payments. Single payment, or immediate, annuities can begin making payments to the contract holder immediately, while periodic, or deferred, annuities have an accumulation phase during which the account grows tax-deferred, with payments to the contract holder set to begin at some point in the future.

SEPARATE ACCOUNTS FOR ANNUITIES

Separate accounts refer to specific investment accounts owned by an insurance company. These accounts are isolated from the insurance company's general investments, which means that they are not guaranteed by the insurance company (the investments provide a variable rate of return), although it also means that the investments are safe if the insurance company becomes insolvent.

COSTS AND FEES ASSOCIATED WITH ANNUITIES

Surrender charges are fees paid based upon an undue cancellation of some account or policy, occurring most often with life insurance policies. The fee is meant to cover the cost for keeping the account on the books, and therefore is usually waived for individuals who notify the insurance company of the cancellation sufficiently in advance.

Mortality and expense charges are fees included in variable annuities. When a life insurance company provides an annuity to some customer, the company calculates risks such as the life expectancy of the annuitant and charges a fee based upon these risks.

ACCUMULATION UNITS AND ANNUITY UNITS

When the annuitant is contributing funds into an annuity, he actually purchases particular units. These units are **accumulation units**, and they vary in price; a series of fixed contributions by the annuitant might purchase more units or fewer, depending on the units. The value of accumulation units depends upon the performance of the underlying investments for the annuity.

When it comes time for the annuitant to receive payouts (i.e., when the accumulation period has ended), the accumulation units will be converted into **annuity units**, and the annuitant will receive an equal number of annuity units per distribution.

IMMEDIATE PAYMENT ANNUITIES

Immediate payment annuities are annuities purchased with one lump sum, in which case distributions begin to occur immediately. These are suitable for retired persons who fear they may outlast their retirement savings, but since these annuity payments are cancelled upon the death of the annuitant, they carry the risk, in cases of early death, of significantly decreasing an inheritance.

WAIVERS OF PREMIUM

A **waiver of premium** is a provision in an insurance contract which waives the policyholder of any obligation to pay further premiums but still be entitled to the insurance benefits. This waiver kicks in due to some serious disability for the policyholder, and usually only after the policyholder has been disabled for some period of time (e.g., six months).

To obtain this provision, a policyholder has to purchase it upfront with the insurance contract, and due to the risk it can afford to the insurance company, policyholders must be sufficiently healthy and young to qualify.

SECTION 1035, EXCHANGES OF VARIABLE ANNUITIES

Section 1035 of the U.S. tax code allows the tax-free exchange, called a 1035 exchange, of an existing variable annuity contract for a new annuity contract, which is often done to obtain a larger death benefit, different annuity payout options, or a wider selection of subaccount (investment) choices. One potential disadvantage of a 1035 exchange is that the contract holder may be assessed a surrender charge on the original annuity if the surrender period has not yet expired (although the charge may be waived for an exchange within the same company), and a new surrender period will begin on the new annuity.

CHARGES, FEES AND PENALTIES ASSOCIATED WITH VARIABLE ANNUITIES

Fees and expenses associated with the purchase and maintenance of a variable annuity include:

Mortality expense – this is a charge assessed on the account value, usually about 1.25% annually, to compensate the insurance company for the insurance risk it assumes.

Underlying investment fees – similar to mutual funds, variable annuity investors pay management fees and other expenses on the investment portfolios (i.e., subaccounts) they choose.

Guaranteed income rider fees – some variable annuity investors may choose to add on specific features or benefits, such as minimum lifetime income, which charge an additional annual percentage fee.

Surrender fee – this is a charge for withdrawing money from the variable before a specified date, usually within 6 to 8 years of purchase.

In addition to surrender fees, because variable annuities are tax-deferred investment products, contract holders who withdraw funds prior to age 591/2 will incur a 10% penalty.

PAYOUT OPTIONS OF ANNUITIES

There are three different options that from which annuity owners can choose when deciding how they want to receive their annuity.

The first one is the simplest, and is called **life income**. With life income, the insurance company pays the annuitant until he dies; after the annuitant dies, no payments are given to beneficiaries.

The second option is **life with period certain**. With this option, the annuitant chooses a period of either 10 or 20 years (the period certain). The annuitant will then be guaranteed payments for life, but if the annuitant dies before the period certain is over, his beneficiary receives payments for the rest of the period certain.

The last option is **joint life with last survivor.** With this arrangement, two parties, usually husband and wife, are entitled to one payment, and when the first party dies, the other party receives the payments until his or her death.

ANNUITIZATION

Annuitization is the process by which an annuity investment is converted into payments.

The **fixed annuitization method** takes the total account balance for the annuitant and divides it by a particular annuity factor (which factor is derived from an IRS table) to arrive at an equal payment that cannot later be changed.

The **fixed amortization method** takes the total account balance and amortizes it over the annuitant's life expectancy, again using IRS tables. The interest rate to be used in the amortization cannot exceed 120% of the federal mid-term rate. As with the fixed annuitization method, this method fixes the periodic payments so that they may not be changed.

The **required minimum distribution method** takes the account balance at December 31 of each year and divides it by the life expectancy of the annuitant, according to the same tables mentioned above. This method allows for different distributions depending on changes in the account balance and life expectancy.

ASSUMED INTEREST RATE (AIR)

The **assumed interest rate** (AIR) is the rate of growth, assumed by the insurance company, that is necessary for the underlying investments of an annuity to cover the insurance company's costs and provide the company with its target profit margin. The AIR enters into the calculation to determine an annuitant's periodic income payments.

TAXATION OF ANNUITIES

In the **accumulation period**, any growth on the underlying investment in an annuity has tax-deferred growth. The annuitant does not have to pay any taxes on it until the distribution period.

The taxes paid on the payouts in the **distribution period** will be at the ordinary income tax rate. Although gains on investments will largely involve capital gains, tax regulations still require that annuity growth be taxed as ordinary income.

The taxable amount will vary according to the nature of the payout. If it is one lump-sum payment, then the annuitant will pay taxes on all the investment growth at that point. If the payouts instead come in a series of periodic payments, then each payment will be considered as partly a return of the original investment (and thus nontaxable) and partly a gain on the investment (and thus taxable).

Early withdrawals to annuities (before the age of 59 ½) are subject to a 10% penalty. Certain early withdrawals can be waived from this penalty, however, if they are for qualified reasons (e.g. purchasing a home, disability, or 55 and unemployed) and are distributed in a certain number of substantially equal periodic payments (SEPPs), at least five.

TAXATION OF FIXED ANNUITIES

If an annuity gives periodic payments to the annuitant during the annuity's distribution period, then each payment will be considered as partly a return of the original investment (and thus nontaxable) and partly a gain on the investment (and thus taxable). For **fixed annuities** (annuities paying a series of fixed payments), the particular composition of principal and gain (i.e., original investment and gain) is determined by an exclusion ratio, which is calculated as follows:

Exclusion Ratio = Original Investment / Expected Total Payout

Since the original investment is nontaxable, then the percentage of each periodic payment attributable to that original investment will be excluded from taxes, hence the name of the ratio.

The **expected total payout** is calculated by multiplying the fixed payment amount by the number of months the annuitant is expected to live, based on IRS tables.

For example, if an annuitant paid $100,000 into an annuity with fixed monthly payments of $800 and was expected to live for 23 years, then the expected payout would be $220,800 ($800 x 12 x 23), and the exclusion ratio would be 45.29% ($100,000 / $220,800). Thus, for a given tax year, the 12 monthly payments totaling $9600 would be deducted by 45.29%, or $4,347.84.

SIMPLER METHOD OF COMPUTING TAXES ON FIXED ANNUITIES

Taxes on fixed annuities are generally taught in terms of an "**exclusion ratio**," where the expected payout of the annuity is calculated so that each monthly payment can be broken up between the original investment and the gain on investment, with only the latter being taxable. This can be on the Series 7 exam, so it is important to know. But there is a shortcut: the nontaxable portion for each annuity payment can also be calculated by ignoring the expected payout altogether. Just divide the original investment by the number of expected years in the annuitant's life to get the yearly deduction.

For instance, in the example from the other card on fixed annuities, calculate it this way:

$100,000 / 23 years = $4,347.82 (The difference from the other method is due to rounding.)

And if you want the nontaxable portion of each monthly annuity payment, simply divide the yearly number by 12 to get $362.32.

TAXATION OF VARIABLE ANNUITIES

Since **variable annuities** do not have a fixed monthly payment, calculating the taxable amount for each payment is different than for fixed annuities. One ignores the expected total payout over the life of the annuity, looking simply at the **original investment amount**. The original investment amount, when divided by the life expectancy of the annuitant (in months), gives the amount of original investment attributable to each monthly payment, regardless of how much gain on investment is included in each monthly payment.

For example, if an annuitant contributes a total of $100,000 to a variable annuity and has a life expectancy of 23 years, then he will have a yearly tax deduction from his annuity income of $4,347.82 ($100,000 / 23 years), or a monthly deduction of $362.32.

On closer inspection, you'll notice that this is simply a shortcut way of making the exact same calculation as for fixed annuities. The formula for taxes on fixed annuities (involving the exclusion ratio) unnecessarily includes the expected payout, when the only relevant variables are the original investment and the life expectancy of the annuitant.

TAXATION OF DEATH BENEFITS ON ANNUITIES

If an annuitant dies in the **accumulation period**, then the money will go to the specified beneficiaries, who will have to pay taxes on any gain earned in the annuity up to that point; they will have to pay ordinary income tax rates.

If an annuitant dies in the **distribution period**, then the insurance company's obligation to make further payments depends on the nature of the agreement. A "life-only annuity" means that payments are made to the annuitant while he is alive, so that the company is not obligated to make any other payments if he dies. A "term-certain option" in the annuity requires payments to be made to a specified beneficiary if the annuitant dies before a particular length of time has passed. A "joint-life annuity" requires payments to be made to the other person associated with the annuity (usually a spouse), so that the company is obligated to make payments until both parties are deceased.

Again, any money received by beneficiaries is subject to ordinary income tax.

REAL ESTATE INVESTMENT TRUSTS (REITs)

Real estate investment trusts (REITs) are companies that own, and often operate, income-producing real estate. REITs provide individual investors with an opportunity to invest in all types of real estate without having to purchase property. The REIT structure is attractive to companies because it allows them to deduct from taxable income all the dividends paid out to shareholders. However, to qualify as a REIT and maintain REIT status, companies must meet certain requirements:

- Distribute at least 90 percent of taxable income to shareholders annually in the form of dividends
- Be taxable as a corporation
- Be managed by a board of directors or trustees
- Have at least 100 shareholders after its first year of existence
- Have shares that are fully transferable
- Have no more than 50% of its shares held by five or fewer individuals
- Derive at least 75% of income from real estate-related activity
- Hold at least 75% of assets in real estate, government securities, or cash

Most REITs are registered with the SEC and are publicly traded on a stock exchange. Benefits to investors include liquidity, steady income and dividends that can be higher than other investments since REITs distribute at least 90% of profits. However, the flipside is that REITs can grow more slowly than other types of investments, which are not required to distribute profits, and dividends may be taxed as ordinary income.

TYPES OF REITs

There are three different kinds of real estate investment trusts (REITs):

Equity REITs purchase real estate equity, owning real estate and making profit off of rent revenue or capital gains when the real estate is sold.

Mortgage REITs purchase various debt securities related to real estate, such as construction loans and mortgages. The income from mortgage REITs is therefore based on interest.

Hybrid REITs are combinations of the above two, investing in both equity and debt securities related to real estate.

ISSUANCE AND TRADING OF REITS

Though REITs are like mutual funds in that they pool investors' money and distribute shares, they are unlike mutual funds in that they have a finite number of shares. Related to this, while REIT securities are originally issued at their initial public offering (IPO) price, they can also be traded on the secondary market; investors are not limited from purchasing REIT shares directly issued by the issuer. And since REITs can be traded on the secondary market, shares will not simply be priced at their net asset value (NAV), but can move above or below NAV, according to market dynamics and sentiments.

TAX TREATMENT OF REITS

The tax treatment of dividends paid by REITs for individual investors depends on how the distribution is classified:

- Dividend payouts that consist of a company's operating profits are treated as ordinary income.
- Dividend payouts that consist of the company's profit from selling a real estate asset are treated as capital gains. If the asset was held for less than one year, gains are taxed at the short-term rate. If it was held for more than one year, gains are taxed at the long-term rate.
- Dividend payouts that consist of a portion of operating profit that was previously sheltered from tax due to depreciation of real estate assets is treated as a return of capital. The investor does not pay taxes on these dividends in the current year, but they do increase taxes when the REIT shares are sold because they reduce the investor's cost basis.

Recently, the Tax Cuts and Jobs Act of 2017 resulted in a policy that allows individual investors in REITs to deduct up to 20% of their ordinary income dividends, with the rest charged at the investor's marginal rate. For investors in a high income-tax bracket, this deduction serves to reduce their taxable rate by several percentage points.

REITs are required to provide shareholders with information about how the prior year's dividends should be allocated for tax purposes early in the subsequent year.

DIRECT PARTICIPATION PROGRAMS (DPPS)

Direct Participation Programs (DPPs) are non-traded pooled investments in real estate or energy related projects that offer investors access to the business' cash flows and tax benefits. Limited partners take interest in the DPP, which is quantified in units. These dollars are then invested by a general partner. Most DPPs are passively managed and have a lifespan of 5 to 10 years. Over this period, all the DPP's income and tax deductions are passed on to the partners.

Direct participation programs are usually organized as a limited partnership, a subchapter S corporation, or a general partnership, as these structures allow the DPP's income, losses, gains, tax credits, and deductions to transfer though to the underlying partner/taxpayer on a pre-tax basis. As a result, the DPP pays no corporate tax. Because DPPs are not traded on an exchange and the secondary market for them is sparse, they are not liquid and their market value can be difficult to determine. For this reason, most states require that investors in DPPs be accredited investors.

DOCUMENTS USED IN THE FORMATION OF PARTNERSHIPS

These three documents are involved with the formation of partnerships and introduction of new partners.

The **certificate of limited partnership** must be sent to the secretary of state for the state where the partnership does business, allowing the partnership to be legally recognized.

The **partnership agreement** is the contract between the partners to form the partnership, outlining the nature of the business, the capital contributions of each partner, the entitlements to profit and liabilities to loss (e.g. 50-50), and other rights and duties.

The **subscription agreement** is an application for a new investor to join a partnership as a limited partner.

LIMITED PARTNERSHIPS
FORMATION OF LIMITED PARTNERSHIPS

Limited partnerships, including direct participate programs, can be sold either through private placement or by public offering. Private placement DPPs are not registered with the SEC and are typically offered to smaller groups of investors who able to meet the high investment minimums. Publicly offered DPPs are registered with the SEC and are typically widely available at lower investment minimums relative to private placements.

Publicly offered direct participation programs are regulated under FINRA Rule 2310, which provides a number of protections that are not available with private placements:

A member that plans to offer the DPP to participants must determine the adequacy of the disclosures contained in the prospectus by examining relevant materials facts and must have reasonable grounds to believe that the participant is or will be in a financial position appropriate to enable him to realize the benefits described in the prospectus, including the tax benefits, and has a fair market net worth sufficient to sustain the risks inherent in the program, including loss of investment and lack of liquidity.

ARRANGEMENTS FOR DISTRIBUTING COSTS AND REVENUES FROM LIMITED PARTNERSHIPS

Investors in oil and gas drilling limited partnerships can hold two types of interest.

Working interest means the investor is directly liable for the ongoing costs related to the project and fully participates in the profits. Working interests can be operated or non-operated. Operated working interest members are designated operators that make operational decisions. Non-operated working interest members are not involved in daily operations but are consulted on decisions. The profit potential for a working interest limited partnership can be high and losses can be used to offset other income for tax purposes. Certain costs are also tax deductible. Working interest income is treated as self-employment income, so investors are expected to make estimated tax payments. Working interests usually require a large investment and costs can be high.

Royalty interest means the investor is not liable for ongoing operational costs and only participates proportionally in the profits of the business. Royalty interests are often held by companies that have ownership rights to an oil field but don't possess the resources to put it into production. Another company capable of producing the oil would take a working interest, while the owner maintains a royalty interest.

GENERAL PARTNERS IN LIMITED PARTNERSHIPS

A **limited partnership** must have at least one general partner and at least one limited partner, although they usually have more. The **general partner** has more responsibilities and liabilities than does the limited partner. The general partner does the actual managing of the business and makes decisions that are legally binding for everyone in the partnership. He may be paid for services as a general partner, and may buy and sell property on behalf of the partnership. The general partner must avoid conflicts of interest with the partnership, and must keep his own funds separate from partnership funds at all times. The general partner may not borrow money from the partnership (although the partnership may borrow from the general partner), and he has a legal responsibility to use the assets of the partnership for the best interests of the partnership. Finally, the general partner is personally liable for all obligations incurred by the partnership.

LIMITED PARTNERS IN LIMITED PARTNERSHIPS

Limited partners, unlike general partners, are not personally liable for obligations incurred by a limited partnership. The limited partner cannot make management decisions, but does have the right to sue the general partner if he believes that the general partner is not acting in the best interests of the partnership. Limited partners are allowed to vote on certain partnership matters, and they can inspect the financial records and accounting books of the partnership if they so desire. But their main role is to put up the money, while the general partner actually runs the business.

EVALUATING LIMITED PARTNERSHIPS

Besides determining whether an investor should invest in limited partnerships generally—i.e. whether the general risks of limited partnerships, in comparison to other investments, fits the investor—the registered representative also ought to evaluate the merits and risks of particular DPPs. This evaluation involves four main considerations:

(1) the program's **economic soundness**

(2) the general partner's **talent, knowledge, and expertise**

(3) the program's **basic objectives**

(4) the DPP's **start-up costs**

DISSOLUTION OF LIMITED PARTNERSHIPS

The process for dissolving a limited partnership should be covered in the partnership agreement. Generally, a limited partner cannot initiate the dissolution of a partnership. The partnership may be dissolved on a specified date if one is indicated in the partnership agreement, or it may be dissolved upon a vote by all general partners and limited partners who collectively own a majority interest. The agreement may identify a triggering event, such as a retirement or majority vote of the partners to terminate the business, that will start the dissolution process. The agreement should also indicate the procedures for winding down the business and how any remaining assets will be distributed among the partners. In cases where the state involuntarily dissolves a limited partnership for failing to comply with state statutes and regulations a different process than the one spelled out in the agreement may be followed.

DEDUCTIBLE EXPENSES FOR LIMITED PARTNERSHIPS

For tax purposes, a limited partnership (such as hedge funds, private equity funds, or natural resource funds) may make standard expense deductions for operating expenses. The main items that generate tax write-offs for investors in the limited partnership are interest expenses, operating and maintenance expenses, depreciation or depletion, and tax credits.

Several of the big-ticket deductions are higher early in the life of a limited partnership - due to leverage and the accelerated depreciation schedules used.

OIL AND GAS PARTNERSHIPS

Oil and gas partnerships aim to make a profit through various investments involving the extraction of oil and gas.

Exploratory oil and gas DPPs search new areas to find new oil and drill for it. This is the riskiest oil and gas DPP, and its activity is also called "wildcatting."

Developmental oil and gas DPPs search for new reserves in areas near wells that are already extracting oil or gas.

Income oil and gas DPPs purchase wells that already exist.

Combination oil and gas DPPs involve any assortment of the previous three.

DEDUCTIBLE EXPENSES FOR OIL AND GAS PARTNERSHIPS

Oil and gas partnerships are eligible for a number of tax benefits.

Tangible drilling costs (TDCs) are any costs for items used in extracting oil or gas that have a salvage value upon disposal (e.g., storage tanks, drills)—basically, the equipment used in drilling. These costs can be deducted as the equipment is depreciated, with the deduction equaling the depreciation expense for that year. They can be depreciated either on a straight-line basis (the same amount every year of their use) or on an accelerated basis (more depreciation earlier and less later).

Intangible drilling costs (IDCs) are costs of extraction that don't involve objects with salvage value (whether or not the costs are "intangible" in the sense of being nonphysical). These costs include wages, fuel, costs for repairs and maintenance, and other things. Unlike TDCs, IDCs are fully deductible in the year the expenses are incurred. However, IDCs can only be deducted for costs related to the drilling and preparation of well; once it is producing oil or gas, IDCs cannot be deducted.

Depletion cost is a tax deduction for the amount of natural resources depleted in a reserve. This is deducted according to the oil or gas sold, not how much of a resource is actually extracted or stored.

REAL-ESTATE PARTNERSHIPS

Real estate limited partnerships or real estate DPPs can invest in a number of different real estate assets, and thus these partnerships can be classified in various ways:

- Public housing partnerships invest in the construction of low-income and retirement housing. Since these housing programs are government-assisted (e.g., missing rent payments are covered by the U.S. Department of Housing and Urban Development), they are considered the safest form of real estate partnership. These partnerships may generate tax credits for the investor.
- Existing properties partnerships invest in properties that are already constructed, with the purpose of earning rental income.

- New construction partnerships invest in properties to be built, aiming to make a profit when the properties are sold. These partnerships generally create tax write-offs during the initial construction phase when the company is operating at a loss.
- Raw land partnerships invest in undeveloped land. Their aim is to earn capital gains as the value of the land increases. These are the riskiest form of real estate partnership, and they typically do not create tax savings.

EQUIPMENT LEASING PARTNERSHIPS

Equipment leasing partnerships seek to make a profit by purchasing and leasing various assets, such as computers, trucks, or machinery. There are two main types of leases for equipment leasing DPPs:

Full payout leases rent out equipment for long periods of time (often the equipment's useful life), so that the first lease is sufficient to cover the cost of the equipment.

Operating leases rent out equipment for rather short periods, or at least for periods where the total rental payments do not cover the cost of the equipment by themselves. In operating leases, the same equipment will be leased out several times. Because of this, they can be riskier than full payout leases.

ESCROW RECEIPTS

When investors transact option contracts, the contract depends upon the fact that one of the investors has the underlying security and will have it for a specific time period, up to the last time when the other investor can exercise the option. When investors want better proof that the other man indeed possesses the underlying security, they can seek an **escrow receipt**, a bank's guarantee that the option writer has the security and that it is easily deliverable.

LISTED OPTIONS

Listed options, also known as exchange-traded options, are standardized derivatives contracts (either calls or puts) that are traded on an exchange. Consequently, listed options are required to follow exchange rules. Listed options have standardized strike prices, expiration dates, and deliverables. Additionally, due to the large market for listed options, they are very liquid, as clearinghouses guarantee execution.

Listed options can be classified as either American style or European style. American style options can be exercised at any time prior to expiration, while European style options can only be exercised at expiration.

UNDERLYING INSTRUMENTS, EXERCISE PRICE, AND EXPIRATION DATE FOR OPTIONS

The underlying instrument of an option is an asset that gives the option its value. For example, an investor may purchase a call option to be able to buy a stock at a specified exercise price. The stock is the underlying instrument, as it is the stock's price that gives the call option its value. If the stock's price goes up, the value of the call option also goes up. Underlying instruments can be any tradeable asset, such as stocks, currencies, commodities, or real estate.

Exercise price is the price at which the underlying instrument can be purchased (in the case of a call option) or sold (in the case of a put option). If a call option's exercise price is below the underlying security's price, the option is said to be "in the money." If a put option's exercise price is above the underlying security's price, the option is "in the money."

The expiration date of an option is the last day on which the contract can be exercised. Before or on this date, contract holders can either exercise the option, close the option by selling the contract (generally this must be done a week prior to the expiration date) or let the contract expire worthless.

OPTION PREMIUMS

An option premium is the market price of an option's contract. In other words, it is what the seller, or writer, of the options contract earns. An option's premium is determined by two factors: intrinsic value and extrinsic value. Intrinsic value is the difference between the option's exercise price and the market value of the underlying asset. Extrinsic value is a product of the amount of time remaining until the option contract expires and implied volatility, which is the amount the underlying asset's market price may move over a specified period of time. Closeness of the expiration date reduces extrinsic value, while increased implied volatility increases extrinsic value.

LONG AND SHORT POSITIONS FOR OPTIONS

There are different "positions" which investors enter into when they buy or sell option contracts. A **long position** is a position where the trader wants the price to increase, and a **short position** is a position where the trader wants the price to decrease. Naturally, then, every single option contract involves one person in the long position and another in the short; someone will profit from the price growing and the other from the price dropping.

For instance, if a trader buys a call option, then he is in a long position with respect to the underlying asset: he wants its actual price to go up, so that when he buys it, he can then sell it for the higher price at a profit. But the seller will be in a short position. And if a trader buys a put option, he is in a short position with respect to the underlying asset, since he wants the actual price to go down, so that he can sell high and buy low.

Note: for put options, the buyer will be in a short position with respect to the underlying asset, but in a long position with respect to the option contract itself. The value of a put option increases as the price of the underlying asset decreases. The key thing to remember is that long position = wants price to increase, and short position = wants price to decrease.

OPENING AND CLOSING TRANSACTIONS FOR OPTIONS

Traders enter into options contract either by **buying** them (purchasing a right to buy or sell something in the future) or **writing/selling** them (being paid to have an obligation to buy or sell something in the future).

Since entering into an option contract involves "opening a position," whether the position is long or short, any opening transaction for an option contract is either **buy-to-open** (if you're buying the contract) or **sell-to-open** (if you're writing/selling the contract).

Likewise, since the termination of the contract, whether by exercising the option or by expiration, involves closing the long and short positions of the traders, then the trader needs to submit a closing order—either a **buy-to-close** order (if it is a call option) or a **sell-to-close** order (if it is a put option).

OPTION ASSIGNMENTS

Option assignments are notices received by the writers (i.e. sellers) of options, informing the writer that the buyer has now exercised the option. Thus, if the option is a put option, then an assignment means that the writer is at that point obligated to buy shares from the option-holder at the strike price. And if the option is a call option, then the writer is obligated to sell shares to the option-holder. (If the writer of a call option already owns the shares he is obligated to sell, then he is said to be **covered**; otherwise he is said to be **naked**, and must buy the shares on the market in order to sell them to the option-holder.)

The exercise date is different from the **settlement date** for options, which is the date by which the actual transaction needs to be made. For options, the settlement date is one business day after the date when the option is exercised.

VOLUME AND OPEN INTEREST FOR OPTIONS

Volume is the number of option contracts that have been traded in a certain time period. It helps to show how meaningful price differences are.

Open interest is the number of option contracts that are still open, i.e., not yet closed, for a certain time period. This number is very closely related to volume, but still different. Suppose X purchased an option from Z, who wrote the option. This transaction would increase volume by 1 and open interest by 1, since a transaction occurred and the option is not yet closed (since it was just bought). But suppose that X then sold the same to Y, so that Y was the option-holder in relation to the writer, Z. In this case, volume would have increased by 1 again, but open interest would not change.

POSITION LIMITS AND EXERCISE LIMITS FOR OPTIONS

Position limits are restrictions placed upon the number of options contracts an investor can hold with respect to a particular security. It is possible for investors to hold a long position on one option contract, and then, with respect to the same asset, hold a short position on a different option contract. To limit the ways these can be exploited, position limits exist.

Exercise limits are restrictions placed upon the number of option contracts an investor can exercise for a given security in a given time period. For instance, an investor (probably an institutional one) might be forbidden from exercising 6,000 option contracts on a particular share of stock in the span of five days. Note, however, that the investor is not limited on the total options he can exercise—only on the total number he can exercise for a particular security.

EFFECT OF STOCK DIVIDENDS ON OPTIONS

The issuance of **stock dividends** by a company requires the strike price and shares per option contract to change, although the number of option contracts stays the same. Stock dividends increase the number of shares that an outstanding option contract can buy and then lowers the strike price accordingly.

For instance, suppose a call option permitted the holder to purchase 100 shares of company X at $30 per share, and company X then issued 5% stock dividends. This call option would now permit the holder to purchase 105 shares according to the contract, a 5% increase from 100 shares. Yet, the price per share would decrease to $28.57 ($30/share x 100 shares / 105 shares).

If a company issues cash dividends, no changes are made to the terms of the option contract. **Cash dividends** affect the stock price (e.g. the stock price decreases by the dividend amount on the ex-dividend date), but not the contract itself.

EFFECT OF STOCK SPLITS ON OPTIONS

Since **stock splits** involve multiplying the quantity of stocks and dividing their value (whether twofold, threefold, or whatever), this could potentially wreak havoc on options contracts. Imagine an investor who had an option to buy various stocks which suddenly were halved, even though the value of the company did not meaningfully change; he would experience unnecessary and great

122

losses. Because of this, the **Options Clearing Corporation (OCC)** ensures that options contracts are adjusted when stock splits occur, so that the value of the adjusted contract is equivalent to the pre-split value. Moreover, the actual number of contracts are multiplied, so that option holders are entitled to purchase the same amount of ownership as they could before the split.

OPTIONS CLEARING CORPORATION (OCC)

Options Clearing Corporation (OCC) is the largest equity derivatives clearinghouse in the world. The OCC operates under the jurisdiction of the SEC and the Commodities Futures Trading Commission (CFTC). Under SEC jurisdiction, OCC clears transactions on exchange-traded options, security futures, and OTC options. Under CFTC jurisdiction, OCC offers clearing and settlement services for transactions in futures and options on futures. OCC provides clearing to 16 participant exchanges, including Cboe Exchange Inc. and Nasdaq Options Market, as well as hundreds of clearing members, including the largest U.S. broker-dealers, futures commission merchants and non-U.S. securities firms, which serve professional traders and public customers.

AMERICAN-STYLE EXERCISING AND EUROPEAN-STYLE EXERCISING FOR OPTIONS

Exercising an option is activating the right contained in the option contract. If a trader exercises a call option, he is at that point entitled to the underlying securities at the strike price. There are different rules governing the exercising of options:

American-style exercising means that, at any time before the option has reached its expiration date, the option-holder is able to exercise it. There are not restrictions on when he can exercise it besides the expiration date.

European-style exercising means that the only time when the option-holder may exercise the option is at the expiration date. Option-holders are prohibited from exercising these options prior to the expiration date.

As you can imagine, since American-style options give the option-holder a much higher chance of profit, they also command a higher price than European-style options, all other things being equal.

LONG-TERM EQUITY ANTICIPATION SECURITIES (LEAPS)

Long-term equity anticipation securities (LEAPS) are publicly traded options contracts with expiration dates of longer than one year and typically up to three years. LEAPS can be used to hedge a long-term holding and are usually less price sensitive to movements in the underlying asset and the passage of time than shorter term options; however, premiums are generally higher and prices can be more sensitive to changes in volatility and interest rates. For some investors, LEAPS are an attractive alternative to rolling over short-term options contracts when they are looking to benefit from a long-term trend.

INTEREST RATE OPTIONS

An interest rate options are a type of derivative that is based on the value of interest rates. They are generally tied to interest rate products like Treasury notes. Interest rate call options are "in the money" when interest rates are rising, and the exercise price is lower than current rates. Interest rate put options are "in the money" when interest rates are falling, and the exercise price is higher than current rates.

Interest rate options are traded on exchanges like the CME Group, and option values are 10 times the underlying Treasury yield for the contract. Interest rate options have European-style exercise provisions, which means the holder can only exercise them at expiration. They are settled in cash, with the seller paying the purchaser the difference between the exercise price and the interest rate value. Interest rate options can be used to speculate on the direction of interest rates or to hedge interest rate exposure during times of uncertainty.

HEDGING FOR EQUITY WITH PUT OPTIONS

Suppose an investor has a number of stocks which have done well over the previous few years, increasing by 30% or so in value. If he is concerned about the price peaking and dropping, he can purchase a put option to ensure that he will not experience losses in selling those stocks should the price drop. This is called **hedging for equity**.

Yet, because determining and acquiring proper put options for each stock can be difficult or otherwise time-consuming, a good idea for the investor would be to purchase a put option on an **index**, so that the option varies with the value of a number of major companies comprising the index (and assuming his investments are in these kinds of companies).

OPTION STRATEGIES

There are four fundamental types of option strategies:

- Long Call - buying a call option, presuming the asset price will rise (or hedging against a rise)
- Long Put - buying a put option, presuming the asset price will fall (or hedging against a fall)
- Short Call - selling a call option, presuming that the asset price will fall (or hedging against a fall)
- Short Put - selling a put option, presuming that the asset price will rise (or hedging against a rise)

EQUITY, INDEX, AND YIELD-BASED OPTIONS

Equity options are contracts that allow a purchaser to buy or sell a set amount of equity shares at a specified equity price. Equity call options are "in the money" when the equity price is rising, and the exercise price is lower than the current market price. Equity put options are "in the money" when the equity price is falling, and the exercise price is higher than the current market price.

Index options are based on the value of an index, such as the S&P 500. They are settled in cash on the expiration date of the option. Index call options are "in the money" when the index value is rising, and the exercise price is lower than the current value. Index put options are "in the money" when index values are falling, and the exercise price is higher than the current index value.

Yield-based options are based on the yield of a security, such as a Treasury bond. They are settled in cash on the expiration date of the option. Yield-based call options are "in the money" when yields are rising, and the exercise price is lower than the current yield. Yield-based put options are "in the money" when yields are falling, and the exercise price is higher than the current yield.

USING OPTIONS TO PROTECT STOCK INVESTMENTS
LONG POSITIONS

A **bullish investor** thinks a stock will go up, and will therefore be long on the stock. But to protect against risk, there are some things a long investor can do to minimize the risk in case the investor is wrong. For short-term protection, the investor can write a call on the stock, giving someone else the right to purchase it for lower than the market price. This limits their upside potential, and is only advisable for stock with low volatility. For long-term protection, the investor can buy a put on the same stock, giving the investor the right to sell the stock at a certain price.

SHORT POSITIONS

A **bearish investor** thinks stock will decline in price and might therefore be a short seller, borrowing shares he doesn't own and hoping to replace them with stocks bought at a lower price down the road. To protect against the risk of loss, a short seller can use options. For partial protection, the short seller can sell a put against the same stock. For full protection, the short seller can buy a call on the same stock. Each approach has its advantages and disadvantages, but both offer some protection against the risks of short selling.

COVERED CALLS

If an investor believes the price of a stock will go down in the future, the investor can write a call on the stock, giving the call buyer the right to purchase the stock from the investor in the future at a specific price. If the stock falls in price or stays even, the call writer makes money on the option premium. However, if the stock rises and the call becomes "in the money," the call writer will have to deliver the stock to the call owner. A call is **covered** if the call writer actually owns the stock he is writing a call on. If the investor does not own the stock, but would have to purchase it to honor the call, it is said to be **uncovered**.

If the investor purchases the stock at the same time he writes the call option, then he is engaging in a "buy-write" strategy.

SPREADS IN OPTIONS TRADING

A **spread** is a pair of options transactions an investor makes at the same time and on the same security. Investors use **straddles** to protect their positions and to take advantage of discrepancies in options pricing. A **call spread** is when the investor buys a call and sells a call on the same stock, and a **put spread** is when the investor buys a put and sells a put on the same stock.

CALL OPTIONS, PUT OPTIONS, SPREADS, AND "IN THE MONEY"

An option with the right to buy is a **call option**, and an option with a right to sell is a **put option**.

The **spread** for a stock option is the difference between the strike price (that is, the price at which one can exercise the right to engage in the transaction) and the current market value of the stock.

"In the money" means that the strike price and market value of the stock are such that exercising the option would be a gain for the investor. For instance, if a trader has a call option and the strike price is less than the market value, then he is in the money. The same goes for a trader with a put option, if the strike price is greater than the stocks' market value. Keep in mind, however, that an option can be "in the money" without necessarily being profitable, because the gain on the closing transaction also needs to make up for the cost of the option itself.

OPTIONS MARGIN

Options margin refers to the minimum amount of cash required to be deposited in an options trading broker account for the trader to begin trading options. Since brokerage firms are liable to cover any traders who are unable to pay their options contracts (as ensured by the OCC), they wish to lower their risk by requiring specific amounts of cash in option traders' accounts. Different brokers have varying **margin requirements.**

DEBIT AND CREDIT SPREAD POSITIONS IN OPTIONS TRADING

Debit and credit spreads are options strategies in which the investor simultaneously buys and sells options of the same class with different strike prices. A debit spread is when the investor pays a larger premium for buying an option than he earns from selling one. A credit spread is when the investor pays a smaller premium for buying an option than he earns from selling one.

Examples of a debit spread include:

Bull Call Spread – an investor buys a call option at a price above the current market price for a $3 premium and sells a call option at a higher strike price than the option purchased but with the same expiration date for a $2 premium, for a debit spread of $1. In this case, the investor is bullish, believing the stock price will increase.

Bear Put Spread – an investor buys a put option for a $3 premium and sells a put option for a $2 premium, for a debit spread of $1. The put sold must have a lower strike price than the put purchased, but the same expiration. In this case, the investor is bearish, believing the stock price will decrease.

Examples of a credit spread include:

Bear Call Spread – an investor buys a call option for a $2 premium and sells one for a $3 premium, for a credit spread of $1. The purchased call must be at a higher strike price than the call sold. The investor profits if the stock falls below the strike price of the option sold.

Bull Put Spread – an investor buys a put option for a $2 premium and sells a put option for a $3 premium (at a higher strike price than the purchased put), for a credit spread of $1. In this case, the investor expects the price to rise above both strike prices.

STRADDLES AND COMBINATIONS

Straddles are a type of combination options strategy where the investor either purchases a call and a put (long straddle) or sells a call and a put (short straddle) on the same underlying instrument, with both having the same expiration date and exercise price. An investor might implement a long straddle if they expect there to be a large price move and/or a significant amount of volatility in the underlying security. If they security price moves up, the investor would exercise the call. If the security price moves down, the investor would exercise the put. An investor might implement a short straddle if they expect there to be very little price movement or volatility in the underlying security. The investor earns premiums from selling both the call and the put but believes that the difference between the exercise price and the market value of the underlying security will be very minimal should the holder of either the call or put choose to exercise their option.

Other combination options strategies do not require the two options to have the same expiration date or strike price.

UNCOVERED WRITING IN OPTION TRADING

Uncovered Writing (also known as Naked Writing) is selling options on securities, which the seller does not own. The option writer collects the premium from selling the option and speculates that the market will not move in a direction that causes the option holder to exercise it. In the case of an uncovered call option, the writer hopes that the market price of the underlying security does not go up, as this would cause the purchaser to exercise the call. As a result, the writer would have to purchase the security in the market at the higher price and deliver it to the purchaser at the lower exercise price.

As an example, an option seller writes a three-month uncovered call option on Stock X and collects a premium of $30. The exercise price is $10 per share, and at the time of the transaction, the stock is trading at a price of $5 per share. Shortly before the call expires, the market price of Stock X jumps to $15 per share on news of a breakthrough innovation, and the option holder exercises the call. The seller must purchase Stock X in the market for $15 per share and deliver it to the call holder for $10 per share.

In the case of an uncovered put option, the writer hopes that the market price of the underlying security does not go down, as this would cause the purchaser to exercise the put. The writer would have to accept delivery of the security at the exercise price, which is above market value.

As an example, an option seller writes a three-month uncovered put option on Stock X and collects a premium of $30. The exercise price is $10 per share, and at the time of the transaction, the stock is trading at a price of $15 per share. Shortly before the put expires, the market price of Stock X falls to $5 per share on news of a scandal, and the option holder exercises the put. The seller must accept delivery of the of the stock at $10 per share but will only receive $5 per share if they choose to sell it.

CURRENCY OPTIONS AND YIELD-BASED OPTIONS

Currency options are options that give the trader the right to purchase (or sell) some currency at a specified exchange rate. This allows investors to profit, or especially to avoid losses, from changes in exchange rate, and is especially utilized by corporations to hedge the value of receivables or payables denominated in a foreign currency.

Yield-based options are options that give the trader the right to purchase (or sell) a bond whose value derives from its yield. The value of the option thus depends on any difference between the option's strike price and the bond's yield.

BREAKEVEN POINTS AND PROFIT AND LOSS FOR OPTIONS

Although option traders always concern themselves with the stock's value in relation to the strike price, their profit or loss is not determined solely by it. Rather, the **breakeven point** for the option trader—that is, the price at which an option trader will make no profit or loss—is determined by the strike price and the option premium, or the price paid for the option.

For the holder of a call option, the breakeven point is the strike price plus the premium. If I have an option to buy stocks at $40/share and I paid $2/share for the option, then the stocks must rise to $42 for me to break even. I would buy the stocks at the strike price of $40, sell them for $42, and cover my premium of $2.

On the other hand, for the holder of a put option, the breakeven point is the strike price minus the premium. If I have an option to sell stocks at $40/share and I paid $2/share for the option, then the stocks must drop to $38 for me to break even. I would sell the stocks at the strike price of $40 and cover my premium of $2.

TAXES FOR OPTIONS

Options are subject to **capital gains taxation**. That is, the underlying asset for options (e.g. stocks) are subject to capital gains and losses, but the option contracts themselves also have value and can be traded, resulting in capital gains or losses.

If the holder of an option chooses not to exercise the option, but trades it to someone else before it expires, then any difference in price is a capital gain or loss. If the holder held the option for less than one year, then it is considered short-term; otherwise it is considered long-term.

If the holder of an option trades it to someone else, the writer of the option does not experience any capital gain or loss; he is still just as obligated as before to fulfill his end of the contract. However, if the writer buys back the option himself, then he will have a capital gain or loss for the difference. Moreover, if an option-writer buys back the option, it will always be considered a short-term capital gain, even if it occurs over one year after being written.

BONDS

A **bond** is a debt instrument, or debt security. Unlike stockowners, investors who purchase bonds receive no ownership in the company and no voting rights. Bonds are issued by private companies, by the federal government, and by state and local governments (municipal bonds) to raise money for various projects, or for operating expenses. The value of bonds fluctuates with interest rates, and not with the success of the company or the stock market. Should a company go bankrupt, bond owners are compensated before stockholders if there are any assets to be liquidated. For this reason, bonds are called **senior securities.**

THE CAPITAL MARKET AND THE MONEY MARKET

The capital markets are where buyers and sellers of investments, such as stocks or bonds, come together to efficiently execute transactions. The capital markets are comprised of primary and secondary markets. Primary markets are where an investor purchases a security directly from the issuer (e.g., an investor purchases a bond directly from the U.S. Treasury). Secondary markets are where previously issued securities are bought and sold among investors.

The money markets are where buyers and sellers of highly liquid, very short-term debt instruments, such as commercial paper or Treasury bills, come together to efficiently execute transactions. The money markets consist of a wholesale market and a retail market. The wholesale market is where financial institutions and companies lend to and purchase from each other. The retail market is where individuals can buy and sell short-term debt instruments, such as money market funds and certificates of deposit, either directly from the issuer (e.g., a CD from a bank) or through an intermediary (e.g., a money market fund through a financial advisor).

COMMERCIAL PAPER

Commercial paper refers to short-term, unsecured promissory notes issued by corporations to cover cash shortages brought on by various factors, such as large accounts receivable or seasonal business fluctuations. Maturity on commercial paper is generally within 90 days, but can range anywhere from 1 to 270 days.

There are two kinds of commercial paper. **Direct paper** is sold directly by the financing institution to the public, without going through dealers. **Dealer paper** is any commercial paper marketed through dealers.

CERTIFICATES OF DEPOSIT (CDs), BROKERED CDs, AND JUMBO CDs

Certificates of deposit (CDs) are financial instruments offered by banks, having a specific term (such as six months or one year) and usually having a fixed interest rate. Due to the decrease in accessibility for money, banks generally have higher interest rates on CDs.

Brokered certificates of deposit are CDs which are not purchased directly from a bank, but instead mediated by a brokerage firm (or from some other entity besides a bank). These CDs are generally pricier.

Jumbo certificates of deposit are CDs with a minimum face value of $100,000. These are, of course, ordinarily purchased only by large institutional investors, and they are considered to be low-risk.

BANKER'S ACCEPTANCE (BA)

A **banker's acceptance (BA)** is commonly used in international transactions. It is the corporate equivalent of a post-dated check, and can have limits of 1 to 270 days. A banker's acceptance is better than a regular postdated check, however, because the holder has the goods being traded as collateral in case the bank underwriting the acceptance goes under. Bankers' acceptances are bought and sold in the money market. They sell at a discount and mature at face value.

EURODOLLARS, EUROBONDS, AND EURODOLLAR BONDS

When U.S. dollars are deposited anywhere in the world outside the United States, they are called **Eurodollars** (even if they're not in Europe). The important thing to remember is that they're in American dollars, and not the currency of the bank where they're deposited.

Likewise, a **Eurobond** is any long-term debt instrument that's sold in a country other than the one whose currency it is in. A **Eurodollar bond** is a U.S. bond, denominated in American currency, which is sold anywhere outside the United States. The U.S. government doesn't issue Eurodollar bonds, but many foreign governments do, and so do some state and local governments in America, as well as foreign and American corporations.

RISKS INVOLVED IN DEBT SECURITIES

Risks to consider for Debt Instruments include:

Credit Risk (Default Risk) - the risk that the company will be unable to make the coupon or principal payments (Principal Risk)

Liquidity Risk - the risk that the investor may not be able to sell the investment quickly.

Reinvestment risk- risk that the proceeds from the bond or future cash flows will need to be reinvested in a security with a lower yield than the bond originally provided. Reinvestment risk may be higher for callable bonds—investments that can be called by the issuer before the maturity rate (Call Risk).

Inflation Risk - the risk that the value of money may decline and reduce the value of future payments more than anticipated.

Interest Rate Risk - A fundamental principle of bond investing is that market interest rates and bond prices generally move in opposite directions. When an investor expects future interest rates to rise, short-term debt is more attractive, and when rates are expected to fall, long-term debt is more attractive. When market interest rates rise, prices of fixed-rate bonds fall. This phenomenon is known as interest rate risk.

TERM BONDS AND SERIAL BONDS

A term bond is an individual bond that matures on a specific date in the future. On this date, the bond's principal must be paid to the bondholder. The bond's term is the time from issuance to the maturity date. The majority of bonds are term bonds.

A serial bond is a multiple bond issue where a portion of the bonds mature at regular intervals. A serial bond may be used to finance a project that provides a consistent stream of revenue to make principal payments. As the total amount of outstanding debt declines, so does the risk of default.

CALL PROVISIONS ON BONDS

Call provisions are arrangements on bonds stating that the bond issuer has the right to purchase back and retire the bond. These provisions ordinarily establish a timeframe when the call can occur, including details on the price and accrued interest paid to the bondholders. Bond issuers will call bonds if the market interest rate is lower than the bond rate, so that they can refinance their bonds to pay less interest. Due to the risk this places on bond investors, bonds with call provisions have a higher yield.

A particular type of call provision is a **make whole call**, whose aim is to properly compensate bond investors for future interest revenues they do not receive because of a bond call. With a make whole call provision, the bond issuer will be required to pay a lump sum equal to the net present value (NPV) of the future interest payments at the time of the call.

FLAT TRADES FOR BONDS

A **flat trade** for a bond occurs if the bond is traded to another investor without accrued interest being included in the price. This can occur either because no interest has actually generated, or because the bond is in default.

Compare this with the meaning of "flat trades" for equity securities, which has the related meaning of "breaking even." A stock trades flat if it is sold for the same price at which it was purchased.

EQUITY-LINKED SECURITIES (ELKSS)

Equity-linked securities (ELKSs) are hybrid securities, partly involving debt and partly involving equity. Fundamentally, they are debt securities which will behave like normal debt securities if a specified stock maintains a specific level of performance, but if that stock drops below the minimum performance level, then the investor receives an amount of stock instead. For instance, suppose that an ELKS is purchased which is linked to a company whose stock is trading at $20 per share, and suppose that the minimum percentage is 80%. If the share price drops below $16 (80% of $20) at any time before the maturity date of the ELKS, then the investor will receive a predetermined quantity of shares at the maturity date, rather than a repayment of the cash principal.

Since ELKSs are riskier, they tend to have a higher coupon rate than convertible debt, which is a different kind of hybrid security.

EXCHANGE-TRADED NOTES (ETNS)

Exchange-traded notes (ETNs) are hybrid securities which serve as a mixture of bonds and exchange-traded funds (ETFs). As their name implies, they are traded on an exchange, although they also have a maturity date like bonds. But with ETNs, the repayment of principal at the maturity date is modified according to the day's market index factor. (Further, the repayment is reduced by investing fees.) The value of an ETN, however, is not simply based on the market index, but also depends on the creditworthiness of the debtor company, since ETNs are unsecured debt instruments.

Unlike ordinary bonds, ETNs do not have periodic coupon payments.

Sovereign Debt

Sovereign debt is a governmental debt security, though it is issued by a foreign national government. It is issued in the foreign country's currency and serves the purpose of funding that country's growth. Sovereign debt has two primary risks: first, since it is usually aiding a developing country, the possible instability of the country lowers the chance of repayment; and second, because the debt is in a foreign currency, there is always the foreign currency exchange risk.

Corporate Debt

Corporate debt is debt issued by a company for the purpose of raising capital. The backing for the debt is generally the ability of the company to repay, which depends on its prospects for future revenues and profitability.

Corporate debt instruments include:

Commercial Paper is an unsecured, short-term debt instrument that is used to fund short-term liabilities. Maturities can range from several days up to nine months.

Corporate Notes are short-term loans that can be used for any purpose, including paying off higher interest rate debt. Notes can be either secured (i.e., backed by collateral) or unsecured, and terms are typically three years or less.

Corporate Bonds are longer-term debt issuances that are typically used to finance large company initiatives, such as expansions or acquisitions. Bonds can be either secured (i.e., backed by collateral) or unsecured, and have short-term (<1 year), medium-term (4 to 10 years) or long-term (10+ years) maturities.

Exchange Rates and Currency Trading

An **exchange rate** is the relationship between any two currencies, and it reflects how many units of one currency are required to obtain one unit of the other currency. They change daily, and many different factors can affect them. This constant change in the exchange rate is known as the float. If the dollar is going down in value with respect to another currency, it is depreciating; it will take more dollars to buy one unit of the other currency. When the dollar is getting strong, it is appreciating, and can buy more of the other currency. Because of the nature of exchange rates, and due to their constant fluctuation, **currency trading** can be quite profitable. But it is very risky, and not suitable for the average investor.

Exchange rates which change according to the supply and demand fluctuations within the market are floating exchange rates, whereas exchange rates pegged by the government as the official rate are fixed exchange rates.

One of the ways in which exchange rates are modified is through the intervention of central banks. A central bank will either buy or sell a particular currency in order to alter the value of its nation's currency against some foreign currency.

Yield to Maturity, Yield to Call, and Yield to Worst

Nominal yield is the same as the coupon rate of the bond. It is a percentage of the bond's par value.

Yield to maturity (YTM) is the percentage rate return assuming the bondholder holds the bond to maturity. If the bondholder buys the bond at a premium, then the YTM will be lower than the coupon rate. If bondholder buys the bond at a discount, then the YTM will be higher than the coupon rate.

Yield to call (YTC) is the percentage rate return assuming the issuer calls the bond on its call date. Callable bonds can be repurchased (or paid off) by the issuer on the call date, which is a date prior to maturity. The call price is determined by the market but is often a premium over par to incent investors to buy the bond. An issuer may choose to call their bond if interest rates have fallen, and they can issue a new bond at a lower rate.

Yield to worst (YTW) is the lowest possible percentage rate return the bondholder can expect to earn. It can either be the YTC or the YTM.

Discount Yield

Discount yield is the percentage rate of return that the bondholder earns if they purchase the bond below par value. The bond's return equals the difference between the par value and what the investor paid for the bond times the time to maturity.

For example, if an investor purchases a $10,000 bond at a $200 discount from par value that matures in 240 days, the discount yield would be calculated as: [($10,000-$9,800)/$10,000] * (360/240) or a 3% yield.

Yield Curves

Yield curves are graphs representing the interest rates for various bonds of the same credit rating but with different maturity dates. The x-axis displays the maturity date while the y-axis displays the interest rate.

A common yield curve compares U.S. Treasury debt for maturities of three months, two years, five years, and thirty years. Such a curve, since it represents the risk-free rate for debt securities, then serves as a basis of comparison for other bond yields.

Yield curves are utilized in forecasting economic changes, especially economic growth and output.

Normal, Inverted, and Flat Yield Curves

Yield curves, in showing the relationship between bond interest rates and maturity dates, can take different shapes. A healthy economy will be reflected by a **normal yield curve**, where the yield (interest rate) increases as the bond's maturity increases. However, with an **inverted yield curve**, bonds with longer maturities are displayed as having a lower yield rate. This generally signifies a future recession.

Yield curves which show minimal to no difference between short-term and long-term yields are **flat yield curves**. These can signify a change from recession to economic health or vice versa.

Calculation of Bond Interest

Bonds pay a stated interest rate, the coupon rate, over the term, or time to maturity, of the bond. The total interest paid is a product of the face value of the bond, multiplied by the coupon interest rate, multiplied by the term of the bond.

As an example, a company issues a 10-year bond with a face value of $1,000 and a 4% coupon rate. The total bond interest paid will be $1,000 x 4% x 10 years, or $400. Interest payments are generally paid twice per year, resulting in semiannual interest payments of $20.

Day-Count Conventions

Day-count conventions are systems used to determine how many days exist between bond coupon payments. This might seem strange, since it would seem to be a simple matter of counting the actual days. But such a method is simply one option—namely, the **actual day-count convention**.

A common convention is the **30/360 day-count convention**, which assumes 30 days per month and thus 360 days per year for the sake of simple calculations with uniform periods.

BOND RATINGS

Many bonds are rated by **bond rating companies**. The three best known are *Moody's*, *Standard & Poor's*, and *Fitch*. These companies assign ratings to bonds based on their evaluation of the creditworthiness of the bond issuer. They evaluate such things as how much debt the company has and the company's ability to manage it, how much cash flow the company can reasonably expect, and the history and performance of the company and its managers at handling debt. As a company's circumstances change, their bond rating can be upgraded or downgraded.

TAXATION OF BONDS

Bondholders' income normally comes from the periodic interest payments of the bond. However, discounts and premiums make things slightly more complicated. For tax purposes, any discount on a bond has to be **accreted** (increased) on a straight-line basis over the bond's term; the annual accretion amount is then added to the investor's reported income on the bond. The opposite occurs for bonds purchased at a premium. Premiums are **amortized** (decreased), with the annual amortization amount being subtracted from the investor's reported income.

For example, suppose an investor purchased at 95 a 10-year bond with a face value of $1,000 and stated rate of 6%. The discount of $50 would be accreted at a rate of $5 per year, and so the bondholder's reported income for each year would be $65 ($60 interest + $5 accretion).

Bonds that are originally issued at a discount are unsurprisingly called **original issue discounts (OIDs)**.

TAX-EQUIVALENT YIELD

The **tax-equivalent yield** is the yield that a taxable bond needs to have before taxes in order to achieve the same return as a nontaxable bond.

Tax-equivalent yield = (desired yield) / (1 – tax rate)

For example, if a nontaxable bond had a yield of 18% and the tax rate were 12%, then any taxable bonds, to be more valuable to the investor, would need to have a yield of 20.45% (18% / 88%).

TYPES OF SECURED BONDS

Secured bonds are bonds backed by some collateral, such that if the issuer defaults, the bond investor has claims on the collateralized asset.

Mortgage bonds are bonds secured by a mortgage on property owned by the issuer. The issuer would then have to liquidate this asset to repay the bondholder if he defaults.

Equipment trusts are bonds issued by transportation companies backed by the assets they employ, such as trucks or airplanes.

Collateral trusts are bonds backed by financial assets, such as stocks and other bonds.

Guaranteed bonds are bonds backed by the promise of a firm besides the issuer, ordinarily a parent company.

In the case of trusts, the collateralized assets are under the authority of a third-party trustee.

TYPES OF UNSECURED BONDS

Unsecured bonds differ from secured corporate bonds because there is no collateral behind them, which means they're riskier than secured bonds. The two main types of unsecured corporate bonds are **debentures** and **subordinated debentures**.

Holders of debentures are treated like other business creditors in the event of liquidation due to bankruptcy; they collect only if any assets remain after employees, taxes, and secured creditors are paid. But they do come before holders of subordinated debentures. Because of this, subordinated debenture investments usually have higher rates of return to make them more attractive to investors.

ZERO-COUPON BONDS AND STEP-UP BONDS

Zero-coupon bonds don't pay interest. Instead, their price is heavily discounted from face value. When the bond matures, bondholders receive the full face value, but they gain no interest in the meantime.

Zero-coupon bonds cost much less to purchase, but are extremely sensitive to changes in interest rates. Small changes in interest rates can have a huge impact on zero-coupon bonds (much more so than on regular bonds), since the present value of the bond is based entirely on the maturity-date payment and not on any coupon payments.

Because the investors profit simply from the principal increase, these are also called **capital appreciation bonds**.

Step-up bonds are bonds whose interest rate increases over the term of the bond. The bond contract specifies how the coupon payments grow over time.

ARBITRAGE TRADING

Arbitrage is a specialized trading strategy that seeks to take advantage of very small differences in a security's price in different markets by buying the security in one market and selling it in another. Market inefficiencies are what make arbitrage possible, but these opportunities are typically short-lived until markets correct to align prices.

There are several different types of arbitrage, including:

- Risk Arbitrage (also called Merger Arbitrage) - buying the acquiree (the company being taken over) and selling short the acquiror, the company doing the takeover.
- Convertible arbitrage – buying a convertible security (e.g., bond, right, warrant, etc.) and short-selling its underlying stock.
- Covered interest arbitrage - exchanging domestic and foreign currency at current spot rate and buying or selling the forward contract in foreign currency. This strategy seeks to take advantage of interest rate differences between two countries while nullifying the currency exchange risk.

CONVERTIBLE BONDS

Convertible bonds are bonds that can be converted into a stated amount of shares of the issuing company's stock. This makes them attractive to investors because they combine features of both financial instruments—they pay interest, which is regular income, and they can also appreciate if the company's stock appreciates. If the stock goes up, the holder of a convertible bond can choose to convert them to stocks, or sell the bond on the market, and receive a premium to reflect the appreciation of the stock.

Some convertible bonds give the issuer the right to force conversions, forcing bondholders to convert their convertible bonds into stock. Companies who force conversions usually do so to refinance their bonds if a lower interest rate is available.

PARITY, THE CONVERSION RATIO, AND THE PARITY PRICE FOR CONVERTIBLE BONDS

Parity occurs when a convertible bond is trading on the market for the same price as the stock to which it can be converted.

The **conversion ratio** gives the number of shares a convertible bond may be converted into. It is calculated by the following formula:

Conversion ratio = (par value of bond) / (conversion price of stock)

For instance, for a bond with a par value of $1,000 and a conversion price of $20, the conversion ratio would be 50 shares.

Since the **parity price** of the bond is the price equivalent to the value of the underlying stock, its formula is as follows:

Parity price = (market price of stock) x (conversion ratio)

For instance, if the conversion ratio is 50 shares, and if the stock is trading on the market at $22/share, then the parity price of the bond would be $1,100 (a premium of $100 over par).

REPURCHASE AGREEMENTS

Some financial institutions raise cash through a **repurchase agreement**. This entails selling some of their securities, usually for a fixed amount of time, after which they agree to buy them back. The securities become the collateral, making it a very safe loan for the lender. This way, the financial institution doesn't have to sell the securities to come up with cash. Not all repurchase agreements, or repos, come with a fixed maturity date. Some are left open, in which case the lender has the right to demand repayment at any time. Whether fixed or open, if the borrower defaults, the lender has the right to sell the securities. Repurchase agreements are sensitive to interest rates—if they rise sharply, the lender's collateral loses value.

MUNICIPAL SECURITIES

As per Section 3(a)(29) of the Securities Exchange Act of 1934, municipal securities are defined as securities which are a direct obligation or obligations for payment of interest and principal by a state or any governmental subdivision, such as a city, county, agency, etc.

Municipal securities fall into two categories:

- Municipal bonds are issued by states, cities, counties and other governmental entities to raise money to build roads, schools and a host of other projects for the public good. Municipal bonds are typically sold in minimum increments of $5,000, pay interest on a semi-annual basis, and have maturities that range from less than one year to 30 years.
- Municipal fund securities are mutual funds for local governments. Municipal fund securities include 529 Savings Plans, which are established by states to provide a way for investors to pay for qualified education expenses, and ABLE Programs, which are savings accounts for individuals with disabilities and their families.

135

GENERAL OBLIGATION BONDS AND REVENUE BONDS

There are two types of municipal bonds:

- General obligation bonds – these bonds are not backed by revenues from a specific project or source. Instead, they may be backed by dedicated taxes or payable from general funds.
- Revenue bonds – these bonds are backed by revenues from a specific project or source. Revenue bonds include airport, industrial, public power, hospital, and housing revenue bonds.

The interest paid on municipal issues is exempt from federal taxes and sometimes state and local taxes as well.

MUNICIPAL SECURITIES PRICING AND REPORTING

Price transparency has always been a challenge in the municipal securities market, given that there are thousands of securities available, and the majority of transactions are conducted by retail investors in over-the-counter markets.

Municipal securities pricing and reporting is governed by several MSRB Rules, including G-13, G-17, and G-30.

MSRB Rule G-13 states that broker-dealers offering quotes in municipal securities have an obligation to determine that the quotes are "bona fide" and reflect the "fair market value" of the security.

MSRB Rule G-17 requires a dealer to disclose to its customer, at or prior to the sale, all material facts about the transaction known by the dealer, as well as material facts about the security that are reasonably accessible to the market. This includes the obligation to give customers a complete description of the security, including a description of the features that likely would be considered significant by a reasonable investor and facts that are material to assessing the potential risks of the investment. Such disclosures must be made at the time of trade, even if the trade is self-directed.

MSRB Rule G-30 requires that dealers trade with customers at prices that are fair and reasonable, taking into consideration all relevant factors. MSRB's Real-time Transaction Reporting System (RTRS), which was implemented in January 2005, allows market participants to monitor market price levels on a real-time basis and assists them in identifying changes in market prices that may have been caused by news or market events. The MSRB now makes the transaction data reported to RTRS available to the public through the Electronic Municipal Market Access (EMMA) system.

OFFICIAL STATEMENT FOR NEW ISSUE MUNICIPAL SECURITIES

MSRB Rule G-32 was implemented to ensure that customers purchasing new issue municipal securities are provided with all available information relevant to the investment decision by settlement of the transaction. The rule requires all dealers selling new issue municipal securities to provide to their customers a copy of the official statement or, if an official statement is not being prepared, a written notice to that effect together with a copy of a preliminary official statement. The Rule also requires underwriters of a primary offering of municipal securities to make certain submissions to the MSRB by electronic completion of Form G-32 through the EMMA Dataport.

Official statements typically contain the following information: the interest rate, the timing and manner of payment of the interest and the principal; the minimum investment denomination, whether the bonds are callable, and if so, on what terms, the sources of payment, consequences in the event of default, a description of outstanding debt, descriptions of required legal documents such as authorizing resolution, indenture and trust agreement, and discussion of any legal matters such as pending proceedings that may affect the securities offered, legal opinions and tax considerations.

MUNICIPAL SECURITIES ACCORDING TO MSRB RULE D-12

MSRB Rule D-12 addresses the municipal fund securities market. Municipal fund securities are issued by state or local governments and sold by investment companies or dealers. However, they are not municipal bond funds (i.e., mutual fund comprised of municipal bonds) and they are not regulated by the Investment Company Act of 1940. Municipal fund securities can hold a wide variety of securities, including corporate stocks, corporate bonds, and Treasury securities and they do not have to offer a prospectus, calculate a daily NAV, or have independent directors on their board as mutual funds do. Municipal fund securities are exempt from federal taxes, and in many cases state and local taxes.

TYPES OF MUNICIPAL SECURITIES

Types of municipal fund securities:

Local Government Investment Pools (LGIPs) – trusts in which municipal governments may invest their cash reserves. By pooling their assets in these trusts, municipalities benefit from economies of scale and diversification. LGIPs offer daily liquidity.

529 Education Savings Accounts – state-sponsored investment plans, named for Section 529 of the Internal Revenue Code, that allow investors to save money on behalf of a beneficiary to pay for education expenses. All 50 states offer at least one 529 plan. 529 plans are managed by investment companies, which offer a variety of mutual fund and exchange-traded fund portfolios through the plans, many of which are age-based, meaning that the portfolio becomes more conservative as the child ages. Withdrawals 529 education savings accounts are tax-free.

ABLE 529A Savings Accounts – accounts that allow individuals with disabilities and their families to save for disability expenses. Like 529 accounts, withdrawals from ABLE accounts are tax-free when used for disability related expenses. Contributions to ABLE accounts can be made by anyone but must be made using post-taxed dollars and are not deductible from federal income tax.

METHODS OF QUOTATION FOR MUNICIPAL BONDS

Municipal bonds are generally quoted in yield. Revenue bonds that are callable may be quoted as a percentage of par value. Because bonds trade in the over-the-counter market, unlike equities which trade on exchanges, pricing information can be difficult to obtain. Typically, investors interested in purchasing a municipal bond must get pricing information from a broker. Brokerages may provide quotes in three ways:

- A firm quote, also known as a bona fide quotation, is a displayed quote on a securities network terminal or a quote given by phone.
- An out-firm quote is a firm quote that is good for a specified duration, such as for 1 hour.
- A workable indication, also called a nominal quote, is a price that the dealer may be willing to buy or sell, but it is not a firm quote, usually because the bond is not actively traded and may not be located.

DIVERSIFICATION OF MUNICIPAL INVESTMENTS

There are three main factors relevant to the diversification of municipal investments: geography, type, and rating.

Geographic diversification involves municipal investments which are outside one's own state or other governmental jurisdiction. The reason for this kind of diversification is that it offsets the risk of certain events that would bear a cost on only one municipality, such as natural disasters or political changes. By diversifying geographically, one can offset these risks.

Type diversification refers to the different types of municipal investments. Most municipal investments are bonds, but municipal bonds can be further subdivided into other categories, such as general obligation bonds and revenue obligation bonds.

Rating diversification refers to the risk that the bond issuer will be unable to repay its bond debts. This simply involves the ordinary investment tradeoff of risk and reward.

ASSESSING GENERAL OBLIGATION (GO) BOND PROSPECTS

General obligation (GO) bonds are issued to pay for improvements that benefit a community, but don't produce income. They are also known as **full faith and credit issues**, because they are repaid from tax revenue raised by the issuing government entity. The merits of a GO bond depend greatly on whether the community of the issuer is likely to be able to raise the funds to pay back the interest and principal. Are property values high? Is the local economy strong and diversified? Is the population growing, or at least stable? How much debt does the issuer have now, and can he manage this new obligation? Do they plan to issue any further debt soon after this issue? What are the sources of the tax revenue, and do they look likely to remain consistent until maturity? These are the types of considerations to make when evaluating GO bonds.

RATIOS USED IN MEASURING MUNICIPAL DEBT

Net debt to assessed valuation: The municipality's debt divided by the value of the purchased property, as assessed for tax purposes. The lower the better, preferably 5% or below.

Net debt to estimated valuation: Similar to the above, but based on estimations, not actual assessments, which vary.

Taxes per capita: Are citizens paying a high tax burden already?

Debt per capita: Is government debt per person high or low?

Collection ratio: How much of the taxes owed are actually collected?

Coverage ratio: How many years' worth of annual revenue will it take to cover the debt? This is calculated as revenues/debt, and it can be based on net or gross revenue, but usually net.

Also, though not a ratio, it is important to look at the municipality's **debt trend**: Is the taxing authority adding to or reducing its debt, generally speaking?

REVENUS BONDS
ASSESSING REVENUE BOND PROSPECTS

Governments issue **revenue bonds** to finance projects and facilities that are expected to generate enough revenue to pay bondholders back without resorting to tax money. Since they are backed not by a government's ability to tax, but by the expected revenue stream generated by the proposed facility or project, careful analysis must be done to ensure that the project will be able to generate enough income to repay bondholders. Is there a legitimate need for the project, and will enough people use it to make it worthwhile? Are there other facilities nearby that serve the same purpose that will draw revenue away from the project? If not, are there plans to build any competing projects? Will the facility bring in enough money to pay for itself and repay investors? These are the types of considerations to make when evaluating revenue bonds.

FEASIBILITY STUDIES, FINANCIAL REPORTS, AND CATASTROPHE CLAUSES

When assessing revenue bond prospects, there are a number of important factors to consider:

Feasibility studies are analyses of the strengths and weaknesses of the activity being financed by the revenue bonds. It is important to know whether the revenue bonds are funding a sensible operation. Municipalities are required to have these studies for revenue bonds, and they hire their own consultants to carry them out.

Financial reports are also required to be provided by the municipalities. These are subject to external audits, which help to provide assurance of the information's reliability to potential investors.

Catastrophe clauses are clauses stating that if a catastrophic event destroys a facility designed to produce funds for repaying the revenue bonds, then the insurance gained from such an event will repay bondholders.

FLOW OF FUNDS

The **flow of funds** explains how a municipality uses the revenue it generates. The revenues normally are distributed to pay various expenses in a particular order:

Operation and maintenance – payments to maintain the facilities and pay the employees

Debt service – repayment of bond principal and interest

Debt service reserve – savings for future debt repayments

Reserve maintenance fund – savings for future maintenance payments

Renewal and replacement fund – payments to renovate or update facilities and to replace old equipment

Surplus fund – payments for miscellaneous expenditures

When a municipality distributes funds in this order—covering operation expenses before repaying bond debts—it is called a **net revenue pledge**, since the municipality pledges to repay investors from net revenue. If the pledge is to pay investors before operations expenditures, then it is called a **gross revenue pledge**.

COVENANTS

Covenants are promises made by the bond issuer, legally binding him to certain courses of action in order to better protect investors. Because the purpose is to protect investors, these are specifically called **protective covenants**. Examples of such covenants are as follows:

Rate covenants are promises to charge adequate rates, so that sufficient revenue is generated to repay bond principal and interest.

Maintenance covenants are promises to preserve and repair the facilities.

Insurance covenants are promises to appropriately insure the facilities.

Other protective covenants can restrict the issuer from paying a certain amount of dividends to shareholders, or from issuing newer and higher-priority debt.

CREDIT ENHANCEMENTS

Credit enhancements are actions taken by a municipality or company to improve its creditworthiness. This can be accomplished with insurance, collateral, the guarantee of a third party, or internal changes that demonstrate the entity is better able to repay debts.

GENERAL OBLIGATION AND LIMITED-TAX GENERAL OBLIGATION (LTGO) BONDS

General obligation municipal bonds are backed by the credit and taxing power of the issuing government rather than the revenue from a given project.

There are two basic kinds of general obligation bonds:

Limited tax general obligation (LTGO) bonds do not allow for an increase in property taxes. Instead, they must be paid from existing revenue sources. LTGO bonds do not require approval by taxpayers.

Unlimited tax general obligation (UTGO) bonds allow for an increase in property taxes. They must be approved by 60% of voters, with a voter turnout equal to at least 40% of those who voted in the most recent general election. At the same time, voters are asked to approve an excess levy which raises their property taxes to cover the debt service payments.

SHORT-TERM MUNICIPAL OBLIGATIONS

There are a number of different ways for municipalities to fund immediate projects with short-term (one year or less) debt securities, classified according to the means of repaying the debt:

Tax anticipation notes (TANs) are issued for an immediate activity or project, which are expected to be repaid with taxes.

Bond anticipation notes (BANs) are similar to TANs, except that the debts are expected to be paid off through the later issuance of bonds.

Revenue anticipation notes (RANs) are similar to the above two, except that the debts are expected to be paid off through the project's own revenue.

Tax and revenue anticipation notes (TRANs) are expected to be paid off with both taxes and revenues.

Grant anticipation notes (GANs) are issued by municipalities who expect to repay the debts with grants from the federal government.

Tax-exempt commercial paper is a short-term loan which gives the investor (lender) various tax benefits at the local, state, or federal levels.

TYPES OF MUNICIPAL BONDS

There are three main types of municipal bonds, categorized according to the way that the bond repayments can be financed.

General obligation (GO) bonds are the first type. These are issued to pay for improvements that benefit a community, but don't produce income. They are also known as "full faith and credit issues," because they are repaid from tax revenue raised by the issuing government entity.

Revenue bonds are issued by governments to finance projects and facilities that are expected to generate enough revenue to pay bondholders back without resorting to tax money.

Double-barreled bonds are revenue bonds that also have the backing of the taxing authority. They are considered GO bonds, even though they depend primarily on revenue generated from the project for repayment.

VARIABLE RATE, AUCTION RATE, AND FIXED RATE SECURITIES

A fixed rate bond is a bond that pays the same coupon rate over its entire term or until called. The value of the bond may rise or fall in an inverse relationship to current interest rates (e.g., if interest rates rise, the bond and its fixed payments become less valuable, if rates fall, the bond and its fixed payments become more valuable.)

A variable rate bond pays a floating coupon rate that is adjusted at specific intervals. Generally, an interest rate index, such as LIBOR, plus or minus a specified percentage, is used to set the interest rate. This type of bond has more price stability than a fixed rate bond since it adjusts to changes in the interest rate environment.

Auction rate securities (ARS) are variable rate debt securities; either long-term bonds (i.e., maturities of 20 to 30 years) or preferred stock issued by a closed-end fund. Interest rates are periodically reset through auctions, typically every 7, 14, 28, or 35 days. ARBs are sold through a Dutch auction where the bond is sold at an interest rate that will clear the market at the lowest yield possible. These bonds are not tradeable in secondary markets. Interest is often exempt from tax.

SPECIAL TAX BONDS AND SPECIAL ASSESSMENT BONDS

Special tax bonds are municipal bonds where bondholders are repaid through a particular tax levied specifically for their repayment. Generally, this tax will be related to the project which the bonds have funded. For example, an excise tax on tobacco might repay bondholders whose bonds funded some public hospital venture.

Special assessment bonds are municipal bonds where bondholders are repaid through the taxation of the particular community which receives the benefits. For example, if a public playground or park is built in some community, then the property taxes of that community might increase to pay off the bondholders, according to the likelihood that such people would utilize it.

MORAL OBLIGATION BONDS

Moral obligation bonds are municipal bonds where the municipality adds a moral pledge to repay the bondholders, with this pledge backed by a reserve fund established in case of default or any other failure to pay. This is a merely moral obligation, not a legally binding one, yet municipalities have an additional incentive to keep their word, since their credit rating would suffer otherwise.

CERTIFICATES OF PARTICIPATION (COPs)

A **certificate of participation (COP)** grants an investor the right to some lease revenues for a facility that is constructed through a municipal bond issuance. Rather than entitling the investor to the rights of the bondholder, a COP participates in the ownership of the facility and the municipality leases it until all the lease payments are made. COPs provide investors with a solid backup plan if the municipality defaults, for they then can sell or utilize the facility as they see fit.

AUCTION-RATE SECURITIES (ARSS)

Auction-rate securities (ARSs) are a form of debt security where the interest rate is determined by a Dutch auction. (A Dutch auction is a "reverse" auction, where the auctioneer begins with a high price and keeps lowering it to some minimum price. The first bidder wins.) These debt securities typically have a long-term maturity, but in practice are treated as shorter-term, since the interest rate is periodically (e.g. monthly) reset through another Dutch auction.

LOCAL GOVERNMENT INVESTMENT POOLS (LGIP)

Local Government Investment Pools (LGIP) are funds (in the form of surplus cash) pooled by state and local governments and placed into a trust of short-term investments. These aggregated funds are deposited in a diverse portfolio of funds including corporate stock and bonds, mutual funds, and a variety of municipal securities. In many states, the state treasurer or the authorized governing board of another governmental entity (such as a county) oversees a pooled investment fund that operates like a money market mutual fund for the exclusive benefit of governments within the entity's jurisdiction.

Unlike mutual funds, local government investment pools (LGIPs) are not registered with the Securities and Exchange Commission (SEC) and are exempt from SEC regulatory requirements because they fall under a governmental exclusion clause. While this exemption allows pools greater flexibility, it also reduces investor protection. Some have a "constant" objective to maintain liquidity and stability. Some have an objective to maximize return and are thus less liquid and more volatile. Investments in these pools are not insured or guaranteed and substantial losses have occurred in the past. By pooling funds, participating governments benefit from economies of scale, full-time portfolio management, diversification, and liquidity (especially in the case of pools that seek a constant net asset value of $1.00). Interest is normally allocated to the participants on a daily basis, proportionate to the size of the investment. Most pools offer a check writing or wire transfer feature that adds value as a cash management tool. The LGIP is typically administered by a board of trustees, and usually managed by a financial services firm. They are also rated by ratings firms in a manner similar to mutual funds. Whether the LGIP is state-sponsored or created through a joint powers agreement, it is important to be aware that the authorizing entity typically does not guarantee investments in the LGIP. Each LGIP has a defined investment objective.

ABLE ACCOUNTS

ABLE Accounts are tax-advantaged savings accounts for individuals with disabilities and their families, created by the ABLE Act of 2014. The beneficiary of the account is the account owner, and income earned by the account will not be taxed. Contributions to the account, which can be made by any person (the account beneficiary, family, friends Special Needs Trust or Pooled Trust), must be made using post-taxed dollars and will not be tax deductible for purposes of federal taxes; however, some states may allow for state income tax deductions for contributions made to an ABLE account. Eligibility for public benefits (SSI, SNAP, Medicaid) needed by people with disabilities requires meeting a means/resource test. For the first time in public policy, the ABLE Act recognizes the extra and significant costs of living with a disability. These include costs related to raising a child with significant disabilities or a working-age adult with disabilities, accessible housing and transportation, personal assistance services, assistive technology and health care not covered by insurance, Medicaid or Medicare. Eligible individuals and their families will be allowed to establish ABLE savings accounts that will largely not affect their eligibility for SSI, Medicaid and means-tested programs such as FAFSA, HUD and SNAP/food stamp benefits. The ABLE Act limits eligibility to individuals with disabilities with an age of onset of disability before 26. If the beneficiary meets the age requirement and is already receiving benefits under SSI and/or SSDI, they are automatically eligible to establish an ABLE account. To meet the requirement, a person must meet Social Security's definition and criteria regarding functional limitations and receive a letter of disability certification from a licensed physician, a doctor of medicine or osteopathy, a doctor of dental surgery or dental medicine, and, for some purposes, a doctor of podiatric medicine, a doctor of optometry, or a chiropractor.

MANDATORY REDEMPTION SCHEDULES

Mandatory redemption schedules lay out specific dates at which a bond issuer is required to call (redeem) outstanding bonds, either all of the bonds in an issuance or only some. Some mandatory redemption agreements require the issuer to call various outstanding bonds when a certain amount of cash is available in a bond sinking fund.

SINKING FUNDS

A sinking fund is a special account into which bond issuers make deposits for the purpose of paying off a portion of the issue early. If a bond indenture includes a sinking fund, it reduces the risk to bondholders and may attract more investors. A sinking fund can be used to redeem callable bonds, or the issue may have a sinking fund provision, which allows the company to repurchase its bonds periodically and at a specified sinking fund price (often par value). An issuer might utilize this provision when interest rates fall because they can repurchase the bond below market value. Sinking funds are most often used for term bonds. A sinking fund may also be used to buy back preferred stock.

EXTRAORDINARY REDEMPTION

Extraordinary redemption refers to bonds that are called by the issuer due to some event that is both unusual and infrequent. There must be a provision for this kind of redemption laid out in the bond contract.

An example of an event which could permit issuers to call outstanding bonds is a disaster which prevents the construction of, or outright destroys, the project financed by the bonds. Another example is if the interest on the bonds was originally planned to be non-taxable, but bond proceeds must be used in such a way that they are now taxable.

PUTTABLE BONDS

A put is the right to sell something to someone. Some bonds, usually municipal bonds, contain a put option. These are known as **puttable bonds**. A bondholder with a puttable bond has the right, after a specified amount of time, to sell the bond back to the issuer at face value, or **par**. Once the put option date has been reached, the bondholder has the right once a year to sell it back at par, and the issuer has the obligation to buy it back at par. This gives bond buyers added protection against changes in interest rates, and makes their bonds more attractive on the open market.

CROSSOVER REFUNDING

Crossover refunding refers to a particular way in which a municipality may issue new bonds to pay off older bonds. When the new bonds are issued, which are called **refunding bonds**, their proceeds are placed in an escrow account (i.e. a third-party account). These proceeds are used to pay off interest payments on the refunding bonds until the older bonds arrive at their maturity date, at which point the proceeds are then used to repay those older debts.

MUNICIPAL SECURITY REFUNDING METHODS

Municipal securities can be refunded using a variety of methods initiated either at or before the issue's maturity:

- Direct exchange – issuing new bonds to raise the funds needed to exchange for the retiring bonds.
- Escrowed to maturity – issuing new bonds and placing the proceeds in an escrow account, where they are invested in Treasury securities, to pay off the original bond's periodic coupon payments and principal. Since the original bonds are backed by Treasury securities, they may receive a higher credit rating.
- Advance refunding – issuing refunding bonds prior to the call date or maturity of the original bond. The proceeds are put in an escrow account to pay off the original bonds at the earliest possible date. This method might be used if interest rates decline, allowing the issuer to pay offer higher interest rate debt with lower interest rate debt.
- Current refunding – an advance refunding done within 90 days of the call or maturity date.
- Crossover refunding – issuing new municipal bonds and placing the proceeds in an escrow account used to make debt service payments on the new bonds until the call date on the original issue. On the call date, the funds in the escrow account crossover to refund the original bonds. After the original bonds are paid off with the funds held in escrow, the new bonds become payable from the original pledged revenue stream.

BOND REFUNDING AND PRE-REFUNDING

Bond refunding is when an issuer sells a new bond issue in order to raise money to redeem a previous bond issue. This is done to take advantage of lower interest rates. Refunding becomes more likely as bonds get closer to the maturity date.

Pre-refunding is when the issuer sells a new set of bonds at a lower interest rate, but doesn't call the previous issue of bonds. The proceeds from the sale are placed in escrow and used to buy federal government securities, and the interest received is used to call the previous issue at the first call date. This is also known as **advance refunding**. Bonds that are pre-refunded have the highest possible bond rating, as the risk of default is virtually nil.

FACTORS THAT AFFECT A BOND'S LIQUIDITY

The following affect **bond liquidity**:

- how well-known or widely owned they are
- the bond rating (higher rating means trades are easier)
- the quality of the bond issuer
- how mature the bond is
- how high the interest rate is
- whether it is trading at, above, or below par
- whether it has any call features

SECONDARY MARKET ORDERS FOR MUNICIPAL SECURITIES

The **secondary market** for municipal securities consists of the transactions for those securities after they have been initially issued by the government body issuing the bond. (Transactions to purchase bonds directly from the issuer comprise the primary market.)

The different types of orders and offerings in this market depend on whether the bond is sold at a discount, at a premium, or at par. These terms depend upon the relation between the bond's coupon rate (the stated interest rate on the bond) and the bond's current yield (the effective rate of interest, given the actual expected cash inflows and the current market price). If the coupon rate is greater than the current yield, then the bond sells at premium; if the coupon rate is lower than the current yield, then it sells at a discount; and if they are equal, then it sells at par.

BROKER'S BROKERS

Most brokers deal with the general public, and primarily with individual investors. However, some municipal bond brokers don't deal with individual investors or the general public at all. They deal only with other municipal brokers, and large financial institutions, such as banks. A broker in this category is known as a **broker's broker**. Because he's dealing with companies who haven't sold all the bonds they've been assigned, confidentiality is very important, and a broker's broker never reveals the names of his clients and customers.

CALCULATING THE INTEREST DUE ON MUNICIPAL SECURITIES

If a municipal bond is purchased between semiannual coupon payment dates, the purchaser must pay the seller accrued interest, or the amount of interest the seller earned while they still owned the bond.

Municipal securities transactions settle on a trade date plus two days (T+2) basis. Accrued interest is calculated based on a 30/360 calendar.

For example, a $5,000 bond with a 5% coupon rate that pays interest on January 1 and July 1 is sold on August 3 at par value. The number of days of accrued interest that the purchaser owes is calculated as 30 days in July, plus 4 days in August (August 3 + 2 days – settlement date, which is not counted in the calculation of accrued interest), or 34 days. The bond pays semiannual coupon payments of $125 ($5000 x 5% / 2), resulting in daily coupon interest of $0.694 ($125/180). This amount is multiplied by the 34 days of accrued interest to equal $23.61. The purchaser would have to pay $5,023.61 (par value + accrued interest).

ODD FIRST COUPON BONDS

Odd first coupon bonds are bonds whose first coupon comes after an irregular period, either shorter or longer than all the other coupon bonds. Since bonds ordinarily have coupon periods of six months, odd first coupon bonds are ones issued in the midst of these six-month intervals.

If the first coupon period is shorter than the other periods, the bond has an **odd short first coupon**, and if it is longer, then it has an **odd long first coupon**.

CAPITAL GAINS AND LOSSES ON BONDS

Accretion of **bond discounts** and amortization of **bond premiums** affect not only reported income but also capital gains and losses on bonds.

For example, suppose a bondholder purchased at 95 a 10-year bond with a face value of $1,000 and stated rate of 6%. Suppose this bondholder sold the bond to another investor for 105, 5 years after the bond's issuance. If so, the capital gain on the sale would be $75—the difference between $1,050 (the selling price) and $975 (the $950 buying price plus $25 accretion over five years).

RELATIONSHIP BETWEEN BOND PRICES AND DIFFERENCE IN COUPON AND MATURITY

The higher the coupon rate of a bond, the more income it produces. For example, a $5,000 bond with a 5% coupon rate will pay $250 per year (usually $125 every six months), while a $5,000 bond with a 10% coupon rate will pay twice as much. The price investors are willing to pay for a bond on the secondary market is based on their perception of future interest rates. If interest rates are expected to fall, the investor would be willing to pay a premium for the bond (i.e., above par value), believing the bond will pay more income than newly issued bonds. If interest rates are expected to increase, the investor would expect to buy the bond at a discount (i.e., less than par value), believing the bond will pay less income than newly issued bonds.

A bond's Maturity Date is the specific date in the future when the face value of the bond will be repaid to the bondholder. A bond may mature in a few months or in a few years. Maturity affects interest rate risk. The longer the period to the bond's maturity, the greater the risk that the bond's value could be impacted by changing interest rates. Therefore, bonds with longer maturities generally have higher interest rate risk than similar bonds with shorter maturities.

TAXABLE EQUIVALENT YIELDS FOR MUNICIPAL SECURITIES

The Taxable Equivalent Yield (TEY) for a municipal security is the return a taxable security would have to earn pre-tax to have the same yield as the tax-exempt municipal security.

For example, if a tax-free municipal bond has a 2.5% yield, and the purchaser's incremental tax rate is 37%, the taxable equivalent yield would be calculated as $\frac{Tax-Free\ Bond\ Rate}{1-Purchaser\ Tax\ Rate}$, or $\frac{2.5\%}{1-37\%}$, or 3.97%.

TAXATION OF CAPITAL GAINS ON MUNICIPAL SECURITIES

Though interest payments on municipal bonds are tax-free on the Federal level, and in many cases on the state and local levels as well, they are still subject to capital gains taxes, either short term or long term. As with other types of investments, the short-term capital gains (i.e., gains on bonds held less than one year) are taxed as regular income, while the long-term capital gains tax rate on municipal bonds can be 0%, 15%, or 20% for those with taxable incomes of over $441,450 ($496,600 for joint filers). In addition, a surtax on net investment income of 3.8% also applies to high-income taxpayers.

For example, a municipal bond with a face value of $1,000 is purchased at a discount for $975. The investor holds the bond to maturity, making it subject to long-term capital gains taxes. In this case, the investor's long-term capital gains rate is 15%. The capital gains tax would be calculated as: $1,000 − $975 = $25, $25 × 15% = $3.75 in capital gains tax owed. By subtracting the capital gains tax from the discount ($25 − $3.75 = $21.25), the investor's yield declines from 2.5% to 2.125% $\left(\frac{\$1,000-\$978.75}{1000}\right)$.

BASIS POINTS

Basis point is a measure used in finance that is equal to 1/100th of 1%, or 0.01%, or 0.0001. In other words, a 100-basis point change is equivalent to a 1% change. Basis points are often used to express changes in interest rates or yields. For example, if a bond was yielding 5% and its yield increased by 25 basis points, its new yield would be 5.25%. Basis points are commonly abbreviated as "bp," "bps," or "bips."

BOND DEFAULTS

A bond default occurs when the bond issuer fails to make interest or principal payments. Defaulting on a bond poses serious consequences for an issuer, including an inability to obtain future credit, lower credit scores, and higher interest rates on current and future debt. An issuer that is unable to make bond payments will often file for bankruptcy, either Chapter 7, which involves the liquidation of assets to pay debts, or Chapter 11, which involves restructuring the terms of the debt. In both cases, bondholders may only receive a portion of what they are owed. Bonds in default usually continue trading, but generally at deep discounts.

TAXATION OF MUNICIPAL BONDS

Gains from investments on municipal bonds are ordinarily not taxed. **Taxable municipal bonds** can be issued if the purpose of the bond revenue has no clear public benefit, but most municipal bonds are tax-exempt.

This means not only that coupon payments are not taxed, but also that gains from original issue discount (OID) bonds are tax-exempt as well. Accretion on the discount of municipal OID bonds is treated as tax-exempt interest income.

Discounts on municipal bonds purchased in the secondary market are not even accreted. These are the only bonds whose discounts are not accreted.

FEDERAL, STATE, AND LOCAL TAXATION

Investors need not pay any taxes on interest income from **municipal bonds**, although they may have to pay state or local taxes, depending on their laws.

U.S. territories (including American Samoa, Guam, Puerto Rico, and the Virgin Islands) and federal districts (Washington, D.C.) are triple tax-free regarding municipal bonds. Bondholders don't have any federal, state, or local taxes to pay on interest.

Most states, but not all, are triple tax-free regarding municipal bonds for investors purchasing bonds issued within their own state.

Despite all these tax exemptions for interest income, capital gains from the sales of bonds is still taxable.

BANK QUALIFIED BONDS

Banks like the benefit of tax-exempt interest earned on municipal bonds. But with the Tax Reform Act of 1986, banks can't deduct the carrying cost of holding municipal bonds in inventory; that is, they can't deduct the interest expenses which are incurred to purchase or carry those bonds. This tends to negate the benefits of tax-exempt interest income.

But there are exceptions to this rule which allow banks to deduct 80% of the carrying cost on particular bonds. Specifically, if the bonds are issued by a qualified small issuer (i.e. an issuer that issues $10 million in tax-exempt bonds or less yearly), issued for some public purpose, and designated as tax-exempt, then they qualify. These types of bonds are often called **bank qualified bonds**.

BLIND POOLS

Blind pools are stock offerings or limited partnerships that pool together investment money without having any stated objectives for the fund. The reason investors are willing to invest in these is due to the reputation of the individuals or company managing the fund. Some blind pools have a good reputation, but naturally, this is very prone to fraud.

Blind pools are also called **blank-check offerings**.

PRIVATE EQUITY

Private equity consists of any equity which isn't quoted on any public exchanges. Private investments might involve funding a private company to develop new technologies, or simply to be more successful in general. Private equity also might involve purchasing a public company for the sake of making it private.

Private equity often involves investors with enormous amounts of capital.

STRUCTURED PRODUCTS

Structured products are securities which are linked to some other underlying asset, such as another security, a group of securities, a commodity, and index, or something else.

Structured products can sometimes have a "principal guarantee" feature, which means simply that the principal is guaranteed to return if the investor holds the investment for long enough (e.g. to maturity for debt securities).

FUNDS OF FUNDS (FOFS) AND HEDGE FUNDS

Funds of funds (FOFs) are investments that invest in other funds, rather than investing directly in securities such as stocks or bonds. It can also be called **multi-manager investment**.

Hedge funds are private investment funds that are legally restricted to very wealthy individuals, individuals who have an income surpassing the requisite threshold and at least a $1 million net worth. Hedge funds are, in essence, mutual funds for the super wealthy.

CHARACTERISTICS OF HEDGE FUNDS

Hedge funds typically have limited liquidity, meaning investors cannot withdraw their investments at will. Most hedge funds have a lockup period during which investors cannot sell or redeem their investment. Hedge funds are generally much less transparent than many types of registered investments. For instance, unlike mutual funds, which are required to disclose their holdings at least every six months, hedge funds do not have to disclose holdings. This lack of available information is why only qualified or accredited investors can invest in hedge funds. Hedge funds often have a "two and twenty" expense structure, which means the hedge fund manager earns 2% of assets under management annually, as well as 20% of any profits made by the fund above a specified benchmark.

Hedge funds are similar in structure to mutual funds, but they are dissimilar in that they are unregulated (because private) and thus have a wider array of investment options. Hedge funds are characteristically very risky and speculative, using purchases on margin, short sales, and other higher-risk investment strategies to aggressively make a profit.

Hedge funds' riskiness seems to contradict their name, since hedging is the reduction of risk—but the reason for the name is that, when hedge funds historically arose, one of their main purposes was to hedge against the risk of a bear market by selling short.

Hedge funds have very limited liquidity, often keeping investors' money for at least one year.

For tax purposes, hedge funds will be arranged as limited partnerships, so that they will qualify as flow-through entities. The manager of the fund (or an affiliate) will be the general partner, and the investors will be limited partners.

HEDGE FUND STRATEGIES

Hedge funds can pursue multiple strategies, including:

Long/short equity – buying stocks (long positions) that are believed to undervalued, and selling stocks (short positions) that are believed to be overvalued, typically in the same industry

Market neutral – maintaining long and short positions of equal market value. This strategy targets zero net market exposure with returns or losses instead generated from stock selection

148

Merger arbitrage – simultaneously buying shares of the target company and selling shares of an acquiring company. Due to the risk that the merger will not close, the target company's shares will typically trade for less than the acquiring company's per share bid price. This means if the merger comes to fruition, the hedge fund will earn a profit.

Convertible arbitrage – buying a convertible bond and selling short a proportion of the stocks into which it converts. This strategy attempts delta neutrality in which the bond and stock positions offset each other as the market fluctuates.

Event-driven – buying the senior debt of companies that are in financial distress and selling short either the company's stock or a more junior class of debt. This strategy is usually employed during times of economic strength when there is a high probability of corporate reorganization.

TAX TREATMENT OF HEDGE FUND DISTRIBUTIONS

Most hedge funds are structured as limited partnerships and as such are pass-through entities, which are not subject to taxation. Distributions are taxed at the partner (i.e., hedge fund investor) level, with gains classified as either short term or long term and taxed accordingly based on the investor's income level, and interest and dividends taxed at their ordinary income tax rate.

COLLATERALIZED MORTGAGE OBLIGATIONS (CMOS)

Collateralized mortgage obligations (CMOs) are issued by private financial institutions. They are bundles of private mortgages, much like the pass-throughs that are put together by the various federal agencies. Although marketed by private companies, CMOs are usually secured with financial instruments from Ginnie Mae, Freddie Mac, and Fannie Mae, and so are rated AAA.

Mortgages are bundled by maturity dates into groups called **tranches**. In a standard CMO, all tranches receive interest payments every month, but only one tranche at a time receives principal payments.

CMOs are considered very safe because they're tied to mortgages guaranteed by the federal government, although they are not themselves backed by the government. Their yield is higher than that of government securities, and payments are received monthly, instead of every six months. There is a big market for CMOs, so they're usually quite easy to sell, although this isn't true of all of them. The more complex ones tend to have lower liquidity. **Prepayment** is a risk, and some varieties of CMOs have other risks that make them unsuitable for less experienced or less wealthy investors. All investors must sign a **suitability statement** saying that they understand the risks of CMOs before purchase.

COLLATERALIZED DEBT OBLIGATIONS (CDOS)

Collateralized debt obligations (CDOs) are similar to CMOs, also being subdivided into tranches bearing different degrees of risks and maturities. The main difference is that they are backed by debts other than mortgages, such as loans or bonds.

ASSET-BACKED SECURITIES (ABSS)

Asset-backed securities (ABSs) are securities which are backed with some sort of asset as collateral. The collateralized asset may be loans, leases, receivables, royalties, and other things. Asset-backed securities offer an alternative for many investors to corporate bonds.

TYPES OF US TREASURY SECURITIES

U.S. Treasury securities ("Treasuries") are issued by the federal government. There are three types: Treasury Bills, Notes, and Bonds. They share several characteristics.

TREASURY BILLS

Treasury bills, also known as T-bills, are short-term debt instruments backed by the U.S. government. T-bill maturities typically range from one month to one year. Denominations range from $100 to $5 million but T-bills are usually sold in $1,000 denominations. T-bills do not pay a stated interest rate; instead, they are issued at a discount and earned interest is the difference between the discount purchase price and par value paid at maturity (i.e., zero-coupon security). T-bill interest is subject to federal taxes but is exempt from state and local taxes. Individual investors can purchase T-bills directly through the U.S. Treasury website or on the secondary market.

TREASURY NOTES

Treasury notes, also known as T-notes, are debt instruments back by the U.S. government with maturities ranging from two to ten years. Denominations range from $100 to $5 million but T-notes are usually sold in $1,000 denominations. T-notes are sold at par value and pay a stated interest rate with semiannual interest payments. T-note interest is subject to federal taxes but is exempt from state and local taxes. Individual investors can purchase T-bills directly through the U.S. Treasury website or on the secondary market.

TREASURY BONDS

Treasury bonds, also known as T-bonds, are debt instruments backed by the U.S. government with maturities ranging from ten to thirty years. Denominations range from $100 to $5 million but T-bonds are usually sold in $1,000 denominations. T-bonds are sold at par value and pay a stated interest rate with semiannual interest payments. T-bond interest is subject to federal taxes but is exempt from state and local taxes. Individual investors can purchase T-bills directly through the U.S. Treasury website or on the secondary market.

TREASURY RECEIPTS AND T-STRIPS

Treasury receipts and STRIPS (Separate Trading of Registered Interest and Principal Securities) are created when a brokerage or other financial institution purchases Treasury notes or bonds directly from the U.S. Treasury then "strips" the interest payments from the principal payments and resells the principal portions as zero-coupon bonds.

TREASURY INFLATION PROTECTION SECURITIES (TIPS)

Treasury Inflation Protection Securities (TIPS) were created to attract investors by offering protection against rising inflation, which erodes the value of fixed-income securities. Every six months, the interest rate paid on TIPS is adjusted to reflect changes in the Consumer Price Index (CPI). When inflation is rising, the interest payment paid on TIPS rises; if the CPI were to drop, interest payments would be lowered. Because of this built-in protection, TIPS are sold at lower interest rates than other government securities. Any raise in interest paid due to the adjustment is taxable in the year the adjustment is received.

CHARACTERISTICS THAT US TREASURY SECURITIES HAVE IN COMMON

U.S. Treasury securities ("Treasuries") are issued by the federal government. There are three primary types: Treasury Bills, Notes, and Bonds, which share several characteristics: safe, liquid, affordable, and easy to obtain.

Safe - Treasuries are considered to be among the safest investments available because they are backed by the "full faith and credit" of the U.S. government.

Liquid - a group of more than 20 primary dealers are required to buy large quantities of Treasuries every time there is an auction and stand ready to trade them in the secondary market.

Affordable – Treasuries can be purchased in denominations as low as $100.

Easy to obtain – Treasuries can be purchased directly from the U.S. Treasury website, as well as through financial institutions, and are also actively traded in the secondary market.

Treasury security investments are subject to inflation risk (if inflation rises, the interest earned on the securities may not match inflation) and interest rate risk (the securities have fixed interest rates and if interest rates rise, the value of the securities declines).

GOVERNMENT AGENCY BONDS

Government agency bonds are not the same as U.S. Treasury or municipal bonds, but pertain to agencies of the federal government. (They also can pertain to quasi-governmental agencies, which are privately operated though either being originally part of the federal government or being sponsored by the federal government.) They are not guaranteed in the same way that Treasury securities are.

Actual federal agencies authorized to **issue debt securities** are the Farm Credit Administration and the Government National Mortgage Association (GNMA, or Ginnie Mae). Quasi-governmental agencies authorized to issue debt securities are: Federal Home Loan Mortgage Corporation (FHLMC, or Freddie Mac), Federal National Mortgage Association (FNMA, or Fannie Mae), and Student Loan Marketing Association (SLMA, or Sallie Mae). Except for Ginnie Mae, securities offered by these agencies are not backed by the full faith and credit of the U.S. government, so they pay higher interest than Treasury securities, though lower interest than private bonds.

GOVERNMENT-SPONSORED ENTERPRISES (GSEs)

Government-sponsored enterprises (GSEs) are privately-owned corporations that make borrowing easier for different groups of people (e.g., homeowners or students). Because they serve this public function, GSEs have the backing of the federal government.

Examples of GSEs are Fannie Mae, Freddie Mac, Sallie Mae, Ginnie Mae, and others.

FANNIE MAE, FREDDIE MAC, AND SALLIE MAE

Fannie Mae is the Federal National Mortgage Association, or FNMA. It is a publicly-traded company aimed at increasing homeownership among Americans with low to middle incomes by expanding the secondary mortgage market.

Freddie Mac is the Federal Home Loan Mortgage Corporation, or FHLMC. It is very similar to Fannie Mae (and thus called Fannie's "little brother"), expanding the secondary mortgage market. The main difference between the two is that Fannie generally purchases mortgages issued by banks whereas Freddie generally purchases mortgages issued by thrifts (i.e. savings and loan associations).

Sallie Mae is the Student Loan Market Association, or SLMA. It is a publicly-traded company that manages student loans, both by providing them and by buying them from other lenders.

GINNIE MAE PASS-THROUGHS

GNMA, or Ginnie Mae, pass-through securities are mortgage-backed securities whose repayment is guaranteed by the Government National Mortgage Association (GNMA) and thus backed by the full faith and credit of the federal government. GNMA does not originate the mortgage loans but purchases them from banks and other financial institutions and pools them to create securities that are sold to investors.

A pass-through security is a pool of fixed-income securities backed by a package of assets, such as home mortgages. A servicing intermediary, in this case GNMA, collects the monthly interest and principal payments and, after deducting a fee, funnels or passes them through to investors.

FINRA RULE 2114 AND RECOMMENDATIONS TO CUSTOMERS IN OTC EQUITY SECURITIES

No member is to recommend a customer purchase or sell short any OTC equity security, unless the member has reviewed the current financial statements and material business information of the issuer and determined that the information provides a reasonable basis. The registered person designated to make this review is to be a **General Securities Principal** or **General Securities Sales Supervisor** with appropriate skills, background, and knowledge. If the issue has not met any of its necessary filing requirements, the review is to include inquiry about the circumstances of the failure to file, and any subsequent recommendation to a customer is to be in writing.

FINRA RULE 2121 AND FAIR PRICING FOR SERVICES AND TRANSACTION COSTS

FINRA Rule 2121 states that in securities transactions, whether in "listed" or "unlisted" securities, if a member buys for his own account from his customer, or sells for his own account to his customer, he must buy or sell at a price which is fair, taking into consideration all relevant circumstances, including: market conditions at the time of the transaction, the expense involved, and the fact that he is entitled to a profit.

If he acts as agent for his customer in any such transaction, he must not charge more than a fair commission or service charge, taking into consideration all relevant circumstances, including market conditions at the time of the transaction, the expense of executing the order and the value of any service he may have rendered by reason of his experience in and knowledge of such security and the market.

5% RULE

In 1943, the NASD Board adopted what has become known as the "5% Policy" to be applied to transactions executed for customers. It was based upon studies demonstrating that the large majority of customer transactions were affected at a mark-up of 5% or less. The 5% rule is a guideline rather than a strict rule in FINRA Rule 2121, but it may be referenced. Factors that should be considered in setting a fair price include:

1. The Type of Security Involved - Some securities customarily carry a higher mark-up than others. For example, a higher percentage of mark-up customarily applies to a common stock transaction than to bond transactions of the same size.
2. The Availability of the Security in the Market - If a security is not actively traded and is difficult to acquire or requires unusual effort, a higher mark-up may be justified.
3. The Price of the Security - As the security price declines, the transaction costs may rise. Even where the amount of money is substantial, transactions in lower priced securities may require more handling and expense and may warrant a wider spread.

4. The Amount of Money Involved in a Transaction - A transaction that involves a small amount of money may warrant a higher percentage of mark-up to cover the expenses of handling.
5. Disclosure - Any disclosure to the customer before the transaction is affected of information which would indicate the amount of commission charged in an agency transaction or mark-up made in a principal transaction is a factor to be considered. Disclosure itself, however, does not justify a commission or mark-up that is unfair or excessive in light of all other relevant circumstances.
6. The Pattern of Mark-Ups - While each transaction must meet the test of fairness, the Board believes that particular attention should be given to the pattern of a member's mark-ups.
7. The Nature of the Member's Business - The Board is aware of the differences in the services and facilities which are needed by, and provided for, customers of members. If not excessive, the cost of providing such services and facilities, particularly when they are of a continuing nature, may properly be considered in determining the fairness of a member's mark-ups.

FINRA RULE 2122 AND CHARGES FOR SERVICES PERFORMED

FINRA Rule 2122 states that charges, if any, for services performed, including, but not limited to, miscellaneous services such as collection of monies due for principal, dividends, or interest; exchange or transfer of securities; appraisals, safe-keeping or custody of securities, and other services must be reasonable and not unfairly discriminatory among customers.

FINRA RULE 2124 AND NET TRANSACTIONS WITH CUSTOMERS

Net transactions with customers (FINRA Rule 2124) - a member executing a net transaction with a customer must first disclose it and obtain consent from the customer. A net transaction is a when a member, after receiving an order from a customer, purchases the security at a different price and subsequently sells it to the customer to fulfill the original order, keeping the proceeds that make up the difference in price.

REQUIREMENTS OF DIRECT PARTICIPATION PROGRAMS

Direct participation program (program) — a program which provides for flow-through tax consequences regardless of the structure of the legal entity or vehicle for distribution including, but not limited to, oil and gas programs, real estate programs, agricultural programs, cattle programs, condominium securities, Subchapter S corporate offerings and all other programs of a similar nature, regardless of the industry represented by the program, or any combination thereof.

Requirements:

- Offering - members may not underwrite or participate in a public offering for a REIT/DPP unless standards of suitability have been established by the program and disclosed in the prospectus.
- Recommending - members must have reasonable grounds to believe the investor will be able to benefit from the tax benefits or other benefits of the REIT/DPP (for example someone in a low tax bracket may never benefit from the tax losses generated).
- Files - members must keep files to document how suitability was determined. Members must have direct written approval from the customer.
- Disclosure - members must obtain adequate disclosure from the REIT/DPP (prospectus, minimum specific facts, etc.) before participating. The member must inform prospective investors of the pertinent facts, including the timeframe of the investment.

- Fees - members must not underwrite or participate in a REIT/DPP offering unless the Organization and Offering fees are fair and reasonable. Defined: 15% maximum, trail commissions to underwriters/broker-dealers 10% maximum. Limited compensation to members associated with the REIT/DPP.
- Prohibitions of various opaque types of REIT/DPP. Non-Cash compensation is limited and must comply with SEA Rule 151-1, Regulation Best Interest.

REQUIREMENTS FOR COMPLETING THE SALE OF A VARIABLE CONTRACT

FINRA Rule 2320 deals with sales of variable contracts of insurance companies. The Rule defines variable contracts as contracts providing for benefits or values which may vary according to the investment experience of any separate or segregated account or accounts maintained by an insurance company. Key provisions of the Rule include:

Receipt of Payment – payments are not deemed to be received until the contract application has been accepted by the insurance company.

Transmittal - members must transmit applications and payments promptly.

Selling Agreements - members cannot sell through other dealers unless the dealers are also FINRA members and there is a sales agreement in effect between the parties. Sales commissions must be refunded if the variable contract is redeemed within seven days of acceptance.

FINRA RULE 2341 AND COMPENSATION TO ASSOCIATED PERSONS FOR SALES OF MUTUAL FUNDS AND VARIABLE ANNUITIES

FINRA Rules 2341 (Investment Company Securities, section l) and 2320 (Variable Contracts of Insurance Companies, section g) set compensation rules for associated persons of a member. The Rules state that associated persons must only accept compensation from the member with which the person is associated, barring specific exceptions.

The Rules also state that no member or person associated with a member may accept any compensation from an offeror which is in the form of securities of any kind, and that no member may accept any cash compensation from an offeror unless such compensation is described in a current prospectus. A member must maintain records of all compensation received by the member or its associated persons from offerors. The records must include the names of the offerors, the names of the associated persons, the amount of cash, the nature and, if known, the value of non-cash compensation received.

The Rules prohibit members or persons associated with a member from directly or indirectly accepting or making payments or offers of payments of any non-cash compensation, except as provided below:

- gifts that do not exceed $100 per person in value and are not preconditioned on achieving a sales target
- occasional meals, tickets to movies, theater or other similar entertainment if not too extensive as to be inappropriate, and not preconditioned on achieving sales targets
- payment or reimbursement related to meetings held by an offeror, if recorded and approved by the member, and not preconditioned on achieving a sales target

FINRA RULE 2341 AND SALES CHARGES ON SALES OF OPEN-END COMPANIES

FINRA Rule 2341, Section D addresses sales charges for sales of shares of open-end companies. The Rule prohibits excessive sales charges and includes a number of provisions that help ensure that charges are not excessive.

For Investment Companies **without Asset-Based Sales Charges**, sales charges may not exceed 8.5% of the offering price. If rights of accumulation (e.g., quantity discounts) are made available on single purchases, they must conform to one of the following two alternatives:

- A maximum aggregate sales charge of 7.75% on purchases of $10,000 or more and a maximum aggregate sales charge of 6.25% on purchases of $25,000 or more.
- A maximum aggregate sales charge of 7.50% on purchases of $15,000 or more and a maximum aggregate sales charge of 6.25% on purchases of $25,000 or more.

If an investment company without an asset-based sales charge pays a service fee, the maximum aggregate sales charge may not exceed 7.25% of the offering price.

INVESTMENT COMPANIES WITH ASSET-BASED SALES CHARGES

For Investment Companies **with Asset-Based Sales Charges**, the aggregate asset-based, front-end and deferred sales charges described in the prospectus, if the investment company has adopted a plan under which **service fees are paid**, shall not exceed 6.25% of total new gross sales plus interest charges on such amount equal to the prime rate plus one percent per annum.

If an investment company with an asset-based sales charge **does not pay a service** fee, the aggregate asset-based, front-end and deferred sales charges described in the prospectus shall not exceed 7.25% of total new gross sales plus interest charges on such amount equal to the prime rate plus one percent per annum.

No member may offer or sell the shares of an investment company with an asset-based sales charge if:

- The amount of the asset-based sales charge exceeds .75 of 1% per annum of the average annual net assets of the investment company.
- Any deferred sales charges deducted from the proceeds of a redemption after the maximum cap described has been attained are not credited to the investment company.

INDEX WARRANTS, CURRENCY INDEX WARRANTS, AND CURRENCY WARRANTS

FINRA Rule 2351 defines the following types of warrants:

Index warrants - instruments that are direct obligations of the issuing company entitling the holder to a cash settlement in U.S. dollars to the extent that the value of the underlying stock index group has declined below (in the case of a put warrant) or increased above (in the case of a call warrant) the pre-stated cash settlement value of the underlying stock index group.

Currency index warrants - instruments that are direct obligations of the issuing company entitling the holder to a cash settlement in U.S. dollars to the extent that the value of the underlying currency index has declined below (in the case of a put warrant) or increased above (in the case of a call warrant) the pre-stated cash settlement value of the underlying currency index.

Currency warrants - instruments that are direct obligations of the issuing company entitling the holder to a cash settlement in U.S. dollars to the extent that the value of the underlying foreign currency has declined below (in the case of a put warrant) or increased above (in the case of a call warrant) the pre-stated cash settlement value of the underlying foreign currency.

The FINRA 2350 series of rules apply to the conduct of accounts, the execution of transactions, and the handling of orders in exchange-listed stock index warrants, currency index warrants, and currency warrants by members who are not members of the exchange on which the warrant is listed or traded.

DEFINITIONS RELATED TO OPTIONS, CURRENCY WARRANTS, CURRENCY INDEX WARRANTS AND STOCK INDEX WARRANT TRANSACTIONS

Option — the term "option" shall mean any put, call, straddle or other option or privilege, which is a "security" as defined in Section 2(1) of the Securities Act.

Call - an option giving the holder the right to purchase a security or receive a dollar equivalent of an index.

Put – an option giving the holder the right to sell a number of units of the underlying security or deliver a dollar equivalent of the underlying index.

Straddle - a type of combination options strategy where the investor either purchases a call and a put (long straddle) or sells a call and a put (short straddle) on the same underlying instrument, with both having the same expiration date and exercise price.

Currency Index Warrant - direct obligation of the issuing company entitling the holder thereof to a cash settlement in U.S. dollars to the extent that the value of the underlying currency index has declined below (in the case of a put warrant) or increased above (in the case of a call warrant) the pre-stated cash settlement value of the underlying currency index.

Currency Warrant - direct obligation of the issuing company entitling the holder thereof to a cash settlement in U.S. dollars to the extent that the value of the underlying foreign currency has declined below (in the case of a put warrant) or increased above (in the case of a call warrant) the pre-stated cash settlement value of the underlying foreign currency.

Index Warrants - direct obligation of the issuing company entitling the holder thereof to a cash settlement in U.S. dollars to the extent that the value of the underlying stock index group has declined below (in the case of a put warrant) or increased above (in the case of a call warrant) the pre-stated cash settlement value of the underlying stock index group.

SECTION 9(A) OF THE SECURITIES EXCHANGE ACT AND MANIPULATION OF SECURITY PRICES

Section 9(a) of the Securities Exchange Act of 1934 deals with activity designed to create the appearance of trading to manipulate the price of a security. It states that it is unlawful for any person, directly or indirectly, or for any member of a national securities exchange—for the purpose of creating a false or misleading appearance of active trading in any security other than a government security, or a false or misleading appearance with respect to the market for any such security to:

- effect any transaction in such security which involves no change in the beneficial ownership
- enter an order for the purchase of such security with the knowledge that an order of substantially the same size, at substantially the same time, and at substantially the same price, for the sale of any such security, has been or will be entered by or for the same or different parties
- enter any order or orders for the sale of any such security with the knowledge that an order or orders of substantially the same size, at substantially the same time, and at substantially the same price, for the purchase of such security, has been or will be entered by or for the same or different parties

PENNY STOCKS

Definition of penny stock (SEC Rule 3a51-1) - Rule 3a51-1 defines penny stock by describing what a penny stock is not. The definition includes any equity security that:

A. is not a security continuously registered on a national securities exchange;

B. is not a registered security on a national securities exchange that meets certain criteria;

C. is not issued by an investment company registered by the Investment Company Act of 1940;

D. is not a put or call option from an Options Clearing Corporation;

E. does not have a price of $5 or more.

EXEMPTIONS FROM THE RULES FOR CERTAIN TRANSACTIONS

Exemptions for certain transactions (SEC Rule 15g-1) - the following transactions are exempt from Rules 15g-2, 15g-3, 15g-4, 15g-5, and 15g-6:

A. Transactions by a broker/dealer whose commissions from penny stock transactions do not exceed 5% of total commissions and who has not been a market maker in a penny stock.

B. Transactions with an institutional investor as the customer.

C. Transactions that meet the requirements in Regulation D.

D. Transactions with the issuer, director, or other person who owns more than 5% of the issuers stock as the customer.

E. Transactions that are not recommended by the broker/dealer.

F. Other transactions exempted by the SEC.

RISK DISCLOSURE DOCUMENT AND DISCLOSURE OF QUOTATIONS

Risk disclosure document relating to the penny stock market (SEC Rule 15g-2) - a broker/dealer must have the customer sign a Schedule 15G document before transacting in penny stocks in the customer's account. The broker/dealer cannot transact in penny stocks on behalf of the customer within two days of sending such document, and must keep a copy of this document in records.

Broker or dealer disclosure of quotations and other information relating to the penny stock market (SEC Rule 15g-3) - a broker/dealer must disclose to the customer the inside bid/offer quotes and the number of shares applicable before transacting in penny stock on behalf of the customer.

DISCLOSURE OF COMPENSATION TO BROKERS OR DEALERS AND THE DISCLOSURE OF COMPENSATION OF ASSOCIATED PERSONS

Disclosure of compensation to brokers or dealers (SEC Rule 15g-4) - a broker/dealer must disclose to the customer the total compensation received in connection with transaction before transacting in penny stock on behalf of the customer.

Disclosure of compensation of associated persons in connection with penny stock transactions (SEC Rule 15g-5) - a broker/dealer must disclose to the customer the total compensation received by any associated person of the broker/dealer in connection with the transaction before transacting in penny stock on behalf of the customer.

ACCOUNT STATEMENTS AND SALES PRACTICE REQUIREMENTS FOR CERTAIN LOW PRICED SECURITIES

Account statements for penny stock customers (SEC Rule 15g-6) - a broker/dealer must send a monthly account statement to customers within ten days following the end of the month during which they have transacted in penny stocks.

Sales practice requirements for certain low-priced securities (SEC Rule 15g-9) - a broker/dealer must approve a customer's account for trading in penny stocks using specific criteria. The broker/dealer must receive an agreement from the customer to a specific transaction in penny stocks, and cannot make the transaction until after two days from sending such document to the customer.

INVESTMENT COMPANY ACT OF 1940

The Investment Company Act of 1940 defines the requirements of investment companies and for any publicly traded investment product offerings, such as open-end mutual funds, closed-end mutual funds, and unit investment trusts. It is enforced and regulated by the Securities and Exchange Commission.

Among the key definitions set forth in the Act are:

Investment company - any issuer which is or holds itself out as being engaged primarily in the business of investing, reinvesting, or trading in securities; is engaged or proposes to engage in the business of issuing face-amount certificates of the installment type, or has been engaged in such business and has any such certificate outstanding; or is engaged or proposes to engage in the business of investing, reinvesting, owning, holding, or trading in securities, and owns or proposes to acquire investment securities having a value exceeding 40% of the value of such issuer's total assets (exclusive of Government securities and cash items) on an unconsolidated basis.

Investment securities - all securities except Government securities, securities issued by employees' securities companies, and securities issued by majority-owned subsidiaries of the owner which are not investment companies, and are not relying on the exception from the definition of investment company.

CLASSES OF INVESTMENT COMPANIES

Investment companies are divided into three principal classes, defined as:

Face-amount certificate company - an investment company which is engaged or proposes to engage in the business of issuing face-amount certificates of the installment type, or which has been engaged in such business and has any such certificate outstanding.

Unit investment trust - an investment company which is organized under a trust indenture, contract of custodianship or agency, or similar instrument, does not have a board of directors, and issues only redeemable securities, each of which represents an undivided interest in a unit of specified securities; but does not include a voting trust.

Management company - any investment company other than a face-amount certificate company or a unit investment trust.

TYPES OF MANAGEMENT COMPANIES DEFINED UNDER THE 1940 ICA

The Investment Company Act of 1940 classifies management companies as either:

- Open-end - a management company which is offering for sale or has outstanding any redeemable security of which it is the issuer; or
- Closed-end company - any management company other than an open-end company

Management companies are further classified as either:

- Diversified - a management company which meets the following requirements: at least 75% of the value of its total assets is represented by cash and cash items (including receivables), government securities, securities of other investment companies, and other securities for the purposes of this calculation limited in respect of any one issuer to an amount not greater in value than 5% of the value of the total assets of such management company and to not more than 10% of the outstanding voting securities of such issuer.
- Non-diversified - any management company other than a diversified company.

INVESTMENT ADVISERS

Section 202(a)(11) of the Act defines an investment adviser as any person or firm that (1) for compensation (2) is engaged in the business of (3) providing advice to others or issuing reports or analyses regarding securities. A person must satisfy all three elements to fall within the definition of investment adviser.

INTERESTED PERSONS

Section 10 of the Investment Company Act of 1940 states that an investment company may not have a board of directors that is comprised of more than 60% of members who are interested persons in the company.

If by reason of the death, disqualification, or bona fide resignation of any director or directors, the requirements of this provision are not met, such provision shall be suspended

- for a period of thirty days if the vacancy or vacancies may be filled by action of the board of directors
- for a period of sixty days if a vote of stockholders is re-quired to fill the vacancy or vacancies

- for such longer period as the Commission may prescribe, by rules and regulations upon its own motion or by order upon application, as not inconsistent with the protection of investors

PRACTICES THAT REGISTERED INVESTMENT COMPANIES ARE PROHIBITED FROM ENGAGING IN

Section 12a of the Investment Company act of 1940 states that it is unlawful for a registered investment company to engage in the following practices:

- to purchase any security on margin, except such short- term credits as are necessary for the clearance of transactions
- to participate on a joint or a joint and several basis in any trading account in securities, except in connection with an underwriting in which such registered company is a participant
- to effect a short sale of any security, except in connection with an underwriting in which such registered company is a participant

ACTIONS THAT REGISTERED INVESTMENT COMPANIES ARE PROHIBITED FROM TAKING

Section 13a of the Investment Company Act of 1940 prohibits registered investment companies, unless authorized by the vote of a majority of its outstanding voting securities to:

- change its classification as open-end or closed-end company or its subclassification from a diversified to a non-diversified company
- borrow money, issue senior securities, underwrite securities issued by other persons, purchase or sell real estate or commodities or make loans to other persons, except in each case in accordance with the policies contained in its registration statement
- deviate from its policy in respect of concentration of investments in any particular industry or group of industries as recited in its registration statement, or deviate from any investment policy which is changeable only if authorized by share-holder vote
- change the nature of its business so as to cease to be an investment company

CONTRACT REQUIREMENTS OF INVESTMENT ADVISERS OF REGISTERED INVESTMENT COMPANIES

Section 15a of the Investment Company Act of 1940 requires that any person serving or acting as an investment adviser of a registered investment company have a written contract in place that has been approved by the vote of a majority of the outstanding voting securities of such registered company, and includes the following elements:

- precisely describes all compensation to be paid
- includes a statement that the contract shall continue in effect for a period more than two years from the date of its execution, only so long as such continuance is specifically approved at least annually by the board of directors or by vote of a majority of the outstanding voting securities of such company
- provides, in substance, that it may be terminated at any time, without the payment of any penalty, by the board of directors of such registered company or by vote of a majority of the outstanding voting securities of such company on not more than sixty days' written notice to the investment adviser
- provides, in substance, for its automatic termination in the event of its assignment

PROVISIONS FOR FILLING VACANCIES ON THE BOARD OF DIRECTORS

Section 16a of the Investment Company Act of 1940 states that no person may serve as a director of a registered investment company unless elected to that office by the holders of the outstanding voting securities of such company, at an annual or a special meeting duly called for that purpose. In cases where vacancies occur between such meetings, they may be filled in any otherwise legal manner, if after filling the vacancy at least two-thirds of the directors then holding office have been elected by the holders of the outstanding voting securities.

If at any time less than a majority of the directors holding office were elected by the holders of the outstanding voting securities, the board of directors must hold a meeting as promptly as possible, and in any event within sixty days, for the purpose of electing directors to fill any existing vacancies, unless the SEC extends such period. This provision does not apply to members of an advisory board.

Nothing in this section precludes a registered investment company from dividing its directors into classes if its organization document so provides and prescribes the tenure of office of the several classes. However, no class may be elected for a shorter period than one year or for a longer period than five years and the term of office of at least one class expires each year.

TYPES OF TRANSACTIONS THAT ARE PROHIBITED BY AFFILIATED PERSONS OF A REGISTERED INVESTMENT COMPANY

Section 17a of the Investment Company Act states that it is unlawful for any affiliated person or promoter of or principal underwriter for a registered investment company or any affiliated person acting as principal to engage in any of the following:

- knowingly sell any security or other property to such registered company or to any company controlled by such registered company, unless such sale involves solely securities of which the buyer is the issuer, securities of which the seller is the issuer and which are part of a general offering to the holders of a class of its securities, or securities deposited with the trustee of a unit investment trust or periodic payment plan by the depositor
- knowingly purchase from such registered company, or from any company controlled by such registered company, any security or other property (except securities of which the seller is the issuer)
- borrow money or other property from such registered company or from any company controlled by such registered company (unless the borrower is controlled by the lender)
- loan money or other property to such registered company, or to any company controlled by such registered company, in contravention of such rules

ASSET COVERAGE RATIO REQUIREMENTS OF CLOSED-END INVESTMENT COMPANIES WHEN ISSUING SENIOR SECURITIES WHICH REPRESENT AN INDEBTEDNESS

Section 18 of the Investment Company Act of 1940 states that it is unlawful for any registered closed-end company to issue any class of senior security, or to sell any such security of which it is the issuer, unless the following conditions are met.

If such class of senior security represents an indebtedness:

- immediately after such issuance or sale, it has an asset coverage of at least 300%
- provision is made to prohibit the declaration of any dividend, unless it maintains an asset coverage of at least 300% (200% for preferred stock)
- provision is made either that, if asset coverage falls below 100% at the end of a 12-month period, the holders of such securities are entitled to elect at least a majority of the board of directors until an asset coverage of at least 110% is reached, or if it falls below 100% at the end of a 24-month period a default is deemed to have occurred

161

ASSET COVERAGE RATIO REQUIREMENTS OF CLOSED-END AND OPEN-END INVESTMENT COMPANIES WHEN ISSUING SENIOR SECURITIES WHICH ARE STOCKS

If such class of senior security is a stock:

- immediately after such issuance or sale it will have an asset coverage of at least 200%
- provision is made to prohibit the declaration of any dividend, unless it maintains an asset coverage of at least 200%
- provision is made to entitle the holders of such senior securities to elect at least two directors at all times, and to elect a majority of the directors if at any time dividends are in arrears for more than two years
- provision is made requiring approval by the vote of a majority of such securities of any plan of reorganization adversely affecting such securities
- such class of stock has complete priority over any other class as to distribution of assets and payment of dividends, which dividends shall be cumulative

Section 18 also states that a registered open-end company is permitted to borrow from any bank, provided that immediately after any such borrowing there is an asset coverage of at least 300%, and that in the event that asset coverage falls below 300%, within three days the borrowing amount is reduced to achieve asset coverage of at least 300%.

SOURCES FROM WHICH REGISTERED INVESTMENT COMPANIES MAY MAKE DIVIDEND PAYMENTS

Section 19 of the Investment Company Act of 1940 states that it is unlawful for any registered investment company to pay any dividend from any source other than accumulated undistributed net income, not including profits or losses realized upon the sale of securities or other properties; or net income so determined for the current or preceding fiscal year, unless the payment is accompanied by a written statement that adequately discloses the source of such payment in a form prescribed by the SEC.

Section 19 also states that it is unlawful in contravention of such rules for any registered investment company to distribute long-term capital gains more often than once every twelve months.

ROLE OF FINRA IN OVERSEEING THE DISTRIBUTION AND REDEMPTION OF REDEEMABLE REGISTERED INVESTMENT SECURITIES

Section 22 of the Investment Company Act of 1940 states that a securities association registered under Section 15A of the Securities Exchange Act of 1934 (i.e., FINRA) may prescribe:

- a method or methods for computing the minimum price at which a member may purchase a redeemable security issued by an investment company and the maximum price at which a member may sell to such company any redeemable security so that the price in each case bears a relationship to the current net asset value of the security
- a minimum period after the sale or issue of such security before any resale or redemption by a member can be executed

This section also prohibits a registered open-end company from restricting the transferability or negotiability of any security of which it is the issuer except in conformity with its registration statement, and states that a registered open-end company may not issue any of its securities in exchange for services or property other than cash or securities, except as a dividend or distribution to its security holders or in connection with a reorganization.

CIRCUMSTANCES UNDER WHICH A REGISTERED CLOSED-END COMPANY MAY SELL SECURITIES OF WHICH IT IS THE ISSUER

Section 23 of the Investment Company Act of 1940 prohibits a registered closed-end company from issuing any of its securities in exchange for services or property other than cash or securities, except as a dividend or distribution or in connection with a reorganization.

It also states that a registered closed-end company may not sell any common stock of which it is the issuer at a price below the current net asset value of such stock, exclusive of any distributing commission or discount, except in the following situations:

- in connection with an offering to the holders of one or more classes of its capital stock
- with the consent of a majority of its common stockholders
- upon conversion of a convertible security in accordance with its terms
- upon the exercise of any warrant outstanding
- under such other circumstances as the Commission may permit by rules and regulations or orders for the protection of investors

CIRCUMSTANCES UNDER WHICH A REGISTERED CLOSED-END COMPANY MAY PURCHASE SECURITIES OF WHICH IT IS THE ISSUER

Additionally, a registered closed-end company may not **purchase** any securities of any class of which it is the issuer, except in the following situations:

- on a securities exchange or such other open market as the Commission may designate, provided that if such securities are stock, that the company inform stockholders of its intention to purchase stock by letter within the preceding six months
- pursuant to tenders, after reasonable opportunity to submit tenders is given to all holders of securities of the class to be purchased
- under such other circumstances as the Commission may permit

FINANCIAL STATEMENT REPORTING REQUIREMENTS TO SHAREHOLDERS AND THE SEC

Section 30 of the Investment Company Act of 1940 states copies of every periodic or interim report containing financial statements and transmitted to the company's security holders must be filed not later than ten days after such transmission. Every registered investment company must transmit to its stockholders, at least semiannually, reports containing the following information and financial statements as of a reasonably current date:

- a balance sheet accompanied by a statement of the aggregate value of investments on the date of such balance sheet
- a list showing the amounts and values of securities owned on the date of such balance sheet
- a statement of income, for the period covered by the report, which shall be itemized at least for each category of income and expense representing more than 5% of total income or expense
- a statement of surplus, which shall be itemized at least for each charge or credit to the surplus account which represents more than 5% of total charges or credits during the period
- a statement of the aggregate remuneration paid by the company during the period to all directors and to all members of any advisory board for regular or special compensation; to all officers; and to each person of whom any officer or director is an affiliated person
- a statement of the aggregate dollar amounts of purchases and sales of investment securities, other than Government securities, made during the period

Financial statements contained in annual reports required pursuant to this section must be accompanied by a certificate of independent public accountants.

DECEPTIVE OR MISLEADING NAMES

Section 34 of the Investment Company Act of 1940 states that it is unlawful for any person, issuing or selling any security of which a registered investment company is the issuer, to represent or imply in any manner whatsoever that such security or company:

- has been guaranteed, sponsored, recommended, or approved by the United States, or any agency, instrumentality or officer of the United States
- has been insured by the Federal Deposit Insurance Corporation
- is guaranteed by or is otherwise an obligation of any bank or insured depository institution

Additionally, any person issuing or selling the securities of a registered investment company that is advised by, or sold through, a bank must prominently disclose that an investment in the company is not insured by the Federal Deposit Insurance Corporation or any other government agency.

It shall be unlawful for any registered investment company to adopt as a part of the name or title of such company, or of any securities of which it is the issuer, any word or words that the Commission finds are materially deceptive or misleading. The Commission is authorized, by rule, regulation, or order, to define such names or titles as are materially deceptive or misleading.

The Rule prohibits the use of the following naming conventions, unless the fund has adopted a policy to invest, under normal circumstances, at least 80% of the value of its Assets in the particular type of investments suggested by the fund's name:

- Names suggesting investment in certain investments or industries
- Names suggesting investment in certain countries or geographic regions, unless the fund has adopted a policy to invest, under normal circumstances
- Names suggesting that the fund's distributions are exempt from federal income tax or from both federal and state income tax

Funds must provide shareholders with at least 60 days prior notice of any change in the policy and such notice must be provided in plain English in a separate written document and contain the following prominent statement, or similar clear and understandable statement, in bold-face type: "Important Notice Regarding Change in Investment Policy."

CIRCUMSTANCES UNDER WHICH A COURT ACTION CAN BE BROUGH AGAINST A PERSON ACTING IN A FIDUCIARY CAPACITY

Section 36 of the Investment Company Act of 1940 states that the Commission is authorized to bring an action in the proper court of the United States alleging that a person who is or was serving or acting in one or more of the following capacities has engaged in any act or practice constituting a breach of fiduciary duty involving personal misconduct:

- as officer, director, member of any advisory board, investment adviser, or depositor
- as principal underwriter, if such registered company is an open-end company, unit investment trust, or face-amount certificate company

If such allegations are established, the court may enjoin such persons from acting in any or all such capacities either permanently or temporarily and award such injunctive or other relief against such person as may be reasonable and appropriate in the circumstances.

Additionally, an action may be brought by the Commission or by a security holder of such registered investment company on behalf of such company, against an investment adviser or affiliated person who has a fiduciary duty and received compensation or payments, for breach of fiduciary duty.

This Section does not apply to compensation or payments made in connection with transactions subject to Section 17, or to sales loads for the acquisition of any security issued by a registered investment company.

For the purposes of this section, the term "investment adviser" includes a corporate or other trustee performing the functions of an investment adviser.

LARCENY AND EMBEZZLEMENT

Section 36 of the Investment Company Act of 1940 states that whoever steals, unlawfully abstracts, unlawfully and willfully converts to his own use or to the use of another, or embezzles any of the moneys, funds, securities, credits, property, or assets of any registered investment company will be deemed guilty of a crime, and upon conviction thereof will be subject to the penalties provided in Section 49. A judgment of conviction or acquittal on the merits under the laws of any State will be a bar to any prosecution under this section for the same act or acts.

RESTRICTIONS ON REGISTERED OPEN-END MANAGEMENT INVESTMENT COMPANIES IN THE DISTRIBUTION OF SHARES

Rule 12b-1 of the Investment Company Act of 1940 states that it is unlawful for any registered open-end management investment company to act as a distributor of securities of which it is the issuer, except through an underwriter, unless any payments made by the company in connection with such distribution are made pursuant to a written plan and that all agreements with any person relating to implementation of the plan are in writing.

Such a plan must meet the following requirements:

- be approved by a vote of at least a majority of the outstanding voting securities of the company, if a public company
- be approved by a vote of the board of directors at a meeting called for the purpose of voting on such plan or agreements
- be specifically approved at least annually
- provide that any person authorized to direct the disposition of monies furnishes to the board of directors, and the directors reviews, at least quarterly, a written report of the amounts and purposes of expenditures; an
- provide that the plan may be terminated at any time by vote of a majority of the members of the board of directors of the company who are not interested persons of the company or by vote of a majority of the outstanding voting securities of such company

CONDITIONS WHICH CAUSE A COMPANY TO BE DEEMED TO BE ACTING AS A DISTRIBUTOR OF SECURITIES OF WHICH IT IS THE ISSUER

A company may not compensate a broker or dealer for any promotion or sale of shares issued by that company by directing to the broker or dealer securities transactions or any remuneration.

For purposes of this section, a company will be deemed to be acting as a distributor of securities of which it is the issuer if it engages directly or indirectly in financing any activity which is primarily intended to result in the sale of shares, including advertising, compensation of underwriters, dealers, and sales personnel, the printing and mailing of prospectuses to other than current shareholders, and the printing and mailing of sales literature.

KEY TERMS IN CBOE RULE 1.1

Cboe Rule 1.1 defines the following terms:

Trading Permit - a license issued by the Exchange that grants the holder or the holder's nominee the right to access one or more of the facilities of the Exchange for the purpose of effecting transactions in securities traded on the Exchange.

Associated Person and Person Associated with a Trading Permit Holder – any partner, officer, director, or branch manager of a Trading Permit Holder, any person directly or indirectly controlling, controlled by, or under common control with a Trading Permit Holder, or any employee of a Trading Permit Holder.

Broker-Dealer - a Trading Permit Holder, a non-Trading Permit Holder broker or dealer in securities (including a foreign broker-dealer), or a joint venture with a Trading Permit Holder and non-Trading Permit Holder participants.

Designated Primary Market-Maker and DPM - a TPH organization that is approved by the Exchange to function in appointed securities as a Market-Maker and is subject to the obligations under Rule 5.54 or as otherwise provided under the Rules.

Market-Maker - a Trading Permit Holder registered with the Exchange pursuant to Rule 3.52 for the purpose of making markets in option contracts traded on the Exchange and that has the rights and responsibilities set forth in Chapter 5, Section D of the Rules.

Clearing Trading Permit Holder - a Trading Permit Holder that has been admitted to membership in the Clearing Corporation pursuant to the provisions of the Rules of the Clearing Corporation and is self-clearing or that clears transactions for other Trading Permit Holders.

Proprietary Trading Permit Holder - a Trading Permit Holder who is authorized to obtain access to the System to submit proprietary orders that are not Market-Maker orders.

Order - a firm commitment to buy or sell option contracts.

Put - an option contract under which the holder of the option has the right to sell to the Clearing Corporation (a) for equity options, the number of units of the underlying security covered by the option contract, at a price per unit equal to the exercise price, or (b) for index options, the current index value times the index multiplier upon the timely exercise of the option.

Call - an option contract under which the holder of the option has the right to purchase from the Clearing Corporation (a) for equity options, the number of units of the underlying security covered by the option contract, at a price per unit equal to the exercise price, or (b) for index options, the current index value times the index multiplier upon the timely exercise of the option.

Covered - the term "covered" in respect of a short position in a call option contract means that the writer's obligation is secured by a "specific deposit" or an "escrow deposit" or the writer holds in the same account as the short position, on a share-for-share basis, a long position either in the underlying security or in an option contract of the same class of options where the exercise price of the option contract in such long position is equal to or less than the exercise price of the option contract in such short position.

Expiration Date - the third Friday of the expiration month of an option contract, or if that Friday is a day on which the exchange is not open for business, the preceding day on which it is open for business.

Short Position - a person's interest as the writer of one or more option contracts.

Long Position - a person's interest as the holder of one or more option contracts.

Closing Purchase Transaction - an Exchange transaction that reduces or eliminates a short position in an option contract.

Closing Writing Transaction - an Exchange transaction that reduces or eliminates a long position in an option contract.

Opening Purchase Transaction - a transaction that creates or increases a long position in an option contract.

Opening Writing Transaction - a transaction that creates or increases a short position in an option contract.

CBOE RULE 4.5(F) AND REQUIREMENTS FOR LISTING LEAPS

Cboe Rule 4.5(f) states that the Exchange may list long-term equity option series (LEAPS) that expire from 12 to 180 months from the time they are listed. There may be up to ten additional expiration months for options on the SPDR S&P 500 ETF and up to six additional expiration months for all other option classes.

CBOE RULE 4.6 AND ADJUSTING OPTIONS CONTRACTS

Cboe Rule 4.6 states that options contracts are subject to adjustments in accordance with the Rules of the Options Clearing Corporation (OCC). OCC has sole discretion for adjustment decisions to ensure those decisions are consistent, efficient and free from undue influence. Generally, the OCC will adjust contracts to reflect the results of corporate actions, such as splits or mergers. Among the items OCC may adjust on a contract are expiration date, symbol, strike price, multiplier and contract size.

CBOE RULE 6.20E AND AMERICAN-STYLE INDEX OPTIONS

Cboe Rule 6.20(e) states that no Trading Permit Holder may at any time prepare, time stamp or submit an exercise instruction for an American-style index option series if the Trading Permit Holder knows or has reason to know that the exercise instruction calls for the exercise of more contracts than the then "net long position" of the account for which the exercise instruction is to be tendered.

For purposes of this Rule, the term "net long position" means the net position of the account in such option at the opening of business of the day of such exercise instruction, plus the total number of such options purchased that day in opening purchase transactions up to the time of exercise, less the total number of such options sold that day in closing sale transactions up to the time of exercise.

CBOE RULE 6.21 AND ALLOCATION OF EXERCISE NOTICES

Cboe Rule 6.21 states that each TPH organization must establish fixed procedures for the allocation of exercise notices assigned in respect of a short position in such TPH organization's customers' accounts. The allocation must be on a "first in, first out", or automated random selection basis that has been approved by the Exchange, or on a manual random selection basis that has been specified by the Exchange.

Each TPH organization must report its proposed method of allocation to the Exchange and obtain the Exchange's prior approval thereof, and no TPH organization shall change its method of allocation unless the change has been reported to and approved by the Exchange. Each TPH organization must also inform its customers in writing of the method it uses and must preserve for a three-year period sufficient work papers and other documentary materials relating to the allocation of exercise notices to establish the manner in which allocation of such exercise notices is in fact being accomplished.

CBOE RULE 8.1 AND PROHIBITED ACTIVITIES FOR TPH

Cboe Rule 8.1 states that no Trading Permit Holder may engage in acts or practices inconsistent with just and equitable principles of trade. Persons associated with Trading Permit Holders must have the same duties and obligations as Trading Permit Holders.

Among the activities prohibited by Chapter 8 of the Cboe Rules are:

- engaging in conduct in violation of the Securities Exchange Act of 1934, the Bylaws or the Rules of the Exchange, or the Rules of the Clearing Corporation
- giving compensation or gratuity in any one year in excess of $50.00 to any employee of the Exchange or in excess of $100.00 to any employee of any other Trading Permit Holder or of any non-Trading Permit Holder broker, dealer, bank or institution, without the prior consent of the employer and of the Exchange
- employing any person in a nominal position on account of business obtained by such person
- making willful or material misrepresentations
- effecting or inducing the purchase, sale or exercise of any security for the purpose of creating or inducing a false, misleading, or artificial appearance of activity in such security or in the underlying security
- circulating rumors of a character which might affect market conditions in any option contract or underlying security; provided, however, that this shall not prohibit discussion of unsubstantiated information, so long as its source and unverified nature are disclosed

CBOE RULE 8.30 AND POSITION LIMITS

Cboe Rule 8.30 states that no Trading Permit Holder may make, for any account in which it has an interest or for the account of any customer, an opening transaction if it has reason to believe that as a result of such transaction the Trading Permit Holder or its customer would, acting alone or in concert with others, directly or indirectly, control an aggregate position in an option contract in excess of 25,000, 50,000, 75,000, 200,000, or 250,000 (depending on trading volume of the underlying security), whether long or short of the put type and the call type on the same side of the market respecting the same underlying security, combining for purposes of this position limit long positions in put options with short positions in call options, and short positions in put options with long positions in call options.

For example, a customer who is long 25,000 calls on Stock A, may at the same time be short 25,000 calls on Stock A, since long call and short call positions in the same class of options are on opposite sides of the market. On the other hand, a customer who is long 20,000 calls on Stock A, may not at the same time be short more than 5,000 puts on Stock A, since the 25,000-contract limit applies to the aggregation of long call and short put positions in options covering the same underlying security.

CBOE RULE 8.31 AND POSITION LIMITS ON BROAD-BASED INDEX OPTION CONTRACTS

Cboe Rule 8.31 states that in determining compliance with Rule 8.30 there are no position limits for broad-based index option contracts (including reduced-value option contracts and micro-option contracts on Cboe S&P 500 AM/PM Basis, Cboe S&P 500 Three-Month Realized Variance, Cboe S&P 500 Three-Month Realized Volatility and on the BXM (1/10th value), DJX, OEX, XEO, NDX, RUT, VIX, VXN, VXD, VXST, S&P 500 Dividend Index, and SPX classes).

All other broad-based index option contracts are subject to a contract limitation fixed by the Exchange.

CBOE RULE 8.32 AND POSITION LIMITS ON INDUSTRY INDEX OPTIONS

In determining compliance with Rule 8.30, option contracts on an industry index are subject to the following position limits:

- 18,000 contracts if the Exchange determines that any single underlying stock accounted, on average, for 30% or more of the index value during the 30-day period immediately preceding the review
- 24,000 contracts if the Exchange determines that any single underlying stock accounted, on average, for 20% or more of the index value or that any five underlying stocks together accounted, on average, for more than 50% of the index value, but that no single stock in the group accounted, on average, for 30% or more of the index value, during the 30-day period immediately preceding the review
- 31,500 contracts if the Exchange determines that the conditions specified above which would require the establishment of a lower limit have not occurred

The Exchange shall make the determinations with respect to options on each industry index at the commencement of trading of such options on the Exchange and thereafter review the determination semi- annually on January 1 and July 1.

CBOE RULE 8.41 AND POSITION LIMITS ON INTEREST RATE OPTIONS

Cboe Rule 8.41 states that in determining compliance with Rule 8.30, interest rate options are subject to a contract limitation (whether long or short) of the put class and the call class on the same side of the market covering no more than 5,000 contracts in the case of an option on an interest rate measure respecting a short-term Treasury Security or Securities; and 25,000 contracts in the case of an option on an interest rate measure respecting a long-term Treasury Security or Securities.

Bona fide hedging positions held in the aggregate by a public customer are exempt from the 25,000-contract limit to the extent that specified procedures and criteria are satisfied.

CBOE RULE 8.42(B) AND EXEMPTIONS TO THE EXERCISE LIMITS ON INDEX OPTIONS

Cboe Rule 8.42(b) states that in determining compliance with exercise limits for index option contracts excluding those for broad-based indexes for which there are no exercise limits), the following criteria apply to situations that qualify for exemption:

- For a Market-Maker granted an exemption to position limits pursuant to Rule 8.30.05, the number of contracts which can be exercised over a five-business day period shall equal the Market-Maker's exempted position
- CAPS and Q-CAPS will not be included when calculating exercise limits for index option contracts

- With respect to index options contracts for which an exemption has been granted in accordance with the provisions of Rule 8.31, the exercise limit shall be equal to the amount of the exemption
- With respect to Individual Stock or ETF Based Volatility Index options contracts for which an exemption has been granted in accordance with the provisions of Rule 8.34.01, the exercise limit shall be equal to the amount of the exemption

CBOE RULE 8.42(F)

Cboe Rule 8.42(f) states that exercise limits for interest rate options shall be equivalent to the position limits prescribed in Rule 8.41.

CBOE RULE 6.20 AND CUT-OFF TIMES FOR TRADING

Cboe Rule 6.20 states that the Exchange may establish procedures and cutoff times for the submission of exercise advices for noncash-settled equity options. In the event the Exchange provides advance notice, on or before 5:30 p.m. on the business day immediately prior to the last business day before the expiration date, indicating that a modified time for close of Regular Trading Hours in noncash-settled equity options on the last business day before expiration will occur, the deadline to make a final decision to exercise or not exercise an expiring option shall be 1 hour 30 minutes following the time announced for the close of Regular Trading Hours on that day.

CONTRARY EXERCISE ADVICE (CEA)

A Contrary Exercise Advice ("CEA", also known as "Expiring Exercise Declaration" or "EED") is a communication to either exercise or not exercise an option that would be automatically exercised under the Clearing Corporation's Ex-by-Ex procedure.

"Ex-by-ex" is an administrative procedure used by the Options Clearing Corporation in which options that are in the money by specified threshold amounts are exercised unless a clearing member submits instructions not to exercise the options.

MUNICIPAL FUND SECURITIES

MSRB Rule D-12 defines "municipal fund security" as a municipal security issued by a company that (if not issued for a government entity) would be an investment company per the Investment Company Act of 1940.

The Investment Company Act of 1940 defines an investment company as any issuer which is either primarily in the business of investing, reinvesting, or trading in securities; in the business of issuing face-amount certificates; or in the business of investing, reinvesting, owning, holding, or trading in securities, and owns or proposes to acquire investment securities having a value exceeding 40% of the value of such issuer's total assets (exclusive of Government securities and cash items) on an unconsolidated basis.

The MSRB has regulatory responsibility for local government pools and higher education trusts when they meet the following three conditions:

- A dealer is conducting transactions in the trusts
- The trusts constitute municipal securities
- The trusts are issued by an issuer that would be considered an investment company, except for its exemption under the Investment Company Act

MSRB RULE G-13

MSRB Rule G-13 states that no broker, dealer or municipal securities dealer shall distribute or publish, or cause to be distributed or published, any quotation relating to municipal securities, unless:

- the quotation represents a bona fide bid for, or offer of, municipal securities by such broker
- dealer or municipal securities dealer
- the price stated in the quotation is based on the best judgment of such broker, dealer or municipal securities dealer of the fair market value of the securities at the time the quotation is made

MSRB RULE G-17

MSRB Rule G-17 states that each broker, dealer, municipal securities dealer, and municipal advisor shall deal fairly with all persons and shall not engage in any deceptive, dishonest or unfair practice in its conduct of municipal securities or municipal advisory activities.

MSRB RULE G-30

MSRB Rule G-30 states that no broker, dealer or municipal securities dealer may purchase municipal securities for its own account from a customer or sell municipal securities for its own account to a customer (i.e., principal transactions), except at an aggregate price (including any mark-up or mark-down) that is fair and reasonable.

The Rule also states that each broker, dealer and municipal securities dealer, when executing a transaction in municipal securities for or on behalf of a customer as agent, must make a reasonable effort to obtain a price for the customer that is fair and reasonable in relation to prevailing market conditions and must not purchase or sell municipal securities as agent for a customer for a commission or service charge in excess of a fair and reasonable amount.

MSRB RULE G-45

MSRB Rule G-45 states that each underwriter of a primary offering of municipal fund securities that are not interests in local government investment pools must report to the Board the information relating to such offering required by Form G-45 by no later than 60 days following the end of each semi-annual reporting period ending on June 30 and December 31 and in the manner prescribed in the Form G-45 procedures and as set forth in the Form G-45 Manual; however, performance data must only be reported annually by no later than 60 days following the end of the reporting period ending on December 31. All submissions of information required under this Rule must be made by means of Form G- 45 submitted in a designated electronic format to the Board.

OWNERSHIP RESTRICTIONS ON REITS

The REIT Modernization Act of 1999 allowed REITs to own up to 100% of the stock of taxable REIT subsidiaries (TRSs), which can provide services to REIT tenants, without jeopardizing their tax status as a REIT. TRSs, however, may not account for more than 25% of the REIT's total assets. The Act also lowered the percentage of taxable income a REIT must distribute from 95% (where it had been since 1980) to 90%.

TAXATION RULES RELATED TO DISTRIBUTIONS OF PROPERTY

Distributions of property are covered under IRS Rule 301 (26 CFR § 301). Distributions can be cash or property, and the value of the cash or property, less liabilities, creates taxable earnings and/or gains. Per section 301(c), the portion of a distribution that is a dividend (as defined in § 316) is included in gross income, and the remaining portion of the distribution is applied first against the adjusted basis of the stock and then treated as gain from the sale or exchange of property. For anyone who holds 20% or more of a company's stock, IRS Rule 312 applies instead.

IRS Rule 316

IRS Rule 316 defines a dividend as any distribution of property by a corporation to its shareholders out of its earnings and profits. The IRS uses last-in-first-out (LIFO) to determine which profits and earnings are distributed, meaning the most recent profits and earnings are distributed first.

IRS Rule 856

IRS Rule 856 define a Real Estate Investment Trust as a special trust that meets the following criteria:

- is managed by one or more trustees or directors
- ownership is by transferable shares or certificates
- would otherwise be taxable as a domestic corporation
- is neither a financial institution referred to in section 582(c)(2), nor an insurance company to which subchapter L applies
- is owned by 100 or more persons
- is not closely held

Additionally, a REIT must satisfy the following income and valuation tests:

- at least 75% of its gross income must be derived from real estate-related sources
- at least 75% of the value of its assets must consist of cash and cash items, real estate assets, and Government securities

IRS Rule 858

According to IRS Rule 858, if a real estate investment trust (REIT) declares a dividend before the time for the filing of its return for a taxable year (including the period of any extension), and distributes such dividend in the 12-month period following the close of such taxable year and not later than the date of the first regular dividend payment made after such declaration, the amount shall, to the extent the trust elects, be considered as having been paid only during such taxable year.

However, these amounts shall be treated as received by the shareholder or holder of a beneficial interest in the taxable year in which the distribution is made. Any notice to shareholders or holders of beneficial interests required under this part with respect to such amounts shall be made not later than 30 days after the close of the taxable year in which the distribution is made (or mailed to its shareholders or holders of beneficial interests with its annual report for the taxable year).

IRS Rule 1035

IRS Rule 1035 allows for the exchanges of insurance products without a tax consequence in the following situations:

- Exchanging an annuity contract for another annuity contract
- Exchanging a life insurance policy for another life insurance policy, endowment policy, or annuity contract
- Exchanging an endowment policy for an endowment policy or an annuity contract
- Exchanging a life insurance policy or an annuity contract for a long-term care insurance policy

To qualify as a tax-free 1035 Exchange, the contract or policy owner cannot accept receipt of funds and cannot change the owner, insured or annuitant.

IRS RULE 1091

IRS Rule 1091 disallows a tax deduction for a loss from the sale of a security if the taxpayer buys, though the same account or different account over which he has control, a substantially similar security within 30 days before or after the sale. Such a transaction is known as a wash sale. For example, if a taxpayer buys 100 shares of XYZ stock at $100 per share ($10,000) on January 2 then sells it for $90 per share on February 1 (a loss of 10x100 = $1,000), then buys it again on March 1 for $85 (100x85=$8,500), he or she would not be allowed to benefit from the $1,000 loss incurred on February 1.

If a transaction is deemed to be a wash sale, the loss is added to the basis of the replacement purchase and the holding period extends back to the original purchase date. For example, the stock purchased on March 1 would have an additional $1,000 of cost basis attributed to it (8,500+1,000=$9,500 basis, or $95 per share), and the stock would be considered held since January 2.

IRS RULE 1233

According to IRS Rule 1233, for income tax purposes, the recognized gain or loss from a short sale is either a capital gain or loss or ordinary gain or loss depending on whether the property constitutes a capital asset in the hands of the taxpayer.

For instance, an ordinary gain or loss results when a short sale closes if the stock used by a dealer to close the short sale was stock which was held primarily for sale to customers in the ordinary course of trade or business, while a capital gain or loss results if the stock used to close the short sale was a capital asset in the dealer's or taxpayer's hands.

The period that a taxpayer holds the property delivered to close a short sale determines whether it is a long-term or short-term capital gain or loss. If a taxpayer makes a short sale of stock and covers it by delivering shares which he held for not more than 1 year, the recognized gain or loss would be considered a short-term capital gain or loss. If the short sale is made through a broker and the broker borrows the stock to make delivery, the short sale is not considered consummated until the obligation of the seller created by the short sale is finally discharged by delivery of the stock to the broker to replace the stock borrowed by the broker.

IRS RULE 1256

IRS Rule 1256 defines a 1256 contract as any of the following:

- any regulated futures contract,
- any foreign currency contract
- any nonequity option,
- any dealer equity option
- any dealer securities futures contract

Each section 1256 contract held by the taxpayer at the close of the taxable year must be treated as sold for its fair market value on the last business day of such taxable year (and any gain or loss shall be taken into account for that taxable year).

Any gain or loss with respect to a section 1256 contract must be treated as:

- a short-term capital gain or loss, to the extent of 40 percent of such gain or loss
- long-term capital gain or loss, to the extent of 60 percent of such gain or loss

Providing Required Disclosures Regarding Investment Products and their Characteristics, Risks, Services, and Expenses

OUTSIDE BUSINESS ACTIVITIES TO REPORT

Registered representatives are required to disclose **outside business activities** which would betray an "**adverse interest**" against the representative's own employer. RRs are permitted to execute trades for people employed at other firms, but they must exercise "**reasonable diligence**" to ensure that such trades do not unduly harm their own employers.

In case a RR does have an interest in an account at another firm, that firm is obligated to notify the RR's employer in writing, deliver duplicate documents for the account, and notify the RR of it doing those two things. This must be done before any transactions are conducted for the account.

Outside business activities can include personal investment accounts which the RR holds elsewhere than his own firm.

FINRA RULE 2262 AND RULE 2269

Rule 2262 states that if common control exists between a member firm and the issuer of a security, the firm must disclose the relationship in writing to any customer wanting to buy or sell said security. For example, if Firm A is selling an equity security in Company B to a customer and Firm A and Company B have a common majority owner, this relationship has to be disclosed to the customer.

Rule 2269 states that if a firm is participating in or has a financial interest in any security either in primary or secondary distribution, this has to be disclosed in writing to the customer. For example, if a firm will receive a financial gain from a specific equity security, this must be disclosed to the customer before selling this same equity to a customer.

PRIVATE SECURITIES TRANSACTIONS

Private securities transactions are transactions where the broker sells a security not recognized or ordinarily sold by his own broker-dealer and/or receives compensation for the transaction. Such transactions are regulated, since registered representatives are forbidden from using their own brokerage firm as mere fronts for less safe transactions. If a broker engages in a private securities transaction which departs from established regulations (such as FINRA Rule 3040), then the broker commits the crime of "**selling away**."

TYPES OF INVESTMENT RISK

Currency risk is the risk that investments will be harmed through changes in currency exchange rates. This type of risk is a problem for international investors.

Inflationary risk is the risk that investments will substantively decrease in value due to the devaluation of the dollar through inflation.

Interest rate risk is the risk that investments will be harmed through fluctuations in interest rates. This type of risk particularly affects bond and mortgage holders.

Liquidity risk is the risk that an investor will not be able to liquidate his assets when he wishes. The investor may want to sell some particular asset, but there may not be much of a market at a price that the investor finds worthwhile.

Systematic market risk is the risk intrinsic to the market taken as a whole or to a market segment. It is the risk that is unavoidable in some capacity, the risk that cannot be diversified away. Since nothing is certain with investments, there will always be some market risk inherent in the system.

Nonsystematic market risk is the risk associated with specific firms, rather than with the market as a whole. This type of risk, unlike systematic market risk, is diversifiable.

Political or legislative risk is the risk that investments could be harmed through some political events or unrest, whether domestically or abroad.

Prepayment risk is the risk that an investment which depends upon some stream of fixed income in the future (such as a bond) will have its principal repaid earlier than expected. This would reduce the overall expected gain on the investment.

Reinvestment risk is the risk that interest or dividends which one receives from different investments have to be reinvested at a lower rate of return.

Timing risk is simply the risk that an investor might make some transaction at the wrong, failing to minimize his losses or maximize his gains.

Call risk is the chance that a callable bond will be called, causing the bondholder to lose the stream of interest payments left until maturity. Because bonds are generally called when interest rates are going lower, the bondholder will have a hard time getting a comparable interest rate with the money received if the bond is called. When calling bonds, the company usually calls the highest coupon bonds first. Bonds may also have a call premium written into the indenture - the call premium protects the investors against losing too much of the expected coupon payment value if the company calls the bonds too soon before the expiration date. The call premium could also be triggered by the bondholders if the debtor company has a change in ownership or management - the call premium is often a type of "poison pill" or cost that can stop a takeover unless the bondholders agree to terms with the new owners/managers. In addition to the call premium that is paid, callable bonds usually have a call protection feature—a period of time during which the issuer may not call the bonds, usually five to ten years in duration.

Capital risk is the risk of losing all the capital one has invested, particularly for options and warrants. Such securities have expiration dates, and therefore investors can lose all their money at those dates. Purchasing investment-grade bonds can help reduce this risk.

Credit risk is the risk for a creditor that principal and interest on a loan he has given will not be paid back to him on time. Bond rating agencies (e.g., Moody's, Standard & Poor's, and Fitch) help investors to properly rate bond investments for their credit risk.

Price Risk is the risk that the value of a security will decrease. A security price could decrease from a variety of factors: earnings volatility, from market changes (i.e., market risk), legislative changes (legislative, tax, or regulatory risk), poor business management (management risk), or any other factor that might change the prices.

Reinvestment Risk - the risk that when coupon payments or dividends are made, the investor will not be able to reinvest those payments at a rate equivalent to the current rate of the security. For

example, the coupon payment of a bond bought at par with a 20% coupon rate may no longer be able to be invested into an investment with a 20% return due to falling interest rates. **Zero coupon bonds are not subject to reinvestment risk since they make no coupon payments - they are bought at a discount. When contemplating Bond Investments for bonds with coupon payments, the greater the duration of the bond, the greater the Price and Reinvestment Risk. Two features of bonds affect the price volatility in response to changes in market interest rates. A bond with a lower coupon rate will be more volatile than a bond with a higher coupon rate. Also, longer-term bonds are more volatile than bonds with a shorter time to maturity.

TYPES OF INVESTMENT RETURNS

A **dividend** is a portion of the company's profit that is returned to shareholders. A dividend can come in the form of cash, in which case a check is sent to the owner or to the owner's brokerage account. When dividends are paid in cash, they are considered income, and taxes must be paid on them during the tax year they're received. Dividends can also be in the form of additional shares of stock given to shareholders. These are not taxable until they're sold, just like all stocks. Because this type of stock dividend increases the number of outstanding shares, it decreases the market value of each share, but does not affect the total market value of the company.

Interest is the fee charged for the use of another's money. It is often expressed as an annual percentage rate (APR). Interest can also be simple or compound; compound interest periodically adds the outstanding interest to the principal, thus increasing the rate at which interest generates.

Tax-exempted interest is interest income that it not subject to federal income tax. Municipal bonds provide tax-exempted interest.

Whenever an investor sells a security for more than he paid for it (the security's cost basis), the investor has received a **capital gain**. If the investor held the security for more than a year, then it is considered a long-term capital gain, and is given favorable tax treatment; it is only taxed at 15 percent. If the investor held the security for less than a year before the sale, it is considered a short-term capital gain, and is taxed at the investor's regular income tax rate, which for most people is higher than 15 percent.

If the investor sells a security for less than its cost basis, then he or she has a **capital loss**. If, after adding up all the investor's capital gains and capital losses for the tax year, it turns out that the investor has a net capital loss, he or she may use that capital loss to offset taxes against earned income, up to a limit of $3,000 a year.

If an investor has an investment returned to him in part or in whole, such that he is not gaining anything beyond the original investment, then it is a **return of capital** (which is very different from return on capital). This is not taxed or considered as income, because it is simply a return of the original investment.

COSTS AND FEES ASSOCIATED WITH INVESTMENTS

When a broker facilitates an investment transaction for you and then charges you some fee for providing that service, he is receiving a **commission**. However, when he does not merely facilitate a trade, but actually acts as a principal—trading securities using his own account—then the profit he makes on such a transaction will occur from an increased price on the security over the price at which he obtained it: a **markup**.

If you take an investment transaction and deduct the commission or fee paid to the broker, you are left with the **net transaction**: what the transaction is when considered by itself.

When investing in shares, one can purchase different kinds of shares, organized into different **share classes** based on the privileges and rights associated with those shares. Firms can charge different fees based on different share classes.

Fee-based accounts differ from other accounts—commission-based accounts—since fee-based accounts compensate the advisor based on a percentage of the client's assets, rather than as a commission for transactions facilitated.

SOFT DOLLAR ARRANGEMENTS

Soft dollar arrangements are set up between broker-dealers and investment advisers, where the investment advisers receive benefits (e.g. research) in exchange for directing trades towards the broker-dealer. They are opposed to **hard dollar arrangements**, which are ordinary transactions of cash.

COST BASIS OF STOCKS GIVEN AS GIFTS OR AS AN INHERITANCE

Stocks acquired as **gifts** will have a basis equal to the donor's basis unless they have decreased in value since the donor acquired them. In that case, their new basis is their value at the time of donation. If they have increased in value since the donor acquired them, the basis for the gift recipient will still equal the donor's basis.

Stock acquired by **inheritance** will have a basis equal to the value per share at the point of the bequeather's death. All securities acquired by inheritance are automatically taxed as long-term.

ANNUAL GIFT TAX EXCLUSION, LIFETIME GIFT TAX EXEMPTION, AND UNIFICATION OF GIFT AND ESTATE TAXES

Gift taxes have an annual exclusion amount of $17,000 for 2023. This means that a person can give gifts to anyone (or any number of people), up to $17,000 per person, without incurring any federal gift tax. Gifts given to U.S. citizen spouses do not count towards this $17,000.

Gift taxes also have a **lifetime exemption amount**. If a person gives gifts in excess of the annual exclusion amount, then those excess gifts will still not be federally taxable so long as they do not exceed the lifetime exemption amount, which is $12,920,000 for 2023. If a person gives $18,000 worth of gifts in a year, and if the annual exclusion amount is $17,000, then the extra $1,000 in gifts will reduce the lifetime exemption amount by $1,000.

Such a large lifetime exemption amount may seem inconsequential for most people, but it is relevant to some. Tax law contains a **unification of gift and estate taxes**, such that the lifetime exemption amount for gift taxes is unified with estate taxes. Specifically, if someone gives gifts in excess of the annual exclusion amount (and thus credits those excess gifts against the lifetime exemption amount), the exemption amount for estate tax will be reduced as well—the amount of assets he can transfer to others upon his death, apart from federal taxation, will be reduced by whatever amount by which his lifetime exemption amount for gift taxes is credited.

SOURCES OF MARKET AND INVESTMENT INFORMATION

Research reports are documents prepared by investment research teams for brokerage firms or investment banks (or by individual analysts in such teams). Research reports can cover a wide array of topics.

Pricing services are, quite simply, entities which provide different prices for stocks and other tradeable assets.

Product-specific periodicals are publications released to provide information on particular products or investment strategies.

Sources of Information

Since a broker should clearly not be concerned only with the changes in prices for stocks and other investments, but ought to be aware of the underlying causes for such investments, he needs to have **good sources of information** on business conditions, business activities, and corporate profits. Information on these topics can come from a wide variety of sources, such as media outlets, but the more easily accessible the sources are, generally speaking, the more careful the broker should be about using them. A broker can also find good data by studying business indices and statistics, as well as U.S. government sources, in order to gain a better perspective on various business and economic data.

Measures of Market Sentiment, Momentum, and Movement

Market sentiment refers to the prevailing consensus attitude of investors toward a market or particular security. Rising prices signal a bullish sentiment and falling prices a bearish sentiment. A common measurement of sentiment is the VIX Index (also known as the "fear" index), which represents the market's expectations for volatility over the next 30 days. A rising VIX indicates greater volatility while a falling VIX indicates less market volatility.

Market momentum refers to the aggregate acceleration or deceleration of a market or security. It is measured as the rate in change of price over a specified period of time.

Market Indices

Market indices are numbers reporting an aggregate value from the combination of several securities' individual values. These indices are valued at a given date and presented in comparison to their base value from some earlier date. The securities which compose the market indices are selected so that the indices can report the market's performance as a whole. A prominent example of a market index is the S&P 500 Index.

Volatility

Volatility is the degree to which a security's price has fluctuated (or will fluctuate) within a given time period, whether it has increased or decreased. Volatility can be distinguished between **historical volatility** (HV), which measures the changes in a security's price over a prior time period, and **implied volatility** (IV), which is the estimated degree of volatility for a security's price in the future—what various market factors imply about the security's potential behavior.

Options volatility is the application of volatility measures to options transactions. The premiums for options are related directly to the volatility for the underlying security; higher volatility increases the option premium, and vice versa.

Put-Call Ratio

The **put-call ratio** is a comparison of the total trading volume of put options in the market to call options.

This ratio is utilized to analyze market sentiment, determining whether that sentiment is bearish or bullish. Since the buyer of a put option gains the right to sell a security in the future, a higher put-call ratio generally signals a bearish market, where investors desire to sell their securities before the price drops further. The opposite is the case for a lower ratio.

SHORT INTEREST

Short interest is the number of shares which investors have sold short but not yet closed out—that is, the number of shares which investors have borrowed and sold, but have not yet repurchased (to return the shares to the lenders). Since the purpose of selling short is to sell the borrowed security at a higher price at which it is later repurchased, a high number of total securities sold short in the market shows that investors believe the market price for many securities will drop. As such, short interest is one way to measure market sentiment.

Expressed mathematically, short interest will be measured as the percentage of shares sold short in comparison to the total number of shares outstanding.

INDEX FUTURES

Index futures are a type of futures contract which correspond to a particular market index. The relation between the index and the price at which the futures contract is fixed may vary among different types of index futures, but they all are similar in their correspondence to a market index.

Portfolio managers will often use index futures as a hedge against risks in their other investments. Many index futures are linked to the S&P 500 Index.

THE BOND BUYER AND MUNIFACTS

The Bond Buyer and *Munifacts* are the two main sources of information on **municipal bonds**, both for new issues and for the trading market for already issued bonds. *The Bond Buyer* comes out every day, and is the authoritative source of municipal bond information. Every Friday it publishes the total volume of bond offerings expected to come to market in the next 30 days, which is known as the 30-day visible supply, and the placement ratio index, which is the percentage of last week's offerings that actually sold. *The Bond Buyer's* companion publication is *Munifacts*, which is delivered by wire to terminals in offices and contains bond news and price information.

VARIOUS BOND BUYER INDICES

Just as the S&P 500 Index is an index commonly used in understanding the stock market, there are a number of **bond indices** to help in understanding the bond market. *The Bond Buyer* presents a number of these helpful indices.

The *20-Bond GO Index* (also called "Bond Buyer 20" or the "20 Bond Index") is an index based on the average yield of twenty municipal general obligation (GO) bonds, all of which have A ratings or better, with twenty years until their maturity date.

The *11-Bond GO Index* (also called "Bond Buyer 11" or the "11 Bond Index") is an index derived from the 20-Bond GO Index. Eleven bonds are taken from the twenty bonds comprising the 20-Bond GO Index, only those with AA ratings or better, and an index is based on them.

The *25 Revenue Bond Index* (also called the "RevDex") is an index representing the average yield for twenty-five different revenue bonds, all of which have A ratings or better, with thirty years to maturity.

The *Municipal Bond Index* (also called the "40-Bond Index") is an index representing the average price of forty highly traded general obligation and revenue bonds, all of which have A ratings or better, with twenty years as their average maturity.

TRENDLINES, SAUCERS, AND INVERTED SAUCERS

Though stocks may fluctuate seemingly unpredictably in a short period of time, they tend to have a definite pattern, a **trendline**, over longer spans of time. If the stock price is gradually increasing over time, then it is in an uptrend, and if the opposite is the case, then it is in a downtrend.

Saucers are a particular type of trendline involving an initial decrease in stock prices followed by an increase. Because the stock first dips before increasing, it looks like a flattened "u," or a saucer. The reverse is the case with **inverted saucers**; they initially increase and then drop in price.

HEAD-AND-SHOULDERS AND INVERTED HEAD-AND-SHOULDERS PATTERNS

Head-and-shoulders patterns are more complicated than saucers. They involve three peaks in the stock price, with the second one being the highest (just as a head is higher than two shoulders on each side). The other two peaks are roughly the same "height," though not necessarily. Between each peak, the stock price dips to some minimum and then rises up to the next peak. After the third peak, the stock price decreases.

Inverted head-and-shoulders patterns are the opposite, having three troughs rather than three peaks, and signaling a stock price increase at the end of the fluctuation.

BEARISH AND BULLISH TRENDS

In all of these trends, the **final activity** of the stock is crucial in determining whether the pattern signifies a **bearish** or a **bullish** trend. For example, saucers and inverted head-and-shoulders patterns both increase at the end of their fluctuation, so they indicate bullish trends; but the head-and-shoulders pattern and the inverted saucer are both bearish signs, since they decrease at the end.

CONSOLIDATION, SUPPORT LEVELS, RESISTANCE LEVELS, AND BREAKOUTS

Consolidation occurs when a stock's trendline is relatively flat over a significant period of time, when its price remains within a particular and narrow trading channel or trading range. When this pattern is plotted on a graph, the minimum price at which the stock is exchanged within this time period is its **support level**, while the maximum price is its **resistance level**. If a stock price exits this channel—whether decreasing below the support level or increasing above the resistance level—then a **breakout** is occurring: the stock is leaving its previous horizontal trend and beginning a new one.

OVERBOUGHT AND OVERSOLD STOCKS

Stocks are **overbought** if their prices have increased beyond their true value, being unjustifiably increased by speculation or other artificial causes. If a stock is overbought, then it has likely reached its peak price and will be declining soon, in which case it would be wise to sell. Similarly, when stock is **oversold**, their prices are artificially lower than their true value, so the proper course of action is to buy.

One possible indicator for this is by comparing the pattern of stock prices in relation to a significant market index, such as the Dow Jones Industrial Average or the S&P 500.

MOVING AVERAGES IN TECHNICAL ANALYSIS

Since stock prices fluctuate to a notable degree on a daily basis, it can be difficult to track long-term patterns of stock price. To solve this, various **moving averages** of stock prices are used, giving an average price of the stock for a given time period, and then plotting those average prices over a period of time to smooth out the stock's price pattern.

There are different kinds of moving average which emphasize different factors in their calculation.

MOVING AVERAGES

A **simple moving average (SMA)** is the most common method, calculated by taking the sum of all the closing prices for a given time period and dividing it by the number of instances used. For instance, a five-day SMA will take the previous five days' closing prices and divide it by five.

A **linear weighted average** places more weight on more recent stock prices within the specified time period. For instance, a five-day linear weighted average might multiply the most recent closing price by five, the next by four, the next by three, etc., and then divide the whole sum of those multiplied prices by the sum of the multipliers (in this case, 5+4+3+2+1=15). This average is the least common method used.

An **exponential moving average (EMA)** also places more weight on more recent stock prices, but uses a smoothing factor that is understood to be more efficient than the linear average in responding to stock price changes. The calculation is more complicated, so most traders complete the calculations electronically.

ACCUMULATION/DISTRIBUTION INDEX

The **accumulation/distribution index** is utilized in technical analysis in order to gauge market momentum at a given time. The goal is to determine whether stocks are being purchased (accumulated) or sold (distributed), and this is done through an analysis of the stock's price and its volume flow. The particular formula is as follows:

$$\frac{A}{D} = \frac{(close - low) - (high - close)}{high - low} \times period's\ volume$$

$Close$ = closing price

Low = low price

$High$ = high price

The goal of this formula is to spot a divergence between the volume flow and the stock price, thus signifying that a current stock trend is about to end.

TECHNICAL ANALYSTS

Whereas fundamental analysts work on determining which securities to purchase, technical analysts work on determining the proper time to purchase a given security. This is done through an analysis of various stock patterns, both for the market as a whole and for individual stocks, with the presupposition that stocks' past activity is an indicator for its future activity. Technical analysts are sometimes referred to as chartists, and they believe that the future course of the market can be determined.

UPTRENDS, DOWNTRENDS, AND CONSOLIDATION

Uptrends occur where prices are making higher highs and higher lows. Up trendlines connect at least two of the lows and show support levels below price.

Downtrends occur where prices are making lower highs and lower lows. Down trendlines connect at least two of the highs and indicate resistance levels above the price.

Consolidation, or a sideways market, occurs where price is oscillating between an upper and lower range, between two parallel and often horizontal trendlines.

CONTINUATION PATTERNS

A continuation pattern denotes a temporary interruption of an existing trend. Common continuation patterns include:

- Flags, drawn with two parallel trendlines
- Pennants, constructed using two converging trendlines
- Wedges, constructed with two converging trendlines, where both are angled either up or down
- Triangles are similar to wedges and pennants, and occur frequently compared to other patterns. The three most common types of triangles are symmetrical triangles, ascending triangles, and descending triangles. These chart patterns can last anywhere from a couple of weeks to several months.
- The cup and handle is a bullish continuation pattern where an upward trend has paused, but will continue when the pattern is confirmed.
    - The "cup" portion of the pattern should be a "U" shape that resembles the rounding of a bowl rather than a "V" shape with equal highs on both sides of the cup.
    - The "handle" forms on the right side of the cup in the form of a short pullback that resembles a flag or pennant chart pattern. Once the handle is complete, the stock may breakout to new highs and resume its trend higher.

EXAMPLES OF REVERSING PATTERNS

When price reverses after a pause, the price pattern is known as a reversal pattern. There are two main types of reversal patterns: bullish and bearish.

- Head and Shoulders, signaling two smaller price movements surrounding one larger movement, generally signaling the reversal of a trend. A topping head and shoulders is bearish (it signals the end of a bullish trend) and an inverse head and shoulders is bullish (it signals the end of a bearish trend)
- Double Tops, representing a short-term swing high, followed by a subsequent failed attempt to break above the same resistance level (i.e., reversal of a bullish trend)
- Double Bottoms, showing a short-term swing low, followed by another failed attempt to break below the same support level (i.e., reversal of a bearish trend)

EVENTS IMPACTING A MUNICIPAL SECURITIES ISSUER THAT MUST BE DISCLOSED

SEC Rule 15c2-12 is designed to prevent fraudulent, deceptive, or manipulative acts or practices, and mandates that any broker, dealer, or municipal securities dealer acting as an underwriter in a primary offering of municipal securities ensure that the state or local government issuing the bonds provide certain information about the securities on an ongoing basis. Among the required disclosures is notification of specific events that have the potential to affect the ability of the government to pay, the value of the bonds if they are bought or sold prior to maturity, or the timing of repayment. The specific events that must be disclosed include:

- Principal and interest payment delinquencies
- Non-payment related defaults
- Unscheduled draws on debt service reserves reflecting financial difficulties
- Unscheduled draws on credit enhancements reflecting financial difficulties
- Substitution of credit or liquidity providers, or their failure to perform

- Adverse tax opinions or events affecting the tax-exempt status of the security
- Modifications to rights of security holders
- Bond calls and tender offers
- Defeasances
- Release, substitution or sale of property securing repayment of the securities
- Rating changes
- Bankruptcy, insolvency or receivership
- Merger, acquisition or sale of all issuer assets
- Appointment of successor trustee
- Financial obligation1 incurrence or agreement
- Default, event of acceleration, termination event, modification of terms or other similar events under the terms of a financial obligation of the obligated person, any of which reflect financial difficulties.

FINANCIAL EXPLOITATION OF SPECIFIED ADULTS

FINRA Rule 2165 provides protection from financial exploitation for adults over 65 or anyone over 18 who the member reasonably believes has a mental or physical impairment that renders the individual unable to protect his or her own interests.

"Financial exploitation" means:

- the wrongful or unauthorized taking, withholding, appropriation, or use of a Specified Adult's funds or securities
- any act or omission by a person, including through the use of a power of attorney, guardianship, or any other authority regarding a Specified Adult, to: obtain control, through deception, intimidation or undue influence, over the Specified Adult's money, assets or property; or to convert the Specified Adult's money, assets or property

PROTECTING ACCOUNTS OF SPECIFIED ADULTS

A member may place a temporary hold on a disbursement of funds or securities from the Account of a Specified Adult if the member reasonably believes that financial exploitation of the Specified Adult has occurred, is occurring, has been attempted, or will be attempted. Within two business days the member must provide notification of the temporary hold and the reason to all parties authorized to transact business on the Account and the Trusted Contact Persons, unless a party is unavailable or the member reasonably believes that the party has engaged, is engaged, or will engage in the financial exploitation of the Specified Adult. The temporary hold will expire within 15 business days but may be extended for no longer than 10 business days, if the member's internal review supports a reasonable belief that the financial exploitation has occurred, is occurring, has been attempted or will be attempted.

The member must also immediately initiate an internal review of the facts and circumstances. A member relying on this Rule must establish and maintain written supervisory procedures reasonably designed to achieve compliance with this Rule. Members must retain all relevant records pertaining to temporary holds placed on the Accounts of Specified Adults.

EXERCISING INVESTMENT DISCRETION REGARDING PAYMENT OF COMMISSION

Section 28(e) of the Exchange Act of 1934 states that no person exercising investment discretion for an account will be deemed to have acted unlawfully solely by reason of having caused the account to pay a member of an exchange, broker, or dealer an amount of commission in excess of the amount of commission another member, broker, or dealer would have charged, if the person determined in good faith that the amount was reasonable in relation to the value of the brokerage and research services provided, viewed in terms of either that particular transaction or his overall responsibilities with respect to the accounts over which he exercises investment discretion.

This subsection also states that a person exercising investment discretion must disclose his policies and practices with respect to commissions that will be paid for effecting securities transactions, at such times and in such manner, as the appropriate regulatory agency may prescribe as necessary.

For purposes of this subsection, brokerage and research services include:

- advice, either directly or through publications or writings, as to the value of securities, the advisability of investing in, purchasing, or selling securities, and the availability of securities or purchasers or sellers of securities
- analyses and reports concerning issuers, industries, securities, economic factors and trends, portfolio strategy, and the performance of accounts
- securities transactions and functions, such as clearance, settlement, and custody

IRS RULE 2503 AND EXEMPTION FROM TAXES FOR GIFTS

IRS Rule 2503 states that the first $10,000 of taxable gifts (defined as the total amount of gifts made during the calendar year, less the deductions provided in subchapter C) to an individual are not included in the total amount of gifts for tax purposes. This amount is increased over time for inflation; the amount in 2023 is $17,000. Excluded from the definition of taxable gifts are future interests in property.

Gifts to individuals under age 21 are not considered gifts of a future interest in property if the property and income from it may be expended by, or for the benefit of, the donee before reaching age 21, or if not expended, will pass to the donee upon reaching age 21.

Excluded from taxable gifts are certain transfers for educational expenses, such as tuition to an educational organization, or medical care expenses.

Communicating with Customers About Account Information, Processing Requests, and Retaining Documentation

FINRA RULE 3150 AND HOLDING MAIL FOR CUSTOMERS

FINRA Rule 3150 states that a member may hold mail for a customer who will not be receiving mail at his or her usual address, provided that the member receives written instructions from the customer that include the time period during which the member is requested to hold the customer's mail. If the requested time period included in the instructions is longer than three consecutive months (including any aggregation of time periods from prior requests), the customer's instructions must include an acceptable reason for the request (e.g., safety or security concerns). Convenience is not an acceptable reason for holding mail longer than three months.

The member must also inform the customer in writing of any alternate methods, such as email or access through the member's website, that the customer may use to receive or monitor account activity and information and obtain the customer's confirmation of the receipt of such information. Finally, the member must verify at reasonable intervals that the customer's instructions still apply.

During the time that a member is holding mail for a customer, the member must be able to communicate with the customer in a timely manner to provide important account information, as necessary, and must take actions reasonably designed to ensure that the customer's mail is not tampered with, held without the customer's consent, or used by an associated person in any manner that would violate FINRA rules or the federal securities laws.

CUSTOMER CONFIRMATIONS

Customer confirmations are notices of a customer's transaction(s) that must be delivered to the customer at or before the settlement date of the transaction. This is ordinarily three business days after the trade date.

Customer confirmations must include:

- The account number of the customer
- The ID number of the registered representative
- The trade date
- The type of transaction (bought or sold—BOT or SLD)
- Number of shares or the par value of bonds in the transaction
- The yield (if bonds are transacted)
- The CUSIP ID number
- The dollar price of the security transacted
- The total amount of money paid or received, excluding commission
- The commission total
- The net amount, that is, the amount the customer paid or received when the commission is taken into account, and when accrued interest is taken into account for bonds

ACCOUNT STATEMENTS

Account statements show an account value as of the statement date based on the market value of the securities held at the time, plus or minus cash or margin amounts. The value may be shown as a summary and also be detailed by security. Certain securities (REITS, DPPs) have specific valuation methods required by FINRA Rule 2231. Broadly speaking, the change in the account value over time may be considered a profit or loss, net of cash contributions or withdrawals and taxes.

For individual investments, the difference in the current value and the cost basis represents an unrealized gain or loss. This is also referred to as "Paper Profit" because it exists only on the account statement. The gain or loss is realized when the security position is closed (i.e., sold, executed, or lapsed). The gain or loss becomes taxable when realized. At year-end, the realized gains and losses in each category (long-term, short-term) may be netted against one another to calculate the taxable profit or loss for the year.

RESTRICTIONS PLACED UPON TENDER OFFERS

Tender offers are regulated by the SEC. All tender offers are subject to anti-fraud provisions and certain procedural requirements relating to how long the offer must remain open, how quickly holders must be paid for their tendered securities, and the conditions required in order for a bidder to extend an offer.

The specific rules and regulations that apply to tender offers depend on a number of factors, including whether the tender offer is for equity or debt and whether the bidder is an issuer or a third party. If the tender offer is for equity securities, requirements depend on whether such securities are registered.

The vast majority of tender offers are subject to additional SEC rules that require bidders to file certain documents with the SEC disclosing important information about the bidders and the terms of the offer. These documents include a Schedule TO and what is typically called an "Offer to Purchase." The rules also provide other protections to security holders, including "withdrawal rights," which are the rights of security holders to withdraw their tender of securities within certain time periods; the requirement that the tender be open to all holders of the class of securities subject to the offer; and the bidder's obligation to provide each tendering holder with the "best price," which means a bidder cannot offer different prices to different holders.

A broker/dealer may exercise discretion regarding what tender offers to forward to customers. Many broker/dealers habitually forward all tender offers, but there are certain types of tenders that may require special disclosure.

CUSTOMER ACCOUNT RECORDS
MAINTAINING AND UPDATING CUSTOMER ACCOUNT RECORDS

SEC Rule 17a-3 requires members to maintain customer account records that include the following information: name, tax identification number, address, telephone number, date of birth, employment status (including occupation and whether the customer is an associated person of a member, broker or dealer), annual income, net worth (excluding value of primary residence), and the account's investment objectives. Members must then furnish to the customer at intervals no greater than 36 months, a copy of the account record with a prominent statement indicating that the customer should mark any correction and return the account record to the member.

For each account record updated to reflect a change in the name or address of the customer, the member must furnish a notification of that change to the customer's old address, or to each joint owner, and the associated person, if any, responsible for that account, on or before the 30th day after the date the member received notice of the change, and maintain documentation that such notification was made.

CHANGING A CUSTOMER ACCOUNT'S INVESTMENT OBJECTIVES

For each change in the account's investment objectives, the member must furnish to the customer, and the associated person, if any, responsible for that account, a copy of the updated customer account record, on or before the 30th day after the date the member received notice of any change, or, if the account was updated for some reason other than the firm receiving notice of a change, after the date the account record was updated, and maintain documentation that such notification was made.

These requirements are not applicable to an account for which, within the last 36 months, the member, broker or dealer has not been required to make a suitability determination. Neglect, refusal, or inability of a customer to provide or update any account record information will excuse the member from obtaining that required information.

MAINTENANCE OF CUSTOMER ACCOUNT RECORDS

Brokers have obligations not only to acquire customer information, but also to **maintain their customer account records**. This includes an appropriate assessment of the customer's changing assets and his investment objectives, as well as any updates for changes in address. Further, brokers must hold customer mail and send required notifications to their customers, such as the notifications required to inform customers of the risks of various accounts.

TRANSFERRING SECURITIES FROM ONE INSTITUTION TO ANOTHER

The Automated Customer Account Transfer Service (ACATS) is a system that facilitates the transfer of securities from one trading account to another at a different brokerage firm. Transfers involving cash, equities, corporate and municipal bonds, government securities, mutual funds, and listed options are readily transferable through ACATS.

All transfers start and end with the new firm. Customers initiate the transfer process by completing a Transfer Instruction Form (TIF) and sending it to the new firm. Once the document is received, the receiving firm submits a request using the client's account number and sends it to the delivering firm.

A transfer through ACATS that encounters no issues should be completed within six business days from the time the new firm enters the transfer form into ACATS. Transfers that are not from one broker to another, such those where one party is a bank, mutual fund or credit union, may take longer to complete. One or both brokers may charge an account transfer fee. The ACATS fee can be as high as $125.

CLOSING AN ACCOUNT

If someone wishes to **close his brokerage account**, whether due to dissatisfaction with his broker, or due to a need for the funds for some other purpose, he can contact his broker with his account information and let him know. He should let his broker know if he wants any of his investment holdings to be sold or transferred to a different broker.

If the account is not closed within three business days of the request, he should notify his broker. Regulations require that the closing of a brokerage account not be delayed except for just cause.

After the account closure, he should check his account for any remaining funds or securities that should not have been left there.

QUARTERLY CUSTOMER ACCOUNT STATEMENTS
FINRA RULE 2231 AND QUARTERLY CUSTOMER ACCOUNT STATEMENTS

FINRA Rule 2231 states that, unless otherwise exempt, a general securities member must, at every calendar quarter, send a statement of account containing a description of any securities positions, money balances, or account activity to each customer. In addition, each general securities member must include in the account statement a statement that advises the customer to report promptly any inaccuracy or discrepancy in their account. Such statement must also advise the customer that any oral communications should be re-confirmed in writing to further protect the customer's rights, including rights under the Securities Investor Protection Act (SIPA).

Quarterly account statements need not be sent if the following conditions are met:

- the customer's account is carried solely for the purpose of execution on a DVP/RVP basis (an arrangement whereby payment for securities purchased is made to the selling customer's agent and/or delivery of securities sold is made to the buying customer's agent in exchange for payment at time of settlement, usually in the form of cash)
- the account does not show security or money positions at the end of the quarter
- the customer consents to the suspension of such statements in writing
- the member undertakes to provide any particular statement or statements to the customer promptly upon request
- the member undertakes to promptly reinstate the delivery of such statements to the customer upon request

CONDUCT RULES REGARDING CUSTOMER ACCOUNT STATEMENTS

A general securities member must include in a customer account statement a per share estimated value of a direct participation program (DPP) or unlisted real estate investment trust (REIT) security, developed in a manner reasonably designed to ensure that the per share estimated value is reliable using one of the following two methodologies:

- Net Investment - At any time before 150 days following the second anniversary of breaking escrow, the member may include a per share estimated value reflecting the "net investment" disclosed in the issuer's most recent periodic or current report ("Issuer Report"). "Net investment" shall be based on the "amount available for investment" percentage in the "Estimated Use of Proceeds" section of the offering prospectus or, where "amount available for investment" is not provided, another equivalent disclosure that reflects the estimated percentage deduction from the aggregate dollar amount of securities registered for sale to the public of sales commissions, dealer manager fees, and estimated issuer offering and organization expenses.
- Appraised Value - At any time, the member may include a per share estimated value reflecting an appraised valuation disclosed in the Issuer Report, which, in the case of DPPs subject to the Investment Company Act ("1940 Act"), shall be consistent with the valuation requirements of the 1940 Act, or in the case of all other DPPs and REITs, shall be based on valuations of the assets and liabilities of the DPP or REIT performed at least annually, by, or with the material assistance or confirmation of, a third-party valuation expert or service; and derived from a methodology that conforms to standard industry practice.

SEC AND FINRA RULES REGARDING CUSTOMER CONFIRMATIONS

Confirmation of transactions (SEC Rule 10b-10) - broker/dealers must disclose certain information to the customer in writing at or before the completion of a transaction. This disclosure must contain specific information including the date and time of the transaction; the identity, price, and number of shares; agency disclosure of the broker/dealer; disclosure of any odd-lot differential fee paid for by the customer; and certain other disclosures for debt securities. There are some exceptions to the Rule such as certain transactions that are part of an investment company plan.

Customer confirmations (FINRA Rule 2232) - a member is to send to the customer a written notification at or before the completion of a transaction.

PROVIDING EDUCATIONAL COMMUNICATION TO FORMER CUSTOMERS
REGARDING ACCOUNT TRANSFERS TO THE MEMBER

FINRA Rule 2273 states that a member that hires or associates with a registered person must provide to a former customer of the registered person, individually, in paper or electronic form, an educational communication prepared by FINRA when:

- the member, directly or through that registered person, individually contacts the former customer of that registered person to transfer assets
- the former customer of that registered person, absent individualized contact, transfers assets to an account assigned, or to be assigned, to the registered person at the member

The member must deliver the communication at the time of first individualized contact with a former customer by the registered person or the member regarding the former customer transferring assets to the member.

If the contact is in writing, the written FINRA-prepared educational communication must accompany the written communication. If the contact is by electronic communication, the member may hyperlink directly to the educational communication. If the contact is oral, the member or registered person must notify the former customer orally that an educational communication that includes important considerations in deciding whether to transfer assets to the member will be provided not later than three business days after the contact. The educational communication must be sent within three business days from such oral contact or with any other documentation sent to the former customer related to transferring assets to the member, whichever is earlier.

IF NO CONTACT HAS TAKEN PLACE BEFORE THE TRANSFER OF ASSETS IS REQUESTED

If a former customer attempts to transfer assets to an account assigned, or to be assigned, to the registered person at the member, but no individualized contact with the former customer by the registered person or member occurs before the former customer seeks to transfer assets, the member shall deliver the educational communication to the former customer with the account transfer approval documentation.

The delivery of the educational communication required by this applies for a period of three months following the date the registered person begins employment or associates with the member.

RETAINING BOOKS AND RECORDS FOR CUSTOMERS AND FIRMS

One of the duties of a broker for his customers is to retain various **books and records**. According to **MSRB Rule G-8**, these include records of original entry, account records, securities records, and subsidiary records, such as records for municipal securities in transfer, municipal securities to be validated, municipal securities borrowed or loaned, and municipal securities transactions not completed on the settlement date. The broker should also maintain records for put options and repurchase agreements, records for agency transactions, records for transactions as principal, records concerning primary offerings, and other records. Essentially, the broker should maintain a paper trail for all of his customer's substantial activity.

FINRA RULES FOR THE PRESERVATION OF BOOKS AND RECORDS

FINRA Rule 4511 requires firms to make and preserve books and records as required under the rules of FINRA and applicable SEA rules; and preserve the books and records in a format and media that complies with SEA Rule 17a-4. In addition, FINRA Rule 4511 requires firms to preserve for a period of at least six years those FINRA books and records for which there is no specified retention period under specific FINRA rules or applicable SEA rules.

Specific FINRA rules that address books and records include the following:

- Rule 4512 addresses the requirements related to customer accounts
- Rule 4513 addresses the requirements related to written customer complaints
- Rule 4514 addresses the requirements related to authorization records for negotiable instruments drawn from a customer's account
- Rule 4515 addresses the requirements related to approval and documentation of changes in account name or designation
- Rule 4517 addresses the requirements related to member filing and contact information
- Rule 4518 addresses requirements related to notification to FINRA in connection with the JOBS Act

FINRA Rule 11870 and Transference of Customers' Securities

Customers who wish to transfer securities from one FINRA member to another may submit an **automated customer account transfer form**, or **ACAT**. Per FINRA Rule 11870, each FINRA member must "expedite and coordinate activities" to comply with the customer's request. Rule 11870 also provides for non-ACAT transfers via non-ACAT forms. ACAT forms will vary from member to member, but will generally contain the same information. The member that receives the instructions must validate (declare valid) the request or claim that the request is not valid (take issue) within one business day. After that, they must act in a reasonably speedy manner to facilitate the request. If the ACAT requests that the securities be liquidated first, it will generally take longer to process.

FINRA Rule 2232

FINRA Rule 2232 - Customer Confirmations generally specifies that a member must "at or before the completion of any transaction in any security effected for or with an account of a customer, give or send to such customer written notification ("confirmation") in conformity with the requirements of SEA Rule 10b-10". The confirmation must include the settlement date, whether it is callable, and how to get more information.

The rule was amended May 14, 2018. to include:

- required disclosures related to mark-ups and mark-downs (calculated according to FINRA Rule 2121) if the member is acting as a principal or trading in that security in quantities larger than the subject transaction.
- for all transactions in corporate or agency debt securities with non-institutional customers:
  - a reference, and hyperlink if the confirmation is electronic, to a web page hosted by FINRA that contains Trade Reporting And Compliance Engine (TRACE) publicly available trading data for the specific security that was traded, in a format specified by FINRA, along with a brief description of the type of information available on that page;
  - the execution time of the customer transaction, expressed to the second.

Preserving Records by Certain Exchange Members, Brokers and Dealers

SEC Rule 17a-4 states that every member, broker or dealer subject to SEC Rule 17a-3 must preserve for a period of not less than 6 years, the first two years in an easily accessible place, all records required by the Rule, except as otherwise indicated.

Every member must preserve for **a period of not less than three years,** the first two years in an easily accessible place the following types of records: ledgers, brokerage orders, confirmations, written customer complaints, compensation records of associated persons, approval of advertisements by a principal, check books, bank statements, cancelled checks and cash reconciliations, bills receivable or payable, trial balances, computations of aggregate indebtedness and net capital, financial statements, branch office reconciliations, and internal audit working papers, guarantees of accounts and all powers of attorney and other evidence of the granting of any discretionary authority, written agreements, and written policies and procedures.

Types of Records Being Preserved

Every member must preserve for **a period of not less than six years after the closing of any customer's account** any account cards or records which relate to the terms and conditions with respect to the opening and maintenance of the account.

Every member must preserve **during the life of the enterprise and of any successor enterprise** all partnership articles or, in the case of a corporation, all articles of incorporation or charter, minute books, and stock certificate books.

If a person who has been subject to Rule 17a-3 ceases to transact a business in securities such person must, for the remainder of the periods of time specified, continue to preserve the required records.

For purposes of transactions in municipal securities by municipal securities brokers and municipal securities dealers, compliance with Rule G-9 of the Municipal Securities Rulemaking Board or any successor rule will be deemed to be in compliance with this section.

Every member subject to this section must furnish promptly to a representative of the Commission legible, true, complete, and current copies of those records of the member that are requested by the representative of the Commission.

REGULATION OF INSIDER TRADING

Insider trading includes those transactions done by individuals who have access to special, non-public information for a company (or by individuals who receive such information). Because of the risks associated with insider trading, legislation exists to regulate it. For example, SEC regulation FD (which stands for "fair disclosure") demands that companies intentionally disclosing material information to someone must also make the information public. If the disclosure is unintentional, then the company is still required to "promptly" make a public disclosure of the information.

REGULATION FD

Adopted on August 15, 2000, **Regulation FD (Fair Disclosure)** is a set of rules with the purpose of addressing three insider trading issues: selective disclosure, insider trading liability, and family member or non-business relationship trades. **Selective disclosure** refers to when a securities issuer releases material nonpublic information, usually to certain industry professionals. The Regulation prohibits this without public disclosure of the information. The Regulation also states that **insider trading liability** (Rule 10b5-1) arises when an individual trades a security while aware of material nonpublic information. It provides for some exception when the individual can prove that the information was not a factor in the decision to trade. The Regulation also defines (Rule 10b5-2) how a family member - or an individual of another non-business relationship - can be liable for insider trading.

TRADING PERMIT HOLDERS

TRANSACTION REPORTING REQUIREMENTS

Cboe Rule 6.1 states that a designated Trading Permit Holder (TPH) must report a transaction within 90 seconds of the execution in a form and manner prescribed by the Exchange.

The Exchange has established the following procedure for reporting transactions. For each transaction on the Exchange both the buyer and seller shall immediately record on a card or ticket, or enter in an electronic data storage medium acceptable to the Exchange, the following information:

- the assigned broker initial code and clearing firm (if a Market-Maker)
- the symbol of the underlying security or index
- the type, expiration month, and exercise price of the option contract
- the transaction price

- the number of contract units comprising the transaction
- the time of the transaction obtained from a source designated by the Exchange
- the name of the contra Clearing Trading Permit Holder
- the assigned broker initial code of the contra Trading Permit Holder

RECORDKEEPING REQUIREMENTS

Cboe Rule 7.1 states that each Trading Permit Holder (TPH) must make, keep current and preserve such books and records as the Exchange may prescribe and as may be prescribed by the Exchange Act as though the TPH were a broker or dealer registered pursuant to Section 15 of such Act.

No Trading Permit Holder may refuse to make available to the Exchange such books, records or other information as may be called for under the Rules or as may be requested in connection with an investigation by the Exchange. TPHs must comply with all applicable recordkeeping and reporting requirements under the Rules.

REPORTING REQUIREMENTS

Cboe Rule 7.2 states that upon request of the Exchange, each Trading Permit Holder (TPH) must submit to the Exchange a report of the total uncovered short positions in each option contract of a class dealt in on the Exchange showing:

- positions carried by such TPH for its own account;
- positions carried by such TPH for the accounts of customers; provided that the TPH shall not report positions carried for the accounts of other TPHs where such other TPHs report the positions themselves

Such report shall be submitted not later than the second business day following the date the request is made.

FINANCIAL REPORTING REQUIREMENTS

Cboe Rule 7.3 states that each Trading Permit Holder (TPH) must submit to the Exchange answers to financial questionnaires, reports of income and expenses and additional financial information in the type, form, manner and time prescribed by the Exchange. TPHs may be subject to fines for violations of this Rule.

Net Capital Computing - TPHs who are net capital computing must file electronically with the Exchange any required monthly and quarterly FOCUS Reports utilizing the system or software prescribed by the Exchange, which will be announced via Regulatory Circular.

Not Net Capital Computing - TPHs who file an annual FOCUS Report and who are not net capital computing must file electronically with the Exchange the annual FOCUS Report and Schedule 1 utilizing the system or software prescribed by the Exchange, which will be announced via Regulatory Circular.

ANNUALLY SUPPLING INDEPENDENTLY AUDITED REPORT OF THEIR FINANCIAL CONDITION

Cboe Rule 7.4 states that each TPH organization approved to do business with the public and each registered Market-Maker must file a report of its financial condition as of a date within each calendar year prepared in accordance with the requirements of SEC Rule 17a-5 and Form X-17A-5. The report of each TPH must be certified by an independent public accountant, and on or before January 10 of each year, each such TPH must notify the Exchange of the name of the independent public accountant appointed for that year and the date as of which the report will be made.

Such report of financial condition, together with answers to an Exchange financial questionnaire based upon the report, must be filed with the Exchange not later than 60 days after the date as of which the financial condition of the TPH is reported, or such other period as the Exchange may individually require.

Any such TPH may file in lieu of the report required by this Rule a copy of any financial statement which he is or has been required to file with any other national securities exchange or national securities association of which it is a member, or with any agency of any State as a condition of doing business in securities therein, and which is acceptable to the Exchange as containing substantially the same information as Form X-17A-5.

In addition to the annual report, the Exchange may require any TPHs to cause an audit of its financial condition to be made by an independent public accountant as of the date of an answer to a financial questionnaire, and to file a statement to the effect that such audit has been made and whether it is in accord with the answer to the questionnaire.

PROVIDING TRADE DATA TO THE EXCHANGE

TRADES ON ITS OWN BEHALF

Cboe Rule 7.5 states that a Trading Permit Holder (TPH) must submit the trade data elements specified below in such automated format as may be prescribed by the Exchange from time to time.

If the transaction was a proprietary transaction effected by the TPH for any account in which it is directly or indirectly interested, such TPH must submit the following information:

- Clearing house number, or alpha symbol as used by the TPH
- Clearing house number(s), or alpha symbol(s) as may be used from time to time, of the TPH(s) on the opposite side of the transaction
- Identifying symbol assigned to the security and where applicable for options the month and series symbols
- Date transaction was executed
- Number of option contracts for each specific transaction and whether each transaction was an opening or closing purchase or sale
- Transaction price
- Account number
- Market center where transaction was executed

TRADES FOR THE ACCOUNTS OF CUSTOMERS

If the transaction was affected by the TPH for any customer account, such TPH must submit the following information:

- All the criteria indicated above
- Customer name, address(es)
- Branch office number, registered representative number, whether order was solicited or unsolicited
- Date account opened
- Employer name and the tax identification number(s)
- Whether the broker-dealer was acting as a principal or agent on the transaction

Assessing and Monitoring Risks Associated With Options Market-Maker Accounts

Cboe Rule 7.7 requires that each TPH organization which clears or guarantees the transactions of options Market-Makers to establish and maintain written procedures for assessing and monitoring the potential risks to the TPH's capital over a specified range of possible market movements of positions maintained in such options Market-Maker accounts.

Current procedures must be filed and maintained with the Exchange, and must specify the computations to be made, the frequency of computations, the records to be reviewed and maintained, and the position(s) within the organization responsible for the risk function.

Assessing and Monitoring Their Potential Risk of Loss

Each affected TPH organization must, at a minimum, assess and monitor its own potential risk of loss from options Market-Maker accounts each business day as of the close of business the prior day through use of an Exchange-approved computerized risk analysis program. The program must comply with at least the minimum standards specified below:

- The estimated loss to the Clearing TPH organization for each Market-Maker account (potential account deficit) must be determined given the impact of broad market movements in reasonable intervals over a range from negative 15% to positive 15%.
- The TPH organization must calculate volatility using a method approved by the Exchange, with volatility updated at least weekly. The program must have the capability of expanding volatility when projecting losses throughout the range of broad market movements.
- Options prices must be estimated through use of recognized options pricing models such as, but not limited to, Black-Scholes and Cox-Ross-Rubinstein.
- At a minimum, written reports must be generated which describe for each market scenario: the projected loss per options class by account; the projected total loss per options class for all accounts; the projected deficits per account and in aggregate.

Effects of Cboe Rule 7.8 on TPH Organizations

Cboe Rule 7.8 requires each TPH organization that maintains any portfolio margin accounts for customers establish and maintain a written risk analysis methodology for assessing and monitoring the potential risk to the TPH organization's capital over a specified range of possible market movements of positions maintained in such accounts.

The risk analysis methodology must specify the computations to be made, the frequency of computations, the records to be reviewed and maintained, and the person(s) within the organization responsible for the risk function.

This risk analysis methodology must be filed with the TPH organization's Designated Examining Authority and submitted to the SEC prior to the implementation of portfolio margining.

Written Risk Analysis Methodology Procedures

In conducting the risk analysis of portfolio margin accounts, each TPH organization must include in the written risk analysis methodology procedures and guidelines for:

- obtaining and reviewing the appropriate customer account documentation and financial information necessary for assessing the amount of credit extended to customers
- the determination, review and approval of credit limits to each customer, and across all customers, utilizing a portfolio margin account

- monitoring credit risk exposure to the TPH organization from portfolio margin accounts, on both an intra-day and end of day basis, including the type, scope and frequency of reporting to senior management
- the use of stress testing of portfolio margin accounts in order to monitor market risk exposure from individual accounts and in the aggregate
- the regular review and testing of these risk analysis procedures by an independent unit such as internal audit or other comparable group
- managing the impact of credit extension on the TPH organization's overall risk exposure
- the appropriate response by management when limits on credit extensions have been extended
- determining the need to collect additional margin from a particular eligible participant, including whether that determination was based upon the creditworthiness of the participant and/or the risk of the eligible position(s)
- monitoring the credit exposure resulting from concentrated positions within both individual portfolio margin accounts and across all portfolio margin accounts

Moreover, management must periodically review, in accordance with written procedures, the TPH organization's credit extension activities for consistency with these guidelines. Management must periodically determine if the data necessary to apply this Rule 7.8 is accessible on a timely basis and information systems are available to capture, monitor, analyze and report relevant data.

ASSIGNING REGULATORY RESPONSIBILITIES TO ANOTHER SELF-REGULATORY ORGANIZATION

Cboe Rule 7.9 states that the Exchange may enter into one or more agreements with another self-regulatory organization to provide regulatory services to the Exchange.

Any action taken by another self-regulatory organization acting on behalf of the Exchange shall be deemed to be an action taken by the Exchange; however, the Exchange shall retain ultimate legal responsibility for, and control of, its self-regulatory responsibilities, and any such regulatory services agreement shall so provide.

So long as a Trading Permit Holder (TPH) or associated person remains subject to the disciplinary jurisdiction of the Exchange, such TPH or associated person shall be obligated to furnish testimony, documentary evidence or other information to the full extent whether or not an investigation has been initiated by the Exchange or another self-regulatory organization acting on behalf of the Exchange.

WRITTEN CONFIRMATIONS OF OPTIONS TRANSACTIONS

Cboe Rule 9.5 states that every TPH organization must promptly furnish to each customer a written confirmation of each transaction in option contracts which must show:

- the underlying security type of option expiration month
- exercise price
- number of option contracts
- premium
- commissions
- date of transaction and settlement date
- whether the transaction is a purchase or sale
- whether the transaction was an opening or a closing transaction
- whether a principal or agency transaction

INFORMATION AND DISCLOSURES TO BE PROVIDED ON CUSTOMER ACCOUNT STATEMENTS

Cboe Rule 9.6 states that every TPH organization must send to its customers statements of account showing security and money positions, entries, interest charges and any special charges that have been assessed against such account during the period covered by the statement.

With respect to options customers having a general (margin) account, such statement must also provide the mark-to-market price and market value of each option position and other security position in the general (margin) account, the total market value of all positions in the account, the outstanding debit or credit balance in the account, and the general (margin) account equity.

The statement must bear a legend stating that further information with respect to commissions and other charges related to the execution of listed option transactions has been included in confirmations of such transactions previously furnished to the customer, and that such information will be made available to the customer promptly upon request. The statement must also bear a legend requesting the customer to promptly advise the TPH of any material change in the customer's investment objectives or financial situation.

Such statements of account must be sent at least quarterly to all accounts having a money or a security position during the preceding quarter and at least monthly to all accounts having an entry during the preceding month.

ACCOUNT TRANSFER PROCEDURES

Cboe Rule 9.14 states that when a customer whose securities account is carried by a TPH organization (the "carrying organization") wants to transfer the entire account to another TPH organization (the "receiving organization") and gives written notice of that fact to the receiving organization, both TPH organizations must expedite and coordinate activities with respect to the transfer.

Upon receipt from the customer of a signed broker-to-broker transfer instruction to receive such customer's securities account, the receiving organization will immediately submit such instruction to the carrying organization. The carrying organization must, within five business days, validate and return the transfer instruction (with an attachment reflecting all positions and money balances as shown on its books) to the receiving organization, or take exception to the transfer instruction. The carrying organization and the receiving organization must promptly resolve any exceptions taken to the transfer instruction.

FAIL-TO-RECEIVE AND FAIL-TO-DELIVER CONTRACTS

Within five business days following the validation of a transfer instruction, the carrying organization must complete the transfer of the customer's securities account to the receiving organization. The carrying organization and the receiving organization must establish fail to receive and fail to deliver contracts at then current market values upon their respective books of account against the long/short positions (including options) in the customer's securities account that have not been physically delivered/received and the receiving/carrying organization must debit/credit the related money account. The customer's securities account shall thereupon be deemed transferred.

Any fail contracts resulting from this account transfer procedure must be closed out within 10 business days after their establishment. Any discrepancies relating to positions or money balances that exist or occur after transfer of a customer's securities account must be resolved promptly. Unless an exemption has been granted, the Exchange may impose upon a TPH organization a fee of up to $100 per securities account for each day such TPH organization fails to adhere to the time frames or procedures required by this Rule and related published interpretations.

MAINTAINING BOOKS AND RECORDS

MSRB Rule G-8 requires that every broker, dealer and municipal securities dealer make and keep current the following books and records:

- Records of Original Entry, such "blotters" or other records of original entry containing an itemized daily record of all purchases and sales of municipal securities
- Account Records
- Securities Records
- Subsidiary Records
- Put Options and Repurchase Agreements
- Records for Agency Transactions
- Records for Transactions as Principal
- Records Concerning Primary Offerings
- Copies of Confirmations, Periodic Statements and Certain Other Notices to Customers
- Financial Records
- Customer Account Information
- Customer Complaints
- Designation of Persons Responsible for Recordkeeping
- Records Concerning Delivery of Official Statements, Advance Refunding Documents and Forms G-36(OS) and G-36(ARD) to the Board or its Designee Pursuant to Former Rule G-36
- Records Concerning Political Contributions
- Records Concerning Consultants
- Negotiable Instruments Drawn from a Customer's Account
- Records Concerning Regulatory Element Continuing Education
- Records of Secondary Market Trading Account Transactions

Brokers, dealers and municipal securities dealers other than bank dealers which are in compliance with Rule 17a-3 of the Commission will be deemed to be in compliance with the requirements of this rule.

RECORDING REQUIREMENTS OF BROKERS, DEALERS AND MUNICIPAL SECURITIES DEALERS

MSRB Rule G-9 prescribes the time periods that records must be preserved.

Records that must be preserved for **six years** include records of original entry, account records, securities records, records concerning primary offerings, records concerning suitability, customer complaints, ledgers, records regarding information on gifts and gratuities and employment agreements, and records concerning secondary market trading account transactions.

Records that must be preserved for **four years** include subsidiary records, records of put options and repurchase agreements, records relating to agency transactions, records of transactions as principal, copies of confirmations, customer account information, records relating to fingerprinting, and each advertisement from the date of each use.

Records that must be preserved for the **life of the enterprise** include all partnership articles or, in the case of a corporation, all articles of incorporation or charter, minute books and stock certificate books.

Brokers, dealers and municipal securities dealers other than bank dealers that are in compliance with Rules 17a-3 and 17a-4 under the Act will be deemed to be in compliance with the requirements of this rule.

CUSTOMER CONFIRMATIONS OF MUNICIPAL SECURITIES TRANSACTIONS

MSRB Rule G-15 requires that at or before the completion of a transaction in municipal securities with or for the account of a customer, each broker, dealer or municipal securities dealer must give or send to the customer a written confirmation that includes the following information:

Transaction information - name, address, and telephone number of the broker, dealer, or municipal securities dealer, customer, whether transaction was a purchase or sale, whether broker, dealer or municipal securities dealer acted as a principal or agent, trade date and time of execution, par value, settlement date, yield and dollar price, final monies, and delivery of securities.

Securities identification information - name of the issuer, CUSIP number, maturity date, and interest rate.

Securities descriptive information - credit backing, features of securities (e.g., callable), information on status of securities (e.g., pre-refunded, escrowed to maturity), and tax information.

Disclosure statements – certain types of transactions require specific disclosures. For example, confirmations for zero coupon securities must include a statement to the effect that "No periodic payments," and, if applicable, "callable below maturity value," and, if callable and available in bearer form, "callable without notice by mail to holder unless registered."

PROCEDURES FOR MUNICIPAL SECURITIES ACCOUNT TRANSFERS

MSRB Rule G-26 states that when a customer whose municipal securities account is carried by a broker, dealer or municipal securities dealer (the "carrying party") wishes to transfer municipal securities account assets, in whole or in specifically designated part, to another broker, dealer or municipal securities dealer (the "receiving party") and gives authorized instructions to the receiving party, both parties must expedite and coordinate activities with respect to the transfer.

Upon receipt from the customer of an authorized transfer instruction to receive such customer's municipal securities account assets from the carrying party, the receiving party must immediately submit such instruction to the carrying party. The carrying party must, within one business day, validate and return the transfer instruction to the receiving party or take exception to the transfer instruction. The carrying party and the receiving party must promptly resolve any exceptions taken to the transfer instruction.

Upon validation of an instruction to transfer municipal securities account assets in whole, the carrying party must "freeze" the account and return the transfer instruction to the receiving party with an attachment indicating all municipal securities positions, safekeeping positions and any money balance to be transferred as shown on the books of the carrying party, including a then-current market value for all assets. If a then-current market value for an asset cannot be determined, the asset must be valued at original cost. However, delayed delivery assets, nontransferable assets, and assets in-transfer to the customer, need not be valued, although the status of such assets must be indicated on the attachment.

STIPULATIONS FOR FAIL-TO-RECEIVE AND FAIL-TO-DELIVER CONTRACTS

Within three business days following the validation of a transfer instruction, the carrying party must complete the transfer of the customer's municipal securities account assets to the receiving party. The receiving party and the carrying party must immediately establish fail-to-receive and fail-to-deliver contracts at the then-current market value as of the date of validation upon their respective books of account against the long/short positions in the customer's accounts that have not been physically delivered/received and the receiving party/carrying party must debit/credit the related money amount. Nontransferable assets and assets in-transfer to the customer are exempt from this requirement. Zero value fail-to-receive and fail-to-deliver instructions shall be established for delayed delivery assets. The customer's account(s) shall thereupon be deemed transferred.

To the extent any assets in the account are not readily transferable, with or without penalties, such assets are not subject to the time frames required by the rule; and, if the customer has authorized liquidation of any nontransferable assets, the carrying member must distribute the resulting money balance to the customer within five business days following receipt of the customer's disposition instructions.

Processing Transactions

Providing Current Quotes

DUTY OF BEST EXECUTION

While trade execution is usually seamless and quick, it does take time, and prices can change quickly, especially in fast-moving markets. Because price quotes are only for a specific number of shares, investors may not always receive the price they saw on their screen or the price their broker quoted over the phone. No SEC regulations require a trade to be executed within a set period of time but if firms advertise their speed of execution, they must not exaggerate or fail to tell investors about the possibility of significant delays. Broker-dealers have a choice of markets to execute a trade, and are responsible to fulfill a duty of best execution:

- a stock exchange
- a market maker
- an Over the Counter (OTC) market like Nasdaq
- Electronic Communications Network (ECN) - especially if it is a limit order
- through the broker's own inventory, called internalization

Once the transaction is completed, the broker-dealer must meet disclosure requirements by the government and SROs. Generally, the broker-dealer must notify the customer of the date, time, identity, price, quantity, and the role the broker-dealer played in the transaction.

BROKERS VS. DEALERS

A **broker** is a person or institution which acts as a middleman between the buyer of a security and the seller of a security. The broker makes his profit by charging a sales charge, or **commission**, for arranging the transaction. Brokers do not own any products for which they arrange transactions, but simply facilitate the transferal of ownership from a seller to a buyer.

A **dealer** is a person or institution which sells its own inventory to buyers (like a used-car dealer). A dealer charges a **markdown** when he purchases inventory, lowering the price he pays for the inventory; and he charges a **markup** when he sells it, increasing the price the customer pays for it. Furthermore, dealers sometimes intend for the inventory to appreciate in value while they hold it.

Whether a firm is acting in the capacity of a broker or dealer must be disclosed on the receipt of trade, or the confirmation. Commissions need to be disclosed, but not necessarily markups or markdowns.

Firms are prohibited from acting as both a broker and a dealer in the same transaction. Either a commission can be charged, or a markup or markdown, but not both.

NASDAQ ACCESS LEVELS

The NASDAQ has three quote levels:

Level 1 supplies basic information. The trading screen for Level 1 used with stock trading displays the best bid-offer-volume quotes in real-time, or the national best bid and offer (NBBO).

Level 2 supplies greater market depth (5-10 best bid and ask prices) and momentum information to traders by providing real-time access to the NASDAQ order book.

200

Level 3 supplies pricing information from a trading service, including real-time bid and ask prices (up to 20), quote size, price and size of the last trade, high and low price for the day. Level III gives institutions the ability to enter quotes, execute orders, and send information, and is restricted to registered Nasdaq market makers.

OTCBB

The OTCBB stands for the Over-the-Counter Bulletin Board. It is an interdealer quotation system that is used by subscribing FINRA members to reflect market making interest in OTCBB-eligible securities (securities not listed on a national securities exchange in the U.S.). Subscribing market makers can utilize the OTCBB to enter, update, and display their proprietary quotations in individual securities on a real-time basis. Quotation entries may consist of a priced bid and/or offer; an unpriced indication of interest (including "bid wanted" or "offer wanted" indications); or a bid/offer accompanied by a modifier to reflect unsolicited customer interest.

BOND QUOTES VS. STOCK QUOTES

A stock quote is the price of a stock on an exchange. It includes the stock's bid and ask price, last traded price, and volume traded. A stock quote is expressed in decimals.

Unlike stocks, bonds are not traded on an exchange, making pricing information less accessible to the average investor. Investors typically receive bond quotes from their brokerage. Bond quotes are the last price at which a bond traded, expressed as a percentage of par value. Different types of bonds are quoted in different fractional increments depending on their liquidity. For instance, government bonds are quoted in 1/32 increments, while corporate bonds are quoted in 1/8 increments.

SECURITIES QUOTES

WORKOUT QUOTES AND FAST MARKETS

A workout quote is a non-firm quote that requires handling and settlement conditions to be worked out between parties prior to the trade. These types of quotes may be used for non-liquid securities for which the securities may have to be located to complete the transaction.

A fast market is when financial markets are experiencing unusually high levels of volatility and heavy trading causing a stock exchange to officially declare it a "fast market." A fast market can cause a delay in the electronic updating of the last sale and brokers may not be able to fill orders in as timely a manner as investors want, meaning they may be filled at different prices than expected.

BIDS, ASKS, SPREADS, FIRM QUOTES, AND SUBJECT OFFERS

A bid is the highest price a buyer will pay to buy a specified number of shares of a stock at any given time.

An ask is the lowest price at which a seller will sell the stock at any given time.

A spread in the difference between the bid and ask prices of a security.

A firm quote is a bid or ask price that is not negotiable.

A subject offer is a conditional offer for which certain information and terms must be established in order to proceed. Subject offers are negotiable and are often used to solicit a counteroffer.

TYPES OF ORDERS

A buy order is an instruction from an investor to a broker to purchase a specific amount of a security.

A sell order is an instruction from an investor to a broker to sell a specific amount of a security.

Short selling involves borrowing a security, selling it, then buying it to return to the lender. Short selling is done when an investor believes the price of the security will decline.

A market order is an order to buy or sell a security immediately. An execution price is not guaranteed but will generally be at or near the current bid or ask price.

A limit order is an order to buy or sell a security at a specified maximum/minimum price. The order will only be filled if it meets or beats that price.

A stop order is an order to buy or sell a security at the market price once the security has reached or traded through a specified price. If the stock does not reach this price, an order is not executed.

UNSOLICITED ORDERS

An unsolicited order is one that the investor initiates versus one that a broker or firm recommends. An order ticket must be marked as solicited or unsolicited. It is difficult to hold a broker or firm liable for losses from an unsolicited order.

ORDERS TERMS

An immediate-or-cancel order is an order to buy or sell a security that must be executed immediately. If the order cannot be executed immediately, then it is cancelled. A partial amount of the order may be filled.

An all-or-none order is an order to buy or sell a specified amount of a security. If the entire amount cannot be purchased or sold, then the order is cancelled.

A fill-or-kill order is an order to buy or sell a security that must be executed immediately in its entirety. If the specified amount cannot be purchased or sold immediately, then the entire order is cancelled.

A not-held order is an order to buy or sell a security where the broker is given the discretion to execute the order when he or she has identified the best available price.

An at-the-open order is an order to buy or sell a security upon the opening of the trading day.

A market-on-close order is an order to buy or sell a security upon the close of the trading day.

Day orders are orders to buy or sell a security which will lose validity (expire) if the transaction is not made within the same day.

Good till cancelled (GTC) orders are orders which are valid until the customer specifically cancels them (as opposed to expiring after a given period of time or when a security reaches a certain price).

Options are contracts to buy or sell a security in the future, where one person has the right to execute the transaction, and another has the obligation to do so upon the other's exercising of his right.

TYPES OF ORDERS ACCORDING TO NYSE RULE 13

Auto ex order - initiates an automatic execution when entered into the system. Includes market orders, limit orders, cancel orders, among others.

Closing offset (CO) order - an order for execution at the close of trading, assuming there is an imbalance at that time.

Day order - expires at end of trading (4 PM Eastern Time).

Do not reduce (DNR) order - the price is not to be reduced according to the amount of the ordinary cash dividend on dividend date.

Do not ship (DNS) order - an order that is not to be shipped to another market. If in standard process the security should be shipped to another market, it will be cancelled.

Do not increase (DNI) order - the price is not to be increased according to the amount of the cash dividend on dividend date.

Limit "at-the-close" order - a limit order set for potential execution at the close of the market day.

Market order - an order to purchase a security at the most advantageous price.

Market "at-the-close" (MOC) orders - a market order set for execution at the close of the market day.

Market "on-the-open" (MOO) orders - a market order set for execution at the opening of the market day.

SHORT-SELLING AND REGULATION SHO

Short selling consists of borrowing stocks, selling them, and then hoping to replace and deliver them later at a lower price. Unlike most stock market transactions, which involve two parties, short selling involves three parties—the short seller, the buyer, and the individual or corporation that loaned the stock to the short seller.

Rule 200 of Regulation SHO requires a broker-dealer to mark sell orders in any equity security as "long" or "short." Rule 200(a) defines a short sale as "any sale of a security which the seller does not own or any sale which is consummated by the delivery of a security borrowed by, or for the account of, the seller.

Rule 201 of Regulation SHO requires that to execute a short sale, the customer must offer a bid higher than 90% of the prior inside bid. Short Sales are also subject to Margin limits and are governed by SEC Regulation T. The Short Sale margin is calculated by netting all positions in that security.

Rule 203 of Regulation SHO requires a broker-dealer to have reasonable grounds to believe that the security can be borrowed so that it can be delivered on the date delivery is due before effecting a short sale order in any equity security. This "locate" must be made and documented prior to effecting the short sale.

SHORT-SELLING STRATEGIES

Speculation - Short selling can be done for speculation, that is, buying investment vehicles that have a high degree of uncertainty regarding their future value and expected earnings. A short sale speculator is watching for the market to experience fluctuations at which point one can make a high-risk investment, banking on a big change in stock price.

Hedging -However, many investors use short selling as an opportunity for hedging, or reducing risk. This can be done in different ways, one of which might be to systematically eliminate the industry risk by doing short sell transactions with shares of competing companies in the same industry.

Arbitrage - Some investors use short sales as a way to take advantage of price inefficiencies in the market. Arbitrageurs (Arbs) look for different securities that should be trading in the same manner but are not. The Arbs will then short one of the two securities and take a long position in the other. The idea is that as the two securities get aligned, the Arb will make a profit from both the one that rose and the one that fell. A good example of this might be Berkshire Hathaway. BRK-A and BRK-B prices should change in tandem. If they have recently stopped moving in tandem, an Arb may use shorting as part of a strategy to profit from when the two classes of BRK align in price.

It is important to understand that short sales are considered risky because if the stock price rises instead of declines, there is theoretically no limit to the investor's possible loss. As a result, most experienced short sellers will use a stop-loss order, so that if the stock price begins to rise, the short sale will be automatically covered with only a small loss. Be aware, however, that the stop-loss triggers a market order with no guaranteed price. This can be a risky strategy for volatile or illiquid stocks.

EASY-TO-BORROW

Easy-to-borrow securities are available to be borrowed for short-selling transactions; the delivery of these securities is assured. These securities are stated on a list, the "Easy-to-Borrow List," which is used by brokerage firms and updated every 24 hours. Securities are categorized as easy-to-borrow generally due being highly accessible and having a high number of shares outstanding.

HARD-TO-BORROW

Hard-to-borrow securities are just the opposite; they are not very accessible or attainable for use in short-selling transactions.

FAILURE TO DELIVER

Failure to deliver occurs when a brokerage representing the seller of a security doesn't deliver the security to the brokerage representing the buyer, or if the brokerage does delivers the security, but it is not in good delivery form. If a failure to deliver occurs, the buyer's broker may buy the security on the open market and charge the seller's firm for the difference. If, after ten days after settlement, the seller still hasn't delivered the security, the seller's broker must buy them on the open market.

BEST EXECUTION OBLIGATIONS

FINRA Rule 5310 states that in any transaction for or with a customer, a member must use reasonable diligence to ascertain the best market for the security and buy or sell in that market so that the resultant price to the customer is as favorable as possible under prevailing market conditions. Among the factors that will be considered in determining whether a member has used "reasonable diligence" are:

- the character of the market for the security (e.g., price, volatility, relative liquidity, and pressure on available communications)
- the size and type of transaction
- the number of markets checked

- accessibility of the quotation
- the terms and conditions of the order which result in the transaction, as communicated to the member

USING THIRD PARTIES TO FULFILL CUSTOMER ORDERS

In any transaction for or with a customer, no member or person associated with a member may interject a third party between the member and the best market for the security in a manner inconsistent with the requirements of this Rule. When a member cannot execute directly with a market but must employ a broker's broker or some other means in order to ensure an execution advantageous to the customer, the burden of showing the acceptable circumstances for doing so is on the member. Failure to maintain or adequately staff an over-the-counter order room or other department assigned to execute customers' orders cannot be considered justification for executing away from the best available market; nor can channeling orders through a third party as described above as reciprocation for service or business relieve a member of its obligations under this Rule. A member through which an order is channeled and that knowingly is a party to an arrangement whereby the initiating member has not fulfilled its obligations under this Rule, will also be deemed to have violated this Rule.

FINRA RULE 4320 AND SHORT SALE DELIVERY REQUIREMENTS

Short sale delivery requirements (FINRA Rule 4320) – if a participant in a registered clearing agency has failed to deliver a security to fulfill a short sale for 13 consecutive days, he is to close out the position and purchase a security of like kind and quality. Until the participant closes out this position and purchases a security of like kind and quality, he is not to accept any additional short sale orders for the security. If the participant in a registered clearing agency reasonably allocates a portion of the failure to deliver to a broker-dealer for whom he clears transactions, then the rule is applied to the broker-dealer, not the participant. The participant is not exempted as stated if he has entered into an agreement to purchase securities for a person that he knows will not deliver during settlement.

ALTERNATIVE TRADING SYSTEMS INFORMATION

FINRA Rule 4551 states that each alternative trading system that accepts orders for security futures must record each item of information described below:

- Date and time (expressed in terms of hours, minutes and seconds) that the order was received
- Security future product name and symbol
- Number of contracts to which the order applies
- An identification of the order as related to a program trade or an index arbitrage trade as defined in New York Stock Exchange Rule 132B
- Designation of the order as a buy or sell order
- Designation of the order as a market order, limit order, stop order, stop limit order or other type of order
- Any limit or stop price prescribed by the order
- Date on which the order expires and, if the time in force is less than one day, the time when the order expires
- Time limit during which the order is in force
- Any instructions to modify or cancel the order
- Date and time (expressed in terms of hours, minutes and seconds) that the order was received

- Security future product name and symbol
- Number of contracts to which the order applies
- An identification of the order as related to a program trade or an index arbitrage trade as defined in New York Stock Exchange Rule 132B
- Designation of the order as a buy or sell order
- Designation of the order as a market order, limit order, stop order, stop limit order or other type of order
- Any limit or stop price prescribed by the order
- Date on which the order expires and, if the time in force is less than one day, the time when the order expires
- Time limit during which the order is in force

FINRA RULE 5210 AND PUBLICATION OF TRANSACTIONS AND QUOTATIONS

Publication of transactions and quotations (Rule 5210) says that no member shall publish communication about a purchase, sale, or quote unless the member has reason to believe it was bona fide. Additionally, 5210.02 added Self Trades - members must have reasonably designed policies and procedures in place to monitor self-trades. 5210.03 adds that no member shall engage in or facilitate disruptive trading.

Two specific types of disruptive trading are mentioned:

- Type 1 - member inputs multiple limit orders on one side of the market at different price levels, the level of supply and demand changes, then orders on the opposite side (Contra-Side orders) of the market that are executed. Then the member cancels the original order.
- Type 2 - member narrows the spread for a security, then executes an order on the opposite side of the market with another market participant.

COMBATING BACKING AWAY

Offers at stated prices (Rule 5220) says that a member may not make an offer unless they are prepared to transact at that price. Though sometimes "backing-away" is constituted, regularly "backing-away" puts into question the validity of the dealers quotes and disrupts the course of regular business.

The term backing away refers to the failure by a market maker in a security to honor the quoted bid and ask prices for a minimum quantity. Backing away constitutes a serious violation of industry regulations, notably FINRA Rule 5220-Offers at Stated Prices and Rule 2010-Standards of Commercial Honor and Principals of Trade. FINRA uses an automated market surveillance system to enable the resolution of backing-away complaints in real-time. Backing away is usually frowned upon and can lead to disciplinary action against the market maker who has backed away.

SPLITTING ORDERS

Order entry and execution practices (Rule 5290) says that an order cannot be split up into smaller orders simply for the purpose of increasing commissions or payments.

There are legitimate reasons to split an order - for example a security may not have enough transaction volume (liquidity) to meet a large order in one transaction. Since most exchanges are automated now, computers handle the splitting of orders. On the other hand, some brokers in the past would split orders for dishonest reasons - simply to increase the per-transaction fee. That practice is specifically forbidden by FINRA Rule 5290.

TRADING HALTS

Prohibition on transactions, publication of quotations, or publication of indications of interest during trading halts (FINRA Rule 5260) - if trading is halted for a specific security, no trading activities can be made on the security.

Trading halts (FINRA Rule 6120) - FINRA will halt the trading of a security otherwise than on an exchange in certain situations when the market in power calls for a trading halt, or to permit dissemination of material news, obtain material information, obtain material information in the public interest. Other reasons include when extraordinary market activity is occurring.

Trading halts due to extraordinary market volatility (FINRA Rule 6121) - FINRA will halt all trading activity otherwise than on an exchange in any stock if other major securities markets have done the same in response to extraordinary market volatility, or if directed by the SEC.

QUOTING AND TRADING OTC EQUITY SECURITIES

The following FINRA rules cover quoting and trading OTC Equity Securities:

6400 - Quoting and Trading in OTC Equity Securities - The 6400 Series sets forth quotation and trading requirements for "OTC Equity Securities" as that term is defined in Rule 6420(f) "OTC Equity Security" means any equity security that is not an "NMS stock" as that term is defined in Rule 600(b)(47) of SEC Regulation NMS; provided, however, that the term "OTC Equity Security" shall not include any Restricted Equity Security. In plain English, any stock that is not covered by the National Market System and its protections is considered an Over the Counter (OTC) Equity stock.

6430 - Recording of quotation information - any OTC market maker that displays real-time quotes must keep record of certain information including the submitting firm, inter-dealer quotation system, trade date, time quote displayed, security name and symbol, bid and bid quote size, offer and offer quote size, prevailing inside bid, and prevailing inside offer.

6438 - Displaying priced quotations in multiple quotation mediums - if a member displays quotes on multiple real-time quotation mediums, the same priced quotes for a security are to be displayed in each medium.

6440 - FINRA may call halts in OTC trading to protect the public interest

6450 - sets maximum pricing for OTC transaction fees

6460 - sets rules for displaying limit orders

6480 - Members need to use the same MPID to report a quote and any subsequent transactions, and must submit written requests for multiple MPIDs.

If a member operates an alternative trading system (ATS), the member must obtain a MPID for each ATS, and must only report transactions from that ATS with each MPID.

QUOTING AND TRADING IN NMS STOCKS

FINRA Rule series 6100 covers quoting and trading in National Market System (NMS) stocks. It consists of 16 specific rules designed to comply with Regulation NMS.

- 6100 - Quoting and trading in NMS stocks
- 6110 - Trading other than on an exchange
- 6120 - Trading halts

- 6121 - Trading halts due to extraordinary market volatility
- 6130 - Transactions related to initial public
- 6140 - Other trading practices
- 6150 - Obligation to provide information
- 6160 - Multiple MPIDS for trade reporting facility participants
- 6170 - Multiple MPIDS for alternative display facility parties
- 6180 - Transaction reporting
- 6181 - Timely transaction reporting
- 6182 - Trade reporting on short sales
- 6183 - Exemption from trade reporting obligation for certain alternative trading systems
- 6184 - Transactions in exchange-traded managed fund shares ("NextShares")
- 6190 - Compliance with Regulation NMS plan to address extraordinary market volatility
- 6191 - Compliance with Regulation NMS plan to implement a tick size pilot program

TIMEFRAMES FOR PUBLICATION OF TRADES AND QUOTES IN OTC STOCKS

FINRA Rule 6110 indicates timeframes for publication of trades and quotes that do not occur through an exchange (i.e., over-the-counter (OTC) trades). The timeframes for publication by FINRA are as follows:

- For Tier 1 stocks (stocks included in the S&P 500 Index, Russell 1000 Index and some exchange-traded funds), trade information must be published no later than two weeks from the end of the trading week.
- For Tier 2 stocks (all other stocks not included in definition of Tier 1), trade information must be published within four weeks.

PROVISION REGARDING TRANSACTIONS RELATED TO IPOS

Transactions related to initial public offerings (FINRA Rule 6130) - a member is not to execute a transaction outside of an exchange in an initial public offering security until the security has been opened for trading on a national securities exchange.

Obligation of lead underwriter - it is the obligation of the lead underwriter to notify NASDAQ the IPO has been released by the SEC.

OPERATION AND USE OF THE OTC BULLETIN BOARD®

FINRA Rule 6500 Series, known as the "OTC Bulletin Board Rules," govern the operation and use of the OTC Bulletin Board® service (OTCBB) by broker-dealers and their associated persons.

The Series consists of five specific rules:

- 6510 - Applicability
- 6520 - Operation of Service
- 6530 - OTCBB-eligible Securities
- 6540 - Requirements Applicable to Market Makers
- 6550 - Transaction Reporting

TRADE REPORTING REQUIREMENTS

FINRA Rule 6600 Series requires aggregated trading information for OTC transactions to be published by FINRA on its public web site within specified time frames. To facilitate this, OTC Reporting Facility Participants must, as soon as practicable but no later than 10 seconds after execution, transmit to the OTC Reporting Facility last sale reports of transactions in OTC Equity

Securities executed during normal market hours. Transactions not reported within 10 seconds after execution shall be designated as late.

CASH ON DELIVERY ORDERS REGULATIONS

FINRA Rule 11860 prohibits cash on delivery transactions for securities unless the transaction adheres to a strict set of rules. Before the transaction is entered into, the FINRA member must be aware that the transaction will be cash on delivery, the transaction should be marked as such, and the customer must receive a confirmation of the transaction by the end of the next business day. The FINRA member must receive a signed agreement from the customer stating that the "customer will furnish his agent instructions with respect to the receipt or delivery of the securities involved in the transaction promptly upon receipt by the customer of each confirmation, or the relevant data as to each execution" to help ensure that good and prompt delivery is made.

IDENTIFICATION OF QUOTATIONS AND INITIATION OR RESUMPTION OF QUOTATIONS

Identification of quotations (Rule 15c2-7) - when a quote is submitted, the inter-dealer quotation system must be informed and must disclose each published quotation. If two broker-dealers enter into an arrangement to each enter certain quotations for a security, it must be disclosed to all broker-dealers with similar quotations.

Initiation or resumption of quotations with specified information (Rule 15c2-11) - in order to publish a quote, a broker-dealer must have certain documents or information regarding the security. These documents or information can include a copy of the prospectus, a copy of the offering circular, or a copy of the issuer's most recent annual report.

SEC RULE 15C2-11 AND QUOTATION RECORDS

SEC Rule 15c2-11 requires a broker or dealer to publish any quotation for a security or, directly or indirectly, to submit any such quotation for publication and to maintain in its records the following documents and information:

- Copy of the prospectus
- Copy of the offering circular
- Current copy of the annual report
- Information concerning the issuer and security, including name and address, state of incorporation or registration, title, class and ticker symbol of the security, and number of shares outstanding.

The documents and information required under this rule must be preserved for a period of not less than three years, the first two years in an easily accessible place.

REQUIREMENTS OF ALTERNATIVE TRADING SYSTEMS

Regulation ATS states that Alternative Trading Systems (ATSs) must comply with the following requirements:

- Register as a broker-dealer under section 15 of the Act
- File an initial operation report on Form ATS
- Provide to a national securities exchange or national securities association the prices and sizes of the orders at the highest buy price and the lowest sell price for such NMS stock
- Not charge any fee to members that is contrary to, that is not disclosed in the manner required by, or that is inconsistent with any standard of equivalent access established by such rules

- Establish written standards for granting access to trading on its system
- Establish reasonable current and future capacity estimates
- Permit the examination and inspection of its premises, systems, and records
- Separately file the information required by Form ATS-R within 30 calendar days after the end of each calendar quarter
- Establish adequate written safeguards and written procedures to protect subscribers' confidential trading information
- Not use in its name the word "exchange," or derivations of the word "exchange," such as the term "stock market"

SHORT SALE REQUIREMENTS

Short sales—that is, when a customer borrows securities, sells them, and seeks to buy them back at a lower price, returning the securities to the lender and pocketing the profit—have special rules governing them, encapsulated in **Regulation SHO**. Regulation SHO demands that all relevant instances must be marked as short sale. Furthermore, the regulation requires brokerage firms to set its own rules for locating, borrowing, and delivering any securities which are intended to be sold short. Such firms must be able to locate and deliver the security on the delivery due date before any short sales occur.

REGULATION SHO BROKER-DEALERS REQUIREMENTS

Regulation SHO, or the SEC Rule 200 Series, establishes four general requirements:

Rule 200 — Requires a broker-dealer to mark all sell orders of any equity security as "long," "short" or "short exempt." A sell order may only be marked "long" if the seller is "deemed to own" the security being sold.

Rule 201 — Requires trading centers to have policies and procedures in place to restrict short selling when a covered security has triggered a circuit breaker by experiencing a price decline of at least 10% in one day. Once the circuit breaker has been triggered, the price test restriction will apply to short sale orders in that security for the remainder of the day and the following day, unless an exception applies.

Rule 203 — Prohibits a broker-dealer from accepting a short-sale order in any equity security from another person, or effecting a short sale order in an equity security for the broker-dealer's own account, unless the broker-dealer has: borrowed the security, entered into a bona-fide arrangement to borrow the security, or has reasonable grounds to believe that the security can be borrowed so that it can be delivered on the date delivery.

Rule 204 — Requires delivery of securities to a registered clearing agency for clearance and settlement on a long or short sale transaction in any equity security by settlement date. If such delivery cannot take place, the broker-dealer must close out a fail to deliver by the times described as follows: for short-sale transactions by no later than the beginning of regular trading hours on the settlement day following the settlement date, for long sales by no later than the beginning of regular trading hours on the third consecutive settlement day following the settlement date.

COA COMPLEX ORDERS

Cboe Rule 5.33 defines several types of Complex Orders and outlines the processes for completing them. Complex Orders are the simultaneous buying or selling of multiple options in one order.

Complex Orders are executed in two ways: Complex Order Auction (COA) or Complex Order Book (COB).

Complex Order Auction (COA) – A "COA-eligible" complex order is a buy (sell) complex order with user instructions to initiate a COA that is priced equal to or lower (higher) than the Synthetic Best Offer (Synthetic Best Bid). Synthetic Best Bid or Offer is the best bid or offer on the exchange for a complex order. Upon receipt of a COA-eligible order in any class, the System initiates the COA process by sending a COA auction message to all subscribers to the Exchange's data feeds that deliver COA auction messages. A COA auction message identifies the COA auction ID, instrument ID (i.e., complex strategy), quantity, and side of the market of the COA-eligible order. This begins a Response Time Interval, which is the time period during which users may submit a response to COA auction message. At the end of the Response Time Interval, the System executes a COA-eligible order (in whole or in part) against contra-side interest in price priority.

COB COMPLEX ORDERS

Complex Order Book (COB) – This refers to the Exchange's electronic book of complex orders maintained by the System. The COB Opening Process occurs at the beginning of each trading session and after a trading halt. Prior to the COB Opening Process, the System accepts order for inclusion in the Process. If there are matching complex orders in a complex strategy, the System determines the COB opening price, which is the price at which the most complex orders can trade. After the System determines a COB opening price, it executes matching complex orders at the COB opening price in price

priority (i.e., orders better than the COB opening price are executed first). If there are no matching complex orders in a complex strategy, the System opens the complex strategy without a trade and enters any orders in the complex strategy in the COB in time priority.

TYPES OF COB COMPLEX ORDERS

Cboe Rule 5.33 defines several types of Complex Orders processed in its Complex Order Book (COB). Among these types are:

All Sessions - a complex order a User designates as eligible to trade during both Global Trading Hours and Regular Trading Hours.

AON – a complex order that is to be executed in its entirety or not at all. An AON complex order may only execute following a COA, and is not eligible to rest in the COB.

Book Only - a complex order the System ranks and executes pursuant to this Rule 5.33 or cancels or rejects, as applicable (in accordance with the User's instructions).

Complex Only - a Day or Immediate-or-Cancel complex order a Market-Maker may designate to execute only against complex orders in the COB and not Leg into the Simple Book.

Compression or PCC Order - a complex order that satisfies the definition of Compression order in Rule 5.6(c). A Compression order is an order in SPX option contracts that may execute without exposure against another Compression order(s) totaling an equal number of option contracts.

Delta-Adjusted at Close or DAC - a complex order for which the System delta adjusts its execution price after the market close.

Index Combo - an order to purchase or sell one or more index option series and the offsetting number of Index Combinations defined by the delta.

Post Only - a complex order the System ranks and executes pursuant to this Rule 5.33 or cancels or rejects, as applicable (in accordance with the User's instructions), except the order may not remove liquidity from the COB or the Simple Book.

Related Futures Cross or RFC - an SPX or VIX complex order comprised of an option combo order coupled with a contra-side order or orders totaling an equal number of option combo orders.

RTH Only - a complex order a User designates as eligible to trade only during Regular Trading Hours or not designated as All Sessions.

QCC with Stock Order - a QCC Order (including a Complex QCC Order), as defined in Rule 5.6(c), entered with a stock component to be electronically communicated by the Exchange to a designated broker-dealer for execution on behalf of the submitting User.

Stock-option Order - the purchase or sale of a stated number of units of an underlying stock or a security convertible into the underlying stock, coupled with the purchase or sale of an option contract(s) on the opposite side of the market.

SYSTEMIZING ORDERS

Cboe Rule 5.7 states that each order, cancellation of, or change to an order transmitted to the Exchange must be "systematized" in a format approved by the Exchange, either before it is sent to the Exchange or upon receipt on the Exchange's trading floor. An order is systematized if the order is sent electronically to the Exchange or the order that is sent to the Exchange non-electronically (e.g., telephone orders) is input electronically into the Exchange's systems contemporaneously upon receipt on the Exchange.

With respect to non-electronic, market and marketable orders sent to the Exchange, the TPH responsible for systematizing the order must input into the Exchange's systems at least the following specific information:

- the option symbol
- the expiration month
- the expiration year
- the strike price
- buy or sell
- call or put
- the number of contracts
- the Clearing Trading Permit Holder

CIRCUIT BREAKER RULE

Pursuant to NYSE Rule 7.12, a market-wide trading halt will be triggered if the S&P 500 Index declines in price by specified percentages from the prior day's closing price of that index. It is often referred to as the "Circuit Breaker Rule". NYSE Rule 7.12 was piloted to comply with SEC Regulation NMS, Rule 608 and is currently in effect until October 18, 2021. The triggers are set at three circuit breaker thresholds: 7% (Level 1), 13% (Level 2), and 20% (Level 3).

A market decline that triggers a Level 1 or Level 2 halt after 9:30 a.m. ET and before 3:25 p.m. ET would halt market-wide trading for 15 minutes, while a similar market decline at or after 3:25 p.m. ET would not halt market-wide trading. A market decline that triggers a Level 3 halt at any time during the trading day would halt market-wide trading until the primary listing market opens the next trading day.

TYPES OF ORDERS AND THEIR MODIFIERS

NYSE Rule 7.31 defines types of orders and the rules for each.

There are two primary order types:

Market Order - An unpriced order to buy or sell a stated amount of a security that is to be traded at the best price obtainable without trading through the National Best Bid and Offer (NBBO).

Limit Order - An order to buy or sell a stated amount of a security at a specified price or better.

Orders also include a modifier for the time in force:

Day Modifier - Any order to buy or sell designated Day, if not traded, will expire at the end of the designated session on the day on which it was entered.

Immediate-or-Cancel (IOC) Modifier - A Limit Order may be designated IOC or Routable IOC. A Limit Order designated IOC is to be traded in whole or in part on the Exchange as soon as such order is received, and the quantity not so traded is cancelled. A Limit Order designated Routable IOC is to be traded in whole or in part on the Exchange as soon as such order is received, and the quantity not so traded routed to Away Market(s). Any quantity not immediately traded either on the Exchange or an Away Market will be cancelled.

AUCTIONS AND THE AUCTION PROCESS

NYSE Rule 7.35 Series defines Auction-related terms and discusses the Auction process.

Auction refers to the process for opening, reopening, or closing of trading of Auction-Eligible Securities on the Exchange, which can result in either a trade or a quote. Orders are ranked for purposes of how they are included in Auction Imbalance Information (i.e., the volume of better-priced buy (sell) shares that cannot be paired with both at-priced and better-priced sell (buy) shares at the Imbalance Reference Price) or for an Auction allocation, first by Price, then by Time. The Exchange disseminates Auction Imbalance Information via a proprietary data feed. Auction Imbalance Information is updated at least every second, unless there is no change to the information, and is disseminated until the Auction begins. The Exchange will not open or reopen a security, if such opening or reopening would be in the last ten minutes of trading before the end of Core Trading Hours. New orders received during the Auction Processing Period will be accepted but will not be processed until after the Auction Processing Period. After auction processing concludes, the Exchange will transition to continuous trading. Orders that are no longer eligible to trade will expire.

TRANSACTING BUSINESS ON THE NYSE FLOOR

NYSE Rule 54 states that only members are permitted to make or accept bids and offers, consummate transactions or otherwise transact business on the Floor in any security admitted to dealings on the Exchange.

However, an appropriately registered and supervised booth clerk working in a member organization's booth premise that is approved by the Exchange's regulatory staff to operate its booth premise similar to the member organization's "upstairs" office shall be allowed to process orders sent to the booth in the same manner that sales traders in a member organization's "upstairs office" are allowed to process orders.

NYSE Rule 64

NYSE Rule 64 states that bids and offers in securities admitted to dealings on an "issued" basis shall be made as "regular way." In addition, the Exchange may allow for any such additional settlement instructions and periods as the Exchange may from time to time determine.

Binding Bid and Offer Prices

NYSE Rule 71 states that all bids made and accepted, and all offers made and accepted, in accordance with Exchange Rules shall be binding, and that any bid that is made at the same or higher price of the prevailing offer shall result in a transaction at the offer price in an amount equal to the lesser of the bid or offer. The same principle shall apply when an offer is made at the same or lower price as the bid.

Block Orders

NYSE Rule 72 states that when a member has an order to buy and an order to sell an equivalent amount of the same security, and both orders are "block" orders and are not for the account of the member or an account over which the member has discretion, the member may "cross" those orders at a price at or within the Exchange best bid or offer.

The member's bid or offer shall be entitled to priority at such cross price, irrespective of pre-existing displayed bids or offers on the Exchange at that price. The member shall follow the crossing procedures of Rule 76, and another member may trade with either the bid or offer side of the cross transaction only to provide a price which is better than the cross price as to all or part of such bid or offer. A member who is providing a better price to one side of the cross transaction must trade with all other displayed market interest on the Exchange at that price before trading with any part of the cross transaction.

For purposes of this rule, a "block" shall be at least 10,000 shares or a quantity of stock having a market value of $200,000 or more, whichever is less.

As an example, if the Exchange's market Security A is quoted 20 to 20.01, 40,000 shares by 30,000 shares, a member intending to effect a 25,000 share "agency cross" transaction at a price of 20 must bid 20 for 25,000 shares and offer 25,000 shares at 20.01. The member's bid at 20 has priority, and the proposed cross could not be broken up at that price. The proposed cross could, however, be broken up at 20.01, as this would provide a better price to the seller. However, a member intending to trade with the offer side of the cross would first have to take the entire displayed 30,000 share offer at 20.01 before trading with any part of the offer side of the cross.

Requirements to Validate a Prior or Better Bid or Offers

NYSE Rule 74 states that a claim by a member who states that he had on the Floor a prior or better bid or offer shall not be sustained if the bid or offer was not made with the publicity and frequency necessary to make the existence of such bid or offer generally known at the time of the transaction.

Resolving Disputes on Bids and Offers

NYSE Rule 75 states that disputes arising on bids or offers, if not settled by agreement between the members interested, shall be settled by a Trading Official. In rendering a decision as to disputes regarding the amount traded, the Trading Official shall give primary weight to statements by any member who was not a party to the transaction and shall also take into account the size of orders held by parties to the disputed transaction, and such other facts as he deems relevant. Members may also proceed to resolve a dispute through long-standing arbitration procedures established under the Exchange's Rules.

214

When there is no dispute regarding a transaction except as to the amount traded and neither party can produce a witness, the transaction must be considered to have been for the smaller amount; provided, however, that if the member claiming the smaller amount held, at the time of the transaction in dispute, an order or orders totaling the larger amount, the Trading Official, in reaching his decision, shall take into consideration that fact and all other facts which he deems relevant.

REQUIREMENTS BEFORE INITIATING "CROSS" TRANSACTIONS

NYSE Rule 76 states that when a member has an order to buy and an order to sell the same security, he or she shall offer such security at a price which is higher than his or her bid by the minimum variation permitted in such security before making a transaction with himself or herself. All such bids and offers shall be clearly announced to the trading Crowd before the member may proceed with the proposed "cross" transaction.

The provisions of this rule apply only to manual transactions.

PROHIBITED ACTIVITIES ON THE FLOOR OF THE NYSE

NYSE Rule 77 states that no member shall offer publicly on the Floor:

1. to buy or sell securities "on stop" above or below the market
2. to buy or sell securities "at the close"
3. to buy or sell dividends
4. to bet upon the course of the market
5. to buy or sell privileges to receive or deliver securities

LENGTH OF IMPOSED TRADING HALTS WHEN THE DJIA DROPS

According to **NYSE Rule 80B**, trades will be stopped if the DJIA drops 10%, 20% or 30% in one day. Each percentage drop is accompanied by a specific length of time for which trades must be halted. If the DJIA drops 30% in one day, all trading is stopped for the remainder of the day. Trading will stop for the remainder of the day if the DJIA drops by 20% at 2:00 PM or later. Trades are stopped for only one hour in two circumstances: the DJIA drops 10% before 2:00 PM or it drops 10% between 1:00 and 2:00 PM. If the DJIA drops 20% prior to 1:00 PM, trades are halted for two hours. Trading will only be halted for thirty minutes if a 10% drop occurs between 2:00 and 2:30 PM.

DESIGNATED MARKET MAKERS

NYSE Rule 104 states that Designated Market Makers (DMMs) registered in one or more securities traded on the Exchange must engage in dealings for their own account to assist in the maintenance of a fair and orderly market insofar as reasonably practicable. The responsibilities and duties of a DMM specifically include, but are not limited to, the following:

- Assist the Exchange by providing liquidity as needed to provide a reasonable quotation and by maintaining a continuous two-sided quote with a displayed size of at least one round lot
- Facilitate openings and reopenings, including the Midday Auction, for each of the securities in which the DMM is registered as required under Exchange rules
- Facilitate the close of trading for each of the securities in which the DMM is registered as required by Exchange rules

RESPONSIBILITIES FOR PARTICIPATING ON THE FLOOR OF THE NYSE

NYSE Rule 123A pertains to the requirements of members and brokers participating in orders on the Exchange, including the following:

- Members will facilitate business on the Floor by sending their orders as early as possible before the opening.
- Members and member organizations who rent telephone spaces on the Floor may use at such spaces order forms, etc., bearing only their own name.
- A broker handling a market order, limit order or at-the-close order is to use due diligence to execute the order at the best price or prices available to him under the published market procedures of the Exchange.

NYSE RULES REGARDING TRADING HALTS

NYSE Rule 123D - Designated market makers (DMMs) are to ensure that registered securities open as close to the opening bell as possible. In the event that this is not possible, there are specific rules to follow. The NYSE has established processes for certain trading halts including equipment changeover, investment company units or index-linked securities, and dissemination of net asset value.

A. Equipment changeover - applicable when trading in a certain security is inhibited due to systems or equipment concerns.

B. Investment company units or index-linked securities - applicable in regards to investment company units or index-linked securities to allow for "closing the room."

C. Dissemination of net asset value - applicable when the NYSE sees that net asset value information is not being disseminated to all market participants at the same time.

PROPOSING BLOCK TRANSACTIONS OUTSIDE THE CURRENT MARKET QUOTATION

A block transaction that is proposed to be priced outside of the current market quotation is subject to NYSE Rule 127. Under this rule, the floor broker must take the following actions:

- inform the DMM of his or her intention to cross the block orders at a specific price
- probe the market to determine whether more stock would be lost to orders in the trading crowd than is reasonable under the circumstances
- fill at least a portion of the limit orders previously entered at the trading post from the block orders
- cross the remaining block orders at the negotiated clean-up price

NYSE Rule 127 sets forth the broker's obligation to fill the limit orders of the DMM and the trading crowd. Such obligations depend, in part, on whether the broker is handling agency orders for both sides of the block transaction or whether all or a part of one side of the block is for the brokerage firm's house account.

NYSE RULES 1000 TO 1004

NYSE Rules 1000-1004 described how NYSE Automatic Executions worked in the past (until August 2019). These rules have been replaced with the 7 series rules, notably rules 7.31, 7.32, and 7.37. The 1000-1004 rules may still be on the Series 7 exam in 2021 since the most recent FINRA study guide still includes them. However, in August 2019, the NYSE applied to the SEC to delete these rules and replace them with Pillar Rules 7.31, 7.32, and 7.37. The 1000-1004 rules no longer apply on the NYSE rules website as of 2021. On August 22, 2019, the Exchange completed its transition of all trading to the Pillar platform. Because the rules that are not applicable to trading on the Pillar trading platform are now obsolete, the Exchange deleted the old rules that have been replaced by a Pillar rule.

Auto Ex Order - (defined by Rule 13 until August 2019) An auto ex order is a limit order of 1099 shares or less priced at or above the Exchange's published offer (in the case of an order to buy) or at or below the Exchange's published bid (in the case of an order to sell), which a member or member organization has entered for automatic execution in accordance with, and to the extent provided by, Exchange Rules 1000- 1004.

BASIC REGULATIONS

Rule 1000 Automatic Execution of Limit Orders Against Orders Reflected in NYSE Published Quotation – only straight limit orders without tick restrictions are eligible for entry as automatic execution (auto ex) orders.

Rule 1001 Execution of Auto Ex Orders - auto ex orders shall be executed automatically and immediately reported.

Rule 1002 Availability of Automatic Execution Feature – security orders are eligible to receive an automatic execution if entered after the Exchange has disseminated a published bid or offer until 3:59 p.m.

Rule 1003 Application of Tick Tests - if a transaction has been agreed upon in the auction market, and an automatic execution involving auto ex orders is reported at a different price before the auction market transaction is reported, any tick test applicable to such auction market transaction shall be based on the last reported trade on the Exchange prior to such execution of auto ex orders.

Rule 1004 Election of Stop Orders and Percentage Orders - automatic executions of auto ex orders shall elect stop orders, stop limit orders and percentage orders electable at the price of such executions.

Processing and Confirming Customers' Transactions Pursuant to Regulatory Requirements and Informing Customers of Delivery Obligations and Settlement Procedures

INFORMATION REQUIRED ON ORDER TICKETS

An **order ticket** must be filed for every stock trade and must include: the account number of the client; the execution price; the time the order was received; the time the order was executed; the representative's ID number; whether the order is cash or margin; whether it is a market, day, or good-till-canceled order; whether the trade was solicited or unsolicited; whether it is a discretionary account; the stock or bond symbol; the number of shares or units; and what sort of trade it is (buy, sell short, etc.).

NASDAQ CONTINUED LISTING STANDARDS FOR PRIMARY EQUITY SECURITIES

NASDAQ Rule 5450 states that a Company that has its Primary Equity Security listed on the Global Market must continue to substantially meet all the requirements set forth below to maintain eligibility for listing:

- a minimum bid price of $1 per share
- at least 400 total shareholders
- at least one of the following:
  - Equity Standard: >=$10M of stockholders' equity, 750,000 publicly held shares with a market value of >=$5M, and at least 2 registered, active Market Makers
  - Market Value Standard: >=$50M of stockholders' equity, 1.1M publicly held shares with a market value of >=$15M, and at least 4 registered, active Market Makers
  - Total Assets/Total Revenue Standard: Total Assets and Total Revenue of at least $50M each for the most recent fiscal year, or 2 of 3 most recent years, 1.1M of publicly held shares with a market value of >=$15M, and at least 4 registered, active Market Makers

NASDAQ INITIAL LISTING STANDARDS FOR PRIMARY EQUITY SECURITIES

NASDAQ Rule 5405 states that a Company applying to list its Primary Equity Security on the Global Market must meet all the requirements set forth below:

- a minimum bid price of $4 per share
- at least $1.1M of unrestricted publicly held shares
- at least 400 shareholders who hold at least a round lot of shares (100 shares), at least half of whom hold unrestricted shares worth at least $2,500
- if the security is trading in the U.S. over-the-counter market as of the date of application, the security must have a minimum average daily trading volume of 2,000 shares over the 30 trading day period prior to listing
- if an ADR, at least 400,000 issued
- at least one of the following:
  - Income Standard - annual income from continuing operations before income taxes of at least $1,000,000, stockholders' equity of at least $15 million, market value of unrestricted publicly held shares of at least $8 million, and at least three registered and active Market Makers
  - Equity Standard - stockholders' equity of at least $30 million, two-year operating history, market value of unrestricted publicly held shares of at least $18 million, and at least three registered and active Market Makers
  - Market Value Standard - market value of listed securities of $75 million, market value of unrestricted publicly held shares of at least $20 million, and at least four registered and active Market Makers
  - Total Assets/Total Revenue Standard - total assets and total revenue of $75 million each for the most recently completed fiscal year or two of the three most recently completed fiscal years, market value of unrestricted publicly held shares of at least $20 million, and at least four registered and active Market Makers

DESIGNATED MARKET MAKER EXECUTION OF ORDERS

Designated market makers have a specific arrangement by which they execute orders in a particular sequence. Orders are executed by priority, parity, and precedence.

Priority refers to the fact that the highest bid and lowest ask prices are the first ones to be executed.

Parity refers to the chronological priority of orders. If multiple orders are placed at the highest bid or lowest ask price, then the orders arriving first are executed first.

Precedence involves the size of orders. Where priority and parity do not break the tie, then the larger orders receive higher priority.

SEC ORDER HANDLING RULES

The SEC has a number of regulations governing trades on the NASDAQ, including various **order handling rules**. These rules, as the name implies, cover how to handle different orders. Two such rules are the Limit Order Display rule and the Quote rule.

The **Limit Order Display rule** requires market makers to include better-priced limit orders in market maker quotes (i.e. better-priced than whatever the market makers' bid or ask price is). The goal is to provide investors with the lower price.

The **Quote rule** requires public quotes to be displayed for the securities on which market makers (or specialists) are making markets. The goal for this rule is to increase transparency.

NYSE LISTING REQUIREMENTS

NYSE Listing Requirements Summarized:

For US Companies to become listed, the company must apply to the NYSE and meet at least one of these criteria:

A. Pre-Tax income of $10M in the prior three years, with $2M or more in the last two and above $0 in all three years

B. If global, $200M of capitalization or if business development $75M a capitalization

C. If a REIT, $60M of shareholders' equity

D. Market Value Test:

For IPO, Spin-off, or Carve Out at least 400 shareholders who own 100 or more shares each and have at least 1.1M shares outstanding worth at least $40M and a price of at least $4 per share -- other types require $100M or more of value, and the criteria are higher for non-US companies.

In order for a stock to be delisted from the New York Stock Exchange (NYSE), the company may voluntarily request de-listing. De-listing requires the approval of both the company's board of directors and the board's audit committee. Additionally, de-listing requires notification to the company's 35 largest shareholders.

If the company does not maintain the appropriate profit, capitalization, shareholder composition or other NYSE requirement, the NYSE will warn the company and may eventually de-list that company.

STABILIZING BIDS

Stabilizing bids occur when underwriters, following an initial public offering, bid to repurchase the issued securities at the offer price. This is done in order to stabilize the secondary market price of the issued securities. Stabilizing bids are not forbidden, but they are regulated; if an underwriter wishes to do a stabilizing bid, he must first notify his regulatory authority.

PENALTY BIDS

Penalty bids are bids to purchase securities which have recently been issued in an initial public offering. These bids carry with them a penalty on the condition that the purchaser resells the securities in a specified amount of time, though the penalty disappears after that duration passes. The purpose of penalty bids is to prevent "flipping" IPO securities, that is, seeking to resell them quickly based on a fluctuation in price and gain a profit.

This penalty may sometimes be borne entirely by the client of a broker, but ordinarily requires the broker to forfeit any commission he gained back to his underwriting syndicate.

OVERALLOTMENTS

Overallotments are options for underwriters to sell additional securities within an initial public offering, normally no higher than 15% of the original issuance. Overallotments may be exercised for different reasons. If the securities have a high demand and/or are trading at a price higher than the initial price, then the overallotment option might be exercised to raise additional capital. However, they can also be used if the security price drops too low; the underwriters can seek to increase the security's trading price by repurchasing them at the lower price, thereby decreasing the supply, and then still have other securities to sell at a higher price.

Overallotments are also called **greenshoe options**, based on their origination with Green Shoe Manufacturing.

PROHIBITION AGAINST TRADING AHEAD OF CUSTOMER ORDERS

Prohibition against trading ahead of customer orders (FINRA Rule 5320) - a member that accepts an order from a customer and does not immediately execute it is prohibited from trading that same security on the same side of the market for its own account at a price that would satisfy the customer's order unless the member immediately after executes the customer order at the same or better price.

DESIGNATED MARKET MAKERS

Designated market makers (DMMs), also called specialists, seek to keep the trade of some particular security active, fair, and orderly in a stock exchange. Designated market makers will have the security in inventory, and will also post bid and ask prices for it. DMMs are broker-dealers.

Designated market makers are obligated to help the market move smoothly, but their ability to do that can also be used to wrongfully manipulate the market. Needless to say, DMMs are prohibited from market manipulation.

OBLIGATIONS OF MARKET-MAKERS

Cboe Rule 5.51 discusses the obligation of Market-Makers to contribute to the maintenance of a fair and orderly market, and includes the following requirements:

- maintain a continuous two-sided market in each of its appointed classes during the trading day
- engage, to a reasonable degree under existing circumstances, in dealings for its own accounts when there exists a lack of price continuity, a temporary disparity between the supply of (or demand for) a particular option contract, or a temporary distortion of the price relationships between option contracts of the same class
- compete with other Market-Makers in its appointed classes
- update quotations in response to changed market conditions in its appointed classes
- maintain active markets in its appointed classes
- make markets that will be honored for the number of contracts entered into the System in its appointed classes

AUTOMATIC TRADING SYSTEMS

Automatic execution systems allow for the placing and executing of trades without manual input. Automatic execution systems apply an algorithm to a specific set of objective indicators, which when at specified levels will trigger a signal to trade automatically. If a trade signal occurs, an order will be deployed and automatically executed within milliseconds if there is liquidity available at the order price.

While automatic execution systems allow traders to quickly deploy a trade when certain conditions are met, they can be disruptive to the marketplace. For instance, in what has become known as the "Flash Crash" of 2010, a decline in the DJIA triggered some automatic execution systems to sell, which in turn lowered the price even further causing more systems to sell, resulting in a nearly 10% decline in just 10 minutes.

The elements that comprise a business continuity plan are flexible and may be tailored to the size and needs of a member. Each plan, however, must at a minimum address:

- Regulatory reporting
- Communications with regulators
- How the member will assure customers prompt access to their funds and securities in the event that the member determines that it is unable to continue its business

Each member must disclose to its customers its business continuity plan in writing, at a minimum, at account opening, posted on the member's Web site, and mailed to customers upon request.

Each member must report to FINRA prescribed emergency contact information for the member. The emergency contact information for the member includes designation of two associated persons, at least one of whom must be a member of senior management and a registered principal of the member.

ELECTRONIC REPORTING SYSTEMS

Regulators and exchanges have created several electronic reporting systems to provide broader access to disclosures and pricing information, and to allow for better surveillance of markets. Among these systems are the following:

Order Audit Trail System (OATS) - an automated computer system established by FINRA for the reporting of information related to orders, quotes, and other trade data for equities traded on the National Market System (NMS), including over-the-counter (OTC) stocks. The purpose of the system is to easily track and review order information in cases of suspected error or market manipulation.

Trade Reporting and Compliance Engine (TRACE) – a system administered by FINRA for the reporting of information on fixed income security trades in the OTC market. The purpose of the system is to ensure broad access to bond pricing information.

Electronic Municipal Market Access (EMMA) – a publicly available system created by the MSRB for collecting and disseminating disclosure documents and other information about municipal securities.

SOURCES OF MARKET AND INVESTMENT INFORMATION

TRACE stands for the Trade Reporting and Compliance Engine. It is a program developed by FINRA to facilitate the reporting of various trades by brokers. The specific trades reported through TRACE involve over-the-counter secondary market transactions in eligible fixed-income securities. Brokers who are FINRA members are obligated to use TRACE for reporting such transactions.

NASDAQ stands for the National Association of Securities Dealers Automated Quotations. Following the New York Stock Exchange, it is the second largest stock exchange in the world,

Rating agencies are independent entities which provide independent opinions on the worthiness of value of various assets, stocks in particular.

A **Trade Reporting Facility (TRF)** is a service used to facilitate automated trade reporting and reconciliation, specifically for trades which are not made on an exchange. TRFs are available for use by FINRA members.

Electronic Municipal Market Access (EMMA) is an online source of information for municipal bonds. EMMA is free of charge and geared towards nonprofessional investors.

MIG-1 ratings are the best ratings which can be received according to Moody's system of municipal bond credit ratings. Brokers should pay careful attention to such ratings.

REAL-TIME TRADE REPORTING

Since the value of securities depends heavily upon the actual market trades which are occurring, it is crucial that trades be reported quickly for others to review the relevant information and come to informed conclusions for their own investment decisions. This shows the importance of **real-time trade reporting**, which requires market makers, and sometimes non-market makers, to report trades immediately following the completion of the transaction. Ordinarily the report time is within ninety seconds.

ORDER AUDIT TRAIL SYSTEM AND TRADE REPORTING FACILITY

The **Order Audit Trail System (OATS)** is an automated computer system which is owned by the National Association of Securities Dealers (NASD) and which tracks information for securities transactions, such as quotes, orders, and other information. By tracking the progress of a transaction from the initial order to the final completion (or cancellation) of the order, the system permits audits for such orders to more easily take place.

ELECTRONIC REPORTING SYSTEM ACRONYMS

Trade Reporting Facility (TRF) – systems from the various security exchanges (i.e., NYSE) for the purpose of providing information on securities trades through the exchanges.

Real-Time Transaction Reporting System (RTRS) – a system created by the MSRB for the purpose of collecting and disseminating transaction data in municipal securities for market transparency, surveillance purposes and analytics.

Automated Confirmation Transaction Service (ACT) – a system established and operated by NASDAQ for the purpose of documenting and reporting the clearing of trades on the NASDAQ exchanges. Brokers and market makers are required to participate in the system by entering all trade confirmations for matching and clearing.

MARKET MAKER REPORTS

FINRA regulations require that **market makers** must file reports during designated hours of their last sales. These reports must include the price, size, whether it was a buy, sell, or cross trade, and the NASDAQ symbol. These reports must be filed within ninety seconds of the transaction. In addition, market makers must file a daily report on the total numbers of shares they traded that day in the stocks they're making a market for.

GOOD DELIVERY

Good delivery refers to the proper transfer of a security from a seller to a buyer. The requirements for good delivery depend on the security type but among the general requirements are:

- certificate must be in good physical condition (i.e., not mutilated)
- certificate must be endorsed by all owners
- the exact number of securities (whether shares or bonds) must be delivered in the correct denomination

GOOD DELIVERY REQUIREMENTS FOR BONDS

Good delivery for bonds depends on the type of bond.

Bearer bonds (aka, coupon bonds), which are not registered to a particular individual, must be delivered with all the related unpaid coupons attached to the certificate and can only be delivered in denominations of $1,000 or $5,000.

Registered bonds, which are registered to a particular individual, require delivery of a physical bond certificate and must be delivered in multiples of $1,000 par value, not to exceed $100,000 par value.

Book entry bonds require no physical certificate and are transferred electronically. Book entry bonds can be purchased in denominations of $25 and above.

GOOD DELIVERY REQUIREMENTS FOR STOCK

Good delivery for stock generally requires delivery in round lots of 100 shares (100, 200, 300, etc.), divisors of 100 shares (5,10,25, 50, etc.), or units that up to 100 shares (30 shares + 70 shares, etc.).

In 2008, FINRA changed the definition of a round lot to 1 share if the stock trades for $175 or more per share. Trades of fewer than 100 shares are termed odd lot trades and may take longer to settle and charge higher commissions.

As an example, in a trade of 430 shares, if the trade were comprised of two 200-share certificates and a 30-share certificate, the trade would be in good delivery form, since the two 200-share certificates would be multiples of 100, and the 30-share certificate would be exempt as an odd lot portion. However, if the trade were comprised of one 300-share certificate and two 65-share certificates, then it would not be in good form, since, while the 300-share certificate is valid as a multiple of 100 shares, the two 65-share certificates do not meet any of the requirements and are not exempt as an odd lot portion.

Business Continuity and Disaster Recovery Planning

FINRA 4370 requires members to create and maintain a written business continuity plan identifying procedures relating to an emergency or significant business disruption. Such procedures must be reasonably designed to enable the member to meet its existing obligations to customers. In addition, such procedures must address the member's existing relationships with other broker-dealers and counter-parties.

Each member must update its plan in the event of any material change to the member's operations, structure, business or location, and must conduct an annual review of its business continuity plan to determine whether any modifications are necessary.

The elements that comprise a business continuity plan are flexible and may be tailored to the size and needs of a member. Each plan, however, must at a minimum address:

- Data back-up and recovery (hard copy and electronic)
- All mission critical systems (any system that is necessary, depending on the nature of a member's business, to ensure prompt and accurate processing of securities transactions0
- Financial and operational assessments
- Alternate communications between customers and the member
- Alternate communications between the member and its employees
- Alternate physical location of employees
- Critical business constituent, bank, and counter-party impact

Endorsements, Transfer Agents, and Registrars

Paper stock certificates and bonds are signed, or endorsed, to reflect ownership.

Registrars maintain records of security ownership on behalf of the issuing company.

Transfer agents function as an intermediary between the investor and the registrar by issuing and cancelling certificates. Transfer agents also ensure that investors receive dividend and interest payments and generally facilitate processes such as proxy voting, tax reporting and annual report distribution.

The registrar and the transfer agent are often the same entity, such as a bank or trust company.

Medallion Signature Guarantee Program

What is the Medallion Signature Guarantee Program? It is also called the Securities Transfer Agents Medallion Program (STAMP), and there are thousands of banks and financial institutions who participate. If an investor holds securities or funds in his or her name, he or she may need a

Medallion Signature Guarantee to trade. A guarantee of a person's signature is required by all Transfer Agents before a security transfer can take place and SEC Rule 17Ad-15 requires that Transfer Agents adopt an equitable methodology for the acceptance of signature guarantees from eligible Guarantor institutions.

- Medallion signature guarantees that an authorized signature to transfer securities is authentic.
- To provide a Medallion signature guarantee, an institution must be a member of one of three Medallion signature guarantee programs. The Securities Transfer Agents Medallion Program, the Stock Exchanges Medallion Program, or the New York Stock Exchange Medallion Signature Program.
- The investor can obtain a Medallion signature guarantee at a financial institution where he or she is already a customer (that institution is guaranteeing the funds so may have special requirements).
- Medallion signature guarantees are generally required when securities are held in physical certificate form.
- Today individual investors rarely have physical possession of their share certificates, preferring electronic records instead.

STOCK CERTIFICATES

A **stock certificate** is a piece of paper stating how many shares of the stock a person owns. It also includes the name of the company, the investor's name, and the CUSIP number. CUSIP stands for Committee on Uniform Securities Identification Procedures. This is a unique identifier of stocks and bonds, much like a serial number, and it can be used to identify the rightful owner of these instruments if they're lost or stolen. To sell stocks, the owner of the shares must sign the back of the certificate, or a stock power, giving the right to his broker to make the transfer.

DUE BILLS

Because of the way dividends are paid, and the lag between the date of record and the payment day, many times the present owner of a share of stock will not be the person who's actually entitled to the dividend. But that doesn't necessarily mean the dividend will automatically be sent to the rightful owner. Mistakes are made, and sometimes the dividend is sent to the present shareholder, and not to the owner of record. If this happens, it is the responsibility of the owner of record's firm to contact the firm of the shareholder who received the dividend, and present a **due bill**, which simply points out the mistake and requests that it be promptly corrected.

WHAT HAPPENS WHEN THE CUSTOMER DIES

When a customer or client dies, the response on the part of the brokerage is pretty straightforward and simple. As soon as the brokerage has been notified of the death of the account holder, they must mark the account "**deceased**" and cancel all open orders. Any power of attorney in place is revoked, also. The assets in the account are then frozen, and left in place, until the brokerage received instructions from the estate of the client.

BOOK-ENTRY SECURITIES AND THE DIRECT REGISTRATION SYSTEM

Securities used to be represented mostly by physical certificates, but **book-entry securities** (also called book-entry receipts) are recorded merely electronically. These securities can be recorded in the **Direct Registration System**, a method of storing and trading shares. Trading electronically has the benefits of increased convenience, reduced time spent for trades, and decreased administrative costs.

Good delivery for book-entry securities carries with it different requirements than for physical certificates (e.g., a different requirement regarding mutilated certificates), according to the different nature of the transactions.

REGULAR WAY SETTLEMENT

Regular-way settlement (RW) refers to the standard settlement cycle for a particular type of security.

Regular-way settlement for stocks, mutual funds, exchange-traded funds, corporate bonds, and municipal securities transactions is T+2 (transaction day plus two days). In 2017, the SEC shortened the period from T+3 due to technology advancements that facilitated faster settlement.

Regular-way settlement for government bills, notes and bonds, as well as options, is T+1.

ASSIGNMENT OF STOCKS

Stock assignment refers to the legal transfer of ownership of stock shares. This can be accomplished by completing a stock transfer form obtained from the stock's transfer agent. The stock certificate must be endorsed, and the owner must receive a Medallion signature guarantee from a financial institution. Then the form and certificates must be sent to the transfer agent.

Individuals can assign, or gift, up to $15,000 each year tax-free to an unlimited number of recipients. Gifts in excess of that amount require the donor to file an estate and gift tax return, but there would be no tax implications unless the gift exceeded their lifetime gift and estate tax exemption.

The recipient of the stock does not owe any capital gains taxes until the shares are sold. If the recipient sells the stock for a gain, the donor's cost basis and purchase date is used to determine the realized capital gain. For example, if the donor bought the stock more than a year ago, it is considered a long-term gain, with tax rates of 0%, 15%, or 20%, depending on the recipient's income tax bracket. If the recipient sells the shares for a loss, the cost basis is the lower of the donor's cost basis or the fair market value (FMV) on the transfer date.

KEY DATES RELATED TO DIVIDENDS

There are four major dates in the process of a dividend distribution:

Declaration date - the date the board of directors approves and announces the dividend. The declaration includes the size of the dividend and identifies the record date and payment date.

Ex-dividend date - the first day that a stock trades without a dividend. Purchasers of the stock on or after this date are not entitled to a dividend. The ex-dividend date is set by the Exchange where the stock trades and is generally three days or less from the record date.

Record date - the date on which the investor must be on the company's books in order to receive a dividend.

Payment date - the date on which the dividend is paid to shareholders.

The stock price generally declines on the ex-dividend date as purchasers on that date will not receive the dividend.

Payment of Cash Dividends

When a corporation pays a cash dividend to investors, the way an investor receives the money depends on the way he or she holds the stock. Many investors hold stock through a brokerage in the broker's street name. The company pays the dividend to the brokerage, and the brokerage credits the accounts of investors holding the stock. Alternatively, an investor could have the shares registered in his or her name. In this case, the company will wire (if the investor set up ACH with the transfer agent) or send a check for the dividend directly to the shareholder.

When, As, and If Issued Transactions

When, as, and if issued transactions—also called **when issued (WI) transactions** for short—are transactions which involve securities that are authorized for sale but not yet issued. If a new issue of securities has not yet had a public offering, investors can still be sought to purchase the securities, and if they purchase the securities prior to the date of issuance, then the orders are "when issued" orders. These orders are **conditional orders**, because the offering may change the terms of the transactions, or even not occur at all.

Cash Settlement

Using cash settlement, which is also known as **same day settlement**, the seller must deliver the securities, and the buyer must pay for the securities, on the day the trade is executed. If the trade takes place before 2:00 p.m. ET, then settlement must take place by 2:30 p.m. If the trade takes place after 2:00 p.m., it must be settled within thirty minutes.

DK Notifications

Trades between dealers are submitted to the **Automated Confirmation Transaction Service (ACT)** via electronic means. On some occasions, the terms that one side submits won't match the terms the other side submits, either because of an error in input, or because one side misunderstood the terms, such as price, number of shares, etc. In this case, the party will receive a **DK notification**, which is short hand for "Don't Know," and the parties must reconcile the discrepancy.

Ex-Rights Shares of Stock

Some stocks have certain rights associated with them, such as the right to buy shares from a corporation at a discount or before the issuance date. Sometimes shares of stock will no longer have these rights attached to them, and when that is the case, the stocks are **ex-rights shares** and worth less. The rights can be gone for whatever reason, whether they are expired, transferred to someone else, or already exercised.

Adjustment of Orders and Short-Interest Reporting

Adjustment of orders (FINRA Rule 5330) - When a member holds an order from another broker-dealer, the member is to adjust the price and/or number of shares to compensate for any dividend, payment, or distribution on the day of the quote for the security, according to guidelines outlined in the Rule.

Short-interest reporting (FINRA Rule 4560) - members are to maintain records of all of the short equity positions in all accounts and report regularly to FINRA such information.

FINRA 6000 Series Quotation, Order and Transaction Reporting Facilities

The FINRA 6000 Series rules address the Quotation, Order, and Transaction Reporting Facilities for members. The rules include:

- The 6100 Rules - Quoting and Trading in NMS Stocks
- The 6200 Rules - Alternative Display Facility
- The 6300 Rules - Trade Reporting Facilities
- The 6400 Rules - Quoting and Trading in OTC Equity Securities
- The 6500 Rules - OTC Bulletin Board Service
- The 6600 Rules - OTC Reporting Facility
- The 6700 Rules - Trade Reporting and Compliance Engine (TRACE)
- The 6800 Rules - Consolidated Audit Trail Compliance Rule

Prohibited Trading Practices

FINRA Rule 6140 specifies prohibited misleading or manipulative trading practices, including:

- Executing purchases of any NMS stock at successively higher prices, or sales of any such security at successively lower prices, for the purpose of creating or inducing a false, misleading or artificial appearance of activity in such security or for the purpose of unduly or improperly influencing the market price for such security
- Executing any transaction in a security which involves no change in the beneficial ownership thereof
- Entering any order for the purchase/sale of such security with the knowledge that an order of substantially the same size, and at substantially the same price, for the sale/purchase of any such security, has been or will be entered by or for the same or different parties
- Executing purchases or sales that are excessive in view of the member's financial resources or in view of the market for such security
- Participating or having any interest in the profits of a manipulative operation or knowingly managing or financing a manipulative operation
- Making any statement or circulating and disseminating any information which the member knows or has reasonable grounds for believing is false or misleading or would improperly influence the market price of such security
- Holding any interest or participation in a joint account for buying or selling a designated security, unless such joint account is promptly reported to FINRA
- Offering that a transaction to buy or sell a designated security will influence the closing transaction in that security

TRACE System
Reporting Requirements

The FINRA Rule 6700 Series outlines the requirements for reporting to Trade Reporting and Compliance Engine (TRACE).

A TRACE-Eligible Security is a debt security that is U.S. dollar-denominated and is issued by a U.S. or foreign private issuer, an Agency or a Government-Sponsored Enterprise; or is a U.S. Treasury Security.

For members of FINRA, participation in TRACE for trade reporting is mandatory. A member must report a transaction in a TRACE-Eligible Security as soon as practicable, but no later than within 15 minutes of the Time of Execution. Transactions not reported within the specified timeframe will be designated as "late."

INFORMATION REQUIRED ON REPORTS

Each TRACE trade report must contain the following information:

- CUSIP number, similar numeric identifier (e.g., a mortgage pool number) or a FINRA symbol
- Size (volume) of the transaction
- Price of the transaction (or the elements necessary to calculate price, which are contract amount and accrued interest)
- A symbol indicating whether the transaction is a buy or a sell
- Date of Trade Execution ("as/of" trades only)
- Contra-party's identifier (MPID, customer, or a non-member affiliate)
- Capacity — Principal or Agent
- Time of Execution
- Reporting side executing broker as "give-up" (if any)
- Contra side Introducing Broker in case of "give-up" trade
- The commission (total dollar amount), if applicable
- Date of settlement
- If the member is reporting a transaction that occurred on an ATS pursuant to Rule 6732, the ATS's separate MPID obtained in compliance with Rule 6720(c)
- Such trade modifiers as required by either the TRACE rules or the TRACE users guide

FINRA 7000-SERIES RULES

The FINRA 7000 Series rules address the Clearing, Transactions and Order Data Requirements and Facility Charges for members. The rules include:

- The 7100 Series - Alternative Display Facilities
- The 7200 Series - Trade Reporting Facilities (NASDAQ, NYSE)
- The 7300 Series - OTC Reporting Facility
- The 7400 Series - Order Audit Trail System (OATS)
- The 7500 Series - Charges for Alternative Display Facilities
- The 7600 Series - Data Products and Charges for Trade Reporting Facility Services
- The 7700 Series - Charges for OTC Reporting Facility, OTC Bulletin Board and Trade Reporting and Compliance Engine Services

INFORMATION PROVIDED FOR REPORTABLE SYSTEM TRANSACTIONS

An AFS-eligible security is a National Market System (NMS) stock.

Participation is mandatory for any FINRA member that has an obligation to report an over-the-counter transaction to FINRA. Participants must transmit trade reports to the System for Reportable System Transactions as soon as practicable but no later than 10 seconds after execution or must accept or decline trades within 20 minutes after execution. Unless the contra side will have an opportunity to provide its own trade information, the Reporting Member is responsible for the complete and accurate submission of information for both sides of the trade, which must include:

- Security identification symbol of the eligible security (SECID)
- Number of shares
- Unit price, excluding commissions, mark-ups or mark-downs

- The time of execution expressed in hours, minutes and seconds based on Eastern Time in military format
- A symbol indicating whether the party submitting the trade report represents the Reporting Member side or the Non-Reporting Party side
- A symbol indicating whether the transaction is a buy, sell or cross
- A symbol indicating whether the trade is as principal, riskless principal, or agent
- Reporting side clearing broker (if other than normal clearing broker)
- Reporting side executing broker as "give-up" (if any)
- Contra side executing broker
- Contra side introducing broker in case of "give-up" trade
- Contra side clearing broker (if other than normal clearing broker)
- Designated indicator for special trades and "step outs"

LOCKED-IN TRADES

Trades may be locked-in in one the following three ways:

- Trade by Trade Match - Both parties to the trade submit transaction data and the System performs an on-line match
- Trade Acceptance - The Reporting Party enters its version of the trade and the contra party reviews the trade report and accepts or declines the trade
- Automatic Lock-in - Any trade that remains open (i.e., unmatched or unaccepted) at the end of its entry day will be carried over for continued comparison and reconciliation. The System will automatically lock in and submit to DTCC as such any carried-over T to T+21 (calendar day) trade if it remains open as of 2:30 p.m. on the next business day

UNIFORM PRACTICE CODE REQUIREMENTS

The FINRA Series 11000 rules outline the requirements set forth in the Uniform Practice Code.

- 11100 Scope of Uniform Practice - All over-the-counter secondary market transactions in securities between members are subject to the provisions of this Code.
- 11200 Comparisons, Confirmations, Don't Know Notices - Each party to a transaction must send a Uniform Comparison or Confirmation on or before the first business day following the date of the transaction.
- 11300 Delivery of Securities - A member must use the facilities of a securities depository for the book-entry settlement of all transactions in depository eligible securities and delivery must be made in accordance with the rules for that type of transaction (e.g., cash, regular way, etc.).
- 11400 Delivery of Securities with Draft Attached - Drafts accompanying the shipment of securities need be accepted only on a business day between the hours established by rule or practice in the community where the draft is presented.
- 11500 Delivery of Securities with Restrictions – Defines situations that would not be considered good delivery of securities.
- 11600 Delivery of Bonds and Other Evidences of Indebtedness - A coupon bond must have securely attached in the correct place proper coupons, warrants, etc., of the same serial number as the bond and interest must be added to the dollar price at the rate specified in the security up to but not including the date of transaction.

- 11700 Reclamations and Rejections - A properly executed Uniform Reclamation Form must accompany securities on reclamation or return. Reclamation may be made due to irregularity in the delivery of a security, or if a specific certificate tendered in settlement of a contract has been refused by the transfer agent.
- 11800 Close-out Procedures - A securities contract that has not been completed by the seller according to its terms may be closed by the buyer not sooner than the third business day following the date delivery was due. Upon failure of the buyer to accept delivery in accordance with the terms of the contract and lacking a properly executed Uniform Reclamation Form the seller may, without notice, "sell-out" in the best available market and for the account and liability of the party in default.
- 11900 Clearance of Corporate Debt Securities - Each member that is a participant in a registered clearing agency must use the facilities of a registered clearing agency for the clearance of eligible transactions between members in corporate debt securities.

SETTLEMENT CYCLE

SEC Rule 15c6-1 states that a broker or dealer may not affect or enter into a contract for the purchase or sale of a security that provides for payment of funds and delivery of securities later than the second business day after the date of the contract unless otherwise expressly agreed to by the parties at the time of the transaction. Additionally, FINRA Rules 6274 and 6350 require members to clear and settle transactions with a clearing agency that uses a continuous net settlement system.

Regulation T outlines the requirements related to the amount of credit that brokerage firms and dealers may extend to customers for the purchase of securities through a margin account. In general, an investor may borrow up to 50% of the purchase price of securities. A Reg-T call is issued when there is not enough equity in the margin account, at which point the investor may deposit funds into the account or if he cannot, the broker or dealer can liquidate securities. Reg-T calls are generally due four days after the call is issued (T+4).

CBOE RULE 6.20 AND EXERCISING OPTIONS CONTRACTS

Cboe Rule 6.20 states that an exercise notice may be tendered to the Clearing Corporation only by the Clearing Trading Permit Holder in whose account such option contract is carried within the time periods established by the Exchange. Generally, an Exercise Advice must be delivered by the TPH no later than 4:20 p.m., or if trading hours are extended or modified in the applicable option class, no later than five minutes after the close of Regular Trading Hours on that business day.

A TPH may choose to communicate a Contrary Exercise Advice (CEA) to either not exercise an option that would be automatically exercised under the Clearing Corporation's Ex-by-Ex procedure, or to exercise an option that would not be automatically exercised under the Clearing Corporation's Ex-by-Ex procedure. In such cases, the CEA is submitted using the Exchange's Contrary Exercise Advice Form or the Clearing Corporation's ENCORE System. CEAs must be delivered within 3 hours 30 minutes following the time announced for the close of Regular Trading Hours in noncash-settled equity options on that same day.

The Rule also states that no TPH may at any time prepare, time stamp or submit an exercise instruction for an American-style index option series if the TPH knows or has reason to know that the exercise instruction calls for the exercise of more contracts than the then "net long position" of the account.

CBOE RULE 6.21 AND ALLOCATION OF EXERCISE NOTICES

Cboe Rule 6.21 states that each TPH organization must establish fixed procedures for the allocation of exercise notices assigned in respect of a short position in customers' accounts. The allocation must be on a "first in, first out", or automated random selection basis that has been approved by the Exchange, or on a manual random selection basis that has been specified by the Exchange.

Each TPH organization must also inform its customers in writing of the method it uses to allocate exercise notices to its customers' accounts and report its proposed method of allocation to the Exchange and obtain the Exchange's prior approval. A TPH organization may not change its method of allocation unless the change has been reported to and approved by the Exchange.

Each TPH organization shall preserve for a three-year period sufficient work papers and other documentary materials relating to the allocation of exercise notices to establish the manner in which allocation of such exercise notices is in fact being accomplished.

GOVERNMENT SECURITIES OPTIONS AND CORPORATE DEBT SECURITY OPTIONS

In the case of Government securities options, the method of allocation may provide that an exercise notice of block size (principal amount is $1 million or more and where the underlying security) be allocated to customers having an open short position of block size and that an exercise notice of less than block size shall not be allocated to a customer having a short position of block size.

In the case of Corporate Debt Security options, the method of allocation may provide that an exercise notice of a round lot (a series of options of 10 contracts) be allocated to a customer or customers having an open short position of a round lot and that an exercise notice of less than a round lot shall not be allocated to a customer having a short position of a round lot.

CBOE RULE 6.22 AND TIMELY PAYMENT OF EXERCISED OPTIONS CONTRACTS

Cboe Rule 6.22 states that as promptly as possible after the exercise of an option contract by a customer, the TPH organization must require the customer to make full cash payment of the aggregate exercise price in the case of a call option contract, or to deposit the underlying security in the case of a put option contract, or to make the required margin deposit.

For Government Securities and Corporate Debt Securities Options, payment of the aggregate exercise price must be accompanied by payment of accrued interest.

PROCESSING, CLEARING AND SETTLING TRANSACTIONS

MSRB Rule G-12 states that transactions must be settled in one of the following ways:

- Cash transactions – on the trade date
- Regular way transactions – second business day following the trade date
- "When, as and if issued" and other transactions – date agreed upon by both parties

Each party to a transaction must send a confirmation to the other party on trade date. Confirmations of cash transactions must be exchanged by telephone, with written confirmation sent within one business day following the trade date.

CONFIRMATIONS OF CASH TRANSACTIONS

Confirmations must contain the following information:

- confirming party's name, address and telephone number
- contra party identification
- designation of purchase from or sale to
- par value of the securities
- description of the securities
- CUSIP number
- trade date
- settlement date
- yield at which transaction was affected and resulting dollar price
- amount of concession, if any, per $1000 par value
- amount of accrued interest
- extended principal amount
- total dollar amount of transaction
- instructions, if available, regarding receipt or delivery of securities

Upon receipt of a confirmation, each party to a transaction must compare and verify such confirmation to ascertain whether any discrepancies exist. If any discrepancies exist, the party discovering such discrepancies must promptly communicate such discrepancies to the contra party and both parties must promptly attempt to resolve the discrepancies. In the event the parties are unable to resolve the discrepancies, each party must promptly send to the contra party a written notice, return receipt requested, indicating nonrecognition of the transaction. Finally, delivery must be made to the purchaser either through physical delivery at his or her office during business hours or via book-entry through a registered clearing agency.

RULE G-14 AND TRANSACTION REPORTING REQUIREMENTS

Brokers, dealers, and municipal securities dealers are required to report to the board information about each purchase and sale of municipal securities to the **Real-Time Transaction Reporting System (RTRS).** The information collected under this rule is used to make public reports about market activity, prices charged, and transaction fees assessed. It allows the board to ensure that the board rules are being followed and identify and be in contact with members who are not in full compliance. There are a few securities that are not subject to the reporting requirements including those that do not have assigned Committee on Uniform Securities Identification Procedures (CUSIP) numbers, municipal funds, and those interdealer transactions (i.e., the movement of the securities are not eligible for comparison in a clearing agency).

NASDAQ AUTOMATED QUOTATIONS

The **National Association of Securities Dealers Automated Quotations (NASDAQ)** is an electronic market that handles more volume than the NYSE, although the market value of the NASDAQ is lower than that of the NYSE. NASDAQ consists of the NASDAQ National Market, for better-known companies, and the NASDAQ Capital Markets, or Small Cap, for newer, smaller enterprises.

NASDAQ 4600 Series

The NASDAQ 4600 Series rules cover the following topics:

- Standards and registration of market makers
- Termination of registration
- Reporting transactions in NASDAQ-listed securities

Clearing and Settling Transactions Through a Registered Clearing Agency

NASDAQ Rule 4618 states that a market maker must clear and settle transactions in Nasdaq securities through the facilities of a registered clearing agency that uses a continuous net settlement system. This requirement may be satisfied by direct participation, use of direct clearing services, or by entry into a correspondent clearing arrangement with another member that clears trades through such an agency.

NASDAQ Rule 4613 and Maintaining a Two-Sided Market

NASDAQ Rule 4613 outlines the following requirements for registered market makers:

- For each security in which a member is registered as a market maker, the member must be willing to buy and sell such security for its own account on a continuous basis and must enter and maintain two-sided quotations in Nasdaq.
- A registered market maker must display a quotation size for at least one normal unit of trading (or a larger multiple thereof) when it is not displaying a limit order.
- A market maker that receives an offer to buy or sell from another Nasdaq member must execute a transaction for at least a normal unit of trading at its displayed quotations, or a size greater if displayed in the quotation.
- A market maker must enter and maintain quotations that are reasonably related to the prevailing market. Should it appear that a market maker's quotations are no longer reasonably related to the prevailing market, Nasdaq may require the market maker to re-enter its quotations, and failure to do so may result in Nasdaq suspending the market maker's quotations in one or all securities.
- A market maker may not, except under extraordinary circumstances, enter or maintain quotations if the display of a bid during regular trading hours is at a price equal to the price of an offer previously disseminated pursuant to an effective national market system plan (locking quotation), as this results in a zero bid-ask spread, or if the display of a bid during normal trading hours is at a price that is higher than the price of an offer previously disseminated pursuant to an effective national market system plan (cross quotation), as this results in a negative bid-ask spread.

NASDAQ 4750 Series Rules Related to Execution

NASDAQ Rule 4750 series relates to Nasdaq Market Center execution service and includes the following specific rules:

- Rule 4752 – Opening Process
- Rule 4753 – Halt and Imbalance Crosses
- Rule 4754 – Closing Cross
- Rule 4755 – Order Entry Parameters
- Rule 4756 – Entry and Display of Quotes and Orders
- Rule 4757 – Book Processing
- Rule 4758 – Order Routing

NASDAQ RULE 4752 AND TIMING OF ORDER OPENING

NASDAQ Rule 4752 states that for trading that occurs prior to normal market hours, at 7:00 a.m., the system shall add in time priority all eligible Orders in accordance with each order's defined characteristics, then at 9:25 a.m., the system shall open all remaining unopened Quotes in accordance with each firm's instructions.

Nasdaq Quoting Market Participants may instruct Nasdaq to open their Quotes as follows:

- At the price of the firm's quote when the quote was closed by the participant during the previous trading day with a normal unit of trading displayed size; or at a price and size entered by the participant between 7:00 a.m. and 9:24:59 a.m.
- System securities in which no Nasdaq Opening Cross occurs shall begin trading at 9:30 a.m. by integrating Market Hours orders into the book in time priority and executing in accordance with market hours rules.

NASDAQ RULE 4754 AND TIMING AND PROCESS OF CLOSING

NASDAQ Rule 4754 states that the Nasdaq Closing Cross will begin at 4:00:00, and post-market hours trading will commence when the Nasdaq Closing Cross concludes. Beginning at 3:50 p.m., Nasdaq shall disseminate by electronic means an Order Imbalance Indicator every 5 seconds until market close.

The Nasdaq Closing Cross will occur at the price that maximizes the number of shares of Eligible Interest in the Nasdaq Market Center to be executed. If more than one price exists, the Nasdaq Closing Cross shall occur at the price that minimizes any Imbalance.

All orders executed in the Nasdaq Closing Cross will be executed at the Nasdaq Closing Cross price, trade reported anonymously, and disseminated via the consolidated tape. When significant trading volume is expected at the close of Market hours, Nasdaq may apply auxiliary procedures for the Closing Cross to ensure a fair and orderly market.

NASDAQ RULE 4757 AND THE BOOK PROCESS

NASDAQ Rule 4757 states that System orders shall be executed through the Nasdaq Book Process set forth below:

- Execution Algorithm - Price/Time — The System shall execute equally priced or better priced trading interest within the System in price/time priority in the following order: Displayed Orders; Non-Displayed Orders, the reserve portion of Quotes and Reserve Orders, in price/time priority among such interest; the discretionary portion of Discretionary Orders.
- Decrementation—Upon execution, an order shall be reduced by an amount equal to the size of that execution.
- Price Improvement—Any potential price improvement resulting from an execution in the System shall accrue to the taker of liquidity.

NSADAQ RULE 4758 AND ORDER ROUTING OPTIONS

NASDAQ Rule 4758 states that the Order Routing Process shall be available to Participants from 7:00 a.m. until 8:00 p.m. Eastern Time, and shall route orders as described below:

- DOT ("DOT")—under this option, after checking the System for available shares, orders are sent to other available market centers for potential execution, per entering firm's instructions, before being sent to the destination exchange, so long as the price at such market centers would not violate the Order Protection Rule. Any un-executed portion will thereafter be sent to the NYSE or AMEX, as appropriate, at the order's original limit order price.
- Reactive Electronic Only ("STGY")—under this option, after checking the System for available shares, orders are sent to other available market centers for potential execution, per entering firm's instructions. When checking the book, the System will seek to execute at the price it would send the order to a destination market center. If shares remain un-executed after routing, they are posted on the book. Once on the book, should the order subsequently be locked or crossed by another accessible market center, the System shall route the order to the locking or crossing market center.
- Electronic Only Scan ("SCAN")—under this option, after checking the System for available shares, orders are sent to other available market centers for potential execution, per entering firm's instructions, in compliance with Rule 611 under Regulation NMS. When checking the book, the System will seek to execute at the price it would send the order to a destination market center. If shares remain un-executed after routing, they are posted on the book. Once on the book, should the order subsequently be locked or crossed by another market center, the System will not route the order to the locking or crossing market center. With the exception of the Minimum Quantity order type, all time-in-force parameters and order types may be used in conjunction with this routing option.

Regardless of the routing option selected, orders sent by the System to other markets do not retain time priority with respect to other orders in the System and the System shall continue to execute other orders while routed orders are away at another market center. Once routed by the System, an order becomes subject to the rules and procedures of the destination market including, but not limited to, order cancellation. If a routed order is subsequently returned, in whole or in part, that order, or its remainder, shall receive a new time stamp reflecting the time of its return to the System.

WHEN ISSUED AND WHEN DISTRIBUTED

NYSE Rule 63 states that bids and offers in securities admitted to dealings on a "when issued" basis shall be made only "when issued," i.e., for delivery when issued as determined by the Exchange. Bids and offers in securities admitted to dealings on a "when distributed" basis shall be made only "when distributed," i.e., for delivery when distributed as determined by the Exchange.

When-issued refers to a conditional transaction for a security that has been authorized but not yet issued.

When-distributed refers to a transaction for a security that has been issued but not yet distributed.

NYSE RULE 130

With regard to the NYSE 130 Series rules, except for manual transactions pursuant to Rule 76, this Rule is not applicable to trading on the Pillar trading platform.

Rule 130 states that each transaction effected on the Exchange shall be processed anonymously and compared or otherwise closed out by the close of business on the Exchange on the business day following the day of the contract. All reports associated with such transactions will indicate the details of such transactions and shall not reveal contra-party identities.

The Exchange will reveal the contra-party identities in the following circumstances:

- for regulatory purposes or to comply with an order of a court or arbitrator
- when a Qualified Clearing Agency ceases to act for a Member Organization or the Member Organization's clearing firm, and determines not to guarantee the settlement of the Member Organization's trades
- if both parties to the transaction consent

NYSE RULES 131, 132, 134, AND 138

Rule 131 states that it shall be the duty of every member to report each transaction made by him on the Floor as promptly as possible, but no later than one hour after the close of business on that day to his office, to the office of the member or member organization clearing for him or his member organization, or to the office of his principal, as the case may be, where adequate facilities to effect comparison are maintained.

Rule 132 states that each party to a contract shall submit data regarding its side of the contract ("trade data") to a Fully-Interfaced Clearing Agency for comparison or settlement, but each party shall be free to select the Fully-Interfaced Clearing Agency of its choice for such purpose.

Rule 134 states that when a clearing member organization submits a transaction in a listed stock or in a listed bond which it executed on the Exchange to the Exchange or to a Qualified Clearing Agency pursuant to the rules of such Exchange or Qualified Clearing Agency as a comparison item, and learns that it is uncompared, it shall resolve such comparison item on the first business day after the trade date through the facilities of the Correction System (the "System") during the time that such System is available for use.

Rule 138 states that an original party to a transaction may give up to the other original party to said transaction, the names of other members or member organizations, but such giving up or the acceptance thereof shall not constitute a substitution of principals.

NYSE RULE 133

NYSE Rule 133 was deleted in its entirety in 2019. It may still show up on the Series 7 exam if FINRA has not yet modernized it.

The old rule was related to the 130 Series and defined a procedure for the comparison of trades for the clearing agency if the clearing agency did not have a clearing method in place. The member would be required to send duplicate copies of the comparison forms to the buyer and seller by 1 pm the next business day. The buyer and seller would confirm the sale by signing it, or they could point out discrepancies. This comparison is now done electronically.

WHEN COMPARISON OF A TRANSACTION DO NOT TAKE PLACE

NYSE Rule 135 indicates the procedures when a comparison of a transaction does not take place:

- When a comparison of a transaction executed on the Exchange which is not submitted to the Exchange or to a Qualified Clearing Agency for comparison is received and the recipient has no knowledge of the transaction, the comparison shall be stamped "Don't Know," dated and initialed by the person so marking the same, and the comparison form, so stamped, shall be returned immediately to the seller, and
- When the buyer has not received a comparison from the seller, or when comparison cannot be made because of a difference, the buyer shall communicate that fact by telephone to the seller as soon as possible, but not later than the opening of the Exchange on the first business day following the day of the transaction; and
- When a comparison form has been returned to the seller stamped "Don't Know," or if, for any reason, comparison cannot be made, the parties shall, as soon as possible, but not later than 12:01 PM on the first business day following the day of the transaction, report the transaction to the executing Floor broker or brokers; and the Floor broker or brokers to whom such a transaction is reported shall investigate it immediately and resolve the transaction as either OK or DK no later than 6:00 PM on such day.

The provisions of this rule do not apply to transactions which are submitted to the Exchange or to a Qualified Clearing Agency for comparison pursuant to the rules of such Qualified Clearing Agency.

NYSE RULE 136

NYSE Rule 136 was deleted in its entirety in 2019. It may still show up on the Series 7 exam if FINRA has not yet modernized it.

Rule 136 required an exchange or clearing agency, if the agency / exchange excluded a transaction, to compare the transaction the same way it would have been under Rule 133 as promptly as possible and reported to all parties.

Informing the Appropriate Supervisor and Assisting in the Resolution of Discrepancies, Disputes, Errors, and Complaints

COMMON ERRORS OCCURRING DURING TRADING

When errors occur, there are several SEC, exchange and SRO rules to follow regarding reporting and resolving the errors. These include FINRA Rules 11892 - Clearly Erroneous Transactions in Exchange-Listed Securities and 11893 - Clearly Erroneous Transactions in OTC Equity Securities, CBOE Rule 5.11, NASDAQs Clearly Erroneous Transactions Policy, and NYSE Rule 134.

Common errors include:

- trading to the wrong account
- using margin instead of cash, or vice versa
- trading the wrong security
- trading at the wrong price
- trading the wrong quantity

TRADING ERRORS PROCEDURES

It is also possible that delays, even short ones, in executing a trade can lead to unintended price fluctuations. The errors could occur due to human error (mis-keys, miscommunication) or computer errors (interface errors, lag, etc.). When a brokerage firm is responsible for the error, the firm may be required to cancel and refund the transaction. In some cases, the brokerage may also need to compensate the customer for any financial damages incurred. Some exchanges (such as the NYSE) require trading firms to maintain error accounts to use for correcting errors. In any case, the firm must maintain clear records of the transactions and the corrections, including correction notices to customers.

For trades made to the wrong account or incorrectly paid for with cash or margin, the brokerage is required to correct the error through a cancel and rebill process. These corrections must be approved by a principal.

In 2009, the SEC approved rules for SROs and exchanges to follow for price/quantity/symbol errors. In general, the new rules allow an exchange to consider breaking a trade only if the price exceeds the consolidated last sale price by more than a specified percentage amount: 10% for stocks priced under $25; 5% for stocks priced between $25 and $50; and 3% for stocks priced over $50. In addition, the erroneous trade review process generally must commence within 30 minutes of the trade and be resolved within 30 minutes thereafter.

HANDLING CUSTOMER COMPLAINTS

Complaints, to be official, must be in writing. FINRA has different proceedings for handling customer complaints: formal and informal. The customer making the complaint decides whether to pursue formal or informal proceedings.

If the customer decides to pursue **formal proceedings** to resolve his complaint, then the complaint must be resolved according to FINRA's **code of procedure**. According to this, the **District Business Conduct Committee (DBCC)** maintains first jurisdiction over complaints, and if the customer is dissatisfied with the DBCC's handling of the issue, he can appeal the outcome to the FINRA Board of Governors and even up to the Supreme Court.

If the customer decides to pursue **informal proceedings**, then the complaint can be resolved according to FINRA's **code of arbitration**. According to this, at least two arbiters will participate in an informal hearing, and their decision will be binding and not open to appeal. Arbitration can be pursued not only by customers, but by any members of FINRA, including complaints that RRs might have with broker-dealers.

Mediation is also available for complaints, where an independent third party provides a nonbinding resolution to the matter.

SIMPLIFIED ARBITRATION IN FINRA DISPUTES

FINRA Rule 12800 applies to arbitrations involving $50,000 or less, exclusive of interest and expenses. All arbitrations administered under this rule will be decided on the pleadings and other materials submitted by the parties. Except as otherwise provided in this rule, all provisions of the Arbitration Code apply to such arbitrations.

All arbitrations administered under this rule will be decided by a single public arbitrator appointed from the FINRA chairperson roster in accordance with the Neutral List Selection System unless the parties agree in writing otherwise.

No hearing will be held in arbitrations administered under this rule unless the customer requests a hearing. If no hearing is requested, no initial prehearing conference or other prehearing conference will be held, and the arbitrator will render an award based on the pleadings and other materials submitted by the parties.

If the customer requests a hearing, the customer must select between one of two hearing options under this rule.

OPTIONS UNDER HEARING REQUESTS

Option One — the regular provisions of the Arbitration Code relating to prehearings and hearings, including all fee provisions.

Option Two — a special proceeding, subject to the regular provisions of the Code relating to prehearings and hearings, including all fee provisions, with the following modifications (simplified arbitration):

1. a special proceeding will be held by telephone unless the parties agree to another method of appearance;
2. the claimants, collectively, are limited to two hours to present their case and ½ hour for any rebuttal and closing statement, exclusive of questions from the arbitrator and responses to such questions;
3. the respondents, collectively, are limited to two hours to present their case and ½ hour for any rebuttal and closing statement, exclusive of questions from the arbitrator and responses to such questions;
4. the arbitrator has the discretion to cede his or her allotted time to the parties;
5. in no event shall a special proceeding exceed two hearing sessions, exclusive of prehearing conferences, to be completed in one day;
6. the parties may not question the opposing parties' witnesses;
7. a customer may not call an opposing party, a current or former associated person of a member party or a current or former employee of a member party as a witness; and
8. members and associated persons may not call a customer of a member party as a witness.

OPTIONS AVAILABLE TO THE ARBITER

The arbitrator may, in his or her discretion, choose to use relevant portions of the Document Production Lists in a manner consistent with the expedited nature of simplified proceedings. The parties also may request documents and other information from each other. All requests for the production of documents and other information must be served on all other parties, and any response or objection to a discovery request must be served on all other parties.

If any pleading increases the amount in dispute to more than $50,000, the arbitration will no longer be administered under this rule, and the regular provisions of the Arbitration Code will apply.

FORM U4 AND REQUIRED SUPERVISORY REVIEW

Form U4 is the Uniform Application for Securities Industry Registration or Transfer. Representatives of broker-dealers, investment advisers, or issuers of securities must use this form to become registered in the appropriate jurisdictions and/or SROs. FINRA, other self-regulatory organizations (SROs) and jurisdictions use the Form U4 to elicit employment history, disciplinary and other information about individuals to register them. The Form U4 requires applicants to provide the following information: basic contact information, employment histories, fingerprint information, requested examinations (e.g., Series 7, 63 or 65), professional designations, education, outside business interests or activities, criminal convictions and civil judgments and liens.

U4 forms must be reviewed by a principal and background checks must be performed. The applicant's employers from the previous three years must be contacted to verify the applicant's employment history within 30 days of receiving the U4 form.

An individual is under a continuing obligation to amend and update information required by Form U4 as changes occur. Amendments must be filed electronically (unless the filer is an approved paper filer) by updating the appropriate section of Form U4. A copy, with original signatures, of the initial Form U4 and amendments must be retained by the filing firm and must be made available for inspection upon regulatory request.

FINRA RULE 4513 AND RECORDKEEPING FOR WRITTEN CUSTOMER COMPLAINTS

FINRA Rule 4513 requires each member to keep and preserve in each office of supervisory jurisdiction either a separate file of all written customer complaints that relate to that office (including complaints that relate to activities supervised from that office) and action taken by the member, if any, or a separate record of such complaints and a clear reference to the files in that office containing the correspondence connected with such complaints. Rather than keep and preserve the customer complaint records required under this Rule at the office of supervisory jurisdiction, the member may choose to make them promptly available at that office, upon request of FINRA. Customer complaint records shall be preserved for a period of at least four years.

For purposes of this Rule, "customer complaint" means any grievance by a customer or any person authorized to act on behalf of the customer involving the activities of the member or a person associated with the member in connection with the solicitation or execution of any transaction or the disposition of securities or funds of that customer.

DISCIPLINARY ACTIONS REQUIRING REPORTING

FINRA Rule 4530 states that each member must promptly report to FINRA, but in any event not later than 30 calendar days, after the member knows or should have known of the existence of any of the following with respect to the member or an associated person of the member:

- has been found to have violated any securities-, insurance-, commodities-, financial- or investment-related laws, rules, regulations or standards of conduct
- is the subject of any written customer complaint involving allegations of theft or misappropriation of funds or securities or of forgery
- is named as a defendant or respondent in any proceeding brought by a domestic or foreign regulatory body or self-regulatory organization, or of any other federal, state or foreign securities, insurance or commodities statute, or of any rule or regulation thereunder
- is denied registration or is expelled, enjoined, directed to cease and desist, suspended or otherwise disciplined by any securities, insurance or commodities industry domestic or foreign regulatory body or self-regulatory organization
- is indicted, or convicted of, or pleads guilty to, or pleads no contest to, any felony; or any misdemeanor that involves the purchase or sale of any security
- is a director, controlling stockholder, partner, officer or sole proprietor of, or an associated person with, a broker, dealer, investment company, investment advisor, underwriter or insurance company that was suspended, expelled or had its registration denied or revoked

- is a defendant or respondent in any securities, commodities, or financial-related insurance related civil litigation or arbitration, or is the subject of any claim for damages by a customer, broker or dealer that relates to a financial transaction, and such civil litigation, arbitration or claim for damages has been disposed of by judgment, award or settlement for an amount exceeding $15,000. However, when the member is the defendant or respondent then the reporting to FINRA shall be required only when such judgment, award or settlement is for an amount exceeding $25,000
- is subject to a "statutory disqualification" or is involved in the sale of any financial instrument, the provision of any investment advice or the financing of any such activities with any person that is subject to a "statutory disqualification"

RESPONSIBILITY TO REPORT DISCIPLINARY ACTIONS

Within 30 days, a member must also report if an associated person is the subject of any disciplinary action taken by the member involving suspension, termination, the withholding of compensation or of any other remuneration in excess of $2,500, the imposition of fines in excess of $2,500 or is otherwise disciplined in any manner that would have a significant limitation on the individual's activities on a temporary or permanent basis.

Each member shall report to FINRA statistical and summary information regarding written customer complaints in such detail as FINRA shall specify by the 15th day of the month following the calendar quarter in which customer complaints are received by the member.

Nothing contained in this Rule shall eliminate, reduce or otherwise abrogate the responsibilities of a member or person associated with a member to promptly disclose required information on the Forms BD, U4 or U5, as applicable, to make any other required filings or to respond to FINRA with respect to any customer complaint, examination or inquiry.

RECTIFYING ERRONEOUS TRANSACTIONS

FINRA Rule 11892 states that an Executive Vice President of FINRA's Market Regulation Department or Transparency Services Department, or any officer designated by such Executive Vice President (FINRA officer), may, on his or her own motion, review any over-the-counter transaction involving an exchange-listed security, provided that the transaction meets specified thresholds.

A FINRA officer acting pursuant to this rule may declare any such transaction null and void if the officer determines that the transaction is clearly erroneous, or such actions are necessary for the maintenance of a fair and orderly market or the protection of investors and the public interest. Absent extraordinary circumstances, the officer shall take action generally within 30 minutes after becoming aware of the transaction. When extraordinary circumstances exist, any such action of the officer must be taken no later than the start of trading on the day following the date of execution(s) under review. If a FINRA officer declares any transaction null and void, each party involved in the transaction shall be notified as soon as practicable by FINRA, and the party aggrieved by the action may appeal.

Determinations of a clearly erroneous execution will be made if the price of the transaction is away from the Reference Price by an amount that equals or exceeds a specified set of Numerical Guidelines. In the event of any disruption or malfunction in the operation of the electronic communications and trading facilities of a self-regulatory organization or responsible single plan processor in connection with the transmittal or receipt of a regulatory trading halt, suspension or pause, a FINRA officer, acting on his or her own motion, shall declare as null and void any transaction in a security that occurs after the primary listing market for such security declares a regulatory trading halt, suspension or pause.

RECTIFYING ERRONEOUS TRANSACTIONS IN OTC EQUITY SECURITIES

FINRA Rule 11893 states that an Executive Vice President of FINRA's Market Regulation Department or Transparency Services Department, or any officer designated by such Executive Vice President, may, on his or her own motion, review any transaction involving an OTC Equity Security arising out of or reported through a trade reporting system owned or operated by FINRA or FINRA Regulation and authorized by the Commission.

A FINRA officer acting pursuant to this rule may declare any such transaction null and void if the officer determines that the transaction is clearly erroneous, or such actions are necessary for the maintenance of a fair and orderly market or the protection of investors and the public interest; provided, however, that the officer shall take action as soon as possible after becoming aware of the transaction, but in all cases by 3:00 p.m., Eastern Time, on the next trading day following the date of the transaction(s) at issue.

If a FINRA officer acting pursuant to this rule declares any transaction null and void, each party involved in the transaction shall be notified as soon as practicable by FINRA, and the party aggrieved by the action may appeal.

Determinations of a clearly erroneous execution will be made if the price of the transaction is away from the Reference Price by an amount that equals or exceeds a specified set of Numerical Guidelines.

INITIATION OF THE ARBITRATION PROCESS

BETWEEN CUSTOMERS AND FINRA MEMBERS

FINRA 12000 Series rules related to arbitration apply to disputes between a customer and a member or associated person of a member arising in connection with the business activities of the member or the associated person.

Parties must arbitrate a dispute under the Code if arbitration is either required by a written agreement or requested by the customer. Parties may elect to arbitrate a dispute under the Code if the parties agree in writing to submit the dispute to arbitration under the Code after the dispute arises. Parties may represent themselves in an arbitration but at any stage of an arbitration proceeding may be represented by an attorney. During an arbitration, no party may bring any suit, legal action, or proceeding against any other party that concerns or that would resolve any of the matters raised in the arbitration.

To initiate an arbitration, a claimant must file with the Director of FINRA Dispute Resolution Services a signed and dated Submission Agreement and a statement of claim specifying the relevant facts and remedies requested. Respondent(s) must serve each other party with required documents within 45 days of receipt of the statement of claim including a signed and dated Submission Agreement and an answer specifying the relevant facts and available defenses to the statement of claim. The answer to the statement of claim may include any counterclaims.

BETWEEN FINRA MEMBERS

Arbitrators are then selected through the Neutral List Selection System, a computer system that generates, on a random basis, lists of arbitrators from FINRA's rosters of arbitrators for the selected hearing location for each proceeding. The parties will select their panel through a process of striking and ranking the arbitrators. If the amount of a claim is $50,000 or less, the panel will consist of one arbitrator and the claim is subject to the simplified arbitration procedures. If the amount of a claim is more than $50,000 but not more than $100,000, the panel will consist of one arbitrator unless the parties agree in writing to three arbitrators. If the amount of a claim is more than $100,000, or is unspecified, or if the claim does not request money damages, the panel will consist of three arbitrators, unless the parties agree in writing to one arbitrator.

Before appointing arbitrators to a panel, the Director will notify the arbitrators of the nature of the dispute and the identity of the parties. Each potential arbitrator must make a reasonable effort to learn of, and must disclose to the Director, any circumstances which might preclude the arbitrator from rendering an objective and impartial determination in the proceeding.

The panel has the authority to interpret and determine the applicability of all provisions under the Code. Such interpretations are final and binding upon the parties. All rulings and determinations of the panel must be made by a majority of the arbitrators. All awards shall be in writing and signed by a majority of the arbitrators. Such awards may be entered as a judgment in any court of competent jurisdiction. Unless the applicable law directs otherwise, all awards rendered under the Code are final and are not subject to review or appeal.

CIRCUMSTANCES CAUSING DISPUTES

The FINRA 13000 Series rules state that a dispute must be arbitrated under the Code if the dispute arises out of the business activities of a member or an associated person and is between or among members, members and associated persons, or associated persons. To initiate an arbitration, a claimant must file with the Director of FINRA Dispute Resolution Services a signed and dated Submission Agreement, and a statement of claim specifying the relevant facts and remedies requested.

The Director will serve the Claim Notification Letter on the respondent(s). Respondent(s) must serve each other party with the following documents within 45 days of receipt of the statement of claim: a signed and dated Submission Agreement, and an answer specifying the relevant facts and available defenses to the statement of claim. The answer to the statement of claim may include any counterclaims.

INITIATION OF THE MEDIATION PROCESS

FINRA 14000 Series rules state that Mediation under the Code is voluntary and requires the written agreement of all parties. No party may be compelled to participate in a mediation. If all parties agree, any matter that is eligible for arbitration under the Customer Code or Industry Code may be submitted for mediation. A matter is submitted to mediation when the Director of Mediation receives an executed Submission Agreement from each party. The Director shall have the sole authority to determine if a matter is eligible to be submitted for mediation. The submission of a matter for mediation will not stay or otherwise delay the arbitration of a matter pending at FINRA. If all parties agree to stay an arbitration in order to mediate the matter, the arbitration will be stayed. Parties may represent themselves in mediation but all parties shall have the right to be represented by an attorney. A mediator may be selected: by the parties from a list supplied by the Director; with the Director's approval upon receipt of the parties' joint request, from a list or other source the parties choose; or by the Director if the parties do not select a mediator after submitting a matter to mediation.

GROUND RULES FOR MEDIATION

The following ground rules apply to mediation:

- Mediation is voluntary and any party may withdraw from mediation at any time prior to the execution of a written settlement agreement.
- The mediator shall act as a neutral, impartial, facilitator of the mediation process.

- The mediator shall determine the procedure for the conduct of the mediation. The parties and their representatives agree to cooperate with the mediator in ensuring that the mediation is conducted expeditiously.
- The mediator may meet with and communicate separately with each party or the party's representative. The mediator shall notify all other parties of any such separate meetings or other communications.
- The parties agree to attempt, in good faith, to negotiate a settlement of the matter submitted to mediation.
- Mediation is intended to be private and confidential.

WHEN AN ORDER IS BINDING IN CASES OF AN ERRONEOUS REPORT

Cboe Rule 5.11 states all bids or offers made and accepted in accordance with the Rules constitute binding contracts. The price at which an order is executed is binding notwithstanding that an erroneous report may have been rendered, or no report rendered. A report is not binding if an order was not actually executed but was in error reported to have been executed.

No comparison or failure to compare, and no notification or acceptance of notification of failure to receive or failure to deliver will have the effect of creating or of cancelling a contract, or of changing the terms thereof, or of releasing the original parties from liability.

CBOE RULE 9.17 AND RECORDKEEPING FOR WRITTEN CUSTOMER COMPLAINTS

Cboe Rule 9.17 states that every TPH organization conducting a non-Trading Permit Holder customer business must make and keep current a separate central log, index or other file for all options-related complaints, through which these complaints can easily be identified and retrieved. The term "options-related complaint" shall mean any written statement by a customer or person acting on behalf of a customer alleging a grievance arising out of or in connection with listed options. The central file shall be located at the principal place of business of the TPH organization or such other principal office as shall be designated by the TPH organization. At a minimum, the central file shall include:

- identification of complainant
- date complaint was received
- identification of Registered Representative servicing the account
- a general description of the matter complained of
- a record of what action, if any, has been taken by the TPH organization with respect to the complaint

Each options-related complaint received by a branch office of a TPH organization shall be forwarded to the office in which the separate, central file is located not later than 30 days after receipt by the branch office. A copy of every options-related complaint shall be maintained at the branch office that is the subject of the complaint.

Addressing Margin Issues

REQUIRED DISCLOSURES AND MARGIN ACCOUNTS AND DAY TRADING ACCOUNTS

Margin trading can be profitable, but it includes risks of loss greater than with buying stocks with cash, and customers wishing to trade on margin must be informed of these risks. This notification must be provided by the broker before the client opens a margin account, and the client must be reminded of the risks every year, in writing. You must let customers know that because since they're using borrowed money, it is quite possible that they'll lose more money than they have in

245

their account. You must also tell them that margin calls must be met immediately, that borrowing rules are subject to change at any time, and that if some of their stocks must be sold to meet a margin call, the brokerage house and not the customer chooses which stocks will be sold.

Some brokerage firms actively encourage **day trading** and specialize in catering to day trading clients. These firms have a special obligation to educate their customers who are potential day traders in order to make sure they have some idea of what day trading entails and the risks involved. They must furnish to the customer a risk disclosure form which outlines all the risks involved in day trading, and they must specifically approve the account for day trading, or have the client sign a form affirming that they don't intend to use the account to day trade.

MARGIN ACCOUNTS

TERMS

Margin refers to any borrowed money that is used to purchase something (in this context, to purchase securities).

Portfolio margin seeks to analyze the risk for a portfolio taken as a whole in the determination of margin requirements. Portfolio margin usually leads to significantly lower margin requirements.

Hypothecation is the name given to the practice of using stocks as collateral for loans. Stock market investors selling on margin give permission for the brokerage to do this when they sign their margin agreement.

Rehypothecation refers to the practice of a brokerage firm using the same stocks as collateral for a loan from a bank, though the commingling of stocks from the accounts of two different customers is prohibited, unless they've both given written permission. The brokerage house may not pledge more than 140 percent of a customer's debit balance.

REQUIRED DISCLOSURES

Due to the **increased risks** of margin accounts, brokerage firms must disclose some of the risks to customers. For instance, customers should know that they can lose more funds than they deposit, that they might be forced to sell assets in their accounts (or that the brokerage firm might itself sell such assets), and that the brokerage firm's maintenance margin requirement might increase.

Since the broker is lending money to the client, it is imperative that the broker or firm disclose the rate of interest the client will be charged for the borrowed money. Likewise, since the client will have to collateralize some assets in order to hold the account, the broker should disclose information to the client regarding such hypothecation.

REQUIREMENTS AND CHARACTERISTICS

Margin accounts are brokerage accounts in which the customer purchases securities using cash he borrowed from the broker.

Since purchasing securities on credit is a riskier venture for the broker than a customer who purchases them with his own cash, it is necessary for the broker to approve any clients wishing to do so. Moreover, customers will generally be required to offer securities and cash as **collateral**. Brokerage firms will also have restrictions on what kind of accounts can be margin accounts, as well as what kind of securities can be purchased in margin accounts.

Margin accounts require a certain portion of the account to be owned by the client, not the broker. If the value of certain stocks drops, then the client might be required to place more cash in the account or to sell off some of the securities. At one time, prior to the stock market crash of 1929, investors could buy stocks with only ten percent down. After the crash and after much blame for the crash was placed on speculators, the rule was changed in order to reduce the leverage and risk in margin trading. Currently, investors must put at least fifty percent of the stock price down in cash. To open an account, they must be approved based on their credit history. For their first purchase on margin, they must use at least $2,000.

CREATING A MARGIN ACCOUNTS

To open a margin account a customer must sign several forms, although these can be combined:

- A Customer Agreement - sets forth the general rule of the relationship
- A margin agreement - this obligates the customer to provide as collateral the securities purchased on margin (hypothecation)
- Customer Loan Consent agreement that allows the customer to loan his or her shares out on short sales.
- Credit Agreement - terms and conditions for the financing of any margin balance; the agreement describes the method of interest charges, provides the terms of credit extension, and sets the specific interest rates to be charged.

In the case of a corporation, the corporation must complete an application that includes personal information of the officers, assigns who is authorized to exercise discretion over the account (Control Person), and identifies beneficial owners of more than 10%. The corporation must include proof of existence and address, a corporate charter, corporate resolution authorizing trading on margin, and certain bank and loan statements.

PRODUCT OR STRATEGY SPECIFIC REQUIREMENTS

Since margin accounts use a broker's money, there can be additional requirements and restrictions placed upon it for different investment products or strategies. Some securities, since they are declared **very low-risk** (e.g., U.S. Treasury bonds) do not fall subject to these restrictions, since the restrictions are meant to regulate the increased riskiness of margin accounts. However, the restrictions do apply to such investments as mutual funds. Per **Regulation T**, the shares of mutual funds (open-end investment companies) may not be purchased on margin. This is due to the fact that they're part of a continuous public offering. Once bought and held for thirty days, however, they may be used as collateral for a margin purchase of other securities.

MARGIN REQUIREMENTS FOR SHORT SALE ACCOUNTS

Since short sales involve the selling of stocks which an investor does not own (so that he can buy them back cheaper and return the stocks to their owner, pocketing the difference), there are stricter **margin requirements**. Whereas ordinary margin accounts have margin requirements of 50% (and long positions also have 50% requirements), short sale accounts, according to Regulation T requirements, have margin requirements of 150%. If an investor engages in a short sale for $5,000, then the margin requirement for his short sale account is $7,500.

LONG AND SHORT MARGIN ACCOUNTS

In a margin account, a client can take two different courses of action: either he can borrow money with which he will buy securities, or he can borrow securities directly. The first type of margin account is a long margin account, and the second is a short margin account.

In a **long margin account**, the customer uses money lent to him by the broker, in addition to some of his money, to purchase a security (or set of securities), hoping to make a profit on the security, pay back the broker, and pocket the extra cash. Long margin accounts are therefore fitting for bull markets, since the customer's profit depends on the increased value of the security.

In a **short margin account**, the customer will generally sell the security (or set of securities) he has just borrowed from the broker, hope for the price to decrease, purchase the security at a lower price, and return the security to the broker while pocketing the extra cash. Short margin accounts are therefore fitting for bear markets, since the customer's profit depends on the decreased value of the security.

Margin Requirement Terms

When a customer wishes to set up a margin account with his broker, he cannot simply request that the entire account be given as a loan. Instead, there is some specific portion of the account which he must contribute himself, and it is this equity which is the **initial margin requirement**. These requirements are not merely stipulated by brokerage firms, either, but are subject to government regulation. The initial margin requirement, as determined by Regulation T of the Financial Reserve Board is 50%. Different brokerage firms are free to establish their own initial margin requirement levels in excess of this percentage.

Long market value (LMV) is the current value of the stocks the investor bought on margin. This should not be confused with the value at time of purchase, but always refers to the current value.

Short market value (SMV) is the current price of stocks a short seller has sold. Do not confuse this with the price of the stock at the time of the original transaction. SMV is always the current value of the stock, and is always fluctuating.

The **debit balance** refers to how much the customer has borrowed from the brokerage firm.

The **credit brokerage** refers to how much the customer has contributed to or received in his account.

The **loan value** is the difference between the margin requirement for the account and the total cost.

Meeting Margin Requirements Regulations

FINRA Rule 4210, Federal Reserve Regulation T, and Cboe Rules section 10 set several key requirements for meeting margin requirements. Although the initial margin requirement set by Regulation T is 50% (i.e., at least 50% must be funded by cash), a decline in the value of the securities may reduce the equity amount below 50%. The general rule is that a margin account must maintain at least 25% equity, though individual firms may set higher minimum standards.

The implication of this is that at times an investor may be required to add cash to an account (i.e., a "margin call") to maintain the minimum, or else risk forced liquidation of the securities to maintain the minimum.

Regulation T prohibits "freeriding" which entails buying then selling a security before paying for it. Freeriding may require the investor's broker to "freeze" the investor's cash account for 90 days. During this 90-day period, an investor may still purchase securities with the cash account, but the investor must fully pay for any purchase on the date of the trade.

Regulation T and the Rules of FINRA and the Exchanges

The rules of FINRA and the exchanges supplement the requirements of Regulation T by placing "maintenance" margin requirements on customer accounts. Under the rules of FINRA and the exchanges, the customer's equity in the account must not fall below 25 percent of the current market value of the securities in the account. Otherwise, the customer may be required to deposit more funds or securities in order to maintain the equity at the 25 percent level. The failure to do so may cause the firm to force the sale of—or liquidate—the securities in the customer's account in order to bring the account's equity back up to the required level.

Firms can raise their maintenance margin requirements for specific volatile stocks to ensure there are sufficient funds in their customers' accounts to cover large price swings. These changes in firm policy often take effect immediately and may result in the issuance of a maintenance margin call.

DETERMINING RESTRICTIONS FOR LONG MARGIN ACCOUNTS

A restricted account is an account that no longer meets the margin requirements set forth by Regulation T. For long margin accounts, this generally occurs when the value of securities declines below the margin threshold. The investor may still meet the maintenance margin required but is restricted from making certain additional margin transactions. The restriction is applied by transaction. Ultimately, the customer may deposit enough cash to un-restrict the account, or the broker-dealer may liquidate assets in the margin account to remove the restriction.

To calculate the restriction amounts for Long Margin Accounts:

1. Start with the basic Long equity equation: $Long\ Market\ Value\ (LMV) - Equity = Debit\ Balance$.
2. Compute the equation from the initial purchase but know that the Debit Balance remains constant. As the LMV fluctuates, the Equity changes.
3. Each time calculate the new restriction: $Restriction = Margin\ requirement - Equity$
4. So, if the account has a 40% maintenance requirement and $10,000 of securities were initially purchased with $5,000 of margin and $5,000 of cost, then the LMV declined to $8,000 the equations would be:

- $Initial\ LMV\ (\$10,000) - Equity\ (\$5,000) = Debit\ (\$5,000)$
- $Current\ LMV\ (\$8,000) - Equity\ (\$3,000) = Debit\ (\$5,000)$
- The current equity percentage is $\frac{Equity}{LMV}$, or $\$3,000/\$8,000 = 37.5\%$.
- The required percentage is 40%, and $LMV\ (\$8,000) \times 0.40 = \$3,200$.
- This is below the maintenance margin requirement. The account is Restricted by $3,000 − $3,200 = $200.

DETERMINING RESTRICTIONS FOR SHORT MARGIN ACCOUNTS

A restricted account is an account that no longer meets the initial margin required by Regulation T. For short margin accounts, this generally occurs when the value of short positions increases in value. The investor may still meet the maintenance margins required but is Restricted from making certain additional margin transactions. The restriction is applied by transaction. Ultimately, the customer may deposit enough cash to un-restrict the account, or the broker/dealer may liquidate assets in the margin account to remove the restriction. To calculate the restriction amounts for Short Margin Accounts:

1. Start with the basic Short equity equation: $Short\ Market\ Value\ (SMV) + Equity = Credit\ Balance$
2. The Equity in a short account must be equal to or greater than 50% of the SMV to meet the Regulation T requirement. Additionally, the investor must leave the proceeds of the short sale in the account, so effectively that is a 150% initial requirement.

3. Compute the equation from the initial purchase but know that the Credit Balance remains constant. As the SMV fluctuates, the Equity changes.
4. Each time calculate the new restriction: $Restriction = SMV \times 0.50 - Equity$
5. So, if the account with $20,000 of securities was initially established on margin, the investor had to deposit $10,000 of cash to meet the Regulation T margin requirement. If the SMV rose to $25,000, the investor would no longer meet the margin requirement and would have a Restricted Account.
   a. *Initial SMV ($20,000) + Equity ($10,000) = Credit Balance ($30,000)*
   b. *Current SMV ($25,000) + Equity ($5,000) = Credit Balance ($30,000)*
   c. The initial equity percentage was $\frac{Equity}{SMV}$, or $\frac{\$10,000}{\$20,000} = 50\%$
   d. The current equity percentage is $\frac{Equity}{SMV}$, or $\frac{\$5,000}{\$25,000} = 20\%$
   e. The required percentage is 50%, and since SMV is $25,000, the investor is below this amount by $12,500 - \$5,000 = \$7,500$.

PERMISSIBLE TRANSACTIONS WITH RESTRICTED MARGIN ACCOUNTS

When an account becomes Restricted (meaning that the equity falls below the 50% Regulation T minimum), only certain transactions are permissible. The rules are applied on a transaction basis.

1. The customer may sell securities and withdraw up to 50% of the value (this can be applied on a net basis if the customer buys and sells on the same day)
2. The customer may buy more securities but must deposit 50% of the value (this can be applied on a net basis if the customer buys and sells on the same day)
3. The customer may exchange currencies, but on a dollar-for-dollar basis - this is called "Same Day Substitution"
4. The customer may withdraw securities by depositing at least 50% of the value into the account.

SPECIAL MEMORANDUM ACCOUNTS (SMAS)

A special memorandum account (SMA) may be maintained in conjunction with a margin account. Excess margin generated from a margin account can deposited in an SMA, providing increased buying power. Special memorandum accounts are like lines of credit, where an investor is permitted to take out more on margin if he has more equity in his margin account. Per FINRA Rule 4210, the account balance must be at least $2,000.

EXCESS EQUITY, BALANCE, AND BUYING POWER FOR SMAS

The balance of an SMA depends upon the initial margin requirement, stipulated by Regulation T as 50% minimum, and higher for different financial institutions. Thus, if the value of the stock he has purchased long on margin in his margin account increases, then the line of credit in his SMA will increase. For instance, 100 shares of stock purchased on margin at $50 per share would require the investor to deposit $2,500 in the margin account. If the stock's price rises to $70 per share, the investor would have excess equity of $2,000 in the SMA, calculated as follows:

Initial Long Market Value - Debit Balance = Initial Equity ($50,000 - $25,000 = $25,000)

Current Long Market Value - Debit Balance = Current Equity ($70,000 - $25,000 = $45,000)

$$\frac{Current\ Equity - Debit\ Balance}{2} = Excess\ Equity\ (\$45,000 - \$25,000)\ /\ 2 = \$10,000$$

Conversely, if an investor sells 100 shares of the same security short, and the price of the security falls to $40 per share he would have excess equity of $ in the SMA, calculated as follows:

$$Initial\ Short\ Market\ Value\ +\ Initial\ Equity\ =\ Credit\ Balance\ (\$50,000\ +\ \$25,000$$
$$=\ \$75,000)$$

$$Credit\ Balance\ -\ Current\ Short\ Market\ Value\ =\ Current\ Equity\ (\$75,000\ -\ \$40,000$$
$$=\ \$35,000)$$

$$Current\ Equity\ -\ Required\ Margin\ =\ Excess\ Equity\ (\$35,000\ -\ \$20,000\ =\ \$15,000).$$

MARGIN ACCOUNT TERMS

Marginable securities are securities that can be used as collateral for margin trades. Stocks listed on the New York Stock Exchange and on the NASDAQ exchange are marginable. Certain Over the Counter stocks can also be bought on margin, or used as collateral. Mutual funds and newly issued stocks can't be bought on margin, but can be used as collateral once 30 days have passed. Options (except for LEAPS) and most OTC stocks can't be bought on margin, or used as collateral.

Exempt securities are not required to be registered under the Securities Act of 1933. These include securities issued by the federal government or its agencies, municipal bonds, securities issued by banks, savings institutions, and credit unions, public utility securities, and securities issued by nonprofit, educational, or religious organizations.

Loan value is the difference between the margin requirement for an account and the total cost. If a client opened up a margin account and wished to buy 100 shares of stock X at $20 per share, and if the margin requirement for the account were 50%, then the client would have to pay $1000 in cash, and the difference—the loan value—would be $1000.

Margin calls occur when equity in a margin account goes below a certain maintenance level. (Official rules say that investors must maintain at least twenty-five percent equity in their position; many brokers have higher requirements that that, usually around thirty-three percent.) If this occurs, the brokerage house will issue a margin call to the investor, telling the investor to deposit enough funds or stocks to get back to the minimum. The investor must do so immediately, or the firm will begin selling stocks out of the investor's account to raise the money.

Special memorandum accounts (SMAs) refer to the amount of purchasing power in the account. When stocks purchased on margin increase in value, SMA is created. For every dollar the value increases, fifty cents of SMA is created, because of the fifty percent margin requirement. The customer can then use the value of the SMA to purchase other stocks or withdraw cash without selling the original stocks bought on margin. It is much like a line of credit. Investors are always free to increase their SMA by depositing cash in their account.

PORTFOLIO MARGIN ACCOUNTS AND DAY TRADING ACCOUNTS

Portfolio margin accounts are a type of margin account where the initial margin requirement differs according to the particular risk of the portfolio. Whereas Regulation T requires all margin accounts to have an initial margin requirement of at least 50%, portfolio margin requirements can be much lower, perhaps between 15% and 20%. However, while the margin requirement is low, customers wishing to have a portfolio margin account must have a specific (and high) absolute amount of equity, usually $150,000.

The portfolio margin is calculated according to the Options Clearing Corporation's (OCC's) **Customer Portfolio Margin system**.

Day trading accounts are especially risky margin accounts used to make a very high number of trades per day, making a profit or loss off of the small upticks and downticks in the daily price. Because of the extremely risky nature of day trading, the rules with respect to margin trading are a bit different when it comes to clients who wish to day trade. For one thing, day traders must always have at least $25,000 in equity in their account if they wish to day trade. If they don't meet this requirement, they are not allowed to day trade. And, unlike regular margin traders, their buying power isn't twice the SMA; instead, it is four times the equity in their account above the twenty-five percent maintenance minimum, which is called maintenance margin excess.

REQUIREMENTS FOR MARGIN DISCLOSURE STATEMENTS

All FINRA members must provide to any non-institutional customers opening a margin account, a **margin disclosure statement** in written or electronic form before or at the time of opening the account. The disclosure is also required to be delivered to each margin customer annually. If customers are able to open an account on the internet, the disclosure statement is to be posted on the website in a clear a conspicuous manner. The statement is provided in FINRA Rule 2264 and makes various statements warning customers of risk.

INITIAL MINIMUM MARGIN AND MAINTENANCE MARGIN

When a customer chooses to purchase securities on margin in an account, there are **minimum initial margin amounts** that must be met. In general this amount is $2,000 of equity, with the exception of pattern day traders, who are required to have an initial margin of $25,000 of equity.

Many customers are required to hold much more than this amount. Specifically, broker-dealers can calculate the margin requirements using the following calculations:

1. 25 percent of the current market value of all long positions
2. The greater of $2.50 per share or 100 percent of the current market value for any short equity positions with a price per share under $5.00
3. The greater of $5.00 per share or 30 percent of the current market value for any short equity positions with a price per share over $5.00
4. The greater of 5 percent of the principal amount or 30 percent of the current market value for any short bond positions
5. 20 percent of the current market value for any short or long futures contract
6. 100 percent of the current market value for any positions that are not margin eligible

FINRA RULE 4210
MARGIN REQUIREMENT TERMS

Basket — a group of stocks eligible to be executed in a single trade.

Designated account — an account of certain banks, investment companies, insurance companies, state or political subdivisions, or pension plans.

Margin — the necessary amount of equity to be maintained for a security position in an account.

Major foreign sovereign debt — a debt security issued by a foreign entity that has debt securities that are subordinated in relation and the security has been ranked in the top rating category by a nationally recognized rating organization.

Exempt account — any member or registered broker-dealer, or certain persons with a net worth of $45 million or more.

Other marginable non-equity securities — includes certain debt securities that are not traded on a national exchange and certain private pass-through securities.

Initial margin - the required opening deposit in a margin account.

Maintenance margin - the required margin which must be maintained in an account.

Additional margin - a procedure must be in place for members to review type and limit of credit extended, to formulate their own margin requirements, and to review the need for instituting higher margin requirements.

Exceptions to rule for offsetting long and short positions - if a security in "long" position is exchangeable or convertible into a security in "short" position, the margin required is 10% of current market value of the "long" security. If the "long" and "short" are for the same security, the margin required is 5%.

EXEMPTIONS TO THE MARGIN REQUIREMENTS

Exempted securities - net "long" and "short" positions in obligations that are guaranteed by the United States or that are highly rated foreign sovereign debt securities are exempted and given their own margin requirements. "Long" and "short" positions in exempted securities other than United States obligations shall maintain a margin of 7% of the current market value.

Non-equity securities - "long" and "short" positions in non-equity securities are to maintain a margin of 10% of the current market value for investment grade securities, and the greater of 20% of the current market value or 7% of the principal for other non-equity securities.

Baskets - a member can make basket transactions for a registered market maker based on a margin determined to be adequate by the concerned parties.

SPECIALISTS' AND MARKET MAKERS' ACCOUNTS

Specialists' and market makers' accounts - a member can have a margin account for an approved market maker based on a margin determined to be adequate by the concerned parties.

BROKER-DEALER ACCOUNTS

Broker-dealer accounts - a member can have a proprietary margin account for another broker-dealer based on a margin determined to be adequate by the concerned parties.

SHELF-REGISTERED AND OTHER CONTROL AND RESTRICTED SECURITIES

Shelf-registered and other control and restricted securities - securities that are part of a continuous or delayed offering (shelf-registered securities) are subject to the same maintenance requirements as other securities. For other control and restricted securities, the margin to be maintained is 40% of the current market value for "long" securities.

PATTERN DAY TRADER AND DAY-TRADING BUYING POWER

Pattern day trader — a customer who executes four or more trades within five business days, unless those trades represent 6% or less of the customer's total trades.

Day-trading buying power — the equity the day-trading customer has in their account less any maintenance margin, multiplied by four (for equity securities).

SPECIAL REQUIREMENTS FOR PATTERN DAY TRADERS

Special requirements for pattern day traders — the special requirements for pattern day traders include:

A. a minimum equity requirement of $25,000;

B. they cannot trade in excess of their day-trading buying power;

C. if a pattern day trader fails to meet maintenance margin calls as required, they will be permitted only to trade on a cash available basis for 90 days or until the margin call is met;

D. minimum equity funds deposited cannot be withdrawn for a minimum of two business days after deposit.

MINIMUM LEVEL OF MARGIN REQUIREMENT

Cboe Rule 10.1. states that no TPH organization may affect a transaction or carry an account for a customer, whether a Trading Permit Holder or non-Trading Permit Holder, without proper and adequate margin in accordance with Chapter 10 of the Cboe Rules, all other applicable rules of the Exchange, and Regulation T of the Federal Reserve Board.

TIME PERIOD REQUIREMENT IN WHICH MARGIN MUST BE OBTAINED

Cboe Rule 10.2 states that for securities other than security futures contracts, the amount of initial margin required by this Rule shall be obtained as promptly as possible and in any event within one payment period as defined in Section 220.2 of Regulation T of the Board of Governors of the Federal Reserve System .(Payment period means the number of business days in the standard securities settlement cycle in the United States, as defined in paragraph (a) of SEC Rule 15c6-1, plus two business days.). The amount of maintenance margin required by this Rule shall be obtained as promptly as possible and in any event within 15 business days.

MINIMUM MARGIN AMOUNT REQUIREMENT FOR LONG AND SHORT POSITIONS

Cboe Rule 10.3 prescribes the minimum amount of margin that must be maintained in margin accounts of customers having positions in options securities as follows:

(1) Long Positions - 25% of the current market value of all "long" in the account; plus

(2) Short Positions

- $2.50 per share or 100% of the current market value, whichever amount is greater, of each security "short" in the account which has a current market value of less than $5 per share; plus
- $5.00 per share or 30% of the current market value, whichever amount is greater, of each security "short" in the account which has a current market value of $5 per share or more.
- For Short Bonds, 5% of the principal amount or 30% of the current market value, whichever amount is greater, of each bond "short" in the account.

Note that this rule is very similar to FINRA Rule 4210 and NYSE Rule 431.

MARGIN AMOUNT REQUIREMENT FOR OTHER TYPES OF SECURITIES

As an alternative to the transaction / position specific margin requirements set forth in Cboe Rule 10.3, a TPH organization may require margin in accordance with the portfolio margin requirements contained in Rule 10.4 for the following instruments: all margin equity securities, listed options, unlisted derivatives, security futures products, and index warrants.

The application of the portfolio margin provisions of this Rule is limited to the following customers:

1. any broker or dealer registered pursuant to Section 15 of the Securities Exchange Act of 1934;
2. any member of a national futures exchange to the extent that listed index options, unlisted derivatives, options on exchange traded funds, index warrants or underlying instruments hedge the member's related instruments, and
3. any person or entity not included in (1) or (2) that is approved for writing uncovered options.

The amount of margin required under this Rule 10.4 for each portfolio shall be the greater of:

- the amount for any of the ten equidistant valuation points representing the largest theoretical loss
- $.375 for each listed option, unlisted derivative, security futures product, and related instrument multiplied by the contract or instrument's multiplier, not to exceed the market value in the case of long positions

VALUING POSITIONS IN ACTIVE SECURITIES REQUIREMENTS

Cboe Rule 10.5 states that positions in active securities, except security futures contracts, dealt in on a recognized exchange (including option contracts) must, for margin purposes, be valued at current market value prices; provided that only the following may be deemed to have market value for the purposes of Rule:

- only those options contracts on a stock or stock index, or a stock index warrant, having an expiration that exceeds 9 months and which are listed or guaranteed by the carrying broker-dealer
- a Credit Option as defined in Rule 4.40

Security futures contracts shall have no value for margin purposes. Positions in other securities shall be valued conservatively in the light of current market prices and the amount of anticipated realization upon a liquidation of the entire position. Substantial additional margin must be required in all cases where the securities carried are subject to unusually rapid or violent changes in value, or where the amount carried is such that they cannot be liquidated promptly.

WHEN ISSUED SECURITIES

Cboe Rule 10.6 covers the valuation of "when issued" and "when distributed" securities for margin purposes. The terms "when issued" and "when distributed" are used synonymously in the rule. Generally, a "when issued" security is one that was purchased conditionally because the security is announced but has not been issued yet. Examples include Treasury Securities, stock splits, and new issues of stocks or bonds. Most frequently, these "when issued" securities are offered by underwriters before an issue.

The rule treats "when issued" securities like issued securities. The minimum amount of margin on any transaction or net position in each "when issued" security is the same as if such security were issued. Each position in a "when issued" security shall be margined separately and any unrealized profit shall be of value only in providing the amount of margin required on that particular position.

When an account has a "short" position in a "when issued" security and there are held in the account securities in respect of which the "when issued" security may be issued, such "short" position shall be marked to the market and the balance in the account shall for the purpose of this rule be adjusted for any unrealized loss in such "short" position.

MARGIN REQUIREMENTS FOR WHEN ISSUED SECURITIES

In connection with any transaction or net position resulting from contracts for a "when issued" security, the following requirements must be met.

- In an account that is not for a TPH organization or other institutions, deposits are required equal to the margin required were such transactions or position in a margin account
- When made for or with a non-TPH broker or dealer, no margin need be required, but such net position must be marked to market
- When made for a TPH organization or other institution, no margin need be required and such net position need not be marked to market. However, where such net position is not marked to market, an amount equal to the loss at the market in such position shall be considered as cash required to provide margin in the computation of the net capital of the TPH organization under the Exchange's capital requirements

MARGIN REQUIREMENTS FOR GUARANTEED ACCOUNTS

Cboe Rule 10.7 states that any account guaranteed by another account may be consolidated with such other account and the required margin may be determined on the net position of both accounts, provided the guarantee is in writing and permits the TPH organization carrying the account, without restriction, to use the money and securities in the guaranteeing account to carry the guaranteed account or to pay any deficit therein.

The guaranteeing account may not be owned directly or indirectly by the TPH organization or an Approved Person of the TPH organization carrying the account or any other Trading Permit Holder, TPH organization or Approved Person of a TPH organization having a definite arrangement for participating in the commissions earned on the guaranteed account.

PROHIBITION AGAINST LIQUIDATING THE SAME SECURITIES

Cboe Rule 10.8 states that no TPH organization shall permit a customer to make a practice of effecting transactions requiring initial or additional margin or full cash payment and then furnishing such margin or making such full cash payment by liquidation of the same or other commitments.

The provisions of this Rule shall not apply to margin calls attributable to security futures contract transactions nor to any account maintained for another broker or dealer, exclusive of the partners, officers and directors of such other broker or dealer, provided such other broker or dealer is a TPH organization or has agreed in good faith with the TPH organization carrying the account that it will maintain a record equivalent to that referred to in Rule 10.11

REQUIRING MARGIN IN EXCESS OF THE LEVELS SPECIFIED

Cboe Rule 10.9 states the amount of margin prescribed by these Rules is the minimum which must be required initially and subsequently maintained with respect to each account; but nothing in these Rules shall be construed to prevent a TPH organization from requiring margin in an amount greater than that specified. The Exchange may at any time impose higher margin requirements in respect of such positions when it deems such higher margin requirements to be advisable.

BOUND BY MARGIN REQUIREMENTS OF THE NYSE VS. CBOE

Cboe Rule 10.10 states that in lieu of meeting the margin requirements set forth in Rules 10.3 through 10.8, a TPH organization that is a member of the New York Stock Exchange may elect to be bound by the initial and maintenance requirements of the New York Stock Exchange. Such election must be made in writing and shall remain effective until the TPH organization shall file with the Exchange a written notice of revocation. Upon the filing of such election, a TPH organization shall be bound to comply with the margin rules of the New York Stock Exchange as though such rules were part of these Rules.

RECORDKEEPING REQUIREMENTS OF DAILY MARGIN ACTIVITY

Cboe Rule 10.11 states that each TPH organization carrying margin accounts for customers shall make and maintain a daily record of every case in which initial or additional margin must be obtained in a customer's account because of the transactions effected in such account. This record shall be preserved for at least 12 months and shall show for each account the amount of margin so required and the time and manner in which such margin is furnished or obtained. The Exchange may exempt any TPH organization which is a member or member organization of another national securities exchange having a substantially comparable rule with which such TPH organization is required to comply.

REGULATION T

The Federal Reserve Board was empowered by the Securities Exchange Act (SEA) in 15 USC 78g to set rules related to broker customer credit backed by securities. From this directive, the FRB created Regulation T. Regulation T governs the extension of credit by broker-dealers, including margin requirements. The regulation empowers the Federal Reserve Board to set the initial (50%) and maintenance (25% basic for long positions) margin rates required, which securities may be purchased on margin, and the dates of payment for transactions (four days as of 2017). Broker Dealers have the discretion to set interest rates, decide how often to loan funds (excluding the 90-day freeze periods that may occur), and set margin requirements more restrictive than the regulation. FINRA has supplemented Regulation T with Rule 4210.

Some securities are exempt from Regulation T, meaning they cannot be purchased on margin, although you can have them in the account. These include

- Exempt securities, such as municipal securities, and US Government and USGA securities
- Some non-Nasdaq OTC securities are non-marginable (you can still own them in the account but not as part of the margin)
- IPO securities are non-marginable initially, but become marginable 30 days after the IPO

Non-Convertible corporate debt has different (lower) margin requirements than equity securities.

GENERAL PROVISIONS

Separation of accounts - requirements of an account may not be met by considering items in another account. If cash or securities are being withdrawn from one account to be used for another account to meet requirements, and it is permitted by Regulation T, written entries need to be made.

Maintenance of credit - credit once extended must be maintained, regardless of:

A. reductions in customer's equity from changing market prices;

B. a security ceasing to be a margin or exempted security; and

C. a change in margin requirements.

Guarantee of accounts - a customer's account cannot be guaranteed.

Receipt of funds or securities - a creditor can accept as immediate payment cash, checks, or securities. If a payment has been sent by another creditor, the funds can be considered received upon written notification from the creditor that it has been sent.

Arranging for loans by others - a creditor can arrange for credit to be extended to customers from another creditor.

REGULATION T TERMS

Creditor - broker/dealers that extend credit.

Customer - a person to whom a creditor extends credit.

OTC margin stock - any equity security traded over-the-counter that meets certain qualifications to be able to be treated as if it were traded on a national exchange.

Margin security - any security traded on a national securities exchange; any security traded on the NASDAQ; any non-equity security; any security issued by certain investment companies; any foreign margin stock; and any debt security convertible into a margin security.

Exempted securities mutual fund - a security issued by certain investment companies provided that the company has 95% of its assets in exempted securities.

Non-equity security - a security that is not an equity security.

REQUIRED PAYMENT TIMELINES TO AVOID VIOLATING REGULATION T

The payment dates to meet to avoid violating Regulation T and/or having securities liquidated:

- Customer Securities in a cash or margin account:
  - Customer Payment: Four business days (S+2, T+4)
  - Trade Settlement: Two business days (T+2)
- Municipal Securities
  - Customer Payment: exempt from Reg. T (generally due at settlement)
  - Trade Settlement: Two business Days (T+2)
- US Gov't Securities
  - Customer Payment: exempt from Reg T (generally due at settlement)
  - Trade Settlement: Next Business Day (T+1)
- Option Trades
  - Customer Payment: Four Business Days (T+4)
  - Trade Settlement: Next Business Day (T+1)

Cash transactions for all securities settle on the same day.

VIOLATION OF REGULATION T

Violations of Regulation T occur as a result of not paying the appropriate amount for an order within 5 days of the transaction. (Note that a customer can request an additional 5-day extension from FINRA or the NYSE.)

In a Cash Account:

- Freeriding - selling a security and then buying more securities before the sale settles (i.e., without having funds in the account).
- Selling Short - borrowing shares to sell
- Borrowing money from the broker

In a margin account:

- Conducting a transaction without having 50% of the value on hand.

When a violation occurs, on the sixth day after the transaction, the broker/dealer will sell off the securities that the customer failed to pay for, and can also sell off other securities in the customer's account. Then the broker/dealer will freeze the account for 90 days - meaning that the customer must pay in cash for any transaction during that time.

Series 7 Practice Test #1

Want to take this practice test in an online interactive format?
Check out the bonus page, which includes interactive practice questions and much more: mometrix.com/bonus948/series7

1. Which of the following is the BEST representation of a net revenue pledge for a municipal bond?

    a. (Gross revenues – operating costs) / debt service
    b. (Net revenues – operating costs) / debt service
    c. (Principal balance – interest payments) / years-to-maturity
    d. (Interest payments + principal balance) / operating costs

2. Each of the following is TRUE of open-end investment companies EXCEPT:

    a. New shares are constantly being issued
    b. Only common stock may be issued
    c. Investors may redeem their shares
    d. Investors purchase shares at the NAV plus a commission

3. Which TWO of the following investors would benefit if the strike price of an option and the market price of the underlying stock remained the same?

    I. The buyer of a straddle
    II. Seller of a straddle
    III. Buyer of an at-the-money put
    IV. Seller of an at-the-money put

    a. I and II
    b. I and III
    c. II and III
    d. II and IV

4. Which NASDAQ level is known as the "Inside market"?

    a. Level I
    b. Level II
    c. Level III
    d. Level IV

5. Diane Doughmestic has a margin account that holds securities with a current market value of $35,000 and a debit balance of $18,000. All of the following are TRUE EXCEPT:

    a. The account is currently restricted
    b. The account has a SMA of $0
    c. Diane will receive a margin call for $500
    d. Diane will receive a maintenance call if the market value drops below $24,000

6. Franche Enterprises deals in widgets in both the U.S. and in Europe. The company accepts most payments within 30 days of billing and wants to take a hedge position to protect itself from moves in the currency markets. Which of the following would accomplish this goal on a bill to an Italian customer?

a. Buy Euro puts
b. Sell Euro calls
c. Buy Euro call
d. None of the above

7. Corporations may issue which of the following debt securities?

I. Mortgage bonds
II. Income bonds
III. Moral obligation bonds
IV. Double barreled bonds

a. I and II
b. I and III
c. I, II, and IV
d. II and IV

8. In a margin account, each of the following transactions will cover a put writer EXCEPT:

a. A cash deposit equal to the exercise price of the put.
b. A purchase of shares of the underlying stock.
c. A short sale of shares of the underlying stock.
d. The purchase of a put option with the same exercise price and expiration.

9. A corporation wishing to open a new margin account would need to provide the firm their:

I. Corporate resolution
II. Corporate charter
III. Income statement
IV. List of issued securities

a. I and II
b. I and IV
c. I, II and III
d. I, II, III and IV

10. A customer has a short margin account with ABC Brokers. The account currently has a short market value of $52,000, a credit balance of $104,000 and SMA of $3000. None of the short stocks have a price less than $5 per share. What is the minimum FINRA required equity maintenance on this account?

a. $15,600
b. $19,900
c. $30,800
d. $31,200

11. When investing in variable annuities, an investor may select the following:

        I. Periodic payment immediate annuity
        II. Periodic payment deferred annuity
        III. Single payment immediate annuity
        IV. Single payment deferred annuity

    a. I and II only
    b. I, II, and IV
    c. II and IV only
    d. II, III, and IV

Use the following to answer questions 12 - 13

Specialist's Book: Mega Corporation		
BID	PRICE	ASK
15 DLJ	35.	
8 Bear Stearns (GTC)	.10	
19 Morgan	.20	9 UBS (stop)
	.30	
	.40	
23 Goldie (stop)	.50	
	.60	9 Merrill
	.70	12 Salamon

12. Given the information in the exhibit, which of the following prices would be an example of an acceptable quote for the specialist to enter for his own inventory?

    a. $35.30
    b. $35.10
    c. $35.65
    d. $35.95

13. Given the information in the exhibit, what is the range that defines the inside market?

    a. 35.00 - 35.70
    b. 35.10 – 35.60
    c. 35.20 – 35.60
    d. 35.50 – 35.60

14. Which of the following government securities has the shortest initial maturity?

    a. Treasury bills
    b. Treasury notes
    c. Treasury bonds
    d. Treasury STRIPs

15. If XYZ has a EPS of $4 and a market price of $64 prior to a straight 2-for-1 stock split, after the split

    a. The EPS will be $4, and the market price will be $32
    b. The EPS will be $2, and the market price will be $64
    c. The EPS will be $8, and the market price will be $32
    d. The EPS will be $2, and the market price will be $32

16. Each of the following is a type of municipal note EXCEPT:

   a. AONs
   b. BANs
   c. PNs
   d. RANs

17. A customer has a margin account which contains securities having a market value of $40,000 and a debit balance of $15,000. Assuming that current SEC regulations apply, how much buying power does the customer have to purchase additional securities?

   a. $15,000
   b. $5,000
   c. $10,000
   d. $20,000

18. An investor places an order of 10,000 shares. He tells a representative that he wants as much as possible very quickly and to cancel the rest. The representative should designate this order as:

   a. Fill or kill
   b. All or none
   c. Firm commitment
   d. Immediate or cancel

19. All of the following statements are FALSE regarding callable municipal revenue bonds, EXCEPT:

   a. Callable bonds increase in price faster than non-callable bonds in a rising interest rate environment.
   b. Callable bonds usually have lower yields than non-callable bonds.
   c. The issuer will typically call their bonds in a decreasing interest rate environment.
   d. When bonds are called, the call premium is set to offset the missed interest payments the investor would have received had the bond not been called.

20. When applying the FINRA 5% rule, each of the following is FALSE EXCEPT:

   a. The 5% rule is a guideline for the sales of open-ended investment companies
   b. Securities sold through a prospectus are exempt from the rule
   c. The security type or class is not a consideration
   d. Riskless arbitrage transactions are exempt from the rule

21. Which of the following MUST be a closed-end fund?

   a. POP - $15, NAV - $13.90
   b. POP - $21, NAV - $19.10
   c. POP - $8, NAV - $7.35
   d. POP - $11, NAV - $10.25

22. Each of the following is TRUE of discretionary accounts, EXCEPT:

   a. All discretionary account must be approved by a principal
   b. Discretionary accounts must be regularly reviewed by a principal
   c. Discretionary account cannot trade on margin
   d. Each order for a discretionary account must be marked as such

23. Sally Shortseller has a short margin account with short market value (SMV) of $5,000 and a credit balance (CR) of $8000. How much excess equity (SMA) does Sally have in her account?

a. $3,000
b. None, the account is restricted.
c. $1,000
d. $500

24. Sara Ross holds a portfolio of stocks and bonds and prefers dividend paying stocks. If she is in the 28% tax bracket and holds a GO bond at 94 with a basis of 7% and a nominal yield of 5.5%, what is the tax equivalent yield Sara receives on this bond?

a. 9.2%
b. 9.7%
c. 7.9%
d. 6.8%

25. Sam Spade is considering investing in mutual funds. He has selected Mighty Sure investments to be his broker. Mighty Sure should tell Sam that which of the following is the most important consideration when deciding how to invest his money?

a. Front loaded versus back loaded
b. Sales charges
c. Investment objectives
d. Management fees

26. Under which of the following circumstances may it be possible to receive a reduction in the maximum sales charge when purchasing the shares of an investment company?

I. Shares are purchased by the trustee of a company pension plan.
II. The purchase represents a significant dollar investment amount in the shares.
III. The investor elects to have all dividend income reinvested.
IV. A unit investment trust purchases the shares as one of many investments for the underlying plan.

a. I only
b. I and II
c. I, II, and III
d. I, II, III, and IV

27. UGMA stands for _____.

a. Uniform Grant to Minors Act
b. Uniform Grant to Minorities Act
c. Uniform Gift to Minors Act
d. Uniform Gift to Minorities Act

28. An investor owns 100 shares of XYZ at $36. She wants to limit her loss per share to $4 or less and will accept a longer time for the order to be executed in order to make sure the loss does not exceed $4. Which of the following orders would be the best recommendation?

a. Sell limit order
b. Sell stop-limit order
c. Sell stop order
d. Buy stop order

29. If a registered representative wishes to purchase shares of a risky private equity fund for a customer, according to FINRA, the due diligence process should require

    a. No special actions by the registered rep
    b. Written notice to FINRA of the trade
    c. Written consent from the customer prior to the trade
    d. That the trade be disallowed

30. Which of the following may NOT be deducted by a limited partnership for tax purposes?

    a. Depletion
    b. Principal expenses
    c. Interest expenses
    d. Depreciation

31. A customer should purchase long term bonds when she believes that:

    a. Long term interest rates are going to decrease
    b. Short term interest rates are going to decrease
    c. Long term interest rates are going to increase
    d. Short term interest rates are going to increase

32. Shareholder approval is required for a corporation to:

    I. Declare a cash dividend
    II. Declare a stock dividend
    III. Split the stock
    IV. Reverse split the stock

    a. II only
    b. I and II
    c. II, III, and IV
    d. III and IV

33. Holding a put option, as opposed to selling short, has each of the following advantages:

    I. No dividend payments will be required
    II. There is limited downside on the position
    III. There is no loss of time value
    IV. A smaller amount of capital provides the same level of exposure

    a. I and II only
    b. I and III only
    c. I, II, and IV
    d. II, III, and IV

34. Alan Capone wants to open an account at Chi-town Brokerage, but does not want his name to appear on the account. How should Chi-town respond to this request?

    a. Chi-town should open a numbered account for Alan
    b. Chi-town should set up an AKA account and give Alan a fictitious name
    c. Chi-town should inform Alan that any account must be in his name
    d. Chi-town should set up a street-named account only if Alan is an accredited investor.

35. A company previously issued 6 percent $100 par cumulative preferred stock. During the following two years, the company pays $6 and $4 in dividends respectively. If the company announces a common dividend in year 3, how much does it owe preferred stockholders?

    a. $2
    b. $8
    c. $11
    d. $16

36. Michael Hunt wants to sell some of the restricted ABC shares he has been holding for the past 18 months. There are 5 million outstanding shares of ABC common and the total trading for the past two, four, and six weeks respectively is 100,000, 240,000, and 500,000. What is the maximum number of shares that Mike can sell under rule 144?

    a. 50,000
    b. 60,000
    c. 75,000
    d. 83,334

37. Each of the following are FALSE when using the "portfolio margining" method to calculate the margin in a customer's account EXCEPT:

    a. Only customers meeting specific criteria may request use of this method
    b. Any customer may request this method be used in their account
    c. Margin requirements are based on the weighted average of each position
    d. This method is always used for accounts with more than 20 positions

38. Which of the following information is found in the official notice of sale in relation to the competitive offering of a municipal bond?

    I. The priority of execution of orders when released to the public
    II. The allotment to each syndicate member
    III. The method of interest-cost calculation used to determine the winner
    IV. The reoffering yields of the bonds with different maturities

    a. III only
    b. I and II
    c. I, II, and IV
    d. III and IV

39. Which of the following investments is a violation of the wash sale rule:

    I. 25 days after selling Xenon Corp common at a loss, the customer buys Xenon put options
    II. 30 days after selling Xenon Corp common at a loss, the customer buys Xenon call options
    III. 35 days after selling Xenon Corp common at a loss, the customer buys Xenon warrants
    IV. 20 days after selling Xenon Corp common at a loss, the customer buys Xenon convertible bonds

    a. I and III only
    b. II and IV only
    c. I, II, and III
    d. I, II and IV

40. Which of the following documents outlines the allocation of orders?

a. Syndicate agreement
b. Indenture
c. Notice of sale
d. Official statement

41. Of the following options investors, which one(s) would receive a dividend payment if the option were to be exercised prior to the ex-dividend date?

a. The seller of a call option
b. The writer of a call option
c. The buyer of a call option
d. The holder of a put option

42. If an investor buys an ABC corporate bond with an 8% coupon and 10 years until maturity for 80, and then sells it 5 years later for 89, what gain or loss is realized by the investor?

a. A gain of $70
b. A loss of $70
c. A gain of $10
d. A loss of $10

43. Which of the following statements is TRUE when using the "portfolio margining" method to calculate the margin in a customer's account?

a. Any customer may request use of this method
b. Margin requirements are determined based on the net risk of the entire portfolio
c. Margin requirements are based on the weighted average of each position
d. The "portfolio margining" method is always used for accounts with more than 20 positions

44. A registered representative requires a written power of attorney to execute which of the following discretionary orders?

    I. A market order that specifies which securities to sell
    II. An order that leaves the execution time and price up to the registered rep
    III. A limit order that specifies the price and quantity of the security to be purchased

a. I and II
b. II and III
c. I and III
d. I, II, and III

45. If a corporation raises $10,000,000 by issuing preferred stock with a par value of $100, which of the following will increase:

    I. Net worth
    II. Current assets
    III. Total liabilities
    IV. Quick assets

a. I and II only
b. I and III only
c. I, II, and IV
d. II, III, and IV

46. Joe Jacobs buys an ABC convertible bond at $85 with a conversion price of $25. If Joe converts the bonds six months later and sells the stock for $23, the whole trade results in a

    a. $50 loss
    b. $50 gain
    c. $70 loss
    d. $70 gain

47. Each of the following statements about variable annuities are false EXCEPT:

    a. The payouts to investors are dependent on the performance of the separate account
    b. "Life with period certain" results in the highest payouts
    c. If investors deposit money into the annuity account by April 15 of the following year, they may claim deductions in the current year
    d. The interest rate is assumed to be the rate required to beat one or more broad equity market indexes

48. Which of the following BEST describes dollar cost averaging:

    a. Purchasing a fixed number of shares at regular intervals
    b. Negotiating a reduced per share cost
    c. Purchasing a fixed dollar amount at regular intervals
    d. Buying when the price of the investment declines

49. Which of the following types of bonds most often require a sinking fund?

    a. Balloon bonds
    b. Series bonds
    c. Serial bonds
    d. Term bonds

50. Dewey, Cheetum & Howe Brokerage acquires a large block of ABC Corp for $39 per share. Two weeks later, shares of ABC are quoted in the market at 34 – 34.15. Which of the following prices must the firm use as its basis when selling shares to its customers?

    a. $39.00
    b. $34.00
    c. $34.15
    d. $36.50

51. Growth stocks would normally have:

    I. Low dividend payouts
    II. High dividend payouts
    III. Low beta ratings
    IV. High beta ratings

    a. I and III
    b. I and IV
    c. II and III
    d. II and IV

52. Determine the purchase price of a 6% corporate bond that carries a 6.5% yield-to-call after five years and a 6% basis.

    a. Above $1,000
    b. $1,000
    c. Below $1,000
    d. Not enough information provided

53. ABC broker-dealer is a member of a syndicate that is offering new shares of XYZ Corp common stock to the public. The size of the total offering is 10,000,000 shares, with ABC's allocation being 1,000,000. After selling its entire allotment, 1,000,000 shares remain unsold by other members of the syndicate. How many of the remaining shares is ABC responsible for?

    I. 0 shares if the offering was on an Eastern account basis.
    II. 0 shares if the offering was on a Western account basis.
    III. 100,000 shares if the offering was on an Eastern account basis.
    IV. 100,000 shares if the offering was on a Western account basis.

    a. II and III only.
    b. I and III only.
    c. II and IV only.
    d. I and IV only.

54. Each of the following is a FALSE statement about an ADR, EXCEPT:

    a. The actual shares are not held in a custodian bank
    b. The investor cannot receive dividends in cash
    c. ADRs represent shares of U.S. securities trading in foreign markets
    d. The investor does not receive the actual certificate

55. Sara Sweet owns 10 of Mega Corporation's convertible bonds at 110, which may be converted at $22. The 8% coupon bonds have 23 years to maturity and form a majority of Sara's non-stock holdings. What is the current yield of the bonds?

    a. 7.3%
    b. 6.9%
    c. 8.5%
    d. 8%

56. The holding period requirements of Rule 144 apply to which of the following?

    a. A nonaffiliated person who has held control stock for 6 months
    b. A nonaffiliated person who has held restricted stock for 3 months
    c. A corporate insider who has held restricted stock for 2 years
    d. A nonaffiliated person who has held registered stock for 3 years

57. None of the following are considered owners of a corporation EXCEPT:

    a. Zero coupon bondholders
    b. Convertible debenture holders
    c. Call option holders
    d. Common stock holders

58. Sally Peterson wants to open a new account at Speedy X Brokers. According to the "know your customer" rule, Michael Hunt, the registered representative at Speedy's should obtain which of the following information:

    I. Sally's investment objectives
    II. Sally's birth date
    III. Sally's level of risk tolerance

    a. I and II only
    b. II and III only
    c. I and III only
    d. I, II, and III

59. An investor has the following investment results for the current year:

- Capital gains: $20,000
- Capital losses: $45,000

What is the tax status for this investor?

    a. $3,000 loss for the current year, $22,000 carried over to the following year
    b. $25,000 loss for the current year
    c. $5,000 loss for the current year, $20,000 carried over to the following year
    d. $3,000 loss for the current year, $3,000 carried over to the following year

60. At a shareholder's meeting, Bill Francis intends to vote for the three open slots on the Board of Directors. If he owns 1000 shares of the corporation's stock and voting is conducted on a cumulative basis, each of the following is an acceptable way for Bill to vote EXCEPT:

    a. 1000 votes for each of the three candidates
    b. 3000 votes for each of the three candidates
    c. 1000 votes for one candidate
    d. 3000 votes for one candidate

61. An investor purchases 3 XYZ Jul 40 puts for 3.50 each and purchases 300 shares of common at $45. Three months later XYZ is trading at $46. At what market price for XYZ does the investor break even?

    a. 41.50
    b. 45
    c. 48.50
    d. It is impossible to tell

62. XYZ Corp. is offering 8,000,000 new shares to the public. The price to the syndicate is $28 and the public offering price will be $29.25. The takedown and concession for each share sold is $0.75 and $0.30 respectively; the managing underwriter will earn $0.25 as an override on all shares. The selling group is allotted 1,000,000 shares and sells them all. How much does the selling group make in revenue?

    a. $250,000
    b. $300,000
    c. $850,000
    d. $2,500,000

63. A client writes a June 40 put for 5 and is exercised before expiration. A month later, the client sells the underlying stock in the market for 44. Assuming no commission, the result of these transactions is:

a. A profit of $100
b. A loss of $100
c. A profit of $900
d. A loss of $900

64. All of the following are TRUE regarding the buyer of a put option EXCEPT:

a. The maximum gain per share is equal to the strike price minus the premium
b. The maximum loss is equal to the premium
c. This position is used as a hedge on a short position
d. The Options Clearing Corporation (OCC) guarantees the exercise of the option.

65. An investor sells XYZ Corp. stock at a loss and buys XYZ call options within 30 days. Which of the following is TRUE?

a. The loss deduction will be allowed for tax purposes
b. The loss deduction will be disallowed for tax purposes
c. The loss deduction can be used to offset capital gains
d. The loss can be used if the holding period would have led to a short-term loss

66. A customer purchased 100 shares of SHC stock at $30 and simultaneously writes 1 SHC Oct 40 call at $2. If the customer closes both positions three months later when SHC is trading at $35 and Oct 40 calls are at $3, what is the realized gain or loss?

a. $600
b. $900
c. $400
d. $1,100

67. An investor has just opened an options account and enters an order to buy 1 XYZ Jul 50 Call for $300. What is the maximum potential gain?

a. $300
b. $4,700
c. $5,000
d. Unlimited

68. In order for an investor to transfer a securities account from one broker to another, each of the following must occur EXCEPT:

a. The investor must fill out a transfer form from the new broker
b. The original broker must cancel any open orders
c. The investor must allow the original broker ten business days to implement the transfer
d. The original broker must validate the investor's account transfer form

69. Betty Brown would like to open a cash trading account at XYZ brokerage and give trading authority to her son Jon. Which of the following forms are needed to open the account?

    I. A joint account agreement
    II. A new account form
    III. A limited power of attorney
    IV. A hypothecation agreement

  a. I and III
  b. II and III
  c. I, II, and III
  d. I, II, III, and IV

70. A double-barreled municipal bond is

  a. backed by income streams from two different municipal projects
  b. pays twice as often as a regular municipal bond
  c. is backed by the full faith and credit of the issuer if the revenues obtained from the backing project are insufficient
  d. is automatically exempt from all federal, state, and local taxes

71. Which of the following is not a part of the cooling off period?

  a. A due diligence meeting
  b. Blue-skying the issue
  c. Issuance of a preliminary prospectus
  d. Placement of a stabilizing bid

72. A Rule 147 offering is

  a. an offering of securities worth $5,000,000 or less in a 12-month period
  b. an offering of securities only within the issuer's home state
  c. an offering of securities to no more than 35 unaccredited investors in a 12-month period
  d. an offering of a large block of previously outstanding securities

73. Which of the following would be of least interest to a fundamental analyst?

  a. The P/E ratio
  b. Working capital
  c. Statement of cash flows
  d. Historical prices

74. Sam Steiner purchases an 8% coupon Billing Corporation Bond with basis of 8%. The bond may be called in 8 more years, with a yield to call of 8.75%. Billings recently received an upgrade from Moody's, but not S&P. How much did Sam pay for the Bond?

  a. $975
  b. $1,000
  c. $1,075
  d. $1,235

75. Jon Bondman purchases a callable municipal revenue bond trading at a current market price of 97.2. The bond may be called after 5 years with a half percent call premium, has a coupon of 6%, and is triple tax-free to Jon. What is the current yield?

a. 6%
b. 6.08%
c. 6.17%
d. 6.67%

76. What is the appropriate action for ABC Brokers to take if they receive one signed and one unsigned stock certificate from their customer Agnes?

a. Return only the unsigned certificate
b. Return both certificates
c. Retain both certificates and send a stock power and instructions
d. Retain both certificates because one signature is sufficient

77. A customer sells a 7% corporate bond on October 4th for regular way settlement. The bond pays interest on January 1st and July 1st. How many days of accrued interest is this customer owed?

a. 98
b. 95
c. 92
d. 96

78. A workable indication is a(n)

a. firm quote
b. unqualified quote
c. likely bid price
d. likely ask price

79. What regulatory body is responsible for determining which OTC securities may be purchased on margin?

a. The FRB
b. The NASD
c. The SEC
d. The exchange upon which the stock is listed

80. When is the latest time (barring an extension of trading hours) that a TPH may send a notice of an option exercise from transactions that day, per rule 6.20?

a. 5:20 p.m. EST on the third Friday of the expiration month
b. 4:20 p.m. EST on the third Friday of the expiration month
c. 8:30 p.m. EST on the Saturday after the third Friday of the expiration month
d. 11:59 p.m. EST on the Saturday after the third Friday of the expiration month

81. **If each of the following bonds were all issued by the same corporation, each bond is callable, and the Federal Reserve has recently raised interest rates by 0.25%, which bond is most likely to be called?**

    a. 7% bond maturing 12/31/18
    b. 4.5% bond maturing 12/31/18
    c. 7% bond maturing 12/31/12
    d. 4.5% bond maturing 12/31/12

82. **Each of the following occurrences would change the strike price of a listed option EXCEPT:**

    a. A 2-for-1 stock split
    b. A 2-for-3 stock split
    c. A $0.15 dividend
    d. A 4% stock dividend

83. **Which of the following statements are true regarding individual retirement accounts (IRAs):**

    I. Contributions to an IRA are made from pre-tax dollars
    II. Contributions to an IRA are made from post-tax dollars
    III. Contributions to a Roth IRA are made from pre-tax dollars
    IV. Contributions to a Roth IRA are made from post-tax dollars

    a. I and III only
    b. II and IV only
    c. II and III only
    d. I and IV only

84. **A customer buying 10 corporate bonds with a 6% coupon rate, a conversion feature at $25 into common, and a call provision after a five-year holding period will receive semiannual payments of:**

    a. $30
    b. $60
    c. $300
    d. $600

85. **A customer owns 200 shares of GHY at $90, and wishes to hedge the position while generating income. What is the best recommendation?**

    a. Sell calls
    b. Sell puts
    c. Buy calls
    d. Buy puts

86. **Which of the following statements is FALSE regarding IDR bonds?**

    a. The bonds are issued and backed by a municipality
    b. They are also known as a special tax bond
    c. They are issued to construct a non-revenue-producing facility
    d. The money raised is used to construct a facility for a private corporation

87. Matty Perry is a 64-year old investor who determines that he should have a defensive investment strategy. Which of the following types of investments would MOST likely meet Matty's needs?

I. Municipal bond fund
II. High yield bonds
III. Global fixed income fund
IV. Exotic options strategies

a. I and III
b. II only
c. I, II, and IV
d. II, and IV

88. A customer purchases a new issue of ABC automotive bonds, anticipating that the government will back the car-maker if times get tough. The confirmation that is sent to the customer must include:

I. The customer's name
II. The settlement date
III. The current yield at the time of the sale
IV. The nominal yield

a. I only
b. I, II, and III
c. II and III only
d. I, II, and IV

89. 65 shares of ABC common trade at $256 per share in the OTC market. Which of the following holdings is considered to have traded for reporting purposes?

a. 65 round lots
b. 1 round lot
c. 65 odd lots
d. 1 odd lot

90. If a technical analyst identifies a "head and shoulders topping formation," this indicates which type of condition?

a. Bullish
b. Bearish
c. Reversal of a bullish trend
d. Reversal of a bearish trend

91. ABC common shares are offered in new issue with a public offering price of $30. After trading commences, the shares begin to drop in price. The XYZ syndicate responsible for the offering may place any of the following stabilizing bids EXCEPT:

a. $30.25
b. $30.00
c. $29.75
d. $29.50

92. Vicky Feather enters an order to buy 200 shares of ABC at 25 stop limit. If the ticker following the order is 24.95, 25, 25.05, 24.98, 25, then the order was triggered and executed at which prices?

    a. Triggered 24.95, executed 25.05
    b. Triggered 25.00, executed 24.98
    c. Triggered 25.00, executed 25.05
    d. Triggered 24.95, executed 25.00

93. What organization is both the issuer and the guarantor of all listed options?

    a. The SEC
    b. The CBOE
    c. The OCC
    d. The OAA

94. Sam Specs purchases 1000 shares of Mega Corp at $30 in his margin account. If this initial transaction is at the outer bounds allowed under Reg T, what is the "loan amount" given to Sam by his broker?

    a. $10,000
    b. $12,000
    c. $14,000
    d. $15,000

95. The indenture of a corporate bond includes all of the following EXCEPT:

    a. the nominal yield
    b. collateral backing the bond (if any)
    c. the rating
    d. the maturity date

96. When a municipality chooses an underwriter to complete the issuance of a new issue, the offering is considered to have taken place

    a. On a negotiated basis
    b. Privately
    c. On a competitive basis
    d. All of the above

97. When a variable annuity is "annuitized," the owner of the contract will receive which of the following number of annuity units?

    a. a fixed number based on the value of the accumulation units
    b. a fixed number based on the number of accumulation units
    c. an adjustable number based on the number of accumulation units
    d. an adjustable number based on the value of the accumulation units

98. An investor opens a long margin account by purchasing $300,000 in securities. She signs a hypothecation agreement, a loan consent agreement, and a credit agreement. Each of the following are TRUE EXCEPT

    a. The securities may be used as collateral for a loan
    b. If the market value of the securities declines, the debit balance will increase
    c. The securities will be held in street name
    d. Interest will be due on the debit balance

99. Unless specifically stated to the contrary, a CMO has an S&P rating of

   a. AAA
   b. AA
   c. A
   d. BBB

100. You determine with your customer Renee Retired, a 65-year-old retiree, that she should have a "defensive" investment strategy. Each of the following would be suitable investments for Renee's account, EXCEPT:

   a. High-yield bonds
   b. Treasury bonds
   c. Blue chip stocks
   d. Money market funds

101. An investor wishes to purchase shares at $6.50 per share. If the shares are outside the risk profile of the investor, and the investor insists on making the investment over the advice of the registered representative, the registered representative should

   a. enter the order but mark it "unsolicited"
   b. give the order to one of the other brokers that you don't like
   c. refuse the order
   d. require the investor to amend his investment objectives before accepting the order

102. A stock's support level is which of the following?

   a. The average trading price of the security.
   b. The lower price of the security's recent trading range.
   c. The upper price of the security's trading range.
   d. The price at which fairly priced call options will be profitable.

103. An investor with the following two option positions has created a:

   • Short 1 XYZ Jul 60 call at 4
   • Write 1 XYZ Jul 55 put a 6

   a. Short straddle
   b. Credit spread
   c. Debit spread
   d. Short combination

104. A customer sells 100 shares of ABC short at $43 and buys 1 ABC Oct 45 Call @3. What is the customer's maximum loss?

   a. $500
   b. $100
   c. Unlimited
   d. $4300

105. XYZ Company is selling additional shares of common stock to existing shareholders through a rights offering. Those shareholders who want to subscribe and receive additional shares must send the rights certificate and the purchase cost to

    a. The company
    b. The trustee
    c. The registrar
    d. The rights agent

106. Which of the following is an advantage of a variable rate municipal bond over a bond with a fixed coupon rate?

    a. a variable rate bond's price remains relatively stable
    b. a variable rate bond is non-callable
    c. a variable rate bond is always issued with a higher coupon rate
    d. a variable rate bond is more likely to increase in value

107. Which of the following securities are exempt from state income taxes in all states?

    I. GNMAs
    II. Puerto Rican Commonwealth bonds
    III. Treasury Bonds
    IV. Revenue bonds issued to improve public schools

    a. I only
    b. I, II, and IV
    c. II and III only
    d. I, II, III, and IV

108. With regard to a customer account, a registered representative with limited trading authorization may:

    a. Automatically collect a monthly fee for handling the account
    b. Buy and sell investment securities for the account
    c. Transfer securities in and out of the client's account
    d. Direct funds to third parties

109. A customer is interested in purchasing equity securities with the objective of receiving dividends. Which of the following is LEAST likely to be a suitable investment recommendation?

    a. ABC common stock
    b. DEF warrants
    c. QRS preferred stock
    d. XYZ convertible preferred stock

110. Which of the following are characteristics of corporate debt securities?

    I. They are senior securities
    II. They represent ownership of the issuing corporation
    III. They are issued to raise working capital
    IV. They represent a loan to the issuing corporation

    a. I and II
    b. I, II, and III
    c. I, III, and IV
    d. IV only

111. Peter Piper has made several very successful options trades over the course of the past six months and would like to use these successes as a basis to attract more customers. If he intends to include these picks in his advertisements, he must also include:

a. All of the options trades made by his firm for the last year
b. All of the options trades made by Peter for the last six months
c. All of the securities recommendations made by his firm for the past year
d. A disclaimer that the advertised trades are just a few of those recommended by the firm

112. Each of the following instruments trade in the "money market" EXCEPT:

a. CDs
b. CDSs
c. Repos
d. T-bills

113. Victor Vance maintains an unrestricted long margin account at BD Securities. After a significant move in the S&P 500, his SMA has risen by $12,000. Given this move, how much did the value of the stocks held in his account move (his equity)?

a. $12,000
b. $18,000
c. $24,000
d. There is not sufficient information provided

114. An investor would NOT pursue a covered call writing program to

a. Increase the yield of a portfolio
b. Hedge a long stock position
c. Reduce the size of a concentrated long position over time.
d. Generate profits when the underlying stock is expected to drop significantly

115. Which of the following investment strategies is a long straddle?

a. Buy 1 ABC Oct 60 call; sell 1 ABC Oct 50 put
b. Buy 1 ABC Oct 60 call; buy 1 ABC Oct 50 put
c. Sell 1 ABC Oct 60 call; sell 1 ABC Oct 60 put
d. Buy 1 ABC Oct 60 call; buy 1 ABC Oct 60 put

116. A principal must review (and in some cases approve) each of the following activities or occurrences EXCEPT:

a. Letters recommending securities to clients
b. Forms establishing discretionary authority by a registered rep
c. Written complaints received by customers
d. Internal communications between registered reps

117. Joan Dwindle is long 1 ABC Oct 60 put at $8 and is short 1 ABC Oct 50 put at $2.50. Each of the following is a TRUE statement about Joan's net position EXCEPT:

a. Joan will profit if the difference in the premiums widens
b. Joan has a debit spread in ABC options
c. Joan will profit only if the options are both exercised
d. Joan needs at least one of the options to be in-the-money to profit

118. When performing strategic asset allocation for a 60-year-old customer, each of the following is TRUE EXCEPT:

a. The customer's retirement plans should be considered.
b. A general rule of thumb is to invest 100 minus the customer's age in stocks (40% here) and the rest in bonds and cash.
c. A large percentage of the customer's portfolio should be in cash if the equity markets have been particularly weak during the previous 12 months.
d. Portfolio rebalancing should be performed regularly when needed.

119. William Torry has a short margin account with a short market value of $40,000, a credit balance of $80,000 and SMA of $2,000. What is the FINRA minimum equity maintenance on this account?

a. $2,000
b. $10,000
c. $12,000
d. $24,000

120. When an investor in a JTWROS account dies, his portion of the account is

a. transferred to the remaining survivor(s) on the account
b. transferred to the investor's estate
c. frozen
d. transferred to the investor's spouse

121. An investor purchases an ABC Jul 45 call for 4 each while ABC trades at 47. If ABC increases to 50, which of the following statements is TRUE?

a. The investor has a cost basis of 49 if the options are exercised
b. The investor will realize a $450 profit if she exercises the option and sells the stock
c. The investor has purchased a long strangle
d. The investor may benefit from offsetting the position with a put

122. All of the following are possible reasons that a broker-dealer may be allowed to deviate from FINRA Rule 2121 "the 5% rule" EXCEPT:

a. The trade involves an illiquid security
b. The trade is very small on an absolute dollar basis
c. The broker's cost basis is more than 5% above the security's current market value
d. The trade involves an odd lot

123. The debt-to-equity ratio of a corporation measures

a. liquidity
b. leverage
c. profitability
d. none of the above

124. If XYZ Corporation is trading at $45, which of the following options is in-the-money?

a. XYZ Jul 40 calls
b. XYZ Jul 45 calls
c. XYZ Jul 40 puts
d. XYZ Jul 35 puts

125. Which of the following documents officially triggers the acceptance by a general partner of a new limited partner?

a. Certificate of limited partnership
b. Agreement of limited partnership
c. Subscription agreement
d. New account form

126. Each of the following must be registered at either the individual state level or with the SEC EXCEPT:

a. Variable annuities
b. Private placements
c. Interstate offerings
d. Intrastate offerings

127. When an investor buys common stock that increases in value, how is the result to be categorized for tax purposes?

a. Capital gain
b. Ordinary income
c. Appreciation
d. Passive income

128. Which of the following is TRUE regarding a Regulation D offering?

a. It is an offering of securities worth $5,000,000 or less in a one-year period
b. It is an offering of securities only within the issuer's home state
c. It is an offering of securities to no more than 35 unaccredited investors in a one-year period
d. It is an offering of a large block of previously outstanding securities

129. Frank Samuelson is the CEO of Mega Corporation, a large multi-national conglomerate that has recently negotiated the acquisition of Accretive Corp. The deal will be announced in a week, but Frank is so excited that he tells his friend Bill, over lunch in a popular restaurant. Their conversation is overheard by the waiter, John, who later phones his uncle Mike to share the news. Bill, John, and Mike all buy shares of Accretive the day after the lunch. The following persons have violated the insider trading rules:

I. Frank
II. Bill
III. John
IV. Mike

a. I only
b. II and III only
c. I, II, III, and IV
d. I and II only

130. Which of the following is true regarding bonds purchased at a premium?

a. Yield to maturity is greater than the coupon rate
b. Yield to maturity is lower than the coupon rate
c. Yield to maturity is equal to the coupon rate
d. None of the above

131. None of the following are covered by the Trust Indenture Act of 1939 EXCEPT:

a. Debentures
b. Treasuries
c. Agencies
d. GO bonds

132. Peter Farnsworth wishes to invest $25,000 into the XYZ Technology Fund, which has a current NAV of $9.00 and a POP of $9.89. The sales charges and breakpoints are listed in Exhibit 1. How many shares can Peter buy?

Exhibit 1

Breakpoint	Sales Charge %
$0 - $9,999	9%
$10,000 - $24,999	7.75%
$25,000 - $49,999	6.5%
$50,000 and up	5%

a. 2,527 shares
b. 2,561 shares
c. 2,596 shares
d. 2,639 shares

133. Barry Bonds purchases an ABC 8 % corporate bond at 80. How much does Barry have to claim on his taxes each year, if the bond matures in ten years and he holds it to maturity?

a. $120
b. $100
c. $80
d. $60

134. Which of the following statements are FALSE with regard to Treasury STRIPS?

I. Principal is paid at maturity, and interest is paid semi-annually
II. Principal and interest are paid at maturity
III. Investors pay taxes annually
IV. Investors pay taxes on maturity

a. I and IV
b. I and III
c. II and IV
d. II and III

135. The par value of a corporation's stock

a. Is directly related to the market value of the stock
b. Is inversely related to the market value of the stock
c. Is the liquidation value of the stock that shareholders would receive in bankruptcy
d. Is an arbitrarily determined placeholder on the company's balance sheet

Answer Key and Explanations for Test #1

1. A: The first step here is to recognize that the question is asking about a municipal revenue bond – the bond is backed by the revenues produced by a revenue producing facility. In a net revenue pledge, the municipality pays for operating expenses (cost of operations plus maintenance) first, and then pledges the remainder to the bond holders. Therefore, to obtain the net revenue pledge, start with the gross revenue of the facility, subtract the operating costs, and divide the remaining revenues by the debt service requirements.

2. D: Open-end investment companies trade in mutual funds and have characteristics that differ from closed-end investment companies. An open-end investment company continuously creates and issues new shares to investors, selling them at the public offering price (POP), not the NAV plus a commission. Investors must redeem the shares directly with the issuer, which may only issue common shares. Closed-end funds may issue common shares, preferred shares, and bonds, and their shares may be traded on the open market between two investors not associated with the company. Closed-end funds do not offer redeemable shares.

3. D: Sellers of options, whether put options, straddles, or any other combination, make money when the options owner does not exercise the option contract because the seller then retains the premium amount. This is the objective of most options selling programs. Since the strike price and the market price of the underlying stock remained the same, neither the buyer of a put, nor the buyer of a straddle is likely to exercise the options, and thus, the seller benefits because the premium received is retained and adds to profit.

4. A: Level I on NASDAQ is the inside market and is defined by the highest bid and the lowest offer – a process ultimately creating the tightest bid / ask spread. Nasdaq is called the inside market because, when all the bids and offers are listed in ascending order, the bid and the offer that are closest together or inside all of the others represents the inside market. NASDAQ displays these inside bids and ask prices as level I quotes. The NASDAQ exchange provides level II and other level data to offer market depth analysis to investors who believe this data benefits their positions.

5. C: To determine the status of Diane's account, the first step is to calculate the account's equity and compare that to the SMA as allowed by Reg T. LMV – DR = EQ, so \$35,000 - \$18,000 = \$17,000. Reg T required equity = 50% * \$35,000 = \$17,500. This tells you that the account is restricted by \$500 and that there is currently no SMA in the account. There is no margin call at this point, however, because the maintenance level has not been reached. To calculate the maintenance call level use (4/3) * DR; in this case (4/3) * \$18,000 = \$24,000. A maintenance call will occur if the current market value of the securities held falls to \$24,000.

6. A: This question is one that involves selecting the "best" answer. The company will be paid in Euros, so its risk is that the euro declines relative to the U.S. dollar between the time it bills its Italian customer and that customer pays. While selling calls will provide the company with some protection against a decline in the euro, that protection is limited and could cost the company significantly should the euro rise sharply. Buying puts is the best hedge against a decline in the euro – buying options will always be the right answer to these types of questions.

7. A: Corporations may issue income bonds and mortgage bonds. Income (adjustment) bonds are issued by corporations that are in the process of reorganization (usually to avoid bankruptcy); income bonds do not receive interest or principal until the corporation can afford it. Mortgage bonds are issued by corporations and are secured by a pledge of property. Statements III and IV are municipal bonds: A double-barreled municipal bond is essentially the combination of a revenue bond, backed by the municipal revenues received through a specific investment in a project, and a general obligation (GO) bond, which is backed by the full taxing authority of the issuing municipality. With a double-barreled bond, if the revenue from the revenue-producing project is insufficient, the municipality uses its taxing power to cover any short-fall. Moral obligation bonds are municipal bonds that are backed by the state in the event of default.

8. B: This questions states that each of the options given will cover the put writer's position, except for one; in essence, the question is asking which of the listed actions WILL NOT cover the put writer's position. Answer A is not a good choice because it will not really neutralize the put writer's position (she will still have market exposure), but it will cover the dollar exposure. Answers C and D will fully neutralize the position, cover the put writer's dollar and market exposure. Answer B will not cover the put writer's position at all; if the put is exercised, the put writer will still be responsible for buying the underlying stock at the strike price; a long position in the stock provides no protection, and thus, does not cover the put writer.

9. A: When opening a corporate margin account, a registered representative is required to obtain the corporate resolution and the corporate charter. An income statement is not required to demonstrate the corporation's ability to take on risk, nor is required to provide a list of outstanding securities issued by the company. Statement I is included in every answer choice, so you know that it must be included. Picking up on the subtle nuances in the way the question is posed will not only help you to answer questions, it will help to save time. If a given statement is obviously correct on the face of it, it is not necessary to spend much time evaluating it.

10. A: The minimum short equity maintenance required to be maintained under FINRA rules in a short margin account is $5.00 per share or 30% of the current market value; the question does not specify the number of shares, so this amount is simply calculated based on the short market value held in the account at a given time. In this case, the short market value of the account is $52,000 so the minimum amount based on the 30% rules ($52,000 * 30%) is $15,600. It is important to note that ABC Brokers may require a higher amount than is required by the rule – this question, however, pertains only to the FINRA and not to the broker's own discretionary limits. Also note that FINRA Rule 4210 is similar to NYSE rule 431, and Cboe Rule 10.3 is also very similar for option trading.

11. D: There are two types of annuities: immediate payment and deferred payment. With an immediate payment annuity, the customer pays a lump sum and begins receiving payments immediately. With a deferred payment annuity, the customer pays a lump sum and begins receiving payments at some point in the future; in this case, the customer may be able to opt for making periodic payments. Under no circumstances will the issuing insurance company allow the customer to begin receiving immediate payments without fully paying the lump sum prior to the commencement of payments.

12. A: Specialists are not allowed to compete with orders from the public market. In order to determine the range of the public market, find the highest bid and the lowest offer (ignoring stop orders which are triggered only if the market trades at or through that price). Any quote entered by the specialist must be between these two prices. In this case, the highest bid is 35.20 and the lowest offer is 35.60. Since the specialist's quote must fall in between these two prices, answer A is the only one that fits this criterion, and thus, is the correct answer.

13. C: When trying to determine the inside market by looking at the specialist's book, find the highest bid and the lowest offer (ignoring stop orders which are triggered only if the market trades at or through that price). This defines the inside market. In this case, the highest bid is at Morgan for 35.20 and the lowest offer is at Merrill for 35.60. The range created by these two extremes is the inside market. These are the prices most commonly quoted as the bid/ ask spread to retail clients.

14. A: Treasury bills (more commonly known as T-bills) are issued in 1 month, 3 month, and 6 month maturities. Treasury notes have maturities ranging from 1 year up to 10 years. Treasury bonds are government-backed debt securities with maturities over 10 years. Treasury strips are longer term as well, and are derived from a combination of treasury notes and bonds. Treasury STRIPS (T-STRIPS) are purchased at a discount and mature at par value, building the return on the investment into a single lump sum payment. This type of security behaves similarly to a corporate zero-coupon bond.

15. D: After a 2-for-1 stock split, there are twice as many shares of XYZ outstanding. The earnings of the company must now be shared by twice as many shares, and thus the earnings per share (EPS) must be cut in half ($2). Since there are twice as many shares, and the market capitalization of XYZ should not have changed, each share must also be worth half as much ($32). Each shareholder will still receive a proportional share of the earnings of the company because they will own twice as many shares (worth 50% as much) and receive the $2 EPS twice as many times (assuming no shares are sold). There are many reasons a company may do a stock split, discussed in various areas of the test material. A very common reason for a stock split is to lower the price of shares, making them more attractive to investors. The corporation may raise additional capital in this way.

16. A: All or none (AON) is a type of underwriting or an order qualifier on certain types of securities orders. Bond anticipation notes (BANs), project notes (PNs), and revenue anticipation notes (RANs) are all short-term municipal notes. The trick in this question is somewhat obvious, and is designed to make sure the test-taker is paying attention. AONs are three letters, making PNs the stand-out. This is roughly the depth of understanding that is required about the specific municipal securities that are commonly encountered on the test.

17. C: The buying power in an account is measured as the dollar value of securities that the customer can buy on margin with the excess equity (SMA) in the account. The customer has LMV of $40,000 and a debit balance (DR) of $15,000, and thus, she has $25,000 of equity ($40,000 - $15,000 = $25,000). Under Reg T, a customer is required to have no less than 50% of her LMV in a margin account; any amount above this minimum requirement is considered excess equity and thus SMA. In this case, the customer needs a minimum equity amount of $20,000 (50% * $40,000 or Ret T * LMV). The excess equity is, therefore, $5,000 ($25,000 - $20,000). The buying power is the dollar value of the securities that can be purchased on margin with the account's SMA (2 * $5,000 = $10,000).

18. D: An order where a customer wants an immediate execution and wishes to cancel any portion that is not executed immediately is termed an immediate or cancel order (IOC). A fill or kill (FOK) order is one where the broker is to take the order to market and if it cannot be filled at the specified price, the order is to be cancelled. An all or none order (AON) is one in which the investor specifies that he or she wants the entire order filled as a block or not at all; AON strategies are far less common with equity orders and tend to be used when trading futures or options contracts.

19. C: The key to the question is in the fact that the bonds are callable; there is no significance to the fact that they are municipal revenue bonds. Callable bonds, like any bonds, decrease in price when interest rates rise, so answer A is false. Callable bonds usually have a higher yield to compensate the bond holder for the risk that the bonds may be called early. Answer D is also false because the call premium (the penalty the issuer is required to pay when the bonds are called) is not tied to the lost coupon payments. If it were, bonds would never be called. Answer C is true, and thus the correct answer, because when rates are falling, issuers will often call outstanding bonds and reissue them at lower rates.

20. B: The FINRA 5% rule is somewhat of a misnomer – it is more of a guideline than a regulatory rule. It states that a brokerage firm should not charge more than 5% for commissions, markups, or markdowns when collecting fees from customers. It was enacted to help ensure that customers were not charged excessively in the over-the-counter (OTC) market. It covers OTC trades with public customers in dealing with outstanding, non-exempt securities. The policy is not intended to cover new securities – like those offered through a prospectus. Each of the other statements is false.

21. B: When evaluating any question on the exam, pay careful attention to words that are emphasized (MUST in this case). Any of the combinations of public offering price (POP) and net asset value (NAV) could indicate a closed-end fund but, under the maximum 8.5% sales charge rule, answer B must be a closed-end fund because its sales charge exceeds 8.5%. The sales charge implied in the combinations given can be calculated as: sales charge = (POP – NAV) / POP. Each of the answer choices results in a sales charge below 8.5%, except for B, which must, therefore, be a closed-end fund.

22. C: All discretionary accounts must have a written power of attorney giving the rep the authority to make investment decisions -on behalf of the client. The Power of Attorney can specify any additional rules which must be followed, including whether or not the rep may employ leverage in the account and the degree to which it may be employed. All discretionary accounts must be approved and reviewed by a principal; the principal should pay particular attention to ensuring that excessive trading (called churning) is not taking place to generate unnecessarily high commissions. Additionally, all orders for discretionary accounts must clearly be marked "discretionary." As some discretionary accounts may trade on margin, the correct answer is C.

23. D: In a short margin account, equity (EQ) is determined using the relationship SMV + EQ = CR. For Sally, that means that she has $3,000 of EQ (the equation $5,000 + EQ = $8,000 solves to $3,000). Remember that the question asks for the level of excess equity (SMA); when Reg T is applied to the SMV, it is determined that the required equity in the account is $2,500 (Reg T * SMV = required equity, 50% * $5,000 = $2,500). Therefore, Sally has $500 of SMA in her account ($3,000 - $2,500 = $500). It is important not to confuse this with buying power, which is twice the SMA, or $1,000 in this example.

24. B: The key to this question is to recognize that the test writers often like to provide you with an excess of information in an effort to confuse you or trick you into believing that the question is more complicated than it actually needs to be. To calculate the tax equivalent yield (TEY), the only information that is needed is the bond's yield to maturity (7% in this question) and the investor's effective tax rate (Sara is in the 28% tax bracket). To calculate the TEY, divide the YTM by 100% less the tax rate (TEY = 7% / (100% - 28%) = 9.7%). The additional information provided in the question can be ignored and the answer determined with a single calculation.

25. C: While each of the answer choices listed is important, Sam's investment objectives are the starting point and most important factor when considering how to invest and which mutual funds are appropriate. Answer A pertains to front and back loaded funds – meaning that brokerage fees are collected at time of purchase or when sold later. It is important to include the front- or back-loaded fees as a percentage of the initial investment or the funds that are returned. No load funds may be a more desirable purchase decision. The sales charge is the amount of commission charged by Mighty Sure and must be disclosed, as must the ongoing management fee that will be charged by the fund manager. All fee and charge information must be contained in the prospectus. Each is important, but the overall investment objectives are critical and of top concern to Sam. It is the overall investment objective which must be discussed and determined with the assistance of Might Sure.

26. C: Statement I is correct, since a reduced maximum sales charge is allowed and possible when a company is buying shares for its own pension plan. Statements II and III are both correct also- the sales charge can be reduced when an investor is either purchasing a significant dollar value of stock or when he or she agrees to have income and dividends automatically reinvested. The discount is provided as an inducement for the large purchase or for the indication that an investor wishes to hold the position for an extended period. Statement IV is incorrect. A unit investment trust may receive a reduction in the maximum sales charge only when the shares are the SOLE investment underlying a contractual plan. The answer which combines the three correct statements is C.

27. C: The Uniform Gifts to Minors Act, commonly known as UGMA, is an act in some states of the United States that allows assets such as securities, where the donor has given up all possession and control, to be held in the custodian's name for the benefit of the minor without an attorney needing to set up a special trust fund.

28. B: A sell stop-limit order would be the best choice because it specifies a price, but will not become a market order. This order will only get executed at the price specified or a more favorable one. Pure stop orders, although quicker in execution, become market orders when the stop price is reached and the customer will not be guaranteed a specific price. Stop-limit orders are somewhat risky, in that the order may or may not get executed. If the price of the stock continues to fall, the order will not get executed and the customer's position will continue to depreciate.

29. C: An investment in a private equity fund is an example of a non-conventional investment (NCI). Other examples include hedge funds, high yield bonds (including both distressed and low-grade debt instruments), equity-linked notes, and shares in real estate or natural resource limited partnerships. When a registered rep purchases these instruments for a customer's account, FINRA rules require the rep to have prior written consent from the customer. This is relatively new material, so it is very likely that it will appear on the test – this rule is a reaction to the financial turbulence of 2008.

30. B: For tax purposes, a limited partnership (such as hedge funds, private equity funds, or natural resource funds) may make standard deductions, including depreciation, depletion, and interest expenses. Principal expenses, such as redemptions (the return of principal invested in the fund to some of the limited partners by the general partner after the liquidation of certain assets), may not be deducted for tax purposes. The fund may treat them differently when calculating performance based on the cost of liquidating the specific assets in question, and based largely on the disclosed policies of the partnership at the time the initial investments were received.

31. A: A customer should buy long term bonds when she feels interest rates are going to decline after the purchase of the bond. The long-term bond purchase locks in the higher rate for a longer period of time and provides her with the opportunity to realize a capital gain as the price of the bonds rise. This is due to the fact that when interest rates decline, bond prices go up. The short-term rates have less of an impact on overall rates, and will not necessarily affect the price of long-term bonds.

32. D: Shareholder approval is required for stock splits, including reverse stock splits. Decisions about dividends, whether cash or stock dividends, is the sole purview of the Board of Directors

(BOD). The shareholders elect the BOD and they are expected to make the bulk of decisions affecting the day-to-day operations of the corporation. Dividends (if the company is performing) are a part of the "regular" operations of the company. Stock splits are far less common, and thus require special approval from the shareholders – the true owners of the corporation.

33. C: The advantages of using an option instead of going short a stock include the downside protection, the ability to maintain the same level of exposure while risking less capital, and the fact that no dividend payments will be made if the position is held over an ex-dividend date. The downside is that the option WILL lose time value as it moves toward expiration. It is the advantages described in statements I, II, and IV that an investor must weigh against the cost described in statement III when deciding whether to buy a put option or sell the stock short.

34. A: A numbered (street-named) account is a common occurrence in brokerage firms; a customer who wishes to remain anonymous in the market can have the account set up as a numbered account. All order tickets contain a number or code; however, the brokerage firm needs to have a customer-signed document on file stating who owns the account. There is no requirement that the customer be accredited (have a net worth over $1,000,000 and/or have had an annual income of $200,000 or more for each of the preceding two years) in order to be able to open up a numbered account.

35. B: When a company issues cumulative preferred stock, this means that it may make the required payments as the Board of Directors best decides. However, before the company pays a dividend to common stockholders, it must first make up any delinquent payments to the cumulative preferred shareholders. The preferred carries an annual dividend of $6. Since the company fell short by $2 in the second year, it must make up this shortfall, as well as making the third year's payment (preferred stockholders receive dividends before any common dividend is paid). The $2 short plus the additional $6 means the company must pay $8 before issuing a common dividend.

36. B: According to rule 144, an individual who has held shares of restricted stock for a minimum of a one year holding period is the greater of 1% of the total number of outstanding shares or the average weekly trading volume as determined by the previous four weeks of trading activity. In this case, with 5 million outstanding shares, 1% of the total outstanding shares is 50,000. However, when the average weekly volume over the most recent four weeks is considered (240,000 / 4 = 60,000 shares), this is the larger of the two numbers and the correct answer to the question. Answer choice D is tempting because it stands out, but this is a common test-writers trick and should be ignored.

37. A: The portfolio margining method considers the net risk of the entire portfolio, rather than on a position by position basis, to determine the margin position of an account. It is only available when certain criteria are met and there is no minimum number of requirements that must be held in the account. As a tip, remember that when two answer choices are opposites of each other (answer A and answer B in this question), only one can be the correct answer.

38. A: The official notice of sale, which is found in The Bond Buyer, contains bidding details for municipal bonds, including the information included in statement III - the method of interest-cost calculation used to determine the winner (net interest cost or true interest cost). The priority of execution of orders and the allotment details are present in the syndicate agreement. The reoffering yields are determined by the market and are generally not published anywhere, certainly not in the official notice of sale for a competitive offering.

39. B: Under the wash sale rule, when a customer sells a security at a loss, the customer cannot buy the same security or anything equivalent or convertible into the same security within 30 days before or after the sale and still claim the loss for tax purposes. The object of the rule is to prevent an investor from "locking in a loss" for tax purposes, while essentially maintaining the same position after the sale. (II) is a violation of the rule because the customer is buying options that are equivalent (and also "convertible" upon exercise) into Xenon common. (IV) is also a violation because a convertible bond is also convertible into shares of Xenon common. Buying put options (I) is acceptable because they are not an equivalent position. (III) is acceptable because it takes place after the required 30-day waiting period.

40. A: The allocation of orders, which details the priority by which customer orders will be filled, is found in the syndicate agreement. The official notice of sale is an invitation to underwriters from municipalities announcing that they're accepting bids on a new issue. The indenture is a contract between a bond issuer and bondholders that states certain contract terms, such as whether the bond is callable, when the bond matures, and the coupon rate. The official statement is a document prepared for municipal offerings that contains similar information as to offerings as a prospectus.

41. C: One of the keys to answering this question correctly is being able to distinguish between a seller, a writer, a buyer and a holder of various options contracts. A seller and a writer are equivalent, and both are short the option in question. A buyer and a holder are equivalent, and both are long the option in question. Of the choices listed, only the buyer (or holder) of a call option would end up owning the stock if the options were exercised (an investor short a put would also end up owning the stock, but this is not one of the listed choices). In order to receive the dividend payment, the investor must own the stock as of the ex-dividend date. Only answer C would result in the investor owning the stock.

42. D: The first step to solving this problem is to properly accrete the bond. Accretion is determined by dividing the discount received in the purchase price (par value minus market price) by the number of years to maturity ($1,000 - $800 / 10 = $20). This amount must be added to the purchase price to determine the investor's ultimate cost basis ($800 + $100 = $900). If the investor sells the bond for 89, he or she receives $890 (89% * $1,000 par value = $890). The difference realized by the investor is, therefore, a loss of $10 ($890 - $900 = -$10). Remembering to add the accretion is the critical step in this problem.

43. B: In determining the margin position of an account, the portfolio margining method considers the net risk of the entire portfolio, rather than on assessing margin limit requirements on the basis of each individual position. It is only available when certain criteria are met and there is no minimum number of requirements that must be held in the account. As a tip, remember that when two answer choices are opposites of each other (answer B and answer C in this question), one must be the correct answer, since one must be true and the other false.

44. B: In order to be exempted from the discretionary order account rules, a customer must specify the security, indicate whether the order is a buy or a sell, and also specify the number of shares or dollar-value of a trade he/she will accept when the trade is executed. If these characteristics are not specifically described in the customer order, the trade will be a discretionary trade and the registered rep will be required to obtain a limited power of attorney from the customer before executing the order. Market orders by definition are executed at the best available market price and thus are not subject to the registered representative's discretion. Limit orders set a particular price range at which to purchase or sell an investment and therefore involve discretion.

45. C: When a company raises cash through either a debt or equity offering, including both the issuance of common and preferred shares, the company's cash position increases, but its liabilities do not (the equity section of its balance sheet is the offset for the higher asset level). Since assets have increased with the debt or equity issue, and liabilities have not, net worth increases. The cash raised qualifies as both a current and quick asset (can be liquidated in less than 6 months). Knowing that total liabilities remain unchanged immediately eliminates answers B and D – even if this is all you know; your chances have improved dramatically. Knowing the definition of a quick asset should point you to answer C.

46. D: The first step is to determine the conversion ratio. The conversion ratio is obtained by dividing the par value by the conversion price ($1,000 / $25 = 40 shares). Once this is accomplished, you can determine that Joe sold 40 shares for $23 (40 shares * $23 = $920). Once you have determined the dollars realized from the sale, subtract the cost basis ($850). The trade resulted in a gain of $70 for Joe. The question does not ask whether the trade is advisable as this is impossible to determine without knowing where the bond was trading at the time it was converted – selling the bond might have resulted in lower transaction costs.

47. A: Variable annuities are retirement plans issued by insurance companies whose payouts are dependent on the performance of a group of securities held in a separate account held by the insurance company. Straight life annuities, as opposed to life with period certain annuities, have the highest payouts because all payments stop after the death of the account holder. Answer C refers to the tax treatment of IRAs, not variable annuities. Finally, the assumed interest rate (AIR) of an annuity contract is unrelated to the performance of any of the U.S. equity market indexes.

48. C: Dollar cost averaging refers to the practice of buying a set dollar amount of certain investment vehicles at regular intervals with the goal of achieving a lower average cost per share. The dollar cost averaging method of buying equities relieves the investor of market-timing uncertainties. As the stock's market price fluctuates, the investor continues to purchase shares regardless of the stock price fluctuations. Dollar cost averaging is a long-term strategy which is founded on the premise that equity market prices always climb over long periods of time. Over time, if the investment ultimately appreciates, the investor's average price per share will be lower compared to the future market price of the investment. Unless an investor is extremely lucky, the alternative method of buying a block of shares at a single price point may not achieve this goal and expose the investor to significant market fluctuation risk.

49. D: A sinking fund is a special account into which bond issuers make regular deposits in order to pay off bond principal at maturity. The key to this question is in understanding that it asks which types of debt issue must have a sinking fund. While balloon bonds often use a sinking fund because of the large payment that is made when the balloon is due, a term bond makes a single payment to cover all of the principal and, for this reason, a sinking fund is a required provision as a protection for bondholders.

50. C: Despite the brokerage firm's wish to sell shares using its own cost basis (the price at which the firm acquired the shares and took them into their inventory), the current market price is the only price at which the shares may be sold (plus the commission charged by the firm). Since the question asks what price the brokerage sells the shares for, the current ask or offer price ($34.15) should be used – the customer is buying at the offer. The brokerage could buy the shares from a customer at the bid, less any commission.

51. B: A growth stock is one issued by an emerging company which is thought to have great potential for upside price increases. Normally, such companies are not in an income position to offer much in dividends, as they are still investing their profit into the company. In addition, these companies tend to be more affected by the direction of the general market and by news events. Investors buy growth stocks for the chance at capital appreciation, rather than income (no dividends means no income). This greater sensitivity to moves in the general market (a higher level of volatility) translates into higher beta – the measure of how much a given stock moves relative to the broad market.

52. B: The key to this question is to recognize that the test writers often like to provide you with an excess of information in an effort to confuse you or trick you into believing that the question is more complicated than it actually needs to be. The fact that the bond carries a call premium after 5 years is completely irrelevant to determining the correct answer. If the basis and the coupon are equal, the investor paid par for the bond. This means that the investor paid $1000 for the bond – what has happened since is not relevant to determining the purchase price.

53. A: There are two types of syndicates that may be set up to offer new shares for sale to the public – those that operate on a Western (or divided) account basis and those that operate on an Eastern (or undivided) account basis. Under the Western basis, each firm is responsible only for those shares which they originally were allotted. Under the Eastern basis, each firm is responsible for any unsold shares on the same percentage basis as in the original allotment. In this case, ABC was originally responsible for 10% of the total shares offered (1,000,000 / 10,000,000). ABC is, therefore, responsible for an additional 100,000 of the unsold shares if the syndicate is operating on an Eastern basis; otherwise, ABC has fulfilled its obligation and is not responsible for any additional shares.

54. D: An American Depository Receipt (ADR) represents the shares of a foreign security trading in the U.S. The very definition eliminates answer C. An investor IS able to receive dividends in cash and the certificates are held in a custodial bank; NOT delivered to the investor. Answers A and B can also be eliminated, leaving only answer D as the one TRUE statement of the four answer choices given in the question. ADR questions tend to be very straightforward and should be an easy place to gain points if you are familiar with the basics.

55. A: The key to this question is to recognize that the test writers often like to provide you with an excess of information in an effort to confuse you or trick you into believing that the question is more complicated than it actually needs to be. This question asks for the current yield (current yield = annual interest / market price = $80 / $1,100 = 7.3%). The bond's duration, its conversion price (or even the issue of its convertibility), or the fact that it is one of Sara's major holdings is completely irrelevant to coming up with the correct answer. In questions that provide a laundry list of details, look for the few that are needed to solve the question being asked.

56. B: Rule 144 applies to restricted stock only; control stock and registered shares are not covered by the rule. Under Rule 144, restricted stock must be held by both affiliated and nonaffiliated persons for a minimum of six months. Of the three different nonaffiliated persons given in the answer choices, the only one who has held the restricted stock less than the required 6 months is the one in answer choice B. This person will be required to hold the shares for an additional 3 months before the shares can be sold.

57. D: All bondholders (including both the holders of zero-coupon bonds and the holders of convertible debentures) are debt holders or creditors of the corporation and do not have an ownership interest. The purchase of bond debt gives investors a higher claim to the company's assets in bankruptcy, but does not give them any of the rights of ownership. Options give the holder the right to buy stock at a given price, but the holder of an option does not become an owner until the options have been exercised. Only stock holders (of both common and preferred) are actual owners of the company.

58. D: According to FINRA Rule 2090 "know your customer" and FINRA Rule 2111 "Suitability", Michael is required to obtain Sally's full name, address, date of birth and Social Security number. It is also advisable, though not strictly required, that he consider her risk tolerance and investment objectives in discussions with her.

59. A: An investor may use any capital losses in a given tax year to offset capital gains, and then carry forward any unused losses to use in future years. However, only $3,000 of losses per year may be written off against income gains. In this case, the investor has a net capital loss of $25,000 ($45,000 losses - $20,000 gains). The investor may, therefore, write off the maximum allowable $3,000 in the current tax year and carry forward the remaining $22,000 into the following year. Next year, any capital gains may be offset against the $22,000, but if additional losses accrue, only another $3,000 may be written off.

60. B: The key to this question is that shareholders are voting using cumulative voting rights, meaning that Bill has a total of 3,000 votes (1,000 shares * 3 open slots = 3,000 votes) to cast in any way he sees fit. Cumulative voting rights are a way for a small investor to gain greater influence by allowing him to combine his votes and get at least one favored individual onto the Board of Directors. Each of the answer choices is possible except for choice B, because that choice would imply that Bill has a total of 9000 votes rather than 3000. Choice C is acceptable because Bill is not required to use all of the votes that accrue to him.

61. C: To determine the breakeven point, look at the two purchase prices ($45 for the stock and $3.50 for each put). This forms the cost basis of $48.50. Much of the other information in the question is extraneous.

62. B: The key to this question is to recognize that the test writers often like to provide you with an excess of information in an effort to confuse you or trick you into believing that the question is more complicated than it actually needs to be. The selling group receives the concession on the shares that it actually sells. In this case, the selling group was allotted 1,000,000 shares and earned $0.30 for each share because it sold all the shares it was allotted (1,000,000 * $0.30 = $300,000).

63. C: The problem involves three steps: the purchase of a put option, the purchase of the underlying stock, and the subsequent sale of that stock. When the client sells the put for 5, he receives $500- this is the premium received when the option is sold or written. When the option is exercised, the client must purchase the stock for $4000; this makes the client's cost-basis on the stock $3,500 ($4,000 - $500). When the client later sells the stock, now trading at $44, the client receives $4,400 in proceeds from the sale of the stock in the open market. The client, therefore, realizes a profit of $900: $4,400 - $3,500 or $500 of premium plus $400 profit on the sale ($4,400 - $4,000).

64. C: The question asks you to identify the false answer in the group of answer choices. Buying a put option protects a long position, not a short position. To protect a short position (when selling short), the investor can buy a call option. The maximum loss when purchasing an option is the premium paid, the maximum gain on a put is equal to the strike price minus the premium paid, and the OCC does guarantee that the holder of the option can exercise the option and receive delivery of the underlying shares.

65. B: Under the wash sale rule, when a customer sells a security at a loss, the customer cannot buy the same security or anything equivalent or convertible into the same security within 30 days before or after the sale and still claim the loss for tax purposes. The object of the rule is to prevent an investor from "locking in a loss" for tax purposes, while essentially maintaining the same position after the sale. This investor bought a call option, which gives him or her the right to buy XYZ stock at a fixed price, thereby violating the wash sale rule. Therefore, the loss is disallowed for tax purposes and the cost basis would have to be adjusted for the purchase.

66. C: The question requires you to determine the gain or loss on both the stock position and the option position. On the stock position alone, the customer realizes a profit of $500 from the $5 / share increase in the price of the stock (100 * ($35 - $30)). On the option position alone, the customer has lost $100 (this is the cost of his or her hedge on the SHC stock position). The loss on the option is calculated by multiplying the $1 increase by 100; remember that a call writer is short a call, so an increase in price represents a loss when the option is later repurchased to close the position. The net gain on the combined position is $400 ($500 - $100).

67. D: The maximum gain for the investor in the purchase of a call option is unlimited. The appreciation of the underlying stock can go up without limits, giving the holder of a call option the right to call (or purchase) the stock at the strike price and sell it at the limitlessly high market value. The maximum loss that the investor can incur by the purchase of the call option is the premium paid of $300. For this reason, buying call options is considered the safest form of options investing and is most readily granted by brokers to retail clients. Selling naked options is the riskiest, and is usually more tightly regulated and limited to certain investors.

68. C: After the investor fills out an account transfer form with the new broker, the new broker must send a copy of the form to the old broker. Upon receipt, the original broker must cancel any and all outstanding orders for the account and place it into frozen account status. The old broker then has three business days to validate the account transfer form received from the new broker and then there is an additional four days allowed to complete the transfer. The old broker does NOT have ten days to effectuate the entire transfer.

69. B: Betty has indicated that she wants Jon to have trading authority, not that he should be a joint owner of the account. Having trading authority means that while Jon can trade, he cannot make withdrawals or issue additional instructions (as a joint owner he would have full authority to do so). The account, therefore, requires a limited power of attorney to give Jon trading authority, but not a joint account agreement. All new accounts require a new account form, so that form is required as well. The question indicated that this is to be a cash account, not a margin account, so a hypothecation form is not required either. Despite the addition of Jon to the joint account agreement, only two of the four forms listed as answer options are needed to open the account.

70. C: A double-barreled municipal bond is essentially the combination of a revenue bond, backed by the municipal revenues received through a specific investment in a project, and a general obligation (GO) bond, which is backed by the full taxing authority of the issuing municipality. With a double-barreled bond, if the revenue from the revenue-producing project or facility is insufficient to service the payments due on the bond, the municipality uses its taxing power to make up any short-fall. This is considered an advantage to the bondholder, so double-barreled bonds tend to trade at a discount to straight revenue bonds.

71. D: The cooling off period is a part of the registration process for a new security, and is a required waiting period prior to the offering going on sale to investors. During this period, due diligence must be exercised, blue-sky laws are observed, and a preliminary prospectus, often called a red herring, is issued. A stabilizing bid is placed by the underwriting brokers if the price of the issue drops too quickly after the security IPOs – this is a part of the sales process and only takes place when the security begins to trade. This happens after the cooling off period is finished, and thus, is not a part of the process itself.

72. B: A Rule 147 offering is an intrastate offering that is exempt from SEC registration, provided the issuer conducts business only in one state and sells securities only to residents of the same state. This provision also includes the 80 percent rule, which states that at least 80 percent of the issuer's assets should be located within the state and at least 80 percent of the offering proceeds should be used within the state. A Regulation D offering is also called a private placement. Regulation D offerings are exempt from SEC registration as long as the securities are sold to no more than 35 unaccredited (small) investors per year. Regulation A offerings are exempt from full registration requirements, provided the issuer doesn't sell more than $5,000,000 worth of securities in a 12-month period.

73. D: Fundamental analysis examines the quality of a company's earnings, its growth prospects, and its position within the industry in which it competes; it also tries to identify securities that are mispriced based on the analyst's view of what the company's stock should be worth. Unlike the technical analyst, who examines the price action of the stock, its volume, and its historical behavior, the fundamental analyst is only trying to determine what the "true value" of the stock is so that appropriate trading decisions can be made. D is the correct answer because the fundamental analyst doesn't track the stock's price action in order to assign value to it. The value is set according to "fundamentals."

74. B: The key to this question is to recognize that the test writers often like to provide you with an excess of information in an effort to confuse you or trick you into believing that the question is more complicated than it actually needs to be. The recent upgrade received by Billings by one, but not both, of the major rating agencies, has absolutely no bearing on the correct answer. The fact that the bond carries a call premium (or even the fact that the bond is callable at all) is also irrelevant. The fact that the coupon and the basis are equal means that Sam paid par, or $1000, for the bond. No calculation is required once this is recognized.

75. C: Again, the key to this question is to recognize that the test writers often like to provide you with an excess of information in an effort to confuse you or trick you into believing that the question is more complicated than it actually needs to be. The only information required to answer this question is the market price and the coupon rate ($972 and $60 respectively). The fact that the bond is a callable muni or that it is triple tax free to Jon has no bearing on determining the correct answer. Simply use the following equation: current yield = annual interest / market price = $60 / $972 = 6.17%.

76. C: In order to diminish the possibility that the certificates will be lost in transit, the broker should retain both certificates and send a stock power to the customer with instructions and a return envelope. A stock power has the same impact as signing the back of the certificate itself. Both of the certificates need to be signed in order for the brokerage to be able to successfully transfer them when the customer decides to do so. Proactively getting the appropriate documentation is the correct course of action asked for by the question.

77. B: Accrued interest is the interest due to the seller of a bond as calculated from the last day that interest was paid until the end of the current interest period (the seller is paid for the interest he or she has earned, but not yet received). Corporate bonds pay on a 30-day basis month and a 360 day basis year. They also settle on the 2nd business day following the trade date (T+2). The trade settles on October 6th. The last pay date was July 1st. The customer is owed 30 days for July, 30 days for

August, 30 days for September and 5 days for October. You do not include the interest due for the settlement day of the 6th.

78. C: A workable indication is the price at which one municipal securities dealer is willing to purchase securities from another municipal securities dealer. Therefore, a workable indication is a likely bid price. One of the key features which distinguishes the bond market from the stock market is the lack of a central clearinghouse. Bonds trade amongst dealers, so when an investor wishes to sell a bond, his or her broker calls other dealers to establish the price at which the bond can be sold. It is in this context that a workable indication would be encountered.

79. A: The Federal Reserve Board (the Fed) determines which securities may be purchased on margin. While both the SEC and the NASD propagate rules, which affect the ability of investors to purchase on margin and to short securities and on what terms, the various exchanges have their own rules about what securities may be listed on each respective exchange. Ultimately, the Fed determines if a given security may be sold short or purchased on margin. An easy way to remember this is to keep in mind that purchasing on margin is a form of borrowing – typically a bank lends, so borrowing and banks is regulated by the Fed as opposed to other securities regulators.

80. A: Per Cboe trading rule 6.20, the last time that a TPH can submit an option exercise advice is at 4:20 p.m. CST on the third Friday of the expiration month. It is important to remember that some test questions may switch from CST to EST because many options are traded primarily in Chicago at the CBOE. Options officially expire at 11:59 p.m. CST on the Saturday after the third Friday of the expiration month.

81. A: While prevailing interest rates do affect the likelihood of a company to call a bond, the recent action by the Federal Reserve is irrelevant to determining which of the listed bonds is MOST likely to be called. All other things being equal, an issuer is most likely to call a bond with the highest coupon interest rate in order to issue new debt at a lower rate. Of the two 7% bonds, the issuer is more likely to call the bond with the longer maturity; the longer maturity is more expensive to the issuer over the remaining life of the bond as the higher rate must be paid for a longer period of time. Therefore, the issuer will select the highest coupon, longest maturity bond to call – answer A.

82. C: Of the possible answers listed, only answer C does not change the number of outstanding shares of the stock, which can have a significant impact on the price of the stock. A stock split or a stock dividend will alter the number of shares outstanding and affect the price of the stock significantly. A cash dividend, while having an indirect impact on the price of the stock, is perceived as being "priced-into" the stock and the price of the options as well. The declaration or payment of a cash dividend does NOT alter the strike price of any of the listed options on the underlying stock.

83. D: The central difference between an IRA and a Roth IRA is when, in the tax stream, the contributions may be made. An IRA allows for contributions to be made from pre-tax dollars, allowing the investment of a greater number of dollars individually. When the money is withdrawn from an IRA, the withdrawals will be subject to applicable income taxes. This allows the money to grow "tax-deferred." In a Roth IRA, post-tax dollars are contributed, but any subsequent growth is not subject to additional tax; these assets are allowed to grow tax-free because taxes were paid on the initial dollars before they were invested. Each type of account has advantages and the specifics will differ according to the tax liability needs of the individual investor.

84. C: The key to this question is to recognize that the test writers often like to provide you with an excess of information in an effort to confuse you or trick you into believing that the question is more complicated than it actually needs to be. The only relevant information is that the investor owns 10 6% bonds, and that the question asks for the semi-annual payment amount, not the annual amount. If par is $1,000, then 6% * $1,000 = $60; and $60 * 10 = $600 (annual amount received). Therefore, $600 / 2 = $300. The correct answer is $300 is received by the investor on a semi-annual basis.

85. A: Of the choices listed, selling options is the only way to create income. The customer should sell calls, which are covered by the underlying stock. If the calls were exercised, the stock would be delivered to meet the obligation, protecting the customer from any sharp moves in the stock. In another sense, the income generated through the sale of the options lowers the investors cost basis on the stock, or increasing the profit received at any given price in the open market. This is known as a call writing program – it is usually reserved for instances when the customer's positions will not seriously deteriorate by losing ownership of the underlying shares.

86. B: Municipalities issue IDRs (industrial development revenue bonds) to fund the construction of a facility for the benefit of a private user (usually a corporation). In spite of the fact that the IDR is a municipal bond, it is backed by lease payments made by the corporation, and it is therefore considered the riskiest municipal bond. Special tax bonds are backed by the taxing power of the municipality (though they are often dependent on a specific segment of that taxing authority), which is NOT true of IDR bonds.

87. A: Matty, with a defensive investment strategy, is attempting to safeguard principal, generate current investment income, and maintain a reasonable degree of liquidity for unexpected events. High yield bond funds and exotic options strategies are considered speculative (risky investments) and would likely not have a significant (if any at all) place in his portfolio. Municipals and global bonds would be appropriate because they are generally considered safe investments, particularly when diversified through a vehicle like a fund. It would be useful to know Matty's tax status, because only certain investors benefit from municipals. Since statement III alone was not an option, answer A is the best choice.

88. D: When a customer purchases a new issue of bonds (even dubious automotive ones), the confirmation that must be sent to the customer must include: the customer's name, the settlement date, the maturity date, and the coupon rate (nominal yield on the bond). The current yield at the time of the sale is not required information on the confirmation. Of the choices listed, only answer D includes all information that is required and none that isn't. It is important to identify which statements contain faulty information and eliminate those because this will provide the most comprehensive answer choice and lead to the correct answer.

89. A: Under OTC equity security trading rules – per FINRA in a notice dated 3/18/08 to define the unit of trade for OTC securities, a single share that trades above $175 is considered a round lot. In this case then, with ABC shares trading at $256, each single share will be considered a round lot, so 65 round lots have traded. For lower priced securities, round lots are considered share blocks of 100 shares. If ABC were trading below $175, this would then be considered a trade of 65 odd lots. Investors should pay attention to this when trading stocks that are very near $175.

90. C: This is another question is which you must determine which is the "best answer." A head and shoulders topping formation is a bearish indicator, but more accurately it signals that a bullish trend is reversing. Therefore, while answer B is technically also correct, the "best" answer is C because it is more complete and more accurate. The type of formation can apply to an individual stock or the market as a whole, and it gets its name from the "picture" of a head and two shoulders "appearing" on the chart of the security being investigated.

91. A: A stabilizing bid is placed by a syndicate offering a new security in the open market when the price of that security begins to drop too quickly after trading in the security commences. Under acceptable regulations, any stabilizing bid must be at or slightly below the initial offering price to prevent the syndicate from over stimulating demand by artificially bidding up the price of the stock in the open market. Each of the bids listed, except for $30.25, is at or below the initial offering price of $30. The correct answer is, therefore, choice A.

92. B: The order must be split into two separate orders – an order to buy if the stock trades at or above 25 and an order to buy for a price of $25 or better. Therefore, looking at the ticker, when the stock trades at $25, the order is triggered. You must then look for the next print at or below $25 – The next trade is at $24.98, so this is the price at which the order was filled (executed).

93. C: The SEC is responsible for the regulation of corporations and the issuance of stock. The Chicago Board Options Exchange (CBOE) is one the exchanges upon which options are traded. The Options Clearing Corporation (OCC) is the issuer and guarantor of all listed options in the United States. The OCC determines which securities are may be sold as options, and guarantees that the holder of any options contract will have the right and ability to exercise that option according to the terms under which it was issued.

94. D: The "loan amount" is the amount of capital advanced or loaned to Sam by his brokerage. Since the question states that this is an initial transaction, we know that we are trying to determine the initial allowable dollar figure as opposed to the maintenance margin required. Initial margin may not exceed 50%, so if the transaction value is $30,000 ($30 * 1,000 shares = $30,000), and the transaction is at the maximum allowed by Reg T, then the loan must be for $15,000 ($30,000 * 50% = $15,000).

95. C: A bond indenture includes important information such as the nominal yield (coupon rate), the collateral backing the bond (if any), and the maturity date. The rating is not on the indenture, however, because it is not static and may change as the issuer's financial condition changes. Companies such as Moody's and Standard & Poor's place ratings on the bonds based on their analysis of the financial condition of the issuer. Bond rating companies may also issue warnings about impending changes in status to signal the market before a significant change has occurred. Over the past year or so, these ratings have been called into question as several companies, which issued bonds receiving high ratings, were not as sound as those bond ratings might indicate.

96. A: When the municipality selects an underwriter (or a syndicate of underwriters) the issue is said to be done on a negotiated basis. In contrast, when the municipality publishes a notice of sale, it is putting various dealers on notice that it is accepting bids on a competitive basis. Answer D can be ruled out since A and C are mutually exclusive (both cannot be correct at the same time). Private placements usually refer only to the issuance of specialized investment vehicles like hedge funds or private equity investments, not the issuance of public debt.

97. A: When a variable annuity is annuitized during the payout phase, the investor receives a fixed number of annuity units based on the value of the accumulation units. This is another very straightforward question that is regularly on the test because it forms the basis of understanding much of the other material. In a sense, it is the opposite of those questions where the test-writers purposefully try to confuse you by giving you far too much information. The only trick in this question is to read carefully and be sure that you pay attention to wording – the distinction between number and value is key in this question.

98. B: The debit balance (DR) is the amount the investor borrowed from the broker-dealer when purchasing the securities on margin. The debit balance changes only when the broker-dealer charges interest on the money borrowed, when more securities are purchased or sold, or when more money comes into the account by way of dividend or payment by the customer. A change in the market value of the securities does not change the debit balance. The investor will be responsible for paying interest on the debit balance held in the account and she may use the securities as collateral with which to borrow more funds to purchase additional securities (within the limits of Reg T). The securities will be held in street name.

99. A: A Collateralized Mortgage Obligation (CMO) normally has a Standard & Poor's credit rating of AAA because they are comprised of GNMAs (directly backed by the U.S. Government), FNMAs and FHLMCs (these are agencies implicitly backed by the U.S. Government as we saw during the recent housing crisis). All of these securities are considered exceptionally safe and receive S&P's highest rating unless they are accompanied by a statement to the contrary. Whether this will remain the case remains to be seen, but for the time being, and for the current test, it is accurate.

100. A: As a retiree, Renee selects a defensive strategy because she is likely to prefer to take less risk- preferring capital preservation and current income. Of the listed choices, treasury bonds and money market funds will provide her with current income at a relatively low risk level. Blue chip stocks also present a lower risk profile and may offer additional income through the payment of dividends. High-yield bonds are considered a riskier investment, and thus inappropriate for Renee's account and her goal of defensive investing.

101. A: In spite of the fact that the shares may not fit into the investor's investment objectives, the registered rep can still accept the order. However, as a precaution, the order should be marked as unsolicited in case the shares lose money. If an order ticket is marked unsolicited, it serves as some protection against the investor later claiming that he was manipulated into purchasing the security. A registered rep is prohibited from accepting unsolicited orders on options and DPPs (limited partnerships), unless the rep previously received an ODD and the options account was reviewed and approved.

102. B: In technical analysis (or charting), a stock's support level refers to the bottom patterning of a stock's recent trading range. Around this price, the stock seems to reverse direction and trade higher, and is said to have "price support." If the stock falls below this bottoming level pattern, and particularly if the stock closes below this level, it is referred to (by technical analysts) as a "breakdown." As a result, the stock price is expected to continue to fall until a new, but lower, trading range is established. The support level is determined by the price action of the stock and has nothing to do with the options.

103. D: This question is best answered through the process of elimination. In order to have a spread, the investor must have purchased one option and sold another – this eliminates answers B and C because this investor has sold two options. To determine whether the investor is holding a straddle or a combination, consider the strikes prices and months of expiration for the two options in question. If the strike and expiration months are both the same, then the investor is holding a straddle. If either is different, as is the case here, the investor is holding a combination.

104. A: The customer sold short at $43 per share and bought a call with a strike price of 45; the call gives the customer the right to buy back the stock at $45. If the stock rises, the call can be used to limit the loss to 2 points. The customer can lose $200 on the stock. The customer also paid a $300 premium. Therefore, the maximum loss on the combined position is $200 + $300 = $500. The maximum gain is $40 * 100 = $4,000 (this would occur only if the stock went all the way to zero).

105. D: When a company performs a rights offering, it hires a rights agent, which is responsible for maintaining records of the names of the rights certificate holders. In addition to rights agents, companies also hire transfer agents who are responsible for maintaining lists of shareholders, retiring old stock certificates, and issuing new certificates when required. In certain instances, the transfer agent may act as a rights agent also; were this the only given answer choice, it would be one of the "best" answers test-writers enjoy so much.

106. A: There is an inverse relationship between interest rates and bond prices – they move in opposite directions. If interest rates rise, outstanding bond prices fall; if interest rates fall, outstanding bond prices rise. The distinction to be made in this question is that, if the bond carries a variable rate, the coupon rate adjusts proportionally to interest rate changes. This leads to far greater stability in the price of the bond, which, under certain circumstances, is an advantage to an investor and a reason to select a variable rate bond over one with a fixed rate.

107. C: Investors in GNMAs must pay both state and federal income tax on the interest they receive. Puerto Rican Commonwealth bonds are known as triple-tax-free as they are exempt from income tax on the state, federal and local levels. Treasury bonds are also tax free in all states under federal law. Municipal revenue bonds are tax free to investors who reside in the same state as the municipality issuing the bonds, but residents of other states must pay state income tax on the interest they receive from these bonds.

108. B: A limited trading authorization gives the registered representative the authority to buy and sell investment securities for the customer's account. A limited trading authorization does not give the registered representative the authority to contribute or withdraw funds from the account, neither in the form of cash nor securities. A limited trading authorization also provides for the necessity of paying a third party or for paying the registered representative for his or her services in the form of a regular monthly fees. A customer is the sole person who may add or subtract capital to and from the account.

109. B: Common stock, preferred stock, and convertible preferred stock all MAY provide the holder with regular dividends payments – the specific features of each will vary from issue to issue and be dependent on the specific company issuing the security. A warrant gives the holder the right to purchase stock at a specified price for a specified period of time, but is not equivalent to stock. Holders do not receive dividends, so warrants would not be an appropriate investment recommendation for a customer whose goal is to receive dividends.

110. C: Debt securities are senior securities, meaning that in the event of issuer bankruptcy, holders of debt securities will receive payment before preferred stockholders and common stockholders. This has been the case excepting recent bankruptcy activity in the automotive industry, in which case it may be difficult to determine. Debt securities (bonds) are loans to the issuer, as compared to stocks, which represent ownership of the issuing corporation. Issuers issue bonds to raise working capital (the amount of money a corporation has available), so statement III is true as well.

111. A: When including previous successful recommendations in an advertisement that will be seen by customers, trading regulations require that any and all similar trades suggested by the firm for the previous year be included in the advertisement. The fact that Peter is only interested in sharing his own recommendations for the past six months does not exempt him from including all options trades suggested by the firm during, the previous twelve months. The rule states that all similar trades must be included, so the rule means that only options trades must be disclosed.

112. B: The "money market" refers to the market for financial instruments with maturities of one year or less. CDs, repos, and T-bills are money market instruments because they are used by investors to manage short-term cash (money) positions. CDSs are credit default swaps and are a derivative instrument that have varying maturities, but are not a part of the more liquid money market. CDSs have received a great deal of press coverage of late because of their role in =f the recent financial crisis. Money market instruments tend to be lower-yielding, but are highly liquid instruments and easily converted into cash.

113. C: Since one must assume that this is a normal, on-shore account that is subject to Reg T, an increase in SMA is one half as big as the increase in equity (since Reg T requires that stocks be 50% paid for by equity). You know that the account had some positive SMA before the move in the market, because the question tells you that the account is unrestricted. Therefore, a $12,000 increase in SMA implies that the long market value of the account must have increased by twice as much, or $24,000 (2 * $12,000 = $24,000).

114. D: A covered call writing program involves systematically selling call options on an underlying long position (hence the options are covered). If the options are exercised, the long underlying position is called away. An investor would pursue this type of program to enhance the yield on an underlying security, to hedge a long position by collecting premiums (this essentially lowers the cost basis), or to slowly reduce the size of a concentrated long position. If an investor believes a security will depreciate significantly, selling the security or purchasing put options would be the appropriate action, not covered call writing.

115. D: A long straddle means buying a call and a put on the same underlying security where the call and the put each have the same expiration month and the same strike price. Answer B is a long combination (long meaning buys and no sells), defined as having two buys ("long" means purchase in the context of options) where the expiration month, the strike price, or both are different. A straddle is used when the investor expects a significant move in the underlying security, but is uncertain as to the direction.

116. D: A principal must review any communication that is to be sent to customers of the firm, any complaints received by a customer of the firm, and any special documents (including those giving discretionary authority to a registered rep) pertaining to a customer's account. Internal memos and regular communications made between employees of the firm are not required to be reviewed by a principal. However, the principal is responsible for all official communications coming into and disseminated by the firm, and thus must review written recommendations and other solicitations sent to customers.

117. C: Joan's net position is a debit spread because she paid more for the option she purchased than she received for the option she sold; her net debit is $5.50. In order for Joan to profit, the difference between the two options must widen as they move towards expiration. As the options theta kicks in (time decay), if ABC stock trades below $54.50, the intrinsic value of her long put will be greater than her debit and both options could be covered for a profit. At this point ($54.50), or any point below this, at least one of the options will be in-the-money and Joan will realize a profit. In this case, one or both of the options may be exercised, but this is not necessary for Joan's trade to be profitable.

118. C: The general rule of thumb is that customers should have 100 minus their age invested in stocks. However, years to retirement, retirement plans, and specific investment objectives should also be taken into account. Furthermore, as the customer ages, appropriate portfolio rebalancing should be conducted as a matter of routine procedure. Answer C is correct for two reasons: first, the question refers to strategic asset allocation, while answer C refers to a decision that would fall into the category of tactical asset allocation. Second, the performance of stocks in the most-recent 12 months is insufficient to guide an advisor with regard to the investment objectives of his or her customers.

119. C: Minimum maintenance equity on a short margin account is 30% of the short market value held in the account. FINRA rule 4210 states that, after meeting the initial Reg T requirements, an investor's account may not fall below 30% equity based on the current short market value. In this case, the short market value of $40,000 must be multiplied by 30% (30% * $40,000 = $12,000). If the account falls below this value, the investor will receive a margin call and be required to deposit more money into the account in order to avoid having his or her positions liquidated. The SMA amount is a distractor.

120. A: Because this account is set up as JTWROS (joint tenants with rights of survivorship), the deceased investor's portion of the account is transferred to the remaining survivor(s) named on the account. This is another very straightforward question that is regularly on the test because it forms the basis of understanding much of the other material. In a sense, it is the opposite of those questions where the test-writers purposefully try to confuse you by giving you far too much information. In this type of question, there is no fluff – either you know the answer or you do not. Don't waste time trying to reason through this type of question; simply mark your best answer and move on.

121. A: The cost basis for a call option is determined by adding the premium to the strike price (45 + 4 = 49). Despite the fact that the investor does not actually own the stock, the cost basis is the break-even point for the option in question. This call had some intrinsic value and some time value when it was purchased; it must appreciate in intrinsic value faster than the time decay occurs for the investor to make money. The cost basis is the price above which the stock needs to trade before the expiration date in order to realize a profit-- 49 in this problem.

122. C: FINRA Rule 2121 is somewhat of a misnomer – it is more of a guideline than a rule which can be legally enforced. The 5% rule states that a brokerage firm should not charge more than 5% for commissions, markups, or markdowns when collecting fees from customers. It was enacted to help ensure that customers were not excessively charged in the over-the-counter (OTC) market. It covers OTC trades by customers who trade in outstanding, non-exempt securities. Each of the listed answers, except answer C, is an exception where a higher fee may be charged because of the difficulty in executing the specific trade. A broker may not attempt to recoup losses by overcharging the customer and this not an allowable exception to the 5% rule. Therefore, Answer C is the best answer.

123. B: The debt-to-equity ratio measures the capitalization of a company. The higher the debt-to-equity ratio, the more leveraged the company is (the more money it owes). A high debt-to-equity ratio often indicates that the company has financed its growth by borrowing large quantities of capital. The earnings for companies with high debt-to-equity ratios tend to be more volatile, so they'd be considered somewhat riskier investments. Examining a company's debt-to-equity ratio relative to its peers is important, as some industries are more prone to high debt levels than others.

124. A: An in-the-money option is trading such that there is already some intrinsic value contained in the price of the option. With regard to calls, this means that the underlying is trading above the strike price and, with regard to puts, this means that the underlying stock is trading below the strike price. An at-the-money option occurs when the underlying stock is trading at the strike price of the option. An out-of-the-money option is trading such that there is no intrinsic value contained in the price of the option: for calls this means that the underlying is trading below the strike price and for puts this means that the underlying is trading above the strike price. Only answer A is an in-the-money option.

125. C: The general partner signs the subscription agreement when he or she officially accepts a new limited partner (a new investor); the subscription agreement is usually accompanied by payment and wiring instructions to fund the new account. The certificate of limited partnership must be filed with the Securities and Exchange Commission (the SEC) prior to a public offering; the agreement of limited partnership describes the roles and responsibilities of limited and general partners; and a new account form is filled out when a registered rep takes on a new customer. While other documents may be involved, it is the subscription agreement that OFFICIALLY triggers the acceptance of the new limited partner.

126. B: Intrastate offerings (those offered only within the borders of a single state) are exempt from SEC registration, but must be registered on the state level. Interstate offerings (those offered across state lines in several states) and variable annuities are required to be registered with the SEC. Under Regulation D, private placements are exempt from SEC registration and are not required to be registered in the individual states in which they are offered. Private placements include such investments as hedge funds and private equity funds and are often subject to other restrictions. Additional restrictions may be placed upon the investors and upon the methods by which they may be marketed (think accredited investor rules).

127. C: The question states that the stock's market value increases, but makes no mention of any additional action taken by the investor. The investor does not have a capital gain or loss until he or she sells the security. Passive income is income received from limited partnerships, and ordinary income is interest received from bonds or dividends received from stock. Passive income also includes income earned through wages or salary, and may include rents received. The increase in stock value by itself, if no other subsequent action is taken, is in the category of appreciation.

128. C: A Regulation D offering is also called a private placement. Regulation D offerings are exempt from SEC registration as long as the securities are sold to no more than 35 unaccredited (small) investors per year. A Rule 147 offering is an intrastate offering that is exempt from SEC registration, provided the issuer conducts business only in one state and sells securities only to residents of that same state. This provision also encompasses the 80 percent rule, which states that at least 80 percent of the issuer's assets should be located within the state and at least 80 percent of the offering proceeds should be used within the same state. Regulation A offerings are exempt from full registration requirements, provided the issuer doesn't sell more than $5,000,000 worth of securities in a 12-month period.

129. D: The insider trading rules apply to those individuals who disclose or receive and act upon non-public material information; a pending takeover that has not yet been made public qualifies as both non-public and material, as it is likely to have a significant impact on the price of the stock. The exception to the insider trading rules applies to those individuals who inadvertently receive this type of information and have no reason to know that the information is privileged. Frank and Bill both know that the information is non-public and material. John may realize that the information is valuable, but has no duty to keep it private- neither he nor Mike violates the rules by acting on the information.

130. B: Bonds purchased at a premium will have a lower yield to maturity than the coupon rate. The coupon rate is based on and paid against the par value of the bond. The premium (price above par) will be lost over the life of the bond, as the face value of the bond moves to par at maturity.

While this premium is lost, that loss is what is figured into the lower yield to maturity and is the reason why it is lower than the coupon. This phenomenon occurs when rates in the general market fall. Investors bid up the price of the bond "chasing" the higher rate until the premium brings the bond's yield to maturity (all other factors being equal) into equilibrium with the prevailing rates available in the market.

131. A: The Trust Indenture Act of 1939 was passed to regulate the issuance of debt by corporations, and only covers corporate bonds. Debentures are a type of corporate bond, and thus, are covered by the Act. Treasuries, agencies, and GO bonds (municipal bonds) are backed by government (or quasi-government) entities and are exempt from the Act. Debentures, which are backed by the issuing corporation, are specifically covered by the Act. While agencies are only implicitly backed by the U.S. Government, they are also exempt from the Act.

132. C: The first step in determining the correct answer is to determine at what price Peter will acquire shares – his price is lower than the POP because he is making a sizeable investment and will receive a breakpoint discount. Keep in mind that the entire transaction takes place at this sales charge percentage. To determine the price Peter will be charged, divide the NAV by 100 percent less the sales charge: Price = NAV / (100% - 6.5%) = $9 / (1.00 – 0.065) = $9.63. Now you can determine how many shares Peter can afford to purchase at this price, determined by dividing $25,000 by the $9.63 sale price.

133. B: Barry's tax liability is determined by calculating the annual interest he receives plus the annual accretion. The interest is calculated by multiplying the annual coupon by the par value of the bond (8% * $1,000 = $80). Accretion is determined by dividing the discount received in the purchase price (par value minus market price) by the number of years to maturity ($1,000 - $800 / 10 = $20). Therefore, Barry's annual tax liability is $80 of interest added to the $20 of accretion, or $100.

134. A: Treasury STRIPS (T-STRIPS) are purchased at a discount and mature at par value, building the return on the investment into a single lump sum payment. This type of security behaves similarly to a corporate zero-coupon bond. Despite the fact that the investor only receives a single payment, he or she must pay taxes on the accretion each year. Remember that the question asked which two statements are false. This is a question on which it is easy to get confused and, even after careful analysis, one may still get the wrong answer.

135. D: The par value of a stock is set by the corporation as a placeholder to be listed on the balance sheet. There is no relationship, direct or inverse, between the par value and the market value – the par value is fixed and does not fluctuate unless the company is attempting to achieve an accounting change unrelated to market conditions. Answer C refers to the liquidation value, which is closer to the stock's book value. The balance sheet will often list the stock's par value plus the additional capital that was raised by the initial public offering (IPO) – classified as "paid-in capital."

Series 7 Practice Test #2

1. Which of the following characteristics are features of preferred stock?

I. A fixed rate of return
II. Priority to assets over common
III. Priority to dividends over common
IV. Fixed date of maturity

a. I, II, and IV
b. I and III
c. II and IV
d. I, II, and III

2. Per the MSRB definition, which of the following is not a trait of a municipal fund security?

a. not issued for a government entity
b. invests in securities
c. issues face-amount certificates
d. securities represent 40% or more of total value

3. How often is the "Easy to Borrow" list for short sales updated, and by whom?

a. weekly, by FINRA
b. weekly, by brokerage firms
c. daily, by FINRA
d. daily, by brokerage firms

4. Which of the following investments have tax advantages?

I. Hedge funds
II. FNMAs
III. IRAs
IV. Municipal bonds

a. I and II
b. II and III
c. III and IV
d. All of the above

5. If ABC has 4,000,000 shares currently outstanding, what will the holder of 20,000 shares receive if ABC plans to issue an additional 200,000 shares through a rights offering?

a. 2,000 rights to buy 1,000 shares
b. 2,000 rights to buy 400 shares
c. 20,000 rights to buy 1,000 shares
d. 20,000 rights to buy 400 shares

6. When a company dissolves, what is the order in which net assets are paid out?

a. Secured creditors, Unsecured creditors, preferred stock, common stock
b. employees, secured creditors, unsecured creditors, preferred stock, common stock
c. preferred stock, secured creditors, unsecured creditors, common stock
d. trade creditors, preferred stock, bondholders, common stock

7. According to Cboe Rule 10.3, what is the minimum amount of margin required for a Long Position in an option account

 a. 10%
 b. 25%
 c. 40%
 d. 50%

8. All of the following are true of an investor's rights in a rights offering except that

 a. in the event the investor chooses to not purchase the shares offered, he or she may sell those rights to another investor.
 b. the investor chooses to purchase the shares.
 c. the investor's rights expire after 35 days due to the current market price dropping below the offering's subscription price.
 d. all of the above are true.

9. A REIT has $100,000 of earnings in a year and pays out dividends of $200,000 that year. The dividends do not meet the exclusion standards of the TCJA and were not due to the sale of any long-term assets. How will the dividends likely be treated by the shareholders?

 a. $200,000 ordinary income
 b. $100,000 ordinary income, $100,000 reduction in basis
 c. $100,000 ordinary income, $100,000 pass-through business income
 d. $200,000 reduction in basis

10. If an effective yield for a bond increases from 5.11% to 6.25%, how is this increase described?

 a. 114 bps
 b. 11.40 bps
 c. 1.14 bps
 d. 1.14 percent

11. Which of the following can be defined as a security?

 a. Fixed annuities
 b. Variable annuities
 c. Individual retirement accounts (IRAs)
 d. All of the above

12. All but which characteristic are considerations for evaluating a limited partnership or DPP?

 a. The program's economic soundness
 b. The DPP's prospectus
 c. The general partner's talent, knowledge, and expertise
 d. The program's basic objectives

13. Which of the following is (are) considered promotional material and thus need approval from a principal?

    I. Form letter
    II. Market letter
    III. Research report
    IV. Official statement abstract

    a. I and II
    b. I, II, and III
    c. II, III, and IV
    d. I, II, III, and IV

14. Which of the following investment instruments has shares that trade in the secondary market?

    a. mutual funds
    b. face-amount certificates
    c. closed-end funds
    d. UITs

15. When a customer fails to pay for a trade and the account is now frozen, when must the customer pay for any subsequent purchase transactions?

    a. Within five business days after the trade date
    b. Prior to the trade
    c. By the settlement date (T+2)
    d. Within five business days after the trade date with the firm's permission

16. Which of these risks are inherent to American depositary receipts (ADRs)?

    a. Risk to capital
    b. Currency risk
    c. Volatility risk
    d. All of the above

17. If a GTC order remains unexecuted, it will be automatically cancelled:

    a. A year after the order was placed
    b. At the end of the fiscal quarter
    c. At the end of the month
    d. Based on the broker's GTC Policy

18. All of the following are TRUE of stock index options EXCEPT:

    a. When exercised, the seller delivers cash
    b. When exercised, the seller delivers shares
    c. When exercised, the buyer may owe the seller money
    d. The writer received a premium for selling the option

19. What types of debt can be bundled into a Collateralized Debt Obligation (CDO)?

    1. Car Loans
    2. Mortgages
    3. Bonds
    4. Credit Cards

    a. 3 only
    b. 1 and 3
    c. 1, 3, and 4
    d. 1, 2, 3, and 4

20. An investor starts a margin account with a $50,000 purchase of stock and a $25,000 cash deposit to meet the 50% initial margin requirement. If the value of the stock rises to $80,000, how much would the investor's SMA be?

    a. $5,000
    b. $10,000
    c. $15,000
    d. $20,000

21. While the U.S. government is thought to "stand behind" a variety of securities, it only directly backs which of the following?

    a. GNMA
    b. FNMA
    c. FHLMC
    d. Federal Farm Credits

22. Each of the following is true of warrants EXCEPT:

    a. Warrants are issued to increase the attractiveness of new offerings
    b. Warrants have a longer duration than rights
    c. Warrants can be separated from the stock or bonds of the issuer
    d. Warrants represent a perpetual interest, similar to stocks

23. Which type of oil and gas DPP offers the GREATEST amount of diversification?

    a. Exploratory program
    b. Developmental program
    c. Income program
    d. Combination program

24. Your existing customer has just been approved by your firm to trade options. How long does the customer have to return a signed options agreement?

    a. 10 days
    b. 15 days
    c. 30 days
    d. 45 days

25. Which of the following money market instruments pay interest?

    I. Commercial paper
    II. Banker's acceptance
    III. Jumbo CDs
    IV. T-bills

    a. I and II
    b. III only
    c. I, II and IV
    d. II and IV

26. When a municipality issues a limited tax bond, which of the following is limited in the debt indenture?

    a. The type of taxes that may be used to pay off the debt
    b. The number of taxes from which funds may be drawn to pay off the debt
    c. The rate of taxes that can be levied to pay off the debt
    d. Limited tax bonds may only be paid from real estate taxes

27. Each of the following would affect the debit balance in a long margin account EXCEPT:

    a. Cash deposit
    b. Stock dividends
    c. Cash dividends
    d. The sale of securities held in the account

28. What is the time value of a XYZ Oct 60 call trading for a premium of 7 if XYZ trades at 62.50?

    a. 3
    b. 4.5
    c. 5.75
    d. 7

29. Corporation XEC proceeds with a 2:1 stock split. An investor currently owns 350 shares of XEC stock with a current value of $70 per share and total value of $24,500. What will this investor's position be in terms of number of shares, share price, and overall value once the stock split is finalized?

    a. 700 shares, $35 per share, $24,500 total value
    b. 175 shares, $35 per share, $6,125 total value
    c. 175 shares, $140 per share, $24,500 total value
    d. 700 shares, $140 per share, $98,000 total value

30. What US government security is tailored to protect investors from inflation?

    a. LGIP
    b. TIPS
    c. T-STRIPS
    d. STRIPS

31. Given the following information, what is the stock price discount a rights holder would receive as a result of this rights offering?

> An investor has shares for corporation XEC purchased previously at $74 per share. He or she has rights to purchase XEC shares through a rights offering at a subscription price of $82 per share, and the current market price of stock XEC is $87.

a. $13
b. $5
c. $8
d. None of the above

32. When an underwriter agrees to keep whatever shares of the offering are not sold, this is characterized as what type of underwriting?

a. Best efforts
b. All or none
c. Mini max
d. Firm commitment

33. What is the most common reason for a municipal bond to trade ex-legal?

a. The bonds are illegal
b. The legal opinion is in doubt
c. No legal opinion was obtained
d. The legal opinion has been withdrawn

34. A floor broker asks a specialist to stop stock. Which of the following is/are TRUE about stopping stock?

> I. The specialist is guaranteeing a price.
> II. The specialist needs permission from an exchange official prior to stopping stock.
> III. This may only be done for public orders

a. I only
b. I and II
c. II and III
d. I and III

35. On the maturity date of a corporate bond, the holders of the bonds will

a. Receive par value from the issuer
b. Receive the current market value plus accrued interest
c. Continue to earn interest until they redeem the bonds
d. Receive the current market value of the bond

36. All of the following transactions settle on the second business day after the trade date EXCEPT:

a. A T-bill
b. 100 shares of common stock
c. A municipal bond
d. A convertible corporate bond

37. Which of the following would be found on a stock certificate?

    I. Committee on Uniform Securities Identification Procedures (CUSIP) number
    II. Number of owned stock shares
    III. Owner's name
    IV. Issuer of the shares

    a. II and III
    b. I, II, and IV
    c. II, III, and IV
    d. I, II, III, and IV

38. An investor has a short margin account with $20,000 of SMV and a credit balance of $35,000. If the value of the shorted stock rises to $30,000, by what amount would the account be restricted?

    a. $2,500
    b. $5,000
    c. $7,500
    d. $10,000

39. What is the ad valorem tax on a property with an assessed value of $550,000, a current market value of $535,000, and a tax rate of 16 mills?

    a. $8,800
    b. $9,600
    c. $10,400
    d. $12,800

40. A client writes a Jan 65 put for 6, is exercised, and is assigned the stock. A month later the client sells the underlying stock in the market for 69. The result of these transactions, assuming no commission, is:

    a. A profit of $100
    b. A loss of $100
    c. A profit of $1,000
    d. A loss of $1,000

41. Corporation PPG has 22 million shares of authorized stock, has sold a total of 17 million shares, repurchased back 5 million from investors, and has 12 million shares remaining in the hands of public investors. What is corporation PPG's current amount in treasury stock?

    a. 12 million
    b. 5 million
    c. 17 million
    d. Unknown without additional information

42. Municipal bonds settle regular way in

    a. one day
    b. three days
    c. five days
    d. seven days

43. After shorting a stock at 75, an investor holds the position as the stock declines to 68. Which of the following strategies could the investor use to protect the gain?

a. Buy stop-limit at 70
b. Write calls
c. Write puts
d. Buy calls

44. Tracy Goepel is expecting a large amount of passive income for the next few years. Which of the following investments has the potential to offset a significant amount of passive income?

a. Oil and gas exploration
b. Junk bonds
c. Corporate bonds
d. Hedge funds

45. Which of the following is NOT important to the marketability of a specific municipal bond?

a. The coupon rate
b. The accrued interest
c. The dollar price
d. The name of the issuer

46. Which of the following terms can be described as the day the decision is made by the corporation's board of directors to provide the common stockholders with a dividend?

a. Declaration date
b. Record date
c. Ex-dividend date
d. None of the above

47. Place the following compensations paid out from a new issue in order from largest to smallest:

I. Concession
II. Reallowance
III. Takedown
IV. Manager's fee

a. I, II, III, IV
b. III, I, II, IV
c. IV, II, I, III
d. II, IV, I, III

48. Which of the following is TRUE of the tax treatment of dividends received from an investment in a foreign corporation?

a. If taxes were withheld abroad, the investor is not required to pay any taxes in the U.S.
b. If no taxes were withheld abroad, the investor has no tax responsibility
c. If taxes were withheld abroad, the investor must match the amount in U.S. taxes
d. If taxes were withheld abroad, the investor can claim a foreign tax credit

49. If a broker/dealer sends two work-related emails, each to 5-10 retail investors and several institutional investors who represent 3-5 retail investors each, in two weeks. These emails would most likely be classified as:

   a. Correspondence
   b. Institutional Communication
   c. Retail Communication
   d. Internal Communication

50. What type of option exercise means that the option may only be exercised on the expiration date?

   a. Chicago Style
   b. New York Style
   c. American Style
   d. European Style

51. What type of preferred stock has a price that tends to most closely tied to the common stock price?

   a. Adjustable Rate
   b. Normal
   c. Callable
   d. Convertible

52. A trade confirmation must be sent to the customer

   a. on the trade date
   b. on or before the settlement date
   c. before the settlement date
   d. before the trade date

53. In a municipal bond underwriting, which group receives the "takedown"?

   a. The members of the managing underwriter
   b. Syndicate members
   c. The selling group
   d. Post-underwriting selling groups

54. An investor purchases 10,000 ABC at $30. After ABC increases to $40, the investor wants to protect his profit. A registered representative could recommend which of the following orders?

   a. Sell limit at $45
   b. Sell limit at $35
   c. Sell stop at $40.25
   d. Sell stop at $39.75

55. Simplified arbitration is used for

   a. member-to-member disputes up to $50,000
   b. member-to-customer disputes up to $50,000
   c. member-to-member disputes over $25,000
   d. member-to-customer disputes over $25,000

56. Which of the following order types will be adjusted downward when a stock goes ex-dividend?

       I. Buy stop
       II. Buy limit
       III. Sell stop
       IV. Sell limit

  a. I and II
  b. I, II, and III
  c. II and III
  d. II and IV

57. If a customer wishes to maximize the allowable margin under Reg T in his purchase of 500 shares of ABC Corp. at $45, what is the minimum he must deposit in the account to make the trade?

  a. $11,250
  b. $12,250
  c. $14,375
  d. $15,500

58. Which of the following is the appropriate response to a customer who has placed a trade but wishes to cancel the trade because of a subsequent negative move in the stock?

  a. The customer owns the stock and must submit payment
  b. The broker-dealer will repurchase the securities
  c. The registered rep will repurchase the securities
  d. The customer should be assured that the stock will recover

59. Which of the following are true of the term equity?

       I. It is interchangeable with the term stock.
       II. It provides the investor with ownership stake in the issuing corporation.
       III. The shares do not mature and are therefore perpetual.
       IV. A corporation's goal in selling shares is to create capital.

  a. II, III, and IV
  b. II only
  c. I, II, III, and IV
  d. I and II

60. When exercising options, what is the time period used to evaluate the exercise limit?

  a. 2 days
  b. 5 days
  c. 30 days
  d. 60 days

61. What documentation must a corporation provide to open a cash account with a broker-dealer?

  a. Corporate charter
  b. Corporate resolution
  c. Corporate bylaws
  d. Margin agreement

62. Which TWO of the following positions have the same directional bias?

      I. Long calls and short calls
      II. Long calls and short puts
      III. Long puts and short puts
      IV. Long puts and short calls

    a. I and III
    b. II and III
    c. I and IV
    d. II and IV

63. Frank Furkel buys an ABC convertible bond at $85 with a conversion price of $25. If Frank converts the bonds six months later and sells the stock for $23, the whole trade results in

    a. $50 loss
    b. $50 gain
    c. $70 loss
    d. $70 gain

64. According to Cboe Rule 10.5, what value is assigned to security futures contracts in a margin account?

    a. 0%
    b. 25%
    c. 50%
    d. 100%

65. Which of the following are TRUE of defined contribution plans?

      I. Employers are required to match employee deposits
      II. Annual contribution amounts are generally fixed
      III. Employer contributions may be discontinued based on company performance
      IV. Benefits increase proportionally with term of service

    a. I and II
    b. I and IV
    c. II and IV
    d. II and III

66. The NYSE has 2,100 advancing stocks and 1,250 declining stocks at a particular point in the day. What is the advance-decline ratio at that time?

    a. 1.68
    b. 0.63
    c. 0.59
    d. 1.74

67. What is not a reason a company would issue Preferred Stock?

    a. fight a hostile takeover
    b. reduce the debt to equity ratio
    c. mitigate dividend exposure
    d. retain existing voting power

68. If an investor exercises an index call option, the assigned seller may deliver which of the following?

   a. 100 shares of the underlying index
   b. Cash equal to the current market value of 100 shares of the index
   c. Cash equal to the intrinsic value of the option times 100 shares at the end of the exercise day
   d. Cash equal to the margin requirement for 100 shares of the underlying index

69. Which of the following can be inferred from a tight money yield curve?

   I. Short maturity bonds are yielding less than long maturity bonds
   II. Short maturity bonds are yielding more than long maturity bonds
   III. Interest rates are rising
   IV. Interest rates are falling

   a. I and III
   b. II and III
   c. I and IV
   d. II and IV

70. Which of the following is a zero-coupon government security?

   a. Treasury bonds
   b. Treasury notes
   c. Treasury receipts
   d. All of the above

71. Determine the purchase price of a 5.5% corporate bond that carries a 6.15% yield-to-call after ten years and a 5.5% basis.

   a. $1,075
   b. $1,000
   c. $930
   d. $925

72. Which of the following is TRUE with regard to IDRs?

   a. The municipality is responsible for payment of the debt
   b. They are not subject to the substantial user requirement
   c. They have few similarities with private activity bonds
   d. They do not need voter approval to be issued

73. A customer in the 28% tax bracket holds a GO bond at 94 with a basis of 7% and a nominal yield of 5.5%. What is the tax equivalent yield on this bond?

   a. 9.3%
   b. 9.7%
   c. 7.9%
   d. 10.1%

74. Which of the following describe aspects of a rights offering?

I. *Cum rights* refers to the trading status of a stock after the declaration of a rights offering.

II. The number of rights to be issued per share will differ from offering to offering.

III. The stock will not trade with the rights attached after the ex-date, but the value of the stock will remain the same.

IV. The underwriting investment bank will have the option to purchase any shares that the rights holders decline to purchase in the offering.

   a. I and IV
   b. II and IV
   c. I, II, and IV
   d. II and III

75. What is the tax added on investment income for high income individuals?

   a. 0%, 15%, or 20% depending on income
   b. 3.80%
   c. 5.00%
   d. 8.00%

76. All are characteristics of Local Government Investment Pools except:

   a. aggregated funds are deposited in a diverse portfolio of funds
   b. pooled by state and local governments and placed into a trust of short-term investments
   c. registered with the Securities and Exchange Commission (SEC)
   d. Interest is normally allocated to the participants on a daily basis

77. Which of the following describe characteristics of a shareholder's preemptive rights?

   a. In the event that the number of new shares proposed to be sold by the corporation causes the amount of outstanding shares to outnumber the amount of shares they are authorized to sell, the current shareholders must approve the increase to authorized shares before the sale can proceed.
   b. Current shareholders are given the first option to purchase any new shares sold by a corporation.
   c. Only after current shareholders have declined the offer to purchase shares from the corporation's new offering can the shares be offered for sale to the general investing public.
   d. All of the above are true.

78. All of the following agencies or departments enforce MSRB rules EXCEPT

   a. FINRA
   b. Comptroller of the Currency
   c. Federal Reserve
   d. FGIC

79. Form 144 is waived for affiliates selling restricted shares when

    I. The net amount of the sale is below $100,000
    II. The net amount of the sale is below $50,000
    III. The sale does not exceed 10,000 shares
    IV. The sale does not exceed 5,000 shares

    a. I and II
    b. I and IV
    c. II and IV
    d. II and III

80. If a broker appears in a public event, what standards apply to the communication?

    a. Comments must be scripted and approved in advance by a qualified principal
    b. Comments based on sound evaluation of facts, not false or misleading, and only predict future performance for one year. Disclose any financial interest. No firm procedures needed.
    c. Comments based on sound evaluation of facts, not false or misleading, and do not predict any future performance. Disclose any significant financial interest. No firm procedures needed.
    d. Comments based on sound evaluation of facts, not false or misleading, and do not predict any future performance. Disclose any significant financial interest. Written procedures needed.

81. All of the following are true of stockholder voting methods except that

    a. the statutory method involves an investor voting equal amounts of his or her votes for each of the candidates they would like to vote for.
    b. special circumstances may allow for a stockholder to vote more than one vote per share for each share he or she owns.
    c. the cumulative method involves an investor choosing to cast all of his or her votes for one candidate.
    d. there are two methods by which stockholders may cast their votes.

82. Michael Gluckman purchases a callable corporate bond trading at a current market price of 98.3. The bond may be called after 6 years with a two percent call premium. The bond has a coupon of 7.8%, and is triple tax-free. What is the current yield?

    a. 6.9%
    b. 7.58%
    c. 7.8%
    d. 7.93%

83. What gain or loss is realized by the owner of a BBB corporate bond with a 6% coupon and 15 years until maturity when the bond is purchased for 85 and sold 5 years later for 92?

    a. A gain of $80
    b. A loss of $80
    c. A gain of $20
    d. A loss of $20

84. Which of the following documents or rules govern the investments which may be purchased for a UGMA account?

I. The legal list
II. The prudent man rule
III. The NASD list of approved investments
IV. The NYSE list of approved investments

a. I, II, and III
b. I and II
c. I, II, and IV
d. II and IV

85. Which of the following TWO statements are false regarding indications of interest during the registration period?

I. They are binding on the broker-dealer
II. They are not binding on the broker-dealer
III. They are binding on the customer
IV. They are not binding on the customer

a. I and III
b. I and IV
c. II and III
d. II and IV

86. Which of the following would BEST meet a customer's goal of current income with only moderate risk?

a. Hedge Funds
b. Common stock of a growth company
c. AA rated corporate bonds
d. Convertible preferred stock

87. Per FINRA rule 4513, for how long must a member maintain records of customer complaints?

a. 2 years
b. 3 years
c. 4 years
d. 5 years

88. Which of the following factors may cause a customer to change his or her investment objectives?

I. Age
II. Investment experience
III. Marital status
IV. The inheritance of a large amount of money

a. I and II
b. I, II, and III
c. II, III, and IV
d. I, II, III, and IV

89. Once shelf registration is obtained, the issuer may delay selling all or part of its stock for up to

    a. 180 days
    b. 1 year
    c. 2 years
    d. 3 years

90. Which of the following is NOT a prohibited activity for a registered rep?

    a. Commingling
    b. Interpositioning
    c. Hypothecation
    d. Backing away

91. Corporate bonds which are secured by securities held by a trustee are called

    a. Guaranteed bonds
    b. Debentures
    c. Collateral trust bonds
    d. Equipment trusts bonds

92. Regulation SHO Price Test Circuit Breaker Rule 201 stops short sales on a security at what level of price change in a day?

    a. 5%
    b. 10%
    c. 13%
    d. 15%

93. When a syndicate member retains shares of a hot issue in hopes of later selling them for a greater profit, the member has violated rules relating to

    a. Withholding
    b. Marking to market
    c. Freeriding
    d. Comingling

94. A technical analyst would draw which TWO of the following conclusions with regard to a stock trading at its resistance levels?

    I. The stock is have difficulty going up
    II. The stock is have difficulty going down
    III. The stock is overbought
    IV. The stock is oversold

    a. I and III
    b. II and III
    c. II and IV
    d. I and IV

95. Place the following types of options in order of ascending position limits:

1. Total Long position in one security's options
2. Cboe S&P 500 AM/PM options
3. Industry Index options, with the largest underlying stock representing 30% of the index
4. Interest rate options related to short-term treasury securities

   a. 1,2,3,4
   b. 4,3,2,1
   c. 4,3,1,2
   d. 3,2,4,1

96. Which of the following is NOT TRUE of treasury stock?

   a. it is part of the outstanding shares
   b. it is issued stock that has been repurchased by the company
   c. it has no voting rights
   d. it has no dividend entitlement

97. Which of the following corporate issues does an investor have the right to vote on as a common stockholder?

   a. Proposed stock splits
   b. Corporate bond issuance
   c. Election of the board of directors
   d. All of the above

98. An investor who wishes to add liquidity to her portfolio could add any of the following EXCEPT

   a. a money market fund
   b. private equity limited partnership
   c. blue chip stocks
   d. T-bills

99. All of the following are good delivery for a trade of 470 shares of stock EXCEPT

   a. forty-seven certificates for 10 shares each
   b. eight certificates for 50 shares each, one certificate for 40 shares, and one certificate for 30 shares
   c. four 100-share certificates and one 70-share certificate
   d. two 100-shar

100. The MSRB suitability standard includes all but which of these standards?

   a. Broker Specific
   b. Customer Specific
   c. Reasonable Basis
   d. Quantitative

101. A Regulation A offering is

   a. an offering of securities worth $5,000,000 or less in a 12-month period
   b. an offering of securities only within the issuer's home state
   c. an offering of securities to no more than 35 unaccredited investors in a 12-month period
   d. an offering of a large block of previously outstanding securities

102. Which of the following is the most appropriate hedge for a customer expecting a large payment in Japanese yen six months forward?

   a. Buy calls on the U.S. dollar
   b. Buy puts on the U.S. dollar
   c. Buy calls on the Japanese yen
   d. Buy puts on the Japanese yen

103. Who can make contributions into an ABLE account?

   a. Only the parent/guardian
   b. The parent/guardian or beneficiary
   c. The parent/guardian, grandparents, or beneficiary
   d. Anyone

104. Which of the following federal laws requires the full disclosure of all material information about new security issues?

   a. The Securities Act of 1933
   b. The Glass-Steagall Act
   c. The Securities Exchange Act of 1934
   d. Regulation T

105. Each of following statements is TRUE regarding civil penalties for insider trading violations EXCEPT:

   a. Civil penalties are only levied against registered persons
   b. They may be as large as three times the gain or loss
   c. They may be levied for improper supervision of a registered rep
   d. They center around the use of material, non-public information

106. In technical analysis, a consolidating market has what type of trend line?

   a. Erratic
   b. Sideways
   c. Upwards
   d. Downwards

107. According to FINRA rule 4511 and SEA 17.4a, how long must members retain general books and records?

   a. 6 years, at least 2 years in an easily accessible place
   b. 6 years, at least 1 year in an easily accessible place
   c. 7 years, at least 2 years in an easily accessible place
   d. 7 years, at least 1 year in an easily accessible place

108. The _____ requires that any recommendations made to a customer by a municipal bond broker or dealer be appropriate for that customer.

   a. Municipal Securities Ruling Bond
   b. Options Trading Board
   c. Options and Securities Rulemaking Board
   d. Municipal Securities Rulemaking Board

109. ABC Corp. shares are trading at $45 per share when the company declares a 5 percent stock dividend. After the dividend is paid, an investor who owned 1,000 shares now owns:

    a. 1,000 shares valued at $47.25 per share
    b. 1,005 shares valued at $45 per share
    c. 1,050 shares valued at $45 per share
    d. 1,050 shares valued at $42.86 per share

110. An investor will be casting votes in an election for board of directors under the statutory method. There are three candidates, and the investor has 1,500 votes to cast. Which of the following is an example of how this investor could cast his or her votes?

    a. 1—0 votes, 2—1,500 votes, 3—0 votes
    b. 1—0 votes, 2—1,000 votes, 3—500 votes
    c. 1—500 votes, 2—500 votes, 3—500 votes
    d. None of the above

111. Regarding the results of a stock split, which of the following is true?

    a. Number of shares, stock price, and overall value of holdings changes.
    b. Number of shares changes, and stock price does not change.
    c. Number of shares changes, and value of holdings does not change.
    d. None of the above is true.

112. Term bonds are quoted

    a. according to a percentage of dollar price
    b. on a yield-to-maturity basis
    c. on a current yield basis
    d. on a nominal yield basis

113. Which of the following statements is TRUE regarding the payouts received from a ten-year certain annuity that has already begun making payments?

    a. If the purchaser dies seven years after payments begin, the annuity will not make any more payments
    b. The annuity will stop making payments after ten years, even if the purchaser is still alive
    c. The annuity will not stop making payments after ten years, if the purchaser is still alive
    d. If the purchaser is still alive after ten years, payments will go to the beneficiary

114. To be eligible for an ABLE account, at what age must the disability have begun?

    a. 18 years
    b. 21 years
    c. 26 years
    d. There is no age limit

115. If a municipal securities dealer offers different quotes to different customers for a municipal bond at the same time, what MSRB rule(s) would possibly be violated?

    1. G-13
    2. G-17
    3. G-30
    4. G-45

a. 1 only
b. 1 and 2 only
c. 1, 2, and 3 only
d. 1, 2, 3, and 4

116. A customer is long 100 shares of ABC at $65 and sells 1 ABC Oct 80 call at 2. Six months later, ABC is trading at $70 per share and the call is trading at 4. If the customer closes both positions, what is the resulting gain or loss?

a. $300
b. $500
c. $700
d. $1,100

117. When can a registered rep open a joint account with a customer?

I. Under no circumstances
II. With approval from a principal
III. With a signed proportionate sharing agreement from the customer

a. I and II
b. II and III
c. I and III
d. I, II, and III

118. According to FINRA rule 2121, service charges (not including commissions) on customer accounts must be

a. no more than 2% per year
b. 5% per year
c. fair and reasonable and not discriminatory
d. adjusted according to account size

119. An investor purchases stock worth $25,000, and then later gives the stock to a friend as a gift when it is worth $15,000. The stock peaks again at $22,000. The friend later sells the stock for $17,000. What is the taxable gain or loss to the friend?

a. $3,000 loss
b. $5,000 loss
c. $10,000 gain
d. $0 - no gain or loss

120. What is stock that has been authorized for sale and sold to investors (regardless of its current ownership) considered to be?

a. Issued stock
b. Authorized stock
c. Treasury stock
d. Outstanding stock

121. An investor purchases stock worth $5,000, and then later gives the stock to a friend as a gift when it is worth $10,000. The stock peaks at $20,000. The friend later sells the stock for $12,000. What is the cost basis to the friend?

    a. $5,000
    b. $10,000
    c. $12,000
    d. $20,000

122. According to the Investment Advisers Act of 1940, who is required to register?

    a. All registered reps
    b. Individuals who execute trades for customers
    c. Persons who give investment advice for a fee
    d. Publications giving general investment advice

123. If a customer owns a convertible bond at 105, with a 7.5% coupon, what is the current yield of the bond?

    a. 7.1%
    b. 6.9%
    c. 8.7%
    d. 8%

124. The REIT Modernization Act of 1999 did all of the following except:

    a. Reduced distribution of taxable earnings from 95% to 90%
    b. Allowed REITS to own up to 100% in a TRS
    c. Allowed REITS to hire independent contractors to run health care properties for limited periods
    d. Allowed REITS to derive less than 75% of income from real estate activity

125. In what type of interest rate environment is call protection valuable on a callable bond?

    a. table
    b. Falling
    c. Fluctuating
    d. Rising

126. Which of the following is TRUE regarding the official disclosure statement of a revenue bond?

    a. It includes information about the tax base of the municipality
    b. It needs to be filed with the SEC
    c. A final version does not need to be prepared
    d. It must only be sent to certain prospective purchasers

127. Which of the following is TRUE with regards to bonds sold out of a firm's inventory?

    a. The total amount of the sale should be considered when determining the markup charged
    b. The sale would be subject to the NASD 5% policy
    c. The rating of the bonds is disclosed on the confirmation sent to the customer
    d. The commission amount is disclosed on the confirmation sent to the customer

128. In a new short margin account, an investor sold short 1,000 shares of XYZ stock at $20 per share. How much cash must the investor have in the account to meet the Regulation T initial margin requirement?

a. $5,000
b. $10,000
c. $20,000
d. $40,000

129. What type of preferred stock typically is covered by a sinking fund provision?

a. Adjustable Rate
b. Normal
c. Callable
d. Convertible

130. An investor would like to initiate a short sale in a margin account. Presuming the short sale is for 1,000 shares at $20 per share, what would be the initial margin requirement?

a. $10,000
b. $20,000
c. $30,000
d. $40,000

131. If an investor wants to limit his loss on the stock to a specific price using options to protect against a sharp decline in the stock, a reasonable recommendation would be to:

a. Buy a call option
b. Sell a call option
c. Buy a put option
d. Sell a put option

132. Which of the following parties prepares the legal opinion prior to the issuance of a municipal bond?

a. The trustee
b. The issuer
c. The syndicate manager
d. The bond counsel

133. Corporations choose to repurchase shares previously sold to the public for which of the following reasons?

I. To decrease the corporation's amount of issued stock
II. In an effort to keep majority control over the company
III. To aid in funding a future merger
IV. To maintain the corporation's earnings per share

a. I, II, and III
b. III and IV
c. III only
d. II and III

134. A broker (in a firm that has been in business for more than a year) would like to send a newly created form letter or email to a group of about 30 customers - some institutional and some retail - to recommend a new mutual fund by highlighting its ranking in the brokerages data. What level of approval is required?

    a. A qualified principal must review/approve before, and file with FINRA within 10 days after it is sent

    b. A qualified principal must review/approve before, and file with FINRA within 10 days before it is sent

    c. A qualified principal must review and file with FINRA within 10 days after it is sent

    d. The broker must file with FINRA within 10 days after it is sent

135. If an investor has $15,000 of excess equity in a long margin account, what would his buying power be, presuming the margin requirement is 50%?

    a. $7,500

    b. $15,000

    c. $22,500

    d. $30,000

Answer Key and Explanations for Test #2

1. D: Preferred stocks have characteristics similar to those of fixed income instruments – priority over common to assets in the case of bankruptcy, priority over common to dividends, and a fixed rate of return. One of the distinguishing features is that preferred stock, unlike fixed income securities, does not have a specified maturity date. This means that answer D is the single answer among all the answer options that combines all of the characteristic features of preferred stock. In addition to the features in the question, holders of fixed income securities take priority to assets over the holders of preferred shares.

2. A: Municipal Fund Securities are issued for government entities, and would be considered investment companies if not for the fact that they are government-issued. The ICA definition includes businesses that primarily invest in securities, face-amount certificates, and/or have 40% or more value tied in investment securities.

3. D: The "Easy-to-Borrow List" is maintained by brokerage firms and updated every 24 hours. Securities are categorized as easy-to-borrow generally due being highly accessible and having a high number of shares outstanding.

4. C: IRAs (individual retirement accounts) and municipal bonds provide tax advantages to investors. Capital invested in a traditional IRA can be written off from the individual's income taxes and not paid until the money is withdrawn. IRAs are not entirely exempt from taxation; payment of taxes on IRA gains is merely deferred. The interest payments received from municipal bonds are tax-free at the federal level (some are tax-free at the state level as well) Investors in higher tax brackets benefit most significantly from this advantage of municipal bonds. Despite being issued by a private corporation which has the implicit backing of the federal government, FNMAs are still taxed in the regular way for all investors.

5. C: There are two steps to answering this question. The first is to know that rights are issued on a 1-to-1 basis for shares held – a customer will receive one right for every share of stock that he or she owns. The next step in the question is to know that a rights offering will be anti-dilutive, meaning that if the company is issuing 5% more stock (200,000 / 4,000,000 = 5%), then every current share holder will be granted a proportional increase in the number of shares they can purchase (20,000 shares * 5% = 1,000 shares). When these two steps are combined, the right number of rights and shares gives you answer C.

6. A: Secured bondholders and other secured creditors are paid first because their money is guaranteed, or secured, by collateral or a contract. Unsecured creditors are to be paid next: this includes bankers, employees, suppliers, and tax authorities. Stockholders are the final group: first preferred and then common stock holders.

7. B: Customer Margin Accounts—the minimum amount of margin which must be maintained in margin accounts of customers having long positions in securities is 25% of the current market value of all long positions in the account.

8. C: Investors' rights expire generally after 16-30 days. Additionally, investors may choose to exercise the rights to purchase additional shares or sell those rights to another investor who would like to buy those shares.

9. B: If REIT dividends exceed that year's earnings, the amount that exceeds the current year income could be treated as return of capital. If the dividend meets TCJA requirements it could become pass-through income subject to a 20% deduction, but that was not the case in this question. If the dividend was based on the sale of a long-term asset then the dividend could become a long-term capital gain, but that is not the case in this question.

10. A: One basis point is equal to 1/100th of 1%, or 0.01%, or 0.0001. 1% change = 100 basis points and 0.01% = 1 basis point. Basis points are typically expressed in the abbreviations "bp," "bps," or "bips."

11. B: A security must be transferable from one individual to another and exposes the owner to risk and loss. Variable annuities are securities because they are transferable and, due to their payments being varied and unpredictable, expose the owner to some financial risk and variability in returns. Fixed annuities are not securities in that they provide for fixed payments, a guarantee on the receipt of earnings and principal, and consequently, no risk to the owner. Individual retirement accounts (IRAs) are not considered securities in that they provide for regular and predictable distributions to the owners, and thus, no risk.

12. B: The evaluation involves four main considerations:

1. the program's economic soundness
2. the general partner's talent, knowledge, and expertise
3. the program's basic objectives
4. the DPP's start-up costs

A Limited Partnership does not have a prospectus

13. D: Each of the items listed is considered promotional material and must be approved by a principal prior to being disseminated to customers. A form letter is a generic letter sent to several customers or potential customers. A market letter is a newsletter that a brokerage firm uses to promote its services. A research report usually states the firm's opinion on a specific security. An abstract is an excerpt or synopsis of the official statement and requires approval as it may adjust the original language but not the overall message of the official statement.

14. C: Closed-end funds issue a set number of shares and then the holders of those shares must trade them with other investors in order to close their respective positions. Mutual funds, UITs, and face amount certificates all have provisions by which the investor holding the respective instrument may redeem the shares when he or she no longer wishes to hold the investment. Mutual funds (open-end funds) create and destroy shares in accordance with investor demand, unlike closed-end funds that only issue a specified number of shares.

15. B: After a customer fails to pay for a trade and the broker-dealer freezes his or her account, any subsequent trades must be paid for ahead of the execution of any new buy orders. Likewise, before the customer will be allowed to execute any sell orders, the securities that are the subject of the planned trade must first be delivered to the broker-dealer. This type of customer activity is tracked, which prevents the customer from simply opening another securities account with another broker-dealer and repeating (potentially) the same mistake which is in violation of regulations.

16. D: Investors of American depositary receipts (ADRs) are subject to the risk of permanent loss of their invested capital due to a company's decline having long-term effects on their ability to successfully conduct their business. Further, currency risk as a result of currency fluctuations and the volatility risk associated with stock price fluctuations are also risks inherent to ADR ownership.

17. D: In order to protect both investors and brokers from having orders executed that were not intended to be filled, and were simply forgotten, or to limit losses from forgotten GTC orders that execute during random wild price swings, many exchanges will not accept these orders. Brokerages will usually still accept them but limit the time period – usually to 30-90 days.

18. B: The key to this question is to remember that index options are always settled for cash – this should make sense since an index option, by definition, has an index representing its underlying value and as such may not be deliverable in pure form (instruments that track an index may have slight performance deviations from the index they follow). As a tip, remember that when two answer choices are opposites of each other (answer A and answer B in this question), one must be the correct answer, since one must be true and the other false.

19. D: collateralized debt obligations (CDOs) consist of a group of loans bundled together and sold as an investment vehicle. However, whereas CMOs only contain mortgages, CDOs contain a range of loans such as car loans, credit cards, commercial loans, and even mortgages.

20. C: The equation for a long account is LMV - Equity = Debit Balance, and the Debit Balance remains constant as LMV fluctuates. The initial values would be $50,000 LMV - $25,000 Equity = $25,000 Debit Balance. If the LMV rises to $80,000, the Equity would increase, too, and the new equation would be: $80,000 LMV - $55,000 Equity = $25,000 Debit Balance. Since LMV is $80,000, the required Equity is now $40,000. Finally, $55,000 - $40,000 = $15,000 is the SMA (Special Memorandum Account) amount for the investor.

21. A: Government National Mortgage Association (GNMA) securities are directly backed by the full faith and credit of the U.S. government. The other listed securities (FNMA's, Farm Credits, and Freddie Mac's) are sponsored by various government agencies, but are, in fact, issued by independent corporations that list and back these securities. During the recent financial crisis, the extent to which the government "stood behind" agency securities was tested, and was shown to be weaker than these securities had historically been treated (often trading at near zero spreads to treasuries).

22. D: This is somewhat of a trick question because there are occasions when warrants may be perpetual. Warrants give the holder the right to buy stock at a fixed price. Warrants are long-term investments and may have an expiration date or they may be perpetual. The question asks for which answer choice is not true. Since answer choice D states that warrants are perpetual (i.e., under all circumstances), this is the correct answer because some warrants have an expiration date, making that answer option (D) false.

23. D: This is somewhat self-explanatory as a combination program offers diversification across the other three types of programs listed in the answer choices. Similarly, each type of program is what it sounds like: an exploratory program attempts to find and recover previously undiscovered oil; a development program drills near already existing oil wells; and income programs invest in currently producing wells to earn a return. Combination programs diversify across all three of the above types in varying degrees, depending on the specific mandate of the given program.

24. B: After an existing customer goes through the approval process and is given permission by the firm to trade option contracts, he or she must return a signed written options agreement to the firm within 15 days of receiving the approval. If the signed written options agreement is not tendered, the customer's trading privileges for options will be permanently suspended until the agreement has been received and the suspension is lifted by one of the broker-dealer's principals. The broker-dealer is required to keep these agreements on file in case a dispute arises in the future.

25. B: The majority of instruments that trade in the money market, including banker's acceptance, T-bills, corporate paper, and repos all sell at a discount to face value and mature at their full value, thus helping the holder to realize the expected profit. Jumbo CDs, however, are an exception as they pay regular periodic interest. They can also be distinguished by the fact that they do not, in most cases, trade in the secondary market. Issued by banks, jumbo CDs usually must be held to maturity to avoid a penalty.

26. C: When issuing a limited tax bond, the municipality is issuing a general obligation municipal bond that has the maximum tax rate increase permissible to service the debt defined in the bond indenture. With the majority of GO bonds, the interest payments are backed by the full taxing authority of the municipality, meaning that it can levy whatever taxes are necessary to service the debt obligation created by the bond. Limited tax bonds fall between GO bonds and revenue bonds in perceived safety from any given municipality.

27. B: Each of the answers given would change the amount of cash held in the account, except for answer B. Cash deposits affect the cash balance in the account, and thus will offset any debit balance held. Cash dividends all lead to a higher level of cash being held in the account, thereby driving down the debit balance. The sale of securities will also raise cash in the account and affect the debit balance. The receipt of additional shares from a stock dividend is the only answer choice which will have no impact on the amount of cash held in the account, or on the debit balance held by the customer.

28. B: The premium of an option is made up of intrinsic value and time value: intrinsic value is by what amount the option is in-the-money (what it could be converted for immediately); and time value is the amount the buyer pays for the time to allow the option to appreciate in value. The question tells you that the premium is 7. For a call option, the intrinsic value is calculated as the market price minus the strike price ($62.50 - $60 = $2.50). Since the total premium is equal to the intrinsic value plus the time value, time value can be calculated by subtracting the intrinsic value from the premium ($7 - $2.50 = $4.50).

29. A: A 2:1 stock split dictates that, for every share an investor owns, they will now own two. Further, the per-share price gets split in half due to the additional shares that resulted from the split. The investor's overall position value in stock XEC, however, does not change.

30. B: Treasury Inflation Protection Securities (TIPS) were created to attract investors by offering protection against rising inflation, which erodes the value of fixed-income securities. Every six months, the interest rate paid on TIPS is adjusted to reflect changes in the Consumer Price Index (CPI).

31. B: The discount the investor would receive is the difference between the current market price of stock XEC and the subscription price offered in the rights offering.

$$\$87 - \$82 = \$5$$

32. D: In a firm commitment underwriting, the broker-dealer serving as the underwriter keeps whatever shares it was not able to sell. Both mini-max and all or none underwritings are examples of best efforts offerings. In a mini-max underwriting, the broker-dealer must sell a minimum number of shares of the offering or the entire underwriting is cancelled. In an all or none underwriting, just as it sounds, unless all of the shares of the underwriting are sold, the entire underwriting will be cancelled. In each case, the broker-dealer agrees to use its best efforts to meet the minimums.

33. C: Most large municipal issuances require a legal opinion to be attached to the bond indenture. A legal opinion is a statement prepared by a bond attorney which states that the interest received from the bond being issued meets the requirements of exemption from federal taxation. When no legal opinion is obtained, the bond trades ex legal. Many small issuances trade ex-legal because the issuance is too small to justify the expense of obtaining a formal legal opinion. In this case, the investor must rely on his or her own resources when preparing annual tax returns.

34. D: Stopping stock is a method a specialist uses to guarantee that a customer's order will be executed at a specific price. Stopping stock may be done only for public orders and cannot be executed for the specialist's own book. Since the specialist has his or her own inventory, a specialist does not need permission to stop stock, but is limited to performing this service on public orders only. The NYSE uses specialists, which is one of the things which distinguish it from the over-the-counter (OTC) market.

35. A: When an investor holds a bond to maturity, the investor receives par value from the issuer on the maturity date. After a bond matures (whether corporate, U.S. government, or municipal), an investor stops earning interest. As the bond gets closer and closer to maturity, its market value is likely to move towards par since that is what will be received at maturity. This is similar to an option contract moving toward its intrinsic value as it gets closer and closer to the expiration date.

36. A: Most securities settle on the second business day after the trade date (T + 2), but U.S. government instruments generally settle (known as regular way settlement) one business day after the trade date. This is another very straightforward question that is regularly on the test because it forms the basis of understanding for much of the other material. In a sense, it is the opposite of those questions where the test-writers purposefully try to confuse you by giving you far too much information. Know regular way settlement for the most common instruments.

37. D: Stock certificates contain a Committee on Uniform Securities Identification Procedures (CUSIP) number, the number of owned shares, the owner's name, and the issuer of the shares.

38. D: Put the values into the equation SMV + Equity = Credit Balance. When SMV changes, the Credit Balance remains constant and Equity Changes. The initial equation is $20,000 SMV + $15,000 Equity = $35,000 Credit Balance. If the SMV rises to $30,000, then the new equation would be $30,000 SMV + $5,000 Equity = $35,000 Credit Balance. Regulation T requires Equity to remain at least 50% of SMV, which in this case is $30,000*0.5 = $15,000. Only $5,000 of equity remains, so the account is Restricted by $15,000 - $5,000 = $10,000.

39. A: There are a few keys to getting the correct answer to this question. Firstly, you have to know that the assessed value, rather than the current market value, is used when calculating taxes. Secondly, it is important to know that a mill is equal to 0.001 or one-thousandth when performing the calculation. These two facts are the key, and if you know them, the question is easy. Therefore, in the instance of this question, the taxes are calculated by multiplying the assessed value of the property ($550,000) by 16 by a mill ($550,000 * 16 * 0.001 = $8,800).

40. C: The question asks you to follow the transaction from the purchase of the option, to the purchase of the underlying stock, to the sale of the stock. In the example provided, the customer sells the put option and receives $600 in premium. However, due to the price action of the stock, the customer is obligated to produce the shares and must buy 100 shares of the stock at its strike price of $65. This phase of the transaction sequence results in a total debit of $5,900 ($600 - $6,500 = $5,900). The customer then sells the stock for proceeds of $6,900 for a total of a $1,000 profit ($6,900 - $5,900).

41. B: Corporation PPG's current amount in treasury stock is 5 million, given that treasury stock is defined as the amount of stock once sold to the public and then repurchased by the issuing corporation. The amount of outstanding shares is 12 million, and 17 million is the total amount of issued stock.

42. B: The settlement date is defined as the day on which ownership officially changes from the buyer to the seller, and the issuer updates its records to reflect the new ownership. Current ownership will determine who has a claim to the next interest payment when it becomes due. Municipal securities settle regular way in three business days after the trade date, which is the same as common stock transactions. "Regular way" is often referred to as "T plus 3." Transactions for cash settle the same business day.

43. D: The investor is concerned about an increase in the price of the underlying security, so the strategy used must be targeted at profiting when the stock rises, and fixing the price at which the trade can be closed. The investor could either use a buy-stop order, which is not offered as an answer choice, or buy calls. The owner of a call is entitled to buy shares at a fixed price. If the stock rises (moves against the investor's short position), the owner of a call can buy back the shares required by the short position and close out the position at a set price.

44. A: In order to offset passive income, Tracy needs to find an investment that provides passive losses, as only passive losses may be used to offset passive gains. Passive income and losses are derived from rental properties and limited partnerships. Oil and gas exploration typically provide large write-offs initially for purchasing land, equipment, and other required costs to get the project started, without yielding any cash flow until oil is found and being pumped out of the ground, a process which could take several years. By employing this strategy, Tracy will be able to offset her current passive gains, in hopes of realizing future gains when the oil project begins to produce.

45. B: Each of the answers given, except accrued interest, affects the quality of the bond. Accrued interest is the amount of interest a buyer has to pay a seller when purchasing a bond in between coupon dates. The investor earns the same amount of interest each day, regardless of the specifics of a given bond (all other factors being held equal), so an investor is indifferent to the amount of accrued interest. Therefore, the accrued interest does not impact the marketability of the municipal bond being considered.

46. A: The declaration date is the date when the board of directors declares the decision to pay out a dividend to common stockholders of record. The record date is when investors must be officially recorded as stockholders on stock certificates in order to qualify for receipt of the declared dividend. The ex-dividend date is the first day that the stock trades without the declared dividend attached and, accordingly, will not be given to anyone purchasing the stock as of this date or after.

47. B: When a syndicate sells a new issue, the spread is broken down into the manager's fee and the takedown. The takedown is the amount that syndicate members earn when selling shares or bonds. If the syndicate hires selling groups to help sell the shares, these groups receive the concession, which is a percentage of the takedown and also paid out of the takedown. Firms outside of the syndicate (also called selling groups) receive the reallowance – this amount tends to be smaller than the concession and is also paid out of the takedown. The manager's fee is the lowest, but the syndicate manager receives a fee on every share (or bond) sold by any of the selling entities.

48. D: A U.S. citizen who owns stock or bonds issued in another country is responsible for federal and state taxes on any interest and dividends received on his or her U.S. tax return. However, if there has been withholding made by the country of origin, the investor may claim a tax credit against the amount of such withholding. If the withholding is greater than the amount of U.S. taxes that would be owed, the investor will not need to make additional payments to the U.S. Government.

49. C: Retail Communication is any written or electronic communication to more than 25 retail investors within a 30-day period. These emails meet those criteria. Institutional Communication would apply if the email was made only to institutional investors - but that is not the case in this instance because it is likely those institutional investors will forward the email or make it available to their customers. Internal Communications would be within the company only. Correspondence is when the email is to 25 people or less within any 30-day period.

50. D: American-style exercising means that, at any time before the option has reached its expiration date, the option-holder is able to exercise it. European-style exercising means that the only time when the option-holder may exercise the option is at the expiration date. New York and Chicago styles are types of pizza, and are also an important distinction in some circles.

51. D: Convertible preferred stock consists of shares that can be converted into common stock if the owner so chooses. The conversion price is preset, and convertible preferred shares tend to rise and fall in value along with common shares because of this feature. They also usually have lower dividend payments than other preferred stocks.

52. B: A trade confirmation must be sent on or before the date that the transaction is completed (the settlement date). This is another very straightforward question that is regularly on the test because it forms the basis of understanding much of the other material. In a sense, it is the opposite of those questions where the test-writers purposefully try to confuse you by giving you far too much information. These are single fact based questions which, if studied and acquired through rote memorization, can accumulate valuable test scoring points.

53. B: The "takedown" refers to the amount divided between the various syndicate members when selling new securities to the public. Questions about the various fees involved in bringing new securities to market, the parties involved, and who is to receive what fees for what services will certainly appear on the test in one capacity or another. Memorizing these relationships is an easy way to accumulate needed points on test day. These questions may be complex, or simple (like this one), but they will show up in some form or another.

54. D: Stop orders, not limit orders, are used to protect a stock position (limit orders are used to protect the investor entering a position). Sell stop orders are placed below the market price, but close enough to limit losses; if the market price of the security drops to or below the stated price, the order is triggered and sold on the next trade. Placing a stop too far beneath the current price does not provide sufficient loss protection, but if it is too near the current price point, it will be too easily triggered since a certain amount of price fluctuation is normal. A registered representative should discuss this with the investor in order to determine how much of the profit the investor is willing to risk in order to gain additional upside potential.

55. B: Simplified arbitration is used to settle disputes between members and customers when the amount in dispute is not more than $50,000. Customer-to-Member disputes are covered in the FINRA 12000 series rules. The customer (the non-member in the dispute) is allowed to decide whether the dispute should go to arbitration or through the FINRA formal procedure for handling complaints. Decisions made in the arbitration process, which is less formal than the code of procedures process, are binding and not subject to appeal. The arbitration procedure also tends to be quicker and generally results in faster resolution of disputes.

56. C: Buy limit orders and sell stop orders change on ex-dividend date, while sell limit and buy stop do not. This makes sense if you consider that the first types of orders generally apply to entering and exiting a long stock position, while the second two generally deal with entering and exiting short stock positions. An investor would likely change his trading decisions around the lower ex-dividend price because he or she may receive the dividend. On the short side, the investor does not receive the dividend (he or she must actually pay it), so he or she is less likely to change trading decisions based on the dividend.

57. A: Initial margins may not exceed 50%, so if the transaction value is $22,500 ($45 * 500 shares = $22,500), and the transaction is done at the maximum allowed by Reg T, then the customer must make a deposit for $11,250 ($22,500 * 50% = $11,250). The remainder of the purchase may be financed on margin, assuming that the broker-dealer is willing to advance this quantity to the customer. In some cases, broker-dealers may place additional constraints on customer accounts, including higher margin requirements or simple caps on the dollar value that the firm is willing to advance to a given client.

58. A: As soon as the trade is executed, the customer is obligated by contract to complete the transaction, regardless of any subsequent moves in the price of the stock, positive or negative. Neither the broker-dealer nor the registered rep is permitted to repurchase the shares (there is the implication that the repurchase would take place at the original purchase price), because this would essentially allow brokers and registered reps to guarantee or backstop customer stock trades. The rep may not assure the customer that the stock will recover because this is guaranteeing performance that may or may not be true.

59. C: Equity is interchangeable with the term stock, provides ownership for the investor, has no maturity, and is sold in order to provide capital to the issuing corporation.

60. B: The period is defined as within any five consecutive business days for that class of option

61. B: In order to open a cash account with a broker-dealer, a corporation must provide a copy of its corporate resolutions. Among its resolutions, the document will specify the individuals who have trading authority. If the corporation wanted to open a margin account, it would also need to provide a copy of its bylaws and a signed margin agreement. The bylaws are required because they will warrant (or might not) that the corporation is allowed to purchase securities on margin and assume debts in its own name for this purpose.

62. D: The question is asking you to distinguish between bearish and bullish strategies and match up the two types of options that have the same directional bias. In general, buying one type of option will produce the same directional bias as selling the opposite type of options. Buying calls and selling puts are both bullish strategies, while buying puts and selling calls are both bearish strategies. Answer D identifies each of these combinations as having the same directional bias; the other choices reflect a combination of bullish and bearish strategies.

63. D: The first step in resolving this question is to determine the conversion ratio – this is done by dividing the par value by the conversion price ($1,000 / $25 = 40 shares). This calculation tells you that Frank will receive 40 shares of stock when he converts the bond into shares of common stock. If he sells those shares for $23, the sale results in proceeds of $920 (40 shares * $23 = $920). Frank bought the bond for $850 (($85 / $100) * $1,000 = $850), so Frank is into the trade for $850. If he closes the trade for $920, then he realizes a $70 profit ($920 - $850 = $70).

64. A: Security futures contracts shall have no value for margin purposes. Positions in other securities shall be valued conservatively in the light of current market prices and the amount of anticipated realization upon a liquidation of the entire position. Substantial additional margin must be required in all cases where the securities carried are subject to unusually rapid or violent changes in value, or where the amount carried is such that they cannot be liquidated promptly.

65. C: A defined contribution plan is distinguished from a defined benefit plan in that the amount an employer will contribute to the plan is defined, as opposed to the amount that will be paid as a benefit upon retirement. The shift toward defined contribution plans is the result of employees switching jobs more and more frequently. In these types of plan, the contribution generally remains fixed, although both the employee and the employers may make adjustments to the amount contributed (by the employee) and the % match provided (by the employer). An employer may not discount its contribution based on the company's performance, but there is no requirement that an employer pay into the plan at all.

66. A: To determine the advance-decline ratio, you need to divide the number of advancing stocks by the number of declining stocks (in this case 2,100 / 1,250 = 1.68). The advance-decline ratio gives an investor a strong indication of the true market movement because it considers breadth. If more stocks are advancing than declining (the ratio is greater than one), this is considered a bullish sign. If more stocks are declining than advancing (the ratio's less than one), this is considered a bearish sign. In addition, when there is a disparity between the direction of the major indexes and the advance-decline ratio, traders may look for a reversal in price levels.

67. C: Preferred Stock can fight takeovers, is often used in lieu of debt financing (although it has many traits in common with bonds), does not affect the existing common shareholders' voting rights since preferred shares confer no voting rights, but since preferred stock usually has fixed dividend payments that must be paid before common shareholders, it does not mitigate dividend exposure.

68. C: The key to this question is to remember that index options are always settled for cash – this should make sense since an index option has an index representing its underlying value and so it may not be deliverable in pure form (instruments that track an index may have slight performance deviations from the index they follow). Investors who exercise their options are required to pay the buyer cash equal to the intrinsic value (the in-the-money amount) multiplied by 100 shares. Index options are settled at the end of the business day.

69. B: A tight money yield curve is one indication that interest rates have recently increased and that short maturity bonds are yielding more than long maturity bonds. This is the opposite of what is generally considered "normal" because, when this occurs, the yield curve is said to be inverted. Normally bond holders are compensated for buying longer maturity bonds by receiving higher rates and charting would show an upward sloping yield curve. When money is tight, often due to an increase in rates, short-term bonds are in greater demand and the yield curve may be temporarily distorted.

70. C: Treasury receipts or treasury STRIPS (T-STRIPS) are purchased at a discount and mature at par value, building the return on the investment into a single lump sum payment. In this way, they behave just as any type of zero-coupon bond. Treasury notes and treasury bonds make regular interest payments at regular intervals until maturity. Treasury bonds and treasury notes are distinguished from T-bills (which also behave like zero-coupon bonds) in that they have maturities over ten and one year respectively; T-bills have maturities under a year.

71. B: This question tests a single fact that needs to be memorized for the test: if the coupon and the basis are equal, the bond was purchased at par. Any additional information is provided only to confuse or distract you. The reason this information is so important for the test is that it may help you to eliminate wrong choices on questions where you're not sure how to perform the needed calculation. If the basis is higher (on a percentage basis), the bond traded at a discount and vice versa if the basis is lower. Knowing this will help to narrow your focus in on correct answers when you're not sure how else to proceed.

72. D: An IDR (industrial development revenue bond) is issued to build a facility for a private user or corporation, but they do not need specific voter approval. Because the facility, owned by a third-party, is responsible for earning the revenue needed to make principal and interest payments, the municipality is not directly responsible for the payments. Furthermore, IDRs are, in fact, subject to the substantial user rule, which prohibits substantial participants in the project from buying their own bonds and receiving tax-free payments from the project.

73. B: This is a straightforward question that is asking you to calculate the tax-equivalent yield (TEY) for the investor in question. The only information needed to do this calculation is the effective tax rate and the yield to maturity; any additional information provided in these types of questions is put there to create confusion. The relationship needed is TEY = YTM / (100% - tax rate). In this case then, TEY = 7% / (100% - 28%) = 9.7%. A prepared test-taker will be readily able to recognize basic municipal bond calculation and make them quickly.

74. A: In a rights offering, stock shares trade cum rights after the declaration of the rights offering, and the underwriting investment bank does have the option to purchase any shares not purchased by the rights holders. Further, rights are issued per share, one to one, and after the ex-date, the stock will trade without the rights attached, and accordingly, the stock's value will be reduced to account for the loss of that right.

75. B: The investment tax on investment income for high income individuals is 3.8%. This only applies to people with income exceeding specific Modified Adjusted Gross Income (MAGI) thresholds who also have investment income.

76. C: Local government investment pools (LGIPs) are not registered with the Securities and Exchange Commission (SEC) and are exempt from SEC regulatory requirements because they fall under a governmental exclusion clause. While this exemption allows pools greater flexibility, it also reduces investor protection. A, B, and D are true. LGIPs are also typically administered by a board of trustees and a financial services firm.

77. D: A shareholder's preemptive rights provide for him or her to receive the first option to purchase shares from any new offering conducted by the corporation, provide for the shares to be offered to the public only after they've been declined by the current shareholders, and require approval from the current shareholders for any increase to the amount of the corporation's authorized shares.

78. D: The MSRB (Municipal Securities Rulemaking Board) rules are enforced by each of the following entities in varying capacities and with varying responsibilities: the SEC, FINRA, the FDIC, the Federal Reserve Board (FRB), and the Comptroller of the Currency. The FGIC is not a regulatory body, but rather is an insurer that underwrites various municipal securities. On the test, the details that you will be expected to know about the MSRB is relatively limited and will generally be limited to straightforward, single fact type questions.

79. C: The de minimus filing threshold feature of Rule 144 provides that no filing is required when the total sale within the defined period is less than $50,000 and the number of shares is less than 5000. This applies to affiliates selling restricted shares in keeping with Rule 144. This is a straight memorization question, but can provide easy points. Rule 144 is a favorite test topic because it covers both ethical and insider behavior in different contexts – the major tenets of the rule should be learned for the test.

80. D: FINRA rule 2210 (f) describes the rules for public appearances of an associated person. Financial interest muse be disclosed unless nominal. Conflict of interest must be disclosed if material. Each firm must have written supervisory and training procedures, with evidence that they have been implemented.

81. B: Stockholders are allowed only one vote for every share owned. The statutory method provides for voting equal amounts of votes over more than one candidate, the cumulative method involves casting all votes for one candidate, and there are two methods for stockholder voting, statutory and cumulative.

82. D: The easiest and fastest way to answer this question is to identify the fact that the current yield will be higher than the coupon since the bond is trading at a discount to par. The only answer that fits this criterion is answer D. To calculate the correct answer, simply divide the annual interest payment by the current market price ($78 / $983 = 7.93%). This question is full of extra information that is meant to serve as distraction in an otherwise simple, straightforward question.

83. C: The first step to solving this problem is to properly accrete the bond. Accretion is determined by dividing the discount received in the purchase price (par value minus market price) by the number of years to maturity (($1,000 - $850)/15 = $10). This amount must be multiplied by the number of years the bond has matured, then added to the purchase price to determine the investor's ultimate cost basis ($850 + $50 = $900). If the investor sells the bond for 92, he or she receives $920 (92% * $1,000 par value = $920). The difference realized by the investor is, therefore, a gain of $20 ($920 - $900 = $20). Remembering to add the accretion is the critical step in this problem.

84. B: Fiduciary accounts such as UGMA (Uniform Gift to Minors Act) accounts are required to follow the prudent man rule or legal list of the state in which the account is set up. The prudent man rule or legal list establishes a guideline of appropriate investments for accounts that involve trusts. UGMA accounts are created to allow the custodian to allocate money to a minor in a tax-advantaged way, but limit the custodian's ability to withdraw the money once it has been "gifted" to the minor.

85. A: During the registration process, a broker-dealer may contact its existing clients to gauge the level of interest those clients will have in purchasing shares of the new issue when it becomes available. The customer may indicate his or her level of interest in the hypothetical purchase of shares, but is not obligated to complete the transaction when the shares are actually available for sale. In spite of a customer's enthusiasm for a new offering, a customer may change his or her mind at any time. Likewise, the broker-dealer is not obliged to have as many shares available for sale as the brokerage initially indicates because the assignment of shares has not yet taken place.

86. C: The best answer is a AA rated bond. Although convertible preferred stock pays a consistent dividend, it's not considered as safe as AA rated bonds. AA rated bonds will provide current income and carry only moderate risk relative to the other answer choices. Hedge funds are generally considered risky investments as an asset class, despite the fact that many hedge funds provide less risk than other, traditional investments. The shares on a growth stock are unlikely to provide current income (through a dividend), and might also be considered speculative.

87. C: Customer complaint records shall be preserved for a period of at least four years.

88. D: All the choices listed may change an investor's investment objectives. A customer may, and often will, change his or her investment objectives for the reasons listed or for no reason at all. The best answer choice is one that represents a significant life change which will require the registered rep to review a customer's investment objective to assure that they are still appropriate. Even in the absence of such apparent changes in life status, the registered rep should still review these investment objectives with a customer on a regular basis.

89. D: This is another very straightforward question that is regularly on the test because it forms the basis of understanding much of the other material. In a sense, it is the opposite of those questions where the test-writers purposefully try to confuse you by giving you far too much information. A shelf-registration gives the issuer the ability to delay the sale of all or a portion of the securities for up to two full years. A shelf-registration gives the issuer the ability to be nimble in planning the precise timing of the offering, without the delay of the registration process.

90. C: Hypothecation is the pledging of the securities bought on margin as collateral for the loan that finances the same purchase; it is not prohibited by regulation and is a common practice. Commingling refers to combining customer securities and firm securities in the same account (or a customer's fully paid securities with those bought on margin). Interpositioning refers to standing between a buyer and a seller to illegally act as a middle-man. Backing away refers to a market maker failing to honor a firm quote and refusing to complete the transaction at the quoted price.

91. C: As the name suggests, a collateral trust bond is collaterized by securities owned by the issuer and held by the trustee. The collateral pool stands in reserve until the issuer misses an interest payment, at which time the trustee sells some of the securities to satisfy the debt service payment. Debentures are backed by the faith and credit of the issuer. Guaranteed bonds are backed by another entity, such as a parent company, which is obligated to make any missed payments on behalf of the issuer. Equipment trust certificates are secured directly by equipment owned by the issuer.

92. B: Rule 201 generally requires trading centers to have policies and procedures in place to restrict short selling when a covered security has triggered a circuit breaker by experiencing a price decline of at least 10 percent in one day. Once the circuit breaker in Rule 201 has been triggered, the price test restriction will apply to short sale orders in that security for the remainder of the day and the following day, unless an exception applies.

93. A: A syndicate member is guilty of the illegal practice of withholding when it does not sell available shares of a hot issue to interested investors, and rather holds the shares in hopes of selling them at an even higher price at a later date. Freeriding is when a customer purchases a security and never sends in payment but sells the security to pay for the trade. Marking to the market is adjusting the market value of the securities in a margin account to determine the equity available within the account; this is a legal practice, although marking to market has come under much discussion in terms of banks and their balance sheets. Commingling is the prohibited practice of holding customer funds and firm funds in the same account.

94. A: The resistance level of a stock is the upper bounds of its recent trading range. When a stock hits a resistance level, the stock has difficulty continuing to appreciate above that price. When a stock is at or near the top of its trading range, this often signifies that the stock is overbought. Many prospective buyers are exhausted and have reached their purchase limits, and the stock encounters resistance to further appreciation. If the stock breaks through a resistance level, a technical analyst would expect the stock to then experience a significant period of appreciation as a new upper ceiling or resistance point is established.

95. C: Short-Term Treasury-Based interest rate options = 5,000 contracts. Industry Index Options with one stock >=30% of the index = 18,000 contracts. For any underlying security, 25,000-250,000 contracts. There is no limit to defined broad-based index options, such as the Cboe S&P 500 AM/PM options.

96. A: Treasury stock is defined as stock that has been issued and then repurchased by the issuing company. The stock is not considered part of the outstanding shares for the company because it is not outstanding in the market. The company neither pays itself dividends on the shares, nor does it acquire voting rights (which would presumably be "against" the public shareholders) when it repurchases the shares. Answers B, C, and D are all true statements about treasury stock, so answer A is the correct or UNTRUE answer. It is important to read the question carefully – you are looking for the false ("NOT TRUE") answer in this question.

97. D: Common stockholders have the right by ownership to vote on proposed stock splits, corporate bond issuance, and the election of the corporation's board of directors.

98. B: Liquidity is essentially the ease with which an investor may move into and out of a given investment. Limited partnerships are generally considered illiquid as they require extensive documentation, approval of the general partner, approval of the registered representative, and often contain a lock-up period (a set amount of time during which the investment may not be sold). In addition, there is generally not a secondary market for these types of investments, so relative to all of the other listed choices, B is the best answer.

99. D: To be considered good delivery, the certificates should be in multiples of 100 shares (100, 200, or 300), divisors of 100 shares (1, 2, 4, 5, 10, 20, 25, 50), or amounts that add up to 100 shares (80 + 20, 70 + 30, 60 + 30 + 10). These rules do not apply to any odd lot portions of the delivery, and only apply to the round lot portion of the trade. The 30 shares portion of answer D is not good delivery because 30 is not a divisor of 100.

100. A: MSRB G-19 specifies (in Supplementary Material .05) Three Components of Suitability Obligations: reasonable-basis suitability, customer-specific suitability, and quantitative suitability. The broker's goals are not relevant.

101. A: Regulation A offerings are exempt from full registration requirements, provided the issuer doesn't sell more than $5,000,000 worth of securities in a 12-month period. A Rule 147 offering is an intrastate offering that is exempt from SEC registration, provided the issuer conducts business only in one state and sells securities only to residents of the same state. This provision also encompasses the 80 percent rule, which states that at least 80 percent of the issuer's assets should be located within the state and at least 80 percent of the offering proceeds should be used within the state. A Regulation D offering is also called a private placement. Regulation D offerings are exempt from SEC registration as long as the securities are sold to no more than 35 unaccredited (small) investors per year.

102. D: Since the customer is concerned that the Japanese yen will weaken against the U.S. dollar while he or she is waiting to receive payment, the best answer is one which will protect the customer against depreciation in the currency. Puts offer downside protection against the value of the Japanese yen relative to the U.S. dollar.

103. D: Contributions to the account can be made by any person (the account beneficiary, family, friends Special Needs Trust or Pooled Trust), but must be made using post-taxed dollars and will not be tax deductible for purposes of federal taxes; however, some states may allow for state income tax deductions for contributions made to an ABLE account.

104. A: The Securities Act of 1933 is the federal law that defines the rules issuers must follow when selling new securities. The Glass-Steagall Act prohibited commercial banks from underwriting securities; the repeal of this law led to banks expanding into multiple areas and has been offered as one of the roots of the financial crisis of 2008. The Securities Exchange Act of 1934 is the federal law that defines the rules governing the treatment of outstanding securities. The Securities Exchange Act of 1934 created the SEC, which regulates the various exchanges and the over-the-counter market. Regulation T regulates the maximum amount of credit that can be extended to customers for cash and margin accounts.

105. A: Civil penalties for insider trading may be imposed on anyone violating insider trading rules, whether they are a registered representative or not. Insider trading results when a party uses non-public material information to make trades within a given security. The penalties levied may be as high as three times the gain or the loss that resulted from the illegal transaction. Insider trading violations are extremely serious for a registered rep and may lead to a loss of license as well. These rule infractions are often referred to as 10b violations.

106. B: If the stock market is consolidating, it is trading in a very narrow range and the trendline will be sideways. The term consolidating comes from the idea that there are roughly an equal number of buyers and sellers who are "consolidating" their positions by bouncing the traded shares back and forth. Consolidation periods are often followed by breakouts, a period during which the narrow range that has persisted over an extended period of time is replaced by a wider range in which the indexes make large moves up or down. Technical analysts tend to believe that the longer the consolidation period, the more severe the breakout is likely to be when it occurs.

107. A: Per Rule 4511, Generally, members must preserve records for six years, barring any other specific requirements. The format and media of the records must comply with SEA Rule 17a-4 (six years, first two years of record retention kept in an easily accessible place. can be produced or reproduced on micrographic media. If records are to be maintained by an outside service bureau, such bureau is to file with the Commission)

108. D: A government regulatory agency that oversees the municipal securities, bonds and notes issued by cities, counties and states. It sets standards for municipal securities dealers. It was established by the U.S. Congress in 1975.

109. D: The key to answering this question correctly is to remember that a dividend will never increase or decrease the total value of the investment. Therefore, if the investor started with 1,000 shares at $45 ($45,000), then the investor must still own a $45,000 investment even though the share amount has changed. To recalculate the share price, first determine the new number of shares, then divide the total dollar investment by the new share amount (1.05 * 1,000 shares = 1,050 shares, $45,000 / 1,050 = $42.86 per share).

110. C: The statutory voting method requires that the investor cast his or her votes equally amongst the candidates for which they would like to vote.

111. C: The results of a stock split would be a change in the number of shares (either an increase or decrease), while holding constant the value of the overall holdings. The split causes an increase or decrease in the number of outstanding shares and, accordingly, the stock's price. The value of the holdings is not affected.

112. A: Term bonds, also called dollar bonds, are quoted as a percentage of the dollar value of their price. For example, a term bond trading for $1,050 would be quoted as 105 (105% * $1,000 par = $1,050). This is another very straightforward question which appears regularly on the test because it forms the basis of understanding much of the other material. In a sense, it is the opposite of those questions where the test-writers purposefully try to confuse you by giving you far too much information.

113. C: When purchasing a period-certain annuity, the annuity is guaranteed to make payments for at least as long as the period-certain states. If the purchaser of a period-certain annuity dies prior to the lapse of the specified period, payments are made for the duration of the specified period to the purchaser's designated beneficiary. However, if the purchaser lives beyond the period specified by contract in the period-certain annuity, the annuity will continue to make payments for as long as the purchaser is alive, with payments stopping immediately upon the death of the purchaser.

114. C: The ABLE Act limits eligibility to individuals with disabilities with an age of onset of disability before turning 26 years of age - the person may be over 26 today, but the age of onset for the disability must have occurred before 26. If the beneficiary meets the age requirement and is already receiving benefits under SSI and/or SSDI, they are automatically eligible to establish an ABLE account.

115. C: G-13 requires quotations to be based on the dealer's best judgement of the FMV of the security - not on who the customer is.

G-17 requires advisors and dealers to deal fairly with all persons

G-30 requires dealers to use fair and reasonable prices

G-45 pertains to reporting on 529 plans or ABLE programs - not applicable to this question.

116. A: The easiest way to answer the question is to break the question into 2 parts and calculate the gain or loss on each side. The customer bought the shares for $65 and sells them for $70, resulting in a profit of $5 per share (100 shares * ($70 - $65) = $500). On the option side, remember that the customer sold the option and has to buy it back to close the position (100 * ($2 - $4) = -$200). When the two sides of the transaction are combined, the result of the overall trade is a gain of $300 ($500 + (-$200) = $300).

117. B: A registered rep may open a joint account with a customer after obtaining approval from a principal of the firm. In addition, the registered rep and the customer are required to sign a proportionate sharing agreement, which states that they will share gains and losses proportionately based on the amount of money invested in the account. Generally speaking, sharing an account with a customer is not an advisable practice as it invites scrutiny and offers little in the way of advantage for either the customer or the registered rep.

118. C: While there are no FINRA rules specifying the percentages that brokerage firms are required to charge customers, rule 2121 and 2122 say charges must be fair and reasonable and must not discriminate between customers. The test writers particularly like to test material that covers the ethical behavior of a registered representative or of the brokerage firm; non-discriminatory practices by each of these entities is of particular interest, so if such discrimination or ethics violations stands out among the answer choices, there is a fair possibility that this answer will be the correct answer.

119. D: The cost basis of stock you received as a gift ("gifted stock") is determined by the giver's original cost basis and the fair market value (FMV) of the stock at the time you received the gift. If the FMV when you received the gift ($15,000) was less than the original basis ($25,000) then the original basis is used for a gain, and the FMV would be used to calculate a loss. If you sell the stock for an amount between these two amounts ($15,000 to $25,000) then there is no gain or loss.

120. A: Stock that is authorized for sale and sold to investors is issued stock, regardless of whether it still remains with investors or has subsequently been repurchased by the corporation. Authorized stock is the largest number of shares that can be sold by the corporation. Treasury stock is the stock that has been sold to the public and then repurchased by the corporation. Outstanding stock is stock that has been sold to investors and still remains with investors, having not been repurchased by the issuing corporation.

121. A: The cost basis of stock you received as a gift ("gifted stock") is determined by the giver's original cost basis and the fair market value (FMV) of the stock at the time you received the gift. If the FMV when you received the gift was more the original cost basis, use the original cost basis when you sell. This is the most commonly-encountered situation.

122. C: Under the 1940 Act, if an individual is receiving a fee for the advice they are giving to clients, as opposed to receiving a commission for executing trades, they must be registered. Individuals who give advice for free, or who provide general information in the form of mass marketing publications are not required to register. The important distinction regarding registration is whether the financial advisor solicits a fee for the advice dispensed. These guidelines do not apply to hedge fund managers, who are subject to a different set of criteria to which they must adhere under the accredited investor rules.

123. A: The question asks you to calculate the current yield (current yield = annual interest / market price = $75 / $1050 = 7.3%). This is a straightforward, single fact question that will be determined by your ability to memorize the preceding formula. The test writers use this type of simple memorization question in cases where the knowledge being tested forms the basis of a great deal of other information. The bond section on the test is important as it covers a sizable percentage of the test.

124. D: REITS must derive at least 75% of income from real estate (and 95% from passive sources). They must distribute over 90% of income as dividends, can own 100% of a taxable REIT subsidiary (TRS), and may hire independent contractors to run health care properties for up to 6 years without a lease.

125. B: Call protection refers to the number of years an issuer would have to wait before calling its callable bonds. When interest rates fall, an issuer will prefer to call its bonds and reissue new bonds at lower rates. Keep in mind, however, that the question is focused on the value of call protection. As rates fall, then, investors will prefer to hold their higher rate bonds, making call protection increasingly more valuable as rates fall. Beware of misdirection in test questions and don't confuse the perspective and interests of the issuer with those of the bond holder.

126. C: The official statement is often left in an intermediate stage without a final version being prepared, even though certain changes have been made. For a revenue bond, the official statement will not include information about the tax base of the municipality because the bond will be backed by revenues from the project rather than by the taxing authority of the municipality. The official statement does not need to be filed with the SEC, but it does need to be sent to all prospective purchasers, regardless of whether they end up purchasing shares or not.

127. A: Firstly, when a firm sells securities out of its own inventory, the firm charges a markup, not a commission. Secondly, the sale is not subject to the NASD 5% policy because municipal bonds are exempt securities. Thirdly, a bond's rating is never reported on the confirmation because ratings are subject to change over time. The firm does consider the overall size of a sale when deciding on the size of the markup that will be charged to a customer – this amount is agreed to in advance of the sale and disclosed on the confirmation sent to the customer.

128. B: Regulation T requires Equity to be at least 50% of the SMV. In this case the SMV is $20,000, so equity must be at least $10,000. Additionally, the investor must leave the proceeds of the sale in the account.

129. C: Callable preferred stock is ordinarily covered by a sinking fund provision. In the same way that corporations can repurchase bonds with a sinking fund, the same can be done for their repurchasing of preferred stock.

130. C: Under Regulation T, the Federal Reserve Board requires all short sale accounts to have 150% of the value of the short sale at the time the sale is initiated. The 150% consists of the full value of the short sale proceeds (100%, or $20,000), plus an additional margin requirement of 50% of the value of the short sale (an additional $10,000).

131. C: A put option gives the holder (buyer), the right, but not the obligation, to sell shares of an underlying security at a specific price until the expiration of the contract. The best way for an investor to protect against a sharp decline in the underlying security is to buy a put. Selling options will help the investor to generate additional income, but the seller is basically transferring the right to exercise the options to others. Buying a call option will benefit the investor if the underlying security rises, but will not protect against a decline in the stock price upon which the option is based.

132. D: When a municipal bond is issued, it is accompanied by a legal opinion. A legal opinion is a statement prepared by a bond attorney which states that the interest received from the bond being issued meets the requirements for exemption from federal taxation. All municipal bonds must be accompanied by such an opinion prepared by the issuer's bond counsel, or the bond must be marked as ex-legal (this makes the bond less attractive as the purchaser will need to obtain his or her own legal opinion or risk violating federal tax law).

133. D: Corporations choose to repurchase shares in an effort to maintain a majority interest and control in the company and to fund future mergers. They would not repurchase shares to decrease a company's issued stock in that issued stock is all stock sold to the public regardless of whether it remains outstanding or is repurchased; that is, the number cannot be decreased. Additionally, they would not repurchase shares to maintain their earnings per share due to the fact that a repurchase would reduce the amount of outstanding shares, which would consequently increase the company's earnings per share.

134. B: Because it is going to more than 25 customers, including retail, it is a Retail Communication. Because it includes non-public rankings of investment companies the letter must be reviewed by both a qualified principal and FINRA 10 days before it is sent.

135. D: Buying Power = SMA / Regulation T requirement. SMA is $15,000 / 0.5 = $30,000

Series 7 Practice Test #3

1. An investor purchased 1 PPG August 73 call for a $5 premium. Which of the following are true regarding this investor's position?

    I. The breakeven amount will be $78.
    II. The breakeven amount will be $68.
    III. The maximum loss will be $5.
    IV. The maximum gain will be unlimited.

    a. I, III, and IV
    b. II and IV
    c. II and III
    d. I and IV

2. Which of the following is an example of a type of corporate money market instrument?

    a. Federal fund loans
    b. Reverse repurchase agreements
    c. Bankers' acceptances
    d. All of the above

3. An investor initiates the following options transaction: He or she pays $2 for 1 PPG May 55 call. Translate the specific details of this options contract.

    a. Paid $200 contract premium, contract option to buy 100 shares of PPG at $55 per share, contract expiration is in May
    b. Paid $2 contract premium, contract option to buy 10 shares of PPG at $55 per share, contract expiration is in May
    c. Paid $2,000 contract premium, contract option to buy 1,000 shares of PPG at $55 per share, contract expiration is in May
    d. Paid $200 contract premium, contract option to sell 100 shares of PPG at $55 per share, contract expiration is in May

4. _____ has the power to register, regulate, and oversee brokerage firms, transfer agents, and clearing agencies as well as SROs.

    a. NASD
    b. FINRA
    c. SEC
    d. MSRB

5. What does the Options Clearing Corporation do?

    I. Publishes Characteristics and Risks of Standardized Options
    II. Issues option contracts on the trade date
    III. Guarantees an option's performance
    IV. Facilitates standardized options to settle on a trade date plus one

    a. II, III, and IV
    b. II and IV
    c. I, III, and IV
    d. IV only

6. Calculate the current yield of a mutual fund with a public offering price (POP) of $17 and an annual paid dividend of $3.

a. 5.11 percent
b. 17.7 percent
c. 5.67 percent
d. None of the above

7. What are securities that have the brokerage firm as the registered nominal owner and the customer as the beneficial owner considered?

a. Transferred and held in safekeeping
b. Transferred and shipped
c. Held in street name
d. None of the above

8. Which of the following are true of an option seller?

I. Has the right to decline having the contract exercised
II. Enters into an option contract with the goal of having it exercised
III. Is considered to be the writer of the contract
IV. Has the intent to profit as the result of premium income

a. II, III, and IV
b. III only
c. III and IV
d. I and III

9. When using testimonials, which of the following points does not need to be clearly stated in the body copy of the material?

a. The testimonial may not be representative of the experience of other clients.
b. The fact that that it is a paid testimonial if a nominal sum is paid.
c. If the testimonial concerns a technical aspect of investing, the person making the testimonial must have adequate knowledge and experience to form a valid opinion.
d. The testimonial cannot be indicative of future performance or success.

10. When opening an account for a customer, what information should a registered representative obtain from that customer?

I. Whether he or she is an employee of a bank
II. His or her citizenship status
III. An estimation of his or her annual income
IV. A bank reference

a. I, II, III, and IV
b. II and III
c. I, II, and III
d. II, III, and IV

11. An investor believes shares of PPG will rise from their current price of $65 per share. Which of the following option contracts should he or she purchase in order to maximize their profits in stock PPG given his or her belief in an impending price increase?

    a. 1 PPG August 72 call
    b. 1 PPG August 64 put
    c. 1 PPG August 66 call
    d. 1 PPG August 52 put

12. What is the premium amount on an August $100,000 Treasury bond 120 call on a 5 percent Treasury being quoted at 2.09?

    a. $2,090
    b. $2,280
    c. $228,000
    d. $2,900

13. Which type of U.S. government security has terms ranging from 1 to 10 years, pays semiannual interest, and is obtained through a Treasury auction held semi-monthly?

    a. Treasury bonds
    b. Treasury bills
    c. Treasury notes
    d. None of the above

14. Mailing instruction rules as they pertain to customer accounts include which of the following?

    I. A brokerage firm may hold a customer's account correspondence for up to 1 month if he or she is away and traveling domestically.
    II. Confirmations may be sent only to the customer on the account.
    III. Account statements are sent to the address noted on the account.
    IV. A brokerage firm may hold a customer's account correspondence for up to 2 months if he or she is away and traveling internationally.

    a. II and III
    b. III and IV
    c. I, II, and III
    d. III only

15. Which of the following describe the rights shareholders possesses?

    I. They retain an interest in residual assets that is proportionate to their investment in the event the corporation declares bankruptcy.
    II. They can access a corporation's financial information that would be otherwise held as confidential.
    III. They receive a shareholder list.
    IV. They can inspect a corporation's books and records.

    a. II, III, and IV
    b. I, III, and IV
    c. I, II, and IV
    d. III and IV

16. PPG corporation issues 6.5 percent bonds worth a total of $850,000. The bonds are set to come due with the entire $850,000 on August 15, 2021. Which type of bond maturity is represented with this issuance?

a. Balloon maturity
b. Term maturity
c. Serial maturity
d. None of the above

17. A representative makes two separate and unrelated statements to a prospective customer. First, in an effort to impress the customer with his distinguished educational background, he says that he graduated from a certain Ivy League institution while knowing that he really only attended that college for a couple of semesters. Second, he announces that a well-renowned biotech securities analyst is employed at his firm as of the prior day. The customer proceeds to sign on with this representative and creates an account. The next day, the representative discovers that the biotech analyst decided to leave the firm effective immediately as of early that morning. Which of these two statements would be considered a misrepresentation and grounds for discipline, given that this customer signed on with this representative based on the truth of both?

a. The statement regarding his educational background
b. Neither statement
c. The statement regarding the biotech analyst
d. Unknown without further information

18. An investor sells short 100 shares of PTR for $42.50 per share. They also sell 1 PTR August 38 put for a $2 premium. What is this investor's total maximum gain on his or her position?

a. $650
b. $6.50
c. $450
d. None of the above

19. What does the NASDAQ opening cross do?

    I. It is the source for what is known as NOOP, the NASDAQ official opening price.
    II. Dissemination of opening order imbalance information begins at 9:20am
    III. It allows for order changes of only a specific type.
    IV. Opening Imbalance Only (OIO) orders reduce liquidity.

a. I, III, and IV
b. I and III
c. II, III, and IV
d. III and IV

20. An investor has purchased a PPG August 33 call with a $3 premium. PPG is currently trading at $36.50 per share. Which of the following describes this investor's call position?

a. At the money
b. In the money
c. Out of the money
d. Unknown without further information

21. _____ trading authority is when a person other than the account holder may invest without consulting the account holder about the price, amount, or type of security or the timing of the trades that are placed for the account.

    a. Discretionary
    b. Nondiscretionary
    c. Privileged
    d. Absolute

22. Which of the following is NOT an example of a fiduciary?

    a. Administrators
    b. Guardians
    c. Executors
    d. None of the above

23. Which of the following would be the dollar price quote for a bond quoted at 93 1/2?

    a. $935.00
    b. $930.05
    c. $931.20
    d. $93,500

24. What is the settlement date for a trade?

    a. The date when payment is due to the broker
    b. The execution date for a trade order
    c. Five business days after trade date
    d. Two business days after trade date

25. Which of the following drilling costs are 100 percent deductible for the year in which they occur?

    a. Wages
    b. Well casings
    c. Geological surveys
    d. All of the above

26. An investor looking to profit from movements in the values of foreign currency would buy calls or sell put options given which of the following circumstances?

    a. Indications that a country's stock market is in decline
    b. Indications that a country is headed for an economic downturn
    c. Indications that a government is experiencing increasing levels of instability
    d. None of the above

27. An account in which customers with large portfolios pay a brokerage firm a flat annual fee that covers the cost of a money manager's services and the cost of commissions is called a _____ account.

    a. Cash
    b. Margin
    c. Collateral
    d. Wrap

28. A bond's yield is directly influenced by all of the following except for

    a. the type of collateral on the bond.
    b. supply and demand.
    c. the bond's term.
    d. the issuer's credit quality.

29. What is an order that enables the broker to have discretion regarding the timing of its execution and price called?

    a. Fill-or-kill order
    b. All-or-none order
    c. Market-on-open order
    d. Not-held order

30. All of the following contribute to the determination of an option premium except for

    a. option class and series.
    b. interest rates.
    c. supply and demand.
    d. the timing of its expiration.

31. What does Convertible Security Arbitrage involve?

    a. Simultaneously buying and selling both a stock and a security that may be converted into that same underlying stock
    b. Buying shares in a company that is being taken over or acquired while shorting shares in the company about to acquire them
    c. Simultaneously buying and selling the same security in two different markets to exploit the price difference between the two
    d. None of the above

32. Which of the following duties does a transfer agent NOT perform?

    a. Maintains the list of stockholders
    b. Verifies owner identity in stock issuance
    c. Verifies the validity and legality of a company's debt in a bond issuance
    d. Handles new issuance of stock certificates

33. An investor puts together the following position:

    Sells 1 PPG August 79 call for $2 premium
    Sells 1 PPG August 79 put for $4 premium

Which of the following describes this position?

    a. Combination
    b. Short straddle
    c. Spread
    d. Long straddle

34. Which type of bond issuance has no physical certificate issued to its holder, leaving the only evidence of ownership the resulting trade confirmation from the purchase transaction?

    a. Principal-only registration
    b. Fully registered
    c. Bearer bonds
    d. None of the above

35. What are some consequences of a violation of Regulation T?

I. The customer may not make any trades for 90 days.

II. The customer is fully responsible for any loss incurred due to the firm selling off securities from the unpaid order, but no other securities held in the account may be sold to cover the loss.

III. On the fifth business day after the trade date, purchased securities will be sold by the brokerage firm for failure to pay.

IV. For 90 days, the customer is required to pay up front for any purchases made.

 a. III and IV
 b. I, II, and IV
 c. II, III, and IV
 d. I and IV

36. A custodian managing a Uniform Gift to Minors Act (UGMA) account will be bound by all of the following guidelines regarding contributions except that

 a. gifts are irrevocable.
 b. the tax-free gift limit is set at $18,000 per year (2023).
 c. his or her authority to utilize account assets for the education of the minor is discretionary.
 d. the gift size is limitless.

37. Registered representatives are required to regularly monitor and keep current all of the following customer information except for

 a. the customer's educational status.
 b. the customer's marital status.
 c. the customer's investment objectives, goals, and philosophy.
 d. that all of the above must be kept current.

38. Which of the following is an example of a calendar spread?

 a. Sell 1 PPG May 23 put and buy 1 PPG August 23 put
 b. Buy 1 PPG May 23 put and sell 1 PPG May 21 put
 c. Sell 1 PPG May 21 put and buy 1 PPG August 23 put
 d. None of the above

39. What is the highest level of NASDAQ subscription service available only to approved market makers?

 a. NASDAQ TotalView
 b. Level II
 c. Level I
 d. Level III

40. What are some characteristics of preferred stock?

 a. Unless noted differently, par value for these shares is $1,000.
 b. Ownership of these shares provides a means of fixed income for an investor through dividend payments.
 c. Due to the fixed income nature of these shares, changes in interest rates have no effect on the price of these shares.
 d. Maturity dates for these shares range from 1 to 25 years.

41. By utilizing information from both a company's balance sheet and/or income statement, which of the following can be determined?

    I. Price-earnings ratio
    II. Debt-to-equity ratio
    III. Debt service ratio
    IV. Earnings per share primary

    a. II, III, and IV
    b. I, II, and IV
    c. II and III
    d. I and IV

42. Which of the following are utilized by fundamental analysts to value stocks?

    a. Company income statement
    b. Liquidity ratios
    c. Valuation ratios
    d. All of the above

43. All of the following are true regarding the listing/delisting requirements for the New York Stock Exchange (NYSE) except that

    a. the singular approval of the board of directors is needed for delisting.
    b. a minimum 400 shareholders, each of which owns at least 100 shares, is necessary for listing.
    c. notification of the 35 largest shareholders is needed for delisting.
    d. a minimum of 1.1 million publicly held shares are necessary for listing.

44. All of the following are categorized as secured bonds except for

    a. income bonds.
    b. mortgage bonds.
    c. equipment trust certificates.
    d. collateral trust certificates.

45. An investor places an order to buy 250 PPG 62.15 GTC DNR. The stock closes the prior day at 63.10. Further, the stock goes ex dividend for 0.15 and accordingly will open with the market the next day at 62.95. Given these developments, which of the following depicts what the investor's buy order will be as of market opening the next day?

    a. Buy 250 PPG 62.95 GTC DNR
    b. Buy 250 PPG 62.15 GTC DNR
    c. Buy 250 PPG 62 GTC
    d. None of the above

46. An investor communicates to his or her representative that his or her primary investment objective is to generate income. Which of the following would be the type of investments that the representative should recommend?

    a. Annuities
    b. Government bonds
    c. Collateralized mortgage obligations (CMOs)
    d. Common stocks

47. All of the following are true of technical analysis except that

a. it considers a company's fundamentals.
b. it examines past performance in trying to predict future performance.
c. it analyzes chart patterns.
d. all of the above are true.

48. All of the following are characteristics of a stock short sale except that

a. the position has unlimited risk.
b. it involves, first, the sale of the stock and then, second, the purchase of the stock intended to fulfill the initial sell transaction.
c. it is motivated by the belief that the stock will depreciate beyond its current price.
d. all of the above are characteristics of a short sale.

49. An investor who has a long position in stock DZE would like to create a hedge of protection against downside price risk. Which of the following would provide the hedge he or she is seeking?

I. Long calls
II. Long puts
III. Short puts
IV. Short calls

a. I and III
b. II only
c. I only
d. II and IV

50. Which of the following contribute to the determination of a corporate bond's pricing in the secondary market?

I. Call features
II. Issuer
III. Interest rates
IV. Term

a. I, II, and IV
b. II and III
c. I, II, III, and IV
d. III only

51. The SEC was created under _____.

a. The Securities Act of 1933
b. The Securities Exchange Act of 1934
c. Investment Company Act of 1940
d. Investment Advisers Act of 1940

52. Which of the following is NOT required to be on an issued bond certificate?

a. Call feature
b. State of issuance
c. Paying agent
d. Dates for interest payments

53. A registered representative has the authority in a discretionary account to do all of the following except to

a. choose the type of transaction, buy or sell.
b. choose the securities amount to buy or sell.
c. choose to close out the account.
d. choose the asset for the buy or sell transaction.

54. State-issued unlimited tax general obligation (GO) bonds are backed by which of the following:

a. income taxes.
b. property taxes.
c. sales taxes.
d. any of the above.

55. The automated confirmation system (ACT)/trade reporting facility (TRF) handles which of the following transactions?

a. NASDAQ convertible bonds
b. Third-market trades
c. Non-NASDAQ over-the-counter (OTC) securities
d. All of the above

56. What does LEAPs stand for?

a. Long-Term Equitable Accumulation Securities
b. Level Equity Asset Securities
c. Long-Term Equity Anticipation Securities
d. Limited Expiration Anticipation Securities

57. Which of the following is not a general consideration regarding communications with the public about variable life insurance and variable annuities?

a. Prospectus delivery
b. Product Identification
c. Liquidity
d. Claims about guarantees

58. An investor can receive his or her cash dividend payment all of the following ways except when

a. a corporation sends payment to the brokerage firm holding the investor's shares in a street name, and the firm applies a credit for that amount to the investor's account.
b. a corporation sends payment to the brokerage firm holding the investor's shares in a street name, and the firm forwards a check in that amount directly to the investor.
c. a corporation sends a check in the amount of the cash dividend directly to the investor.
d. all of the above are appropriate ways for an investor to receive their cash dividend payment.

59. What is buying and selling two options of the same class but with either different exercise prices, months, or both, at the same time called?

    a. Long straddle
    b. Short straddle
    c. Spread
    d. Combination

60. Which of the following item(s) can affect an investor's risk tolerance?

    a. Age
    b. Time frame
    c. Personal experience
    d. All of the above

61. A dealer proceeds on a principal basis to fill a customer's order to buy 425 shares of PPG. Given that the dealer does not have the shares currently in his or her own inventory, he or she must buy the shares first in order to sell them to the customer. The current bid quote on the shares of PPG is $7.87, and the dealer actually purchases the shares at $8.00 per share. What is the maximum the dealer could charge this customer including a 5 percent markup for executing and filling the order?

    a. $3,512
    b. $3,238
    c. $3,570
    d. undetermined without further information

62. In relation to option contracts, a bearish outlook would result in all of the following except that

    a. buyers and sellers believe that the stock price will do down.
    b. option contract buyers would pursue purchasing call contracts.
    c. option contract sellers would pursue writing call contracts.
    d. option contract buyers would pursue purchasing put contracts.

63. Given the following four exchange symbols, what are the exchange names that match these symbols (in the same order)?

    X, P, C, Q

    a. Philippines, Philadelphia, Cincinnati, NASDAQ
    b. Philadelphia, Philippines, Cincinnati, NASDAQ
    c. Philippines, Philadelphia, Chicago, NASDAQ
    d. Philadelphia, Philippines, Chicago, NASDAQ

64. An investor over time makes each of the following 9 percent bond purchases. Which of them represents what will be the LOWEST yield to maturity for this investor?

    a. Bond purchased at 98
    b. Bond purchased at 103
    c. Bond purchased at 100
    d. Bond purchased at 100 1/4

65. An investor would use index options for all of the following strategies except for

   a. buying calls or selling puts to hedge a short portfolio.

   b. buying puts or selling calls to hedge a long portfolio.

   c. buying puts or selling calls to hedge a short portfolio.

   d. taking advantage of market movements in terms of direction and magnitude.

66. How are options classified?

   a. By series

   b. By type

   c. By class

   d. By all of the above

67. States and municipalities may need to issue short-term notes to obtain needed financing. All of the following are examples of the types of notes they may issue except for

   a. bond and revenue anticipation notes (BRANs).

   b. bond anticipation notes (BANs).

   c. tax and revenue anticipation notes (TRANs).

   d. revenue anticipation notes (RANs).

68. When considering anyone but the beneficial owner of an account having the authority to enter orders for that account, which of the following accounts must get confirmation of that authority in writing?

   a. Trust account

   b. Fiduciary account

   c. Individual account

   d. Joint tenants in common (JTIC)

69. An investor places an order to buy 220 PPG 66 GTC. PPG declares a 3:2 stock split. Given that the order must be adjusted for the stock split, what would the investor's new order be?

   a. Buy 330 PPG 44 GTC

   b. Buy 146 PPG 99 GTC

   c. Buy 440 PPG 33 GTC

   d. None of the above

70. What is a customer account that requires the account assets of a deceased party to become the property of that party's estate rather than go to the surviving party called?

   a. Joint tenants in common (JTIC)

   b. Transfer on death (TOD)

   c. Joint tenants with rights of survivorship (JTWROS)

   d. Joint

71. What would be the calculated profit on the purchase of a 1 May 60 put for a $3 premium if rates fall to 5 percent by the expiration of this option?

   a. $700

   b. $200 loss

   c. $970

   d. $70

72. Which of the following terms refers to printed or processed analysis covering individual companies or industries?

    a. Advertisement
    b. Market letter
    c. Research report
    d. Sales literature

73. Given the requirements for transacting in a new margin account, what would be the required deposit for a customer purchasing 500 EXL at 2?

    a. $2,000
    b. $1,000
    c. $1,500
    d. $500

74. An investor purchases 1 SPX May 509 call for a $3 premium. When the option expires, the index is quoted at $522.31. First, how much will this investor's account be credited as a result of the index's current quote and the index call that was purchased? Second, what will be the net profit made from this position?

    a. $1,331, $1,631
    b. $1,331, $1031
    c. $1,031, $731
    d. None of the above

75. In relation to the opening of a new customer account, all of the following are true except that

    a. the principal and representative must both sign the new account card.
    b. a principal of the firm must accept and sign off on the account prior to the execution of the first trade.
    c. the customer must be sent a copy of the new account form within 30 days of the account opening.
    d. at least every 36 months, the firm must validate or update the information on the account.

76. An investor owns 100 shares of PPG at $31.25 per share. He or she sells 1 PPG August 38 call with a $1 premium. What would be the breakeven price and maximum total gain for this investor on his or her position?

    a. $30.25, $7.75
    b. $30.25, $775
    c. $31.75, $675
    d. Unknown without further information

77. Locally issued general obligation bonds are backed primarily by property taxes. A given property has a market value of $375,000 and a town assessment rate of 80 percent. What will be this property's assessed value?

    a. $75,000
    b. $375,000
    c. $260,000
    d. $300,000

78. Which characteristics of Treasury Separate Trading of Registered Interest and Principal of Securities (STRIPs) include?

I. A range in denominations of multiples of $10
II. A zero coupon bond
III. A principal portion that may be purchased by an investor to become due in full on some future date
IV. Selling to investors as a bundle of both principal and semiannual interest payments

 a. I, II, and IV
 b. I and III
 c. II and IV
 d. II and III

79. Which of the following types of securities are backed by the full faith and credit of the U.S. government?

 a. Federal National Mortgage Association (FNMA)
 b. Federal Farm Credit System (FFCS)
 c. Government National Mortgage Association (GNMA)
 d. Federal Home Loan Mortgage Corporation (FHLMC)

80. What is a dealer violation involving a dealer not honoring his or her published NASDAQ quote called?

 a. Backing away
 b. Pulling out
 c. Canceling
 d. Revocation

81. The following are all types of trust accounts except for

 a. irrevocable.
 b. basic.
 c. complex.
 d. revocable.

82. Which type of account is most often used for personal estate planning due to potential tax benefits?

 a. Joint account
 b. Joint tenants in common
 c. Individual account
 d. Family limited partnership

83. An investor is selling 320 shares of SRN. In order to make good and complete delivery, which of the following round lot combinations would allow him or her to do that?

 a. Three certificates for 100 shares each and one certificate for 20 shares
 b. Xix certificates of 50 shares each
 c. Thirty certificates of 10 shares each and four certificates of 5 shares each
 d. All of the above round lot combinations

84. All of the following balance sheet transactions result in a reduction in cash except for

a. securities issuance.
b. paying off bond principal in cash.
c. equipment purchased with cash.
d. a dividend payout.

85. An investor with the opinion that interest rates will fall will do which of the following?

I. Buy interest rate put options.
II. Buy interest rate call options.
III. Sell interest rate put options.
IV. Sell interest rate call options.

a. II and III
b. II only
c. I and IV
d. IV only

86. Under Rule 203, a broker dealer is prohibited from initiating an equity short sale for either his or her own account or a customer's unless which of the following is true?

I. They know the security can be borrowed.
II. They have already borrowed the security.
III. They have arranged for the loan of the security.

a. II only
b. II and III
c. I, II, and III
d. I only

87. What can the party responsible for the management of a fiduciary account do?

I. He or she may not work the account and assets in it to benefit him- or herself.
II. He or she acts according to the prudent man rule.
III. He or she may have limited power of attorney to buy and sell securities and withdraw only securities, not cash.
IV. He or she may have full discretion, buying and selling securities from the account and withdrawing cash and securities.

a. I, II, and IV
b. I, II, and III
c. I, III, and IV
d. I and III

88. A specialist can handle all of the following types of orders except for

a. stop orders.
b. market orders.
c. AON orders.
d. buy limit orders.

89. All of the following would be considered long-term liabilities except for

a. notes.
b. accounts payable owed to vendors.
c. mortgages.
d. bonds.

90. What does a buy limit order do?

a. Allows an investor to set a maximum price he or she is willing to pay for a security
b. Allows an investor to set a minimum price at which he or she is willing to sell a security
c. Guarantees execution
d. All of the above

91. A customer places an order with a brokerage firm to sell 320 shares of PPG. The current bid quote for PPG is $5.10. Considering a customary 5 percent dealer markdown charge for execution of the order, what would be the total proceeds due to the customer upon completion of the sell order?

a. $81.60
b. $1,550.40
c. $1,468.80
d. None of the above

92. What is an investment that involves investors receiving interest and principal payments on a monthly basis as a result of individual mortgages being paid down known as?

a. A pass-through
b. Separate Trading of Registered Interest and Principal of Securities (STRIP)
c. Collateralized mortgage obligation
d. TIPS

93. What is the dollar value that any gift from or to a member or person associated with a member may not exceed in one year?

a. $0.00 (gifts are not allowed)
b. $50.00
c. $100.00
d. $150.00

94. Which of the following are true of interest rate options?

a. They can be either a put or a call.
b. They are used to profit from interest rate movements.
c. They are used as a hedge for Treasury securities.
d. They do all of the above.

95. Rule 80B was established to protect against the creation of a disorderly market during times of extraordinary and high volatility, and is currently enforced by the new Pillar Rule 7.12. If the S&P 500 falls by certain percentage amounts (within a day), all trading must stop. Which of the following is one of the percentage drops that enacts the halt in trading?

a. 8 percent
b. 13 percent
c. 15 percent
d. 18 percent

96. Which of the following are considered to be actions falling under the role of a dealer?

    I. Charges a commission for their services
    II. Participates in the trade by trading in and out of his or her own account
    III. Fills the role of market maker
    IV. May facilitate only the order execution for a customer

    a. II only
    b. I, II, and III
    c. I and IV
    d. II and III

97. Which of the following are requirements for a Uniform Gift to Minors Act (UGMA) account?

    I. A minor
    II. Assets that are currently registered in the child's name as the nominal owner
    III. An account title stating it's a UGMA account and within which state it is located
    IV. A custodian

    a. I and IV
    b. I, III, and IV
    c. I, II, III, and IV
    d. IV only

98. Which of the following dollar amounts is represented by a Treasury bond quote of 97.08?

    a. $97.25
    b. $972.50
    c. $970.80
    d. None of the above

99. The parents of three children (A, B, and C) would like to set up a Uniform Gift to Minors Act (UGMA) account for them. Which of the following account setups would be approved under the UGMA account requirements?

    a. The father as the sole custodian of the accounts for children A and B and the mother and father as joint custodians of an account for child C
    b. The mother and father as joint custodians for their three children under one account
    c. The father as sole custodian of individual accounts each for children A, B, and C, and the mother as sole custodian of individual accounts each for children A, B, and C
    d. The mother and father as joint custodians of individual accounts each for children A, B, and C

100. Which of the following persons are considered corporate insiders?

    a. Officers
    b. Directors
    c. Employees
    d. All of the above

101. Which of the following are necessary for a floor broker to cross orders, executing both a buy and sell order for the same security at the same time?

   a. The floor broker must announce the orders.
   b. The specialist for that stock must allow it.
   c. The sell order must be presented at a price that is higher than the current best bid.
   d. All of the above are necessary.

102. An individual is in the beginning stages of forming a limited partnership and first needs to file a certificate of limited partnership within the state he or she plans to do business. Which of the following must be included on the certificate?

   I. Specifics regarding how to approve and incorporate new limited partners into the partnership
   II. Educational and professional backgrounds of all partners, limited and general
   III. Specifics regarding how the partnership will be dissolved, if necessary
   IV. Details of the business that the partnership will engage in

   a. I, II, III, and IV
   b. IV only
   c. I, III, and IV
   d. I and IV

103. What should mutual fund sales literature do?

   a. It should utilize graphs to illustrate the fund's performance against a broad-based index.
   b. It should not contain general statements comparing the relative safety of mutual funds versus other investments.
   c. It should note the sources for any graphs.
   d. It should do all of the above.

104. Which of the following would be appropriate investment recommendation(s) for an investor seeking investments with tax benefits?

   I. Direct participation programs
   II. Annuities
   III. Corporate bonds
   IV. Municipal bonds

   a. III and IV
   b. I, II, and IV
   c. IV only
   d. I and III

105. An investor purchased all of the following option contracts. Given the current pricing for each stock, which of the contracts should he or she move to exercise in order to maximize his or her investment and potential profit?

   I. PPG August 25 call, PPG is currently trading at $24.75
   II. HKP August 75 put, HKP is currently trading at $72.50
   III. RPT August 81 call, RPT is currently trading at $82.75
   IV. TJN August 63 put, TJN is currently trading at $64.25

   a. I and IV
   b. II only
   c. II and III
   d. I and III

106. Of the different types of preferred stock, which one often has the feature of enabling its owner to receive both the preferred and the common dividend?

    a. Cumulative preferred
    b. Callable preferred
    c. Participating preferred
    d. Convertible preferred

107. Which of these categories of earnings listed on an income statement is the source for paying out dividends to shareholders?

    a. Earnings available to common
    b. Operating income
    c. Net income after taxes
    d. None of the above

108. A firm representative is found to have entered a market order that was influenced by information from a report that has not been made public yet. Which prohibited practice is he or she guilty of?

    a. Front running
    b. Capping
    c. Trading ahead
    d. Painting the tape

109. A registered representative in opening a corporate account may have to obtain which of these from the corporation?

    I. Corporate charter
    II. Certificate of incumbency
    III. Corporate resolution
    IV. Corporate bylaws

    a. I, III, and IV
    b. III only
    c. I, II, III, and IV
    d. I and II

110. An investor establishes a position involving a bear call spread:

    Sell 1 DZE March 75 call for a $4 premium
    Buy 1 DZE March 83 call for a $1 premium

What would be this investor's maximum total gain on this position?

    a. $3
    b. $400
    c. $500
    d. $300

111. On a corporation's balance sheet, assets minus liabilities represents which of the following?

    I. Retained earnings
    II. Current liabilities
    III. Corporation's net worth
    IV. Shareholder's equity

    a. III and IV
    b. I and III
    c. I only
    d. III only

112. Which of the following Chicago Board Option Exchange (CBOE) floor personnel are actual employees of the exchange?

    a. Option market maker
    b. Order book official
    c. Two-dollar broker
    d. Commission house broker

113. Which of the following is true of commercial paper?

    a. It is sold only through dealers who act as the middlemen reselling to investors.
    b. It is issued at a discount to face value.
    c. The interest rate is slightly higher than what a commercial bank would charge.
    d. Its maturities range from 1 to 150 days.

114. Which of the following are considered institutional investors?

    a. A governmental entity
    b. An employee benefit plan that meets the requirement of Section 403(b) or Section 457 of the Internal Revenue Code and has at least 100 participants
    c. A qualified plan as defined in Section 3(a)(12)(C) of the Exchange Act and that has at least 100 participants
    d. All of the above

115. Which of the following is a type of account ownership?

    a. Partnership
    b. Trust
    c. Joint
    d. All of the above

116. Given a bond purchased at a premium, all of the following are true except that

    a. it will demonstrate the inverse relationship between investment price and bond yield.
    b. the investment yield will be less than the bond's coupon rate.
    c. higher than par price indicates an expected higher yield than what is stated coupon rate.
    d. the purchased price is higher than par value.

117. An investor has sold short 275 shares of stock PPG at $26 per share. The market currently has PPG trading at $11 per share. The investor sees news of the company that may indicate a price increase over the short term. Which of the following would provide this investor with guaranteed protection against missing a purchase of PPG at a level at which he or she can still make a profit given the short position?

    a. Buy 275 PPG at $21 stop
    b. Unknown without more information
    c. Buy 275 PPG at $32 stop
    d. None of the above

118. All of the following are true of convertible bonds except that

    a. share appreciation will benefit the bondholder in capital appreciation and upon conversion of the bond to common stock.
    b. the bondholder holds a senior creditor position.
    c. they have characteristics that benefit both the issuer and the investor.
    d. they usually have a higher interest rates than nonconvertible bonds.

119. What is the maximum amount that may be contributed to a 529 plan in 2023 before the excess must be reported on IRS form 709?

    a. $2,000
    b. $5,500
    c. $6,500
    d. $17,000

120. What is the amount of a corporation's earnings that would be attributed to all of its common shareholders as dictated by each of the outstanding and individual shares called?

    a. Earnings per share fully diluted
    b. Earnings per share
    c. Earnings available to common
    d. None of the above

121. Which of the following is true of the NASDAQ?

    a. Communications between broker dealers via phone are strictly prohibited.
    b. Prices are negotiated directly between broker dealers on an electronic network.
    c. Proposed negotiation terms regarding a security are disseminated amongst all interested parties via memoranda.
    d. It stands for National Association of Securities Dealers Auction Quotation System.

122. Which of the following bond terms represents the amount loaned by an investor to an issuer, which in most cases is $1,000?

    a. Principal amount
    b. Par value
    c. Face value
    d. All of the above

123. Which of the following securities are exempt from TRACE reporting requirements?

    I. Municipal debt
    II. Securities & Exchange Commission (SEC)-registered corporate debt, both domestic and foreign
    III. Mortgage-backed securities
    IV. Collateralized mortgage obligations (CMOs)

    a. I only
    b. II only
    c. I, III, and IV
    d. III and IV

124. A father is named as the fiduciary of an account for his minor child. He has traded in and out of the account with low to moderate risk securities, reinvested the account distributions in a timely manner, named the child's mother with equal discretionary authority over the account, and avoided participating in option transactions. Which of the actions named above is not approved and within the set guidelines regarding a fiduciary's duty in managing an account?

    a. Trading within the account with low to moderate risk securities
    b. Reinvesting the account distributions in a timely manner
    c. Naming the child's mother with equal discretionary authority over the account
    d. Avoiding participating in option transactions

125. Which of the following are true of a warrant for stock PIX?

    I. Its subscription price is set at the current market value of stock PIX at the time of the warrant's issuance.
    II. It is a security that provides the holder the chance to purchase PIX preferred stock.
    III. As compared to a right, a warrant is more valuable due to its longer life.
    IV. It provides the opportunity to purchase stock PIX for possibly up to ten years at the subscription price.

    a. I and III
    b. III and IV
    c. I, II, and III
    d. II, III, and IV

126. Calculate the current yield on a 9.5 percent bond, having paid $1,250 for the bond.

    a. 7.6 percent
    b. 7.2 percent
    c. 8 percent
    d. None of the above

127. Which of the following actions regarding stock PIX would be considered a violation for any registered representative?

   a. Rushing a customer to purchase stock PIX specifically to qualify prior to the ex-dividend date

   b. Making a customer recommendation to purchase stock PIX simply to benefit from a pending dividend payment

   c. Recommending a purchase of stock PIX to a customer by highlighting the pending dividend payment as an incentive while neglecting to educate him or her on the stock's fundamentals, appropriateness, risks, and rewards

   d. All of the above are violations.

128. Which of the following investments would not be considered appropriate for an investor with an objective of current income?

   a. Growth stock

   b. Municipal bond

   c. Corporate bond

   d. Utility stock

129. Which of the following is not a purpose of the Securities Act of 1933?

   a. Require that investors receive financial and other significant information

   b. Guarantee the financial information received by investors is accurate

   c. Prohibit deceit, misrepresentations, and fraud in the sale of securities

   d. Require the registration of securities

130. All of the following are true of discretionary accounts except that

   a. the registered representative on the account is solely responsible for reviewing the account on a continual basis.

   b. the discretionary authority granted to the registered representative may not be transferred to another individual.

   c. the limited power of attorney that provides discretionary authority is signed by the customer and can be durable or non-durable.

   d. the termination of a registered representative's employment with his or her firm also terminates the discretionary authority he or she was given over the customer's account.

131. What role(s) do corporate bondholders take?

   I. They take on the role of partial owners of the company as a result of the investment capital they have contributed into the company.

   II. They possess unrestricted voting rights.

   III. They have priority over preferred and common stockholders in terms of payment following a company liquidation.

   IV. They are considered creditors of the company.

   a. II, III, and IV

   b. I and III

   c. IV only

   d. III and IV

132. All of the following are options for an investor who possesses a warrant to purchase common stock except when

 a. the warrant will expire as long as the current stock price is above the subscription price.
 b. the investor sells the warrant to another investor.
 c. the investor exercises the warrant and uses it to purchase common stock at the warrant's subscription price.
 d. all of the above are options for an investor who owns a warrant.

133. A registered representative trading an equity based on non-public information in his or her own account before trading for clients is called _____.

 a. Churning
 b. Rebalancing
 c. Market timing
 d. Front running

134. How would the consolidated tape show 4,500 shares of PPG traded at 32.77?

 a. 45s.PPG32.77
 b. 450s.PPG32.77
 c. 4,500s.PPG32.77
 d. None of the above

135. Technical analysis follows chart patterns in order to predict future price performance. Which of the following are chart patterns recognized and used by these analysts?

 I. Resistance
 II. Cyclical trend lines
 III. Upward trend lines
 IV. Consolidation

 a. I, II, III, and IV
 b. I, III, and IV
 c. III only
 d. I and III

Answer Key and Explanations for Test #3

1. D:

$$\text{breakeven} = \text{strike price} + \text{premium}$$

$$\$78 = \$73 + \$5$$

The breakeven amount is the where the gain and loss of the transaction equalizes so as to come out no better and no worse for having participated in the transaction. Here, that amount is $78 per share.

$$\text{premium paid} = 100 \times \$5 = \$500$$

The maximum loss is the most that this investor stands to lose for having purchased this option contract. If the share price for PPG drops to below the strike price of $73 and remains there up through the contract's expiration date, the investor will not exercise the option, and the most he or she will be out is the premium paid for the contract, here $500.

The maximum gain for this investor is unlimited given that the option contract provides them with the option to buy shares at $73 per share. Every dollar of increase in share price above the breakeven price will provide a gain to the investor. With this, the potential for gain is unlimited.

2. D: All of the above are types of corporate money market instruments. Federal fund loans are made between banks, short term in length, and for $1 million or more. Reverse repurchase agreements involve an institutional investor selling securities to a dealer with the intention of repurchasing them back at a later date. Bankers' acceptances are like postdated checks, to provide payment to whomever brings them to the issuing bank for processing on the stated due dates.

3. A: The investor's option contract dictates that he or she paid a $200 contract premium for an option to buy 100 shares of PPG at $55 per share with the expiration of that contract being in May. The option premium must be multiplied by 100, and each contract is for one round lot of 100 shares of the contracted stock.

4. C: The SEC has the power to register, regulate, and oversee brokerage firms, transfer agents, and clearing agencies as well as SROs.

5. C: The Options Clearing Corporation publishes a disclosure document called the Characteristics and Risks of Standardized Options, provides a guarantee as to an option's performance, and facilitates standardized options to settle on a trade date plus one. They do not, however, issue option contracts on the trade date but instead the day after the trade date.

6. B:

$$\text{current yield} = \frac{\text{annual income}}{\text{current price (POP)}}$$

$$\text{current yield} = \frac{\$3}{\$17} = 0.1765 = 17.7\%$$

7. C: Securities that have the brokerage firm as the registered nominal owner and the customer as the beneficial owner are considered held in street name. Transfer and ship securities and transfer and held-in-safekeeping securities are both registered in the customer's name.

8. C: An option seller is the writer of the contract and his or her goal is primarily not to have the option contract exercised but instead to profit off of the premium income resulting from writing the contract itself. Further, the seller does not have the right to decline having the contract exercised. The seller, by writing the contract, does not retain rights to decline exercising the contract but assumes the role instead of having the obligation to the buyer to either sell (call) or buy (put) if the buyer of the option should choose to exercise his or her option.

9. B: If only a nominal sum is paid, the body copy of the material does not need to clearly state that it is a paid testimonial. If more than a nominal sum is paid, however, the fact that it is a paid testimonial must be indicated.

10. A: When opening an account for a customer, a registered representative should obtain from that customer whether he or she is an employee of a bank, citizenship status, an estimation of annual income, and a bank reference.

11. C: An investor who believes shares of PPG will rise is said to be bullish for PPG. With that, they will want to purchase an option contract that will allow him or her to maximize profits. Purchasing 1 PPG August 66 call will allow him or her to make the most potential profit in the event the share price rises above its current $65 per share. The 66 call will maximize profits above the 72 call whether the stock price rises above $72 or not. Either put contract would not be appropriate, given the investor anticipates the share price rising. Any increase in PPG's share price above its current $65 will negate the investor wanting to purchase the option to sell at 52 or 64.

12. B:

$$2.09 = 2\ 9/32\% = 2.28125\%$$

$$0.0228 \times \$100,000 = \$2,280$$

The calculated premium to be paid to buy this call would be $2,280.

13. C: Treasury notes have terms ranging from 1 to 10 years, pay semiannual interest, and are obtained through Treasury auctions held semi-monthly: 3 and 10 year notes are auctioned in the first half of the month and 2, 5, and 7 year notes are auctioned in the second half of the month. Treasury bonds have maturities ranging from 20 to 30 years. Treasury bills have maturities ranging from 4 to 52 weeks, do not pay semiannual interest, and are obtained through weekly Treasury auctions.

14. D: Account statements are sent to the address noted on the customer's account. Duplicate confirmations can be sent to someone with power of attorney, but that request must be made in writing. Brokerage firms may hold a customer's account correspondence for up to two months (not one), if he or she is traveling domestically, and up to three months (not two), if he or she is traveling internationally.

15. B: Shareholders will retain proportionate interest in residual assets in the event of bankruptcy, may receive a list of shareholders, and may inspect a corporation's books and records. They do not have the right to access and review a corporation's confidential financial information.

16. B: The type of maturity represented by this example is a term maturity in that the entire issued amount of $850,000 becomes due in its entirety on one date set in advance. A balloon maturity involves the principal amount being paid over years with the largest coming due on the last date. A serial maturity bond also matures over years with the largest portions due in the later years.

17. A: The statement regarding his educational background would be considered a misrepresentation and grounds for discipline. In order for it to qualify as a misrepresentation and cause for discipline, it must have been untrue and knowingly communicated to the customer. Here, this representative knowingly lied and mischaracterized his education with the intent to impress this prospective customer. The statement regarding the biotech analyst would not qualify as a misrepresentation given that, at the time, the representative made the statement that the analyst was employed by his firm. The representative cannot be held responsible for the analyst leaving even though that is largely the reason the customer signed with him and opened a brokerage account with the firm.

18. A: First, it's necessary to establish what this investor's breakeven price is. This is done by taking into account any money that he or she has obtained to this point as a result of this position, the per share price for selling short the shares of PTR, and the premium on the sale of the put.

$$\$42.50 + \$2 = \$44.50$$

The breakeven here is $44.50. This is the price at which this investor will neither gain nor lose on this position.

Next, in order to calculate the total maximum gain, it's necessary to take the breakeven price and subtract the share price he or she will receive as a result of the put being exercised.

$$\$44.50 - \$38 = \$6.50$$

This is the most he or she can profit, given the amounts taken in for selling shares short and receiving put premium minus the amount he or she will pay out to cover the exercised put option.

The total maximum gain is: $\$6.50 \times 100 = \$650$

19. B: The NASDAQ opening cross is the source for the NASDAQ official opening price (NOOP). Dissemination of imbalance information begins at 9:28am, some order types (MOO splits) are not allowed from 9:28-9:30, while other types will be reclassified to Imbalance Only orders. Cancel requests of regular hours orders (Day, GTC, IOC, market) are not allowed from 9:28-9:30 and will be pended until after the cross occurs. Imbalance Only orders increase liquidity.

20. B: This investor would have a call that is in the money given that the current stock price is greater than the option's strike price. The call provides them with the option to purchase PPG at $33 per share. With it currently trading at $36.50, he or she could exercise the option, purchase the shares at $33, and benefit from the price appreciation between the two.

21. A: Discretionary trading authority is when a person other than the account holder may invest without consulting the account holder about the price, amount, or type of security or the timing of the trades that are placed for the account.

22. D: Examples of a fiduciary include an administrator, a guardian, and an executor.

23. A: Given that corporate bonds are priced as a percentage of their par value of $1,000, the following calculation would provide a dollar price quote of $935 for this bond.

$$93\ 1/2\ \% = 93.50\% = 0.935$$

$$0.935 \times \$1,000 = \$935.00$$

24. D: The settlement date is two business days after trade date. The payment date is when payment is due to the broker and is also four business days after trade date. The execution date for the trade order is the trade date.

25. D: Intangible drilling costs are 100 percent deductible for the year in which they occur and include wages, well casings, and geological surveys.

26. D: An investor looking to profit from foreign currency options would buy foreign currency calls or sell foreign currency puts, given indications that a country's stock market is experiencing levels of price increase, not decrease; indications that a country is experiencing an economic upswing, not downturn; and indications that a country is experiencing a period of government stability, not instability.

27. D: A wrap account is an account in which customers with large portfolios pay a brokerage firm a flat annual fee that covers the cost of a money manager's services and the cost of commissions.

28. B: A bond's yield is not directly influenced or determined by the concept of supply and demand. It is influenced by the type of collateral on the bond, the bond's term, and the issuer's credit quality.

29. D: A not-held order gives discretion to the broker as to timing and price for the order's execution. A fill-or-kill order must be executed immediately upon receipt, or it must be cancelled. An all-or-none order indicates that the investor would like all of the securities bought or sold in the transaction or none at all. A market-on-open order indicates the investor's wish to have it executed right at the opening of the market or as close to it as possible.

30. A: An option's premium is an extension of what its value is to the market and potential investors. The determination of the premium paid by an investor purchasing the option will be based on factors such as interest rates, supply and demand, and the timing of the option's expiration. It will not be based on the option's class and series.

31. A: Convertible Security Arbitrage involves the simultaneous purchase and sale of both a stock and a security that may be converted into that same underlying stock. Buying shares in a company that is being taken over or acquired, while shorting shares in the company about to acquire them, is risk arbitrage. Simultaneously buying and selling the same security in two different markets in order to exploit the price difference between the two is market arbitrage.

32. C: A transfer agent does not verify company debt; this is the role of the registrar. A transfer agent does maintain the list of stockholders, verifies the correct issuance of shares, and handles the new issuance of stock certificates.

33. B: This position, selling a call and a put with the same stock, strike price, and expiration, is a short straddle. A long straddle is the same with the exception of being a purchase of a call and put. A combination is like a straddle except it's a purchase or sale of a call and put with same stock and expiration but different expirations. A spread is buying and selling two options at the same time of the same class but with either different exercise prices, months, or both.

34. D: Book entry bonds are not evidenced by an actual physical certificate and instead have as proof of ownership the trade confirmation from the purchase transaction. Principal-only registration bonds are evidenced by an actual bond certificate printed with the owner's name. Fully registered bonds are recorded for interest and principal payments with the owner's name. Bearer bonds are issued with a bond certificate that does not have the owner's name printed on it.

35. A: A violation of Regulation T has consequences that include the firm selling the securities from the unpaid order after the fifth business day following trade date (a customer has four days to pay). For 90 days, the customer must pay up front for any purchases made through firm, but can still trade. The customer will be fully responsible for any loss incurred by the firm in selling off the securities from the unpaid order; however, the firm may sell any other securities from that customer's account in order to provide financial settlement for the loss.

36. B: Uniform Gift to Minors Act (UGMA) guidelines regarding contributions include gifts being irrevocable, discretionary authority for account assets to be used for the minor's education, and a limitless gift size. Additionally, the tax-free gift limit is set at $17,000 per year (as of 2023), not $18,000 per year.

37. A: Registered representatives are not required to obtain or keep current information regarding their customers' educational statuses or backgrounds. They do need to maintain current information regarding their customers' marital statuses and investment objectives, goals, and philosophies.

38. A: A calendar spread consists of a long and short option with same class but different expirations:

Sell 1 PPG May 23 put

Buy 1 PPG August 23 put

A price spread consists of a long and short option with the same class but different strike prices:

Buy 1 PPG May 23 put

Sell 1 PPG May 21 put

A diagonal spread consists of a long and short option with the same class but different strike prices and expirations:

Sell 1 PPG May 21 put

Buy 1 PPG August 23 put

39. D: The highest level of service for a NASDAQ subscription is level III. NASDAQ TotalView is a quotation service covering all securities traded over NASDAQ. Level II is provided to order-entry firms and enables them to view the quotes associated with all market makers and allows for order execution. Level I offers the lowest level of service and provides quotes for registered representatives.

40. B: Ownership in preferred stock provides a fixed income to the investor through dividend payments. The par value of shares is generally $100, not $1,000. Due to the fixed income nature of these shares, they are more sensitive to changes in interest rates, demonstrating an inverse relationship between rates and pricing. These shares have no maturity date and are therefore considered perpetual.

41. A: Utilizing information from a company's balance sheet and/or income statement, the debt service ratio, debt-to-equity ratio and earnings per share primary can be calculated. The Price/Earnings Ratio of the stock requires the current stock price, which is not shown on either the Balance Sheet or the Income Statement.

42. D: Fundamental analysts will refer to company income statements, liquidity ratios, and valuation ratios in trying to determine a stock's value.

43. A: In order for a stock to be delisted from the New York Stock Exchange (NYSE), the approval of both the company's board of directors and the board's audit committee are necessary. Additionally, delisting requires notification of the company's 35 largest shareholders. Listing requires a minimum of 400 shareholders each owning at least 100 shares and a minimum of 1.1 million publicly held shares.

44. A: Income bonds are considered to be unsecured bonds in that interest will only be paid to the investor if the corporate issuer has the income to do it. Mortgage bonds, equipment trust certificates, and collateral trust certificates are considered to be secured bonds in that they are all backed by a specific type of asset as collateral.

45. B: The investor's order will be to buy 250 PPG 62.15 GTC DNR. The buy order remains exactly the same due to the investor stipulating the order to be do not reduce (DNR), and accordingly, the order will not be reduced to reflect the distribution of dividends.

46. B: Government bonds are the type of investment that this representative should recommend given this investor's primary objective of generating income. Annuities and collateralized mortgage obligations (CMOs) are investments more appropriate to an investor seeking liquidity. Common stocks are more suitable for an investor with capital appreciation as his or her primary investment objective.

47. A: Technical analysis does not consider a company's fundamentals in its attempt to predict price performance. Instead, a technical analyst will examine chart patterns of past price performance in order to predict the direction and magnitude of future price performance.

48. D: A short sale transaction involves first the sale of a stock and, second, a buy transaction intended to fulfill the initial sell transaction. The motivating belief in initiating this position is that the stock price will depreciate, offering the short seller the opportunity to purchase the stock at a lower price than sold in the short sale. The risk in this position is unlimited in that the price of the stock has the unlimited potential to rise beyond the sale price received.

49. D: An investor who is long a stock ideally would like to achieve some downside price protection against loss given the possibility of the share price falling in general, and then specifically, below the original purchase price. There are two options for them doing that here.

By purchasing a put he or she is essentially purchasing the option to sell the shares of DZE at a set price that will allow profit taking, given the original purchase price. Even if the DZE share price drops, the investor will retain the option to sell the shares at the put strike price until the expiration of the contract.

By selling a call, he or she is essentially selling to another investor the option to buy the DZE shares at a set price that will allow profit taking, given the original purchase price. The investor will profit from the option being exercised by the buyer of the call due to the fact that the strike price of the call will have been set at a price above the investor's original purchase price, thereby protecting him or her from any loss in the event of a DZE share price drop. By selling the call, the investor retains the opportunity to sell the shares at a profit."

50. C: The price of a corporate bond is determined by many different factors that include the bond's call features if any, its issuer, interest rates, and the term of the bond.

51. B: Congress created the Securities and Exchange Commission (SEC) under the Securities Exchange Act of 1934.

52. B: Bond certificates, when issued, are not required to have the bond's state of issuance. They are required to have the call feature, paying agent, and dates of interest payments.

53. C: In a discretionary account, a registered representative cannot choose to close out an account without the client's approval, but can choose whether to buy or sell, choose the amount to buy or sell, and choose the type of asset to buy or sell.

54. D: State-issued unlimited tax general obligation (GO) bonds are backed by any taxes it collects.

55. D: The automated confirmation system (ACT)/trade reporting facility (TRF) provides reporting for trades and includes NASDAQ convertible bonds, third-market trades, and non-NASDAQ over-the-counter (OTC) securities.

56. C: LEAPS stands for Long-term Equity Anticipation Securities.

57. A: Prospectus delivery is not a general consideration regarding communications with the public about variable life insurance and variable annuities. Product identification, liquidity, and claims about guarantees are general considerations.

58. B: In the event a corporation pays a cash dividend to investors, an investor may receive that payment as a credit to his or her brokerage account as applied by the brokerage firm or as a check for that amount sent directly to him or her from the corporation paying the dividend. A brokerage firm holding the shares in a street name would not send the investor a check in that amount directly.

59. C: Buying and selling two options at the same time of the same class but with either different exercise prices, months, or both, is called a spread. Buying a call and a put at the same time with the same stock, strike price, and expiration is called a long straddle. Selling a call and put at the same time with the same stock, strike price, and expiration is called a short straddle. Buying or selling at the same time a call and a put with the same stock and expiration but with different strike prices is called a combination.

60. D: Age, time frame, and personal experience can all affect an investor's risk tolerance.

61. C:

$$1.00 + 0.05 = 1.05 = 105\%$$

$$8.00 \times 1.05 = \$8.40 \text{ cost per share}$$

$$8.4 \times 425 = \$3,570 \text{ total cost charged to customer}$$

When a dealer fills an order on a principal basis, it is considered a riskless principal transaction. He or she does not own the shares in inventory and therefore must go out and buy them only then to turn around and sell them in order to fill the customer's buy order. Given that, the 5 percent markup charged to the customer for this order will be based on the dealer's actual cost per share, not the current market bid price per share.

62. B: A bearish outlook points to the opinion that stock prices will fall. In relation to an options contract, it points to the opinion that the stock that is the subject of the contract has a future outlook of price decline. Given this, contract sellers would pursue writing call contracts so as to hopefully avoid the buyer exercising a contract to buy higher a stock whose price is in decline and profit from the premium gained by simply writing the contract. Option contract buyers would pursue purchasing put contracts so as to exercise an option to sell high a stock whose price is currently in decline. Conversely, option contract buyers would not pursue purchasing call contracts. There would be no need to purchase the option to buy high a stock in an open-end decline.

63. B: The exchange names that match X, P, C, and Q are Philadelphia (PHLX), Philippines (PSE), Cincinnati (CINN), and NASDAQ.

64. B: A bond's yield to maturity is largely a combination of considering its annual income and the difference in price paid above, at, or below par. A bond purchased at the highest premium will produce the lowest yield to maturity, here being the bond purchased at 103. All the purchases represented here had the same coupon rates (and accordingly, the same annual income) with one purchased at 98 (a discount), 100 (at par), and two at a premium, 100 1/4 and 103. The par value received at maturity for the 103 bond will represent the largest loss to the investor of these purchases, given that he or she paid the most over par for that bond.

65. C: An investor would not utilize index options to hedge a short portfolio by buying puts or selling calls. He or she would, however, hedge a short portfolio by buying calls or selling puts and hedge a long portfolio by buying puts or selling calls.

66. D: Classification of options is by series, type, and class. The series classification provides that options of the same class with the same expiration month and exercise price be grouped together. There are two types of options, calls and puts. Calls provide the buyer the option to purchase a stock for a specific price and only for a specific period of time. Puts provide the buyer the option to sell a stock for a specific price and only for a specific time period. The option class provides groups according to the type of option and underlying stock.

67. A: The types of short-term notes that a municipality or state may issue include bond anticipation notes (BANs), tax and revenue anticipation notes (TRANs), and revenue anticipation notes (RANs).

68. B: A fiduciary account requires that anyone but the beneficial owner of an account intending to enter orders for that account must provide confirmation of the authority to do so in writing.

69. A: Once adjusted for the 3:2 stock split, the investor's new order would be buying 330 PPG 44 GTC.

70. A: A joint tenants in common (JTIC) account requires that, once deceased, that party's assets from the account become the property of the estate and do not go to the surviving party of the account. In a transfer on death (TOD) account, the parties are provided the opportunity to designate in advance who they would like their portion of the account to go to in the event they die. In a joint tenant with rights of survivorship (JTWROS) account, the death of one party of the account provides for the surviving party to retain all assets in the account. A joint account requires that all parties of the account be alive.

71. A:

$$premium = \$3 \times 100 = \$300$$

Given a strike price of 60 on this put, the interest rate is 6 percent. Rates falling to 5 percent indicate that the investor who purchased this put is in the money 10 points at expiration.

$$60 - 50 = 10 \text{ pts.}$$

Accordingly, this investor's account will be credited $1,000.

$$10 \text{ pts.} \times 100 = 1,000 = \$1,000$$

This investor paid a premium of $300 for this put option. The total profit will be as follows:

$$\$1,000 \text{ credit} - \$300 \text{ premium paid} = \$700 \text{ profit}$$

72. C: The term research report refers to printed or processed analysis covering individual companies or industries.

73. B: With regards to transacting in a new margin account, investors are required to deposit either $2,000 in equity or half of the purchase price of the securities, whichever is greater:

Minimum equity required:

$2,000

Half of the securities' purchase price:

$$500 \times \$2 = \$1,000$$

$$\$1,000 \times 0.50 = \$500$$

In this example, the required deposit would be $1,000. The minimum equity requirement of $2,000 is greater than half of the purchase price of the securities, which is $500. Even with that, a customer's required deposit will never be more than the purchase price of the securities. Here, $2,000 is greater than the purchase price of $1,000; therefore, the purchase price of $1,000 will be the required deposit.

74. B: The credited amount is a result of subtracting the call strike price paid by the investor, as they exercised their option contract, from the current index quote.

$$\$522.31 - \$509.00 = \$13.31$$

$$\$13.31 \times 100 = \$1,331$$

The net profit from this position comes from subtracting the premium he or she paid for the call from the amount credited to the account.

$$\$3 \times 100 = \$300 \text{ premium paid}$$

$$\$1,331 - \$300 = \$1,031$$

75. B: A principal of the firm must accept and sign off on the new account either prior to or soon after the execution of the first trade.

76. B: The breakeven takes into account the investor's original purchase price and the premium he or she was paid for selling the call. Here:

$$\$31.25 - \$1 = \$30.25$$

Selling their shares of PPG at $30.25 will allow them to neither gain nor lose on this position. A sale for any price above $30.25 will produce a gain.

The maximum gain for the position takes into account both the breakeven for the investor and the strike price for the call if exercised. Here:

$$\$38 - \$30.25 = \$7.75$$

$$\$7.75 \times 100 \text{ shares} = \$775$$

If the buyer of the call exercises his or her option to buy 100 shares of PPG at $38 per share, the seller of that call will achieve the maximum gain above the original purchase price (having taken into account the premium he or she received for selling the call).

77. D: In the determination of property value in relation to assessments and general obligation bonds, a property's value will not be its market value, but instead, its assessed value will be determined using the local assessment rate.

$$80\% = 0.80$$

$$\$375,000 \times 0.80 = \$300,000$$

78. D: Treasury Separate Trading of Registered Interest and Principal of Securities (STRIPS) are zero coupon bonds offering the option to an investor to purchase separately (not bundled) the principal or interest portions of the securities' cash flow streams. The minimum face value is $100, and any par amount must be in multiples of $100.

79. C: Government National Mortgage Association (GNMA) securities are backed by the full faith and credit of the U.S. government. Federal National Mortgage Association (FNMA) is a public for-profit corporation in the business of purchasing mortgages and then bundling them to create mortgage-backed securities. Federal Farm Credit System (FFCS) is made up of privately owned lenders who sell securities that are backed by their own obligations. Federal Home Loan Mortgage

Corporation (FHLMC) is a publicly traded company that purchases residential mortgages and bundles them into pools in order to then sell off interest in them to investors.

80. A: Once quotes are published over the NASDAQ workstation, they must be honored. They are considered to be firm quotes, and a dealer refusing to honor his or her firm quotes is committing a violation known as backing away. Backing Away is covered by NASDAQ Rule 4613 and FINRA Rule 5520.

81. B: Trust accounts can be revocable, irrevocable, complex, or simple (not basic).

82. D: A family limited partnership is most often utilized for personal estate planning as a vehicle for parents to transfer ownership of assets to their children and is preferred due to potential tax benefits that favor the parents versus other options.

83. A: In order to provide good and complete delivery, certificates must be delivered in round lots that can be easily combined to form 100. Here, that is three certificates of 100 shares each, with one certificate for 20 shares. Six certificates of 50 shares each does not provide a complete delivery, and 30 certificates of 10 shares each with four certificates of five shares each does not qualify as good round lots.

84. A: A securities issuance would result in an increase in a corporation's cash by the amount gained in the offering, net other costs. Paying off bond principles in cash, buying equipment with cash, and a dividend payout would all result in a reduction in a corporation's cash position.

85. C: If the investor believes that interest rates will fall, he or she should purchase interest rate puts and sell interest rate calls. The puts will allow the investor to profit when the interest rate falls lower than the exercise price, and at the same time the calls they sold will expire worthless, leaving them with the income from the premiums.

86. C: Under Rule 203, a broker dealer cannot initiate an equity short sale transaction unless he or she has already borrowed the security, he or she has arranged to borrow the security, or he or she reasonably believes he or she can borrow the security.

87. A: The managing party of a fiduciary account may not work the account and assets in it to benefit itself, should always act according to the prudent man rule, and may have full discretion with the authority to buy and sell securities and withdraw cash and securities. They may also have a limited power of attorney giving them the authority to buy and sell securities without the ability to withdraw securities.

88. B: A specialist cannot accept market orders in that the nature of those types of orders dictates that they be executed as soon as they are presented to the market, and accordingly, there would be at that point no order to leave with the specialist.

89. B: Accounts payable that are owed to a corporation's vendors are considered to be current liabilities, not long-term liabilities. They must be paid within 12 months. Notes, mortgages, and bonds are all long-term liabilities and are due to be paid by the corporation after 12 months.

90. A: A buy limit order allows protection to an investor by providing the chance to set a maximum price they are willing to pay for a security. A sell limit order allows an investor to set a minimum price at which he or she is willing to sell a security. A buy limit order provides price protection to the investor in that it guarantees he or she will not pay over a certain price for that security, but accordingly, it will NOT guarantee execution of that order in the event that the price level of that security does not reach the investor's desired price or below.

91. B:

$$1.00 - 0.95 = 0.05 = 5\%$$

$$5.10 \times 0.95 = \$4.845 \text{ proceeds per share sold}$$

$$4.845 \times 320 = \$1,550.40 \text{ total proceeds after execution of the sell order}$$

92. A: Pass-throughs provide investors with interest and principal payment income relative to their initial investments in pools of mortgages. The payments flow through to them on a monthly basis as the individual mortgages in the pools are paid down. A Separate Trading of Registered Interest and Principal of Securities (STRIP) is an investment that provides the opportunity to purchase separately either the principal or interest payment cash flow stream of a Treasury security. Collateralized mortgage obligations (CMOs) are similar to pass-throughs except that they are separated into different maturity schedules, or tranches, each being paid in full one at a time. Treasury inflation protected securities (TIPS) are securities whose interest payments and principal amounts are influenced by the level and movement of inflation.

93. C: Any gift from or to a member or person associated with a member may not exceed $100.00 per year.

94. D: Interest rate options can be either puts or calls and are used to profit from interest rate movements or as a hedge for Treasury securities.

95. B: Rule 80B goes into effect following the S&P 500 dropping by 7, 13, or 20 percent within a day of trading.

96. D: Actions falling under the role of a dealer include participating in trades by trading in and out of his or her own account, such as using securities in the account to fill a buy order or buying securities for the account to fill a customer's sell order. Further, making a market in a security is also an action performed by a dealer. Conversely, a broker simply facilitates order execution for a customer, while not participating in the transaction, and charges a commission for their services.

97. B: Requirements for a Uniform Gift to Minors Act (UGMA) account include that there be one minor, one custodian, and an account title stating it's a UGMA account and the state of origin for the account. Further, the assets within the account would not be registered currently in the child's name as the nominal owner but, instead, registered in the custodian's name with the child named as the beneficial owner.

98. B: Treasury bonds are quoted as a percentage of par and, accordingly, in terms of 32nds of 1 percent. Here, 97.08 translates to 97 8/32 percent.

$$97.08 = 97 \ 8/32 \ \% = 97.25\%$$

$$0.9725 \times \$1,000 = \$972.50$$

99. C: The Uniform Gift to Minors Act (UGMA) requires that each account have only one custodian and one minor. A custodian may oversee more than one separate account, and minors can have more than one separate account themselves. As applied to this example here, the father and mother each may be sole custodians of separate accounts for each of their three children A, B, and C.

100. D: Officers, directors, and employees are all persons that are considered to be corporate insiders.

101. D: In order for a floor broker to execute cross orders for the same stock at the same time, the specialist for that stock first must allow it, the floor broker must announce the orders, and the sell order must be presented at a price higher than the current best bid on that stock.

102. C: This individual should ensure that the certificate of limited partnership he or she files includes specifics regarding how to approve and incorporate new limited partners into the partnership, specifics regarding how the partnership will be dissolved, if necessary, and details of the business that the partnership will be engaging in. It will not be necessary to include the educational and professional backgrounds of all partners, limited and general.

103. D: Mutual fund sales literature should utilize graphs to illustrate the fund's performance against a broad-based index, not contain general statements comparing the relative safety of mutual funds versus other investments, and note the sources for any graphs contained therein.

104. C: Municipal bonds would be the choice for an investor seeking investments with tax benefits. Direct participation programs and annuities are appropriate with investors primarily seeking liquidity. Corporate bonds are great for investors seeking income.

105. C: Considering all of this investor's option positions, two of the four are currently in the money. These options would maximize both his or her investment and profit if exercised now.

HKP August 75 put

Shares of HKP are currently quoted at $72.50 per share. If exercised, this contract would provide the investor with the option of selling 100 shares of HKP at $75 per share when the quoted current market price is below that. To go further, the investor's profit is higher selling the shares via the option contract than selling them in the current open market.

RPT August 81 call

Shares of RPT are currently quoted at $82.75 per share. If exercised, this contract would provide the investor with the option of buying 100 shares of RPT at $81 per share when the quoted current market price is higher than that. To go further, the investor's profit is higher buying shares of RPT via the option contract than buying them in the current open market.

106. C: Participating preferred stock ownership provides the investor the right to receive the preferred dividend and also additional dividends when specific targets are met. These specific targets may often include participating in common dividend payments, too. Cumulative preferred shares not only allow the owner payment of the preferred dividend but also provide protection against missed dividend payments by requiring back payment of those dividends. Callable shares afford the corporation the right to call in those shares, often at a premium price. Convertible shares allow for the option to exchange preferred shares for common shares at a conversion price.

107. C: The earnings category on the income statement that provides the source for paying out dividends to shareholders is net income after taxes.

108. C: This representative, in entering a market order that was influenced by information from a report that had not been made public yet, would be guilty of trading ahead. Front running involves entering a firm order before entering a customer's much larger order with the intent to profit from the market effect of that customer's large order. Capping is done with the intent to prevent the further rise of a stock price. Painting the tape is practiced by two or more individuals and involves them creating the false appearance of activity in a given security only in an effort to attract new buyers to that security.

109. C: In opening a corporate account, a registered representative may, if necessary, obtain a corporate charter and the corporation's bylaws that confirm his or her ability to buy securities on margin, a corporate resolution that stipulates individuals with authority to enter orders, and a certificate of incumbency stipulating the officers who can do business on behalf of the corporation.

110. D: The maximum gain on this bear call spread would be the net result of the premium he or she gained on selling the call and the amount paid when buying the call.

$$\$4 - \$1 = \$3$$

$$\$3 \times 100 = \$300$$

This $300 total maximum gain will be attained if neither option is exercised and they both expire.

111. A: On a corporation's balance sheet, assets minus liabilities represents both the corporation's net worth and its shareholders' equity. A corporation's retained earnings are the balance of net income beyond what may be paid out as dividends. Current liabilities are the financial obligations of the corporation that come due within the next 12 months.

112. B: The order book official actually is employed by the exchange and has the job of maintaining a fair and orderly market. An option market maker is an exchange member, a two-dollar broker is an independent member of the exchange, and a commission house broker is employed by an exchange member organization.

113. B: Commercial paper is issued at a discount to face value. It is issued in two ways, direct paper and dealer paper. In the former, the sale is made without the use of a dealer, and in the latter, the paper is sold to dealers who then resell it to investors. The interest rate for commercial paper is actually lower than what a commercial bank would charge, and the maturities range from 1 to 270 days.

114. D: A governmental entity, an employee benefit plan that meets the requirement of Section 403(b) or Section 457 of the Internal Revenue Code and has at least 100 participants, and a qualified plan as defined in Section 3(a)(12)(C) of the Exchange Act and has at least 100 participants are all considered institutional investors.

115. D: Types of account ownership include partnership, trust, and joint.

116. C: The investment purchase price of bonds and their yields demonstrate an inverse relationship in that, as prices rise, yields fall. Therefore, a higher than par price will not indicate an expected higher yield than what is the stated coupon rate. A bond purchased at a premium indicates a purchase price paid that is above par and, consequently, an expected investment yield that will be less than the bond's coupon rate.

117. A: A buy 275 PPG at $21 stop order will allow this investor to pay no more than $21 per share in filling the short position, which has a sell price of $26 per share. A profit will still be made. Conversely, a buy 275 PPG at $32 stop order will enable their order to go as high as $32 a share before being executed, thus potentially eliminating a profit being made by this investor on the short position.

118. D: Convertible bonds usually pay a lower interest rate versus nonconvertible bonds due to the convertible feature of the bond. The lower rate of interest benefits the corporate issuer of the bond in reducing the interest expense he or she pays over the life of the bond. Share appreciation could result in capital appreciation in the bond price for the bondholder and further appreciation upon conversion of the bond to common stock. Finally, the bondholder holds a senior position as a creditor of the corporation.

119. D: The maximum amount that may be contributed to a 529 plan in 2023 is $17,000.

120. B: Earnings per share are the amount of a corporation's earnings owed to its common shareholders as divided by each of the outstanding common shares. Earnings per share fully diluted are a corporation's earnings attributed to each individual share after the conversion of any convertible securities. Earnings available in common are the amount of earnings available to common shareholders after taxes and the payout of any preferred dividend.

121. B: The NASDAQ is a negotiated market where security prices are negotiated directly between broker dealers using an electronic network. Communications between the dealers may be via phone, and any negotiated terms regarding a given security are kept between the two negotiating parties only. Last, NASDAQ stands for National Association of Securities Dealers Automated Quotation System.

122. D: The amount loaned to an issuer by an investor, which in most cases is $1,000, can be described as the principal amount, par value, or face value of the bond.

123. A: The Trade Reporting and Compliance Engine (TRACE) system reports the transactions of fixed-income securities that are eligible for reporting. Securities that are exempt include municipal debt, money market instruments, or foreign sovereign debt. Securities & Exchange Commission (SEC)-registered corporate debt transactions, domestic and foreign, must be reported through the TRACE system.

124. C: The father's action as fiduciary that is outside of the fiduciary guidelines and not allowed is the naming of the child's mother with equal discretionary authority over the account. The custodian does not have the authority to transfer or share discretionary authority of the account with a third party.

125. B: A warrant for stock PIX would be more valuable than a right due to its longer life and would provide the opportunity to purchase stock PIX for possibly up to 10 years at the subscription price. Its subscription price, however, is set above the current market value of stock PIX at the time of the warrant's issuance, and further, the warrant provides the holder the chance to purchase PIX common stock, not preferred.

126. A:

$$\text{current yield} = \frac{\text{bond's annual income}}{\text{current market price}}$$

$$\text{annual income} = \text{coupon rate} \times \text{par value of the bond}$$

$$9.5\% = 0.095$$

$$\text{annual income} = 0.095 \times \$1,000 = \$95$$

$$\text{current yield} = \frac{\$95}{\$1,250} = 0.076 = 7.6\%$$

127. D: A registered representative would be committing a violation by rushing a customer to make a purchase solely to meet the ex-dividend date, recommending a purchase simply to benefit from a pending dividend, or promoting a stock by highlighting the benefit of the pending dividend while neglecting to educate him or her as to the fundamentals or appropriateness this stock may have as an investment.

128. A: A growth stock would not be considered appropriate for an investor with an objective of current income.

129. B: The Securities Act of 1933 requires that investors receive financial and other significant information and that securities be registered, but it does not guarantee the information is accurate. The act also prohibits deceit, misrepresentation, and fraud in the sale of securities.

130. A: It is the principal of the firm who must take additional responsibility in monitoring these accounts over time, closely and more often than usual. A registered representative's discretionary authority is not transferable, requires a limited power of attorney that can last up to three years, and ends with the termination of his or her employment with the firm.

131. D: Corporate bondholders are considered to be creditors of the company, not owners. They only possess voting rights in the event the company fails in its ability to deliver timely interest and principal payments to them and take priority over preferred and common stockholders when owed funds that result from a company liquidation.

132. A: It is false that the warrant will expire when the current stock price is below the subscription price of the warrant. Warrants have stated expiration dates. They are typically issued at a price above the market price at the time, but when the underlying stock price rises above the warrant exercise price the warrant becomes valuable. The investor may sell the warrant to another investor or exercise the warrant in order to purchase common stock at the subscription price.

133. D: Front running is the prohibited activity of a registered representative trading based on non-public information in his or her own account prior to trading for clients.

134. A: The consolidated tape would display the trade as 45s.PPG32.77.

135. B: Chart patterns recognized and utilized by technical analysts in charting price performance are resistance, upward trend lines, and consolidation.

Series 7 Practice Tests #4 and #5

To take these additional Series 7 practice tests, visit our bonus page:
mometrix.com/bonus948/series7

How to Overcome Test Anxiety

Just the thought of taking a test is enough to make most people a little nervous. A test is an important event that can have a long-term impact on your future, so it's important to take it seriously and it's natural to feel anxious about performing well. But just because anxiety is normal, that doesn't mean that it's helpful in test taking, or that you should simply accept it as part of your life. Anxiety can have a variety of effects. These effects can be mild, like making you feel slightly nervous, or severe, like blocking your ability to focus or remember even a simple detail.

If you experience test anxiety—whether severe or mild—it's important to know how to beat it. To discover this, first you need to understand what causes test anxiety.

Causes of Test Anxiety

While we often think of anxiety as an uncontrollable emotional state, it can actually be caused by simple, practical things. One of the most common causes of test anxiety is that a person does not feel adequately prepared for their test. This feeling can be the result of many different issues such as poor study habits or lack of organization, but the most common culprit is time management. Starting to study too late, failing to organize your study time to cover all of the material, or being distracted while you study will mean that you're not well prepared for the test. This may lead to cramming the night before, which will cause you to be physically and mentally exhausted for the test. Poor time management also contributes to feelings of stress, fear, and hopelessness as you realize you are not well prepared but don't know what to do about it.

Other times, test anxiety is not related to your preparation for the test but comes from unresolved fear. This may be a past failure on a test, or poor performance on tests in general. It may come from comparing yourself to others who seem to be performing better or from the stress of living up to expectations. Anxiety may be driven by fears of the future—how failure on this test would affect your educational and career goals. These fears are often completely irrational, but they can still negatively impact your test performance.

> **Review Video: 3 Reasons You Have Test Anxiety**
> Visit mometrix.com/academy and enter code: 428468

Elements of Test Anxiety

As mentioned earlier, test anxiety is considered to be an emotional state, but it has physical and mental components as well. Sometimes you may not even realize that you are suffering from test anxiety until you notice the physical symptoms. These can include trembling hands, rapid heartbeat, sweating, nausea, and tense muscles. Extreme anxiety may lead to fainting or vomiting. Obviously, any of these symptoms can have a negative impact on testing. It is important to recognize them as soon as they begin to occur so that you can address the problem before it damages your performance.

> **Review Video: 3 Ways to Tell You Have Test Anxiety**
> Visit mometrix.com/academy and enter code: 927847

The mental components of test anxiety include trouble focusing and inability to remember learned information. During a test, your mind is on high alert, which can help you recall information and stay focused for an extended period of time. However, anxiety interferes with your mind's natural processes, causing you to blank out, even on the questions you know well. The strain of testing during anxiety makes it difficult to stay focused, especially on a test that may take several hours. Extreme anxiety can take a huge mental toll, making it difficult not only to recall test information but even to understand the test questions or pull your thoughts together.

> **Review Video: How Test Anxiety Affects Memory**
> Visit mometrix.com/academy and enter code: 609003

Effects of Test Anxiety

Test anxiety is like a disease—if left untreated, it will get progressively worse. Anxiety leads to poor performance, and this reinforces the feelings of fear and failure, which in turn lead to poor performances on subsequent tests. It can grow from a mild nervousness to a crippling condition. If allowed to progress, test anxiety can have a big impact on your schooling, and consequently on your future.

Test anxiety can spread to other parts of your life. Anxiety on tests can become anxiety in any stressful situation, and blanking on a test can turn into panicking in a job situation. But fortunately, you don't have to let anxiety rule your testing and determine your grades. There are a number of relatively simple steps you can take to move past anxiety and function normally on a test and in the rest of life.

> **Review Video: How Test Anxiety Impacts Your Grades**
> Visit mometrix.com/academy and enter code: 939819

Physical Steps for Beating Test Anxiety

While test anxiety is a serious problem, the good news is that it can be overcome. It doesn't have to control your ability to think and remember information. While it may take time, you can begin taking steps today to beat anxiety.

Just as your first hint that you may be struggling with anxiety comes from the physical symptoms, the first step to treating it is also physical. Rest is crucial for having a clear, strong mind. If you are tired, it is much easier to give in to anxiety. But if you establish good sleep habits, your body and mind will be ready to perform optimally, without the strain of exhaustion. Additionally, sleeping well helps you to retain information better, so you're more likely to recall the answers when you see the test questions.

Getting good sleep means more than going to bed on time. It's important to allow your brain time to relax. Take study breaks from time to time so it doesn't get overworked, and don't study right before bed. Take time to rest your mind before trying to rest your body, or you may find it difficult to fall asleep.

> **Review Video: The Importance of Sleep for Your Brain**
> Visit mometrix.com/academy and enter code: 319338

Along with sleep, other aspects of physical health are important in preparing for a test. Good nutrition is vital for good brain function. Sugary foods and drinks may give a burst of energy but this burst is followed by a crash, both physically and emotionally. Instead, fuel your body with protein and vitamin-rich foods.

Also, drink plenty of water. Dehydration can lead to headaches and exhaustion, especially if your brain is already under stress from the rigors of the test. Particularly if your test is a long one, drink water during the breaks. And if possible, take an energy-boosting snack to eat between sections.

> **Review Video: How Diet Can Affect your Mood**
> Visit mometrix.com/academy and enter code: 624317

Along with sleep and diet, a third important part of physical health is exercise. Maintaining a steady workout schedule is helpful, but even taking 5-minute study breaks to walk can help get your blood pumping faster and clear your head. Exercise also releases endorphins, which contribute to a positive feeling and can help combat test anxiety.

When you nurture your physical health, you are also contributing to your mental health. If your body is healthy, your mind is much more likely to be healthy as well. So take time to rest, nourish your body with healthy food and water, and get moving as much as possible. Taking these physical steps will make you stronger and more able to take the mental steps necessary to overcome test anxiety.

Mental Steps for Beating Test Anxiety

Working on the mental side of test anxiety can be more challenging, but as with the physical side, there are clear steps you can take to overcome it. As mentioned earlier, test anxiety often stems from lack of preparation, so the obvious solution is to prepare for the test. Effective studying may be the most important weapon you have for beating test anxiety, but you can and should employ several other mental tools to combat fear.

First, boost your confidence by reminding yourself of past success—tests or projects that you aced. If you're putting as much effort into preparing for this test as you did for those, there's no reason you should expect to fail here. Work hard to prepare; then trust your preparation.

Second, surround yourself with encouraging people. It can be helpful to find a study group, but be sure that the people you're around will encourage a positive attitude. If you spend time with others who are anxious or cynical, this will only contribute to your own anxiety. Look for others who are motivated to study hard from a desire to succeed, not from a fear of failure.

Third, reward yourself. A test is physically and mentally tiring, even without anxiety, and it can be helpful to have something to look forward to. Plan an activity following the test, regardless of the outcome, such as going to a movie or getting ice cream.

When you are taking the test, if you find yourself beginning to feel anxious, remind yourself that you know the material. Visualize successfully completing the test. Then take a few deep, relaxing breaths and return to it. Work through the questions carefully but with confidence, knowing that you are capable of succeeding.

Developing a healthy mental approach to test taking will also aid in other areas of life. Test anxiety affects more than just the actual test—it can be damaging to your mental health and even contribute to depression. It's important to beat test anxiety before it becomes a problem for more than testing.

> **Review Video: Test Anxiety and Depression**
> Visit mometrix.com/academy and enter code: 904704

Study Strategy

Being prepared for the test is necessary to combat anxiety, but what does being prepared look like? You may study for hours on end and still not feel prepared. What you need is a strategy for test prep. The next few pages outline our recommended steps to help you plan out and conquer the challenge of preparation.

STEP 1: SCOPE OUT THE TEST

Learn everything you can about the format (multiple choice, essay, etc.) and what will be on the test. Gather any study materials, course outlines, or sample exams that may be available. Not only will this help you to prepare, but knowing what to expect can help to alleviate test anxiety.

STEP 2: MAP OUT THE MATERIAL

Look through the textbook or study guide and make note of how many chapters or sections it has. Then divide these over the time you have. For example, if a book has 15 chapters and you have five days to study, you need to cover three chapters each day. Even better, if you have the time, leave an extra day at the end for overall review after you have gone through the material in depth.

If time is limited, you may need to prioritize the material. Look through it and make note of which sections you think you already have a good grasp on, and which need review. While you are studying, skim quickly through the familiar sections and take more time on the challenging parts. Write out your plan so you don't get lost as you go. Having a written plan also helps you feel more in control of the study, so anxiety is less likely to arise from feeling overwhelmed at the amount to cover.

STEP 3: GATHER YOUR TOOLS

Decide what study method works best for you. Do you prefer to highlight in the book as you study and then go back over the highlighted portions? Or do you type out notes of the important information? Or is it helpful to make flashcards that you can carry with you? Assemble the pens, index cards, highlighters, post-it notes, and any other materials you may need so you won't be distracted by getting up to find things while you study.

If you're having a hard time retaining the information or organizing your notes, experiment with different methods. For example, try color-coding by subject with colored pens, highlighters, or post-it notes. If you learn better by hearing, try recording yourself reading your notes so you can listen while in the car, working out, or simply sitting at your desk. Ask a friend to quiz you from your flashcards, or try teaching someone the material to solidify it in your mind.

STEP 4: CREATE YOUR ENVIRONMENT

It's important to avoid distractions while you study. This includes both the obvious distractions like visitors and the subtle distractions like an uncomfortable chair (or a too-comfortable couch that makes you want to fall asleep). Set up the best study environment possible: good lighting and a comfortable work area. If background music helps you focus, you may want to turn it on, but otherwise keep the room quiet. If you are using a computer to take notes, be sure you don't have any other windows open, especially applications like social media, games, or anything else that could distract you. Silence your phone and turn off notifications. Be sure to keep water close by so you stay hydrated while you study (but avoid unhealthy drinks and snacks).

Also, take into account the best time of day to study. Are you freshest first thing in the morning? Try to set aside some time then to work through the material. Is your mind clearer in the afternoon or evening? Schedule your study session then. Another method is to study at the same time of day that you will take the test, so that your brain gets used to working on the material at that time and will be ready to focus at test time.

STEP 5: STUDY!

Once you have done all the study preparation, it's time to settle into the actual studying. Sit down, take a few moments to settle your mind so you can focus, and begin to follow your study plan. Don't give in to distractions or let yourself procrastinate. This is your time to prepare so you'll be ready to fearlessly approach the test. Make the most of the time and stay focused.

Of course, you don't want to burn out. If you study too long you may find that you're not retaining the information very well. Take regular study breaks. For example, taking five minutes out of every hour to walk briskly, breathing deeply and swinging your arms, can help your mind stay fresh.

As you get to the end of each chapter or section, it's a good idea to do a quick review. Remind yourself of what you learned and work on any difficult parts. When you feel that you've mastered the material, move on to the next part. At the end of your study session, briefly skim through your notes again.

But while review is helpful, cramming last minute is NOT. If at all possible, work ahead so that you won't need to fit all your study into the last day. Cramming overloads your brain with more information than it can process and retain, and your tired mind may struggle to recall even previously learned information when it is overwhelmed with last-minute study. Also, the urgent nature of cramming and the stress placed on your brain contribute to anxiety. You'll be more likely to go to the test feeling unprepared and having trouble thinking clearly.

So don't cram, and don't stay up late before the test, even just to review your notes at a leisurely pace. Your brain needs rest more than it needs to go over the information again. In fact, plan to finish your studies by noon or early afternoon the day before the test. Give your brain the rest of the day to relax or focus on other things, and get a good night's sleep. Then you will be fresh for the test and better able to recall what you've studied.

STEP 6: TAKE A PRACTICE TEST

Many courses offer sample tests, either online or in the study materials. This is an excellent resource to check whether you have mastered the material, as well as to prepare for the test format and environment.

Check the test format ahead of time: the number of questions, the type (multiple choice, free response, etc.), and the time limit. Then create a plan for working through them. For example, if you have 30 minutes to take a 60-question test, your limit is 30 seconds per question. Spend less time on the questions you know well so that you can take more time on the difficult ones.

If you have time to take several practice tests, take the first one open book, with no time limit. Work through the questions at your own pace and make sure you fully understand them. Gradually work up to taking a test under test conditions: sit at a desk with all study materials put away and set a timer. Pace yourself to make sure you finish the test with time to spare and go back to check your answers if you have time.

After each test, check your answers. On the questions you missed, be sure you understand why you missed them. Did you misread the question (tests can use tricky wording)? Did you forget the information? Or was it something you hadn't learned? Go back and study any shaky areas that the practice tests reveal.

Taking these tests not only helps with your grade, but also aids in combating test anxiety. If you're already used to the test conditions, you're less likely to worry about it, and working through tests until you're scoring well gives you a confidence boost. Go through the practice tests until you feel comfortable, and then you can go into the test knowing that you're ready for it.

Test Tips

On test day, you should be confident, knowing that you've prepared well and are ready to answer the questions. But aside from preparation, there are several test day strategies you can employ to maximize your performance.

First, as stated before, get a good night's sleep the night before the test (and for several nights before that, if possible). Go into the test with a fresh, alert mind rather than staying up late to study.

Try not to change too much about your normal routine on the day of the test. It's important to eat a nutritious breakfast, but if you normally don't eat breakfast at all, consider eating just a protein bar. If you're a coffee drinker, go ahead and have your normal coffee. Just make sure you time it so that the caffeine doesn't wear off right in the middle of your test. Avoid sugary beverages, and drink enough water to stay hydrated but not so much that you need a restroom break 10 minutes into the test. If your test isn't first thing in the morning, consider going for a walk or doing a light workout before the test to get your blood flowing.

Allow yourself enough time to get ready, and leave for the test with plenty of time to spare so you won't have the anxiety of scrambling to arrive in time. Another reason to be early is to select a good seat. It's helpful to sit away from doors and windows, which can be distracting. Find a good seat, get out your supplies, and settle your mind before the test begins.

When the test begins, start by going over the instructions carefully, even if you already know what to expect. Make sure you avoid any careless mistakes by following the directions.

Then begin working through the questions, pacing yourself as you've practiced. If you're not sure on an answer, don't spend too much time on it, and don't let it shake your confidence. Either skip it and come back later, or eliminate as many wrong answers as possible and guess among the remaining ones. Don't dwell on these questions as you continue—put them out of your mind and focus on what lies ahead.

Be sure to read all of the answer choices, even if you're sure the first one is the right answer. Sometimes you'll find a better one if you keep reading. But don't second-guess yourself if you do immediately know the answer. Your gut instinct is usually right. Don't let test anxiety rob you of the information you know.

If you have time at the end of the test (and if the test format allows), go back and review your answers. Be cautious about changing any, since your first instinct tends to be correct, but make sure you didn't misread any of the questions or accidentally mark the wrong answer choice. Look over any you skipped and make an educated guess.

At the end, leave the test feeling confident. You've done your best, so don't waste time worrying about your performance or wishing you could change anything. Instead, celebrate the successful completion of this test. And finally, use this test to learn how to deal with anxiety even better next time.

> **Review Video: 5 Tips to Beat Test Anxiety**
> Visit mometrix.com/academy and enter code: 570656

Important Qualification

Not all anxiety is created equal. If your test anxiety is causing major issues in your life beyond the classroom or testing center, or if you are experiencing troubling physical symptoms related to your anxiety, it may be a sign of a serious physiological or psychological condition. If this sounds like your situation, we strongly encourage you to seek professional help.

Tell Us Your Story

We at Mometrix would like to extend our heartfelt thanks to you for letting us be a part of your journey. It is an honor to serve people from all walks of life, people like you, who are committed to building the best future they can for themselves.

We know that each person's situation is unique. But we also know that, whether you are a young student or a mother of four, you care about working to make your own life and the lives of those around you better.

That's why we want to hear your story.

We want to know why you're taking this test. We want to know about the trials you've gone through to get here. And we want to know about the successes you've experienced after taking and passing your test.

In addition to your story, which can be an inspiration both to us and to others, we value your feedback. We want to know both what you loved about our book and what you think we can improve on.

The team at Mometrix would be absolutely thrilled to hear from you! So please, send us an email at tellusyourstory@mometrix.com or visit us at mometrix.com/tellusyourstory.php and let's stay in touch.

Additional Bonus Material

Due to our efforts to try to keep this book to a manageable length, we've created a link that will give you access to all of your additional bonus material:

mometrix.com/bonus948/series7

Made in United States
Orlando, FL
07 April 2023

31838436R00220